Napoleon Bonaparte Broward

A Florida Sand Dollar Book

Yours truly
N B Broward

Napoleon Bonaparte Broward

Florida's Fighting Democrat

SAMUEL PROCTOR

University Press of Florida
Gainesville/Tallahassee/Tampa/Boca Raton
Pensacola/Orlando/Miami/Jacksonville

Library of Congress Cataloging-in-Publication Data

Proctor, Samuel.
    Napoleon Bonaparte Broward, Florida's fighting Democrat / Samuel
Proctor. — 1st pbk. ed.
        p.   cm. — (A Florida sand dollar book.)
    Originally published: 1950.
    Includes bibliographical references and index.
    ISBN 0-8130-1191-4
    1. Broward, Napoleon Bonaparte, 1857-1910.   2. Governors—Florida
—Biography.   3. Florida—Politics and government—1865-1950.
I. Title. II. Series.
F316.B878P7   1993
975.9'061'092—dc20
[B]   92-39694
                                                                     CIP

The University Press of Florida is the scholarly publishing agency for the
State University System of Florida, comprised of Florida A & M University,
Florida Atlantic University, Florida International University, Florida State
University, University of Central Florida, University of Florida, University of
North Florida, University of South Florida, and University of West Florida.

Orders for books should be addressed to
University Press of Florida
15 Northwest 15th Street
Gainesville, FL 32611

*For my three ladies
Bessie, Rebecca, and Madison*

Contents

Illustrations

(After page 208)

Preface to the 1993 Edition

NAPOLEON BONAPARTE BROWARD was elected governor of Florida in 1904 after a bitter battle against the railroads and the corporations. He was hailed as the leader of the populist progressive movement that was moving across the South and throughout the country. It was a time of growth and of economic and political change. Governor Broward was recognized as a politician with an agenda that spoke to the needs and aspirations of the laborer and the farmer. Just as important was his skill as a political leader who was able to have much of his program enacted into law. Now, almost a century later, Broward continues to be recognized as one of the ablest and most effective governors in Florida's history.

Most of Florida was still a wilderness at the beginning of the twentieth century. With 528,000 people, according to the 1900 census, it had the smallest population of any southern state. It had more acreage and more frontier characteristics than any state east of the Mississippi. But it was beginning to change.

Henry M. Flagler, the Standard Oil baron, had great plans for Florida when he arrived in the 1880s. He would conquer its frontier with a railroad, a string of luxury hotels, a steamship company, and land that would be converted into farms and towns. His Florida East Coast Railroad reached West Palm Beach in 1894 and Miami two years later. Almost overnight South Florida began to grow. Miami's population increased from 496 in 1896 to more than 5,000 four years later. In central Florida, the Tampa Bay area, and the Gulf Coast, another Yankee millionaire, Henry B. Plant, was also building grand hotels and railroads.

There was some industrial growth. Phosphate and lime-rock mining were important industries by 1900, and Jacksonville had become a major shipping port. Lumbering, turpentining, the manufacture of fertilizer, and cigar making in Tampa were *growing industries. Tourism was expanding throughout the state. For years St. Augustine had attracted winter visitors, and now Flagler's railroad was enabling tourists to travel farther south. Palm Beach was being touted as the Newport of the South. Rich northerners were constructing elaborate "cottages" along the ocean and lake fronts. The most splendid was Flagler's own great marble palace, Whitehall, built as a wedding present for Mary Lily Kenan, his young bride and third wife. It cost more than $2 million. To marry her, he had to divorce his mentally incompetent second wife. The maneuvering to get a divorce bill passed in 1901 greatly stirred Florida's political cauldron. N. B. Broward was a member of the 1901 legislature and voted for Mr. Flagler's bill, an action that would need an explanation in his populist-progressive gubernatorial campaign in 1904.*

Florida was an agricultural state: over one-half the population grew cotton, tobacco, citrus, and vegetables. The historic freeze of February 1895 had forced the citrus growers to move their groves out of the frosty northern counties onto the peninsula. In order to recoup their losses, many grove owners began to cultivate vegetable crops. Refrigerated freight cars carried Florida's vegetables and fruit to northern and midwestern markets. Fish from Florida's lakes and rivers and Apalachicola oysters were gourmet items on menus of fashionable restaurants throughout the country.

Florida was a poor state when Broward became governor. In 1900 the estimated annual per capita income was $112, compared with an estimated national average of $202. People needed almost everything—housing, education, medical care, social services. The state's infrastructure was a disaster. There was a need for farm-to-market roads, for river and harbor improvements, for schools and public buildings, for hospitals, sewers, street lighting, and more. Providing for these necessities called for money that Florida did not have and that was not forthcoming from the federal government. The South had relegated the Republican party to minority status, and neither the

Congress nor the White House was enthusiastic about funding dollars for the region.

While blacks constituted a sizable segment of Florida's population, they no longer counted in politics. The freedoms that black Floridians had won after the Civil War were gradually nullified. There was no longer a place in Florida for a black secretary of state like Jonathan Gibbs or a black congressman like Josiah T. Walls or black leaders in the Florida House and Senate. Most blacks had been disfranchised by the time Broward became governor.

Floridians suffered from neglect, ignorance, and poverty. Government on every level—local, county, and state—was controlled by a privileged few. Blacks did not vote, nor did many poor whites. Poll taxes, literacy tests, and the like discriminated against both groups. Legislation enacted by the conservative Democrats in power after 1876 mainly benefitted wealthy landowners, railroads, and the business elite. Florida politics operated on the concept that what was good for business was good for everyone. Tax breaks and mammoth giveaway land arrangements were prices not too extravagant to pay for investment capital, jobs, and payrolls.

Florida government—state and local—was white and Democratic by 1900, but the Democratic party was fragmented. The Bourbons in control since Reconstruction were desperately trying to hold on to power, but the populist-progressives were taking over. Time was also taking its toll. Men whose political careers reached back into the past were retiring or dying. Energetic, ambitious, young men were moving onto the political scene. One was Napoleon Broward of Jacksonville.

Broward's predecessor, William Sherman Jennings of Brooksville, was nominated in 1900 by the Democratic party convention meeting in Jacksonville. It was the last nominating convention in Florida history. Jennings was anti-corporation and anti-railroad, and he was elected. His inauguration on January 8, 1901, marked the beginning of a new era in Florida politics. Under his leadership some 3 million acres of public land were *saved for the state. Jennings was setting the stage for Governor Broward's progressive administration.*

Broward was dedicated to the state's growth. "Water will run down hill," he proclaimed. Drainage canals would carry off the surplus water in the Everglades, and millions of acres of rich muckland could be turned into productive farmland and pasture. Farmers could harvest two or three vegetable crops a year, and citrus groves would thrive in a frost-free climate. Broward's agenda also spoke to education. Under his leadership the legislature passed the Buckman Act, which unified the institutions of higher learning under a Board of Control. This act has been described as the most progressive educational legislation enacted by any southern state up to that time.

Broward was the leader of the "wool hat" faction in Florida politics. While his heritage was antebellum planter aristocracy, he had clothed himself in a populist mantle from the beginning of his political career. Growing up in the post–Civil War South had been a struggle against economic adversity, and he could identify with laborers, farmers, and tradesmen. He was determined to better their lot and in doing so to advance Florida. Broward pushed through tax reform, child labor restrictions, a law forbidding selling or giving cigarettes to minors, railroad regulation, increased pay for teachers, programs to stimulate tourism, conservation laws, and support for highway construction and other needed programs.

Napoleon Broward moved into a position of political leadership at a moment when a man with his ability, charisma, and courage was greatly needed in Florida. In any evaluation of effective southern leaders during this period, his name is high on the list. Broward rates as one of Florida's outstanding twentieth-century governors.

Preface to the 1950 Edition

IT IS FREQUENTLY STATED that the office of governor of Florida serves as a political graveyard. Most of the Florida governors who have sought to advance themselves in national politics have failed; their so-called gubernatorial political machines have usually proved to be myths. Florida history reveals, moreover, that the office of chief executive may also serve as a historical graveyard. Many of Florida's governors have fallen into obscurity after their terms of office have been completed, and today their lives and their achievements are almost forgotten. In most instances a governor's influence and popularity have not extended beyond his administration. An exception is Napoleon Bonaparte Broward, one of Florida's truly dramatic and spectacular figures. The Broward administration is considered one of the most important in Florida's history; the Broward Era is regarded as a focal point in the state's development; Broward's influence in politics is still a force apparent today.

Few men in the political life of Florida have been the object of either as much bitter hatred or as much adulation as Broward. No one will deny that his achievements were remarkable; all agree that his career, his activities, and his place in history are unique. And yet Broward, like other great men, shows the truth of Emerson's pronouncement: "To be great is to be misunderstood." Throughout his life Broward was bitterly indicted as a hot-head, a demagogue, and a radical. Critics leveled the charge that he was inconsistent; his political enemies saw him as an ambitious, ruthless upstart. He was accused of fraud in his dealings with the Cuban junta, of speculating in Everglades lands, and of stealing public funds. Many believe that he left office a very wealthy man. Research has revealed little to substantiate these charges and beliefs, and

xiii

*the fact that Broward ended his career as a relatively poor
man stands as his finest and most durable monument.*

*In gathering materials for this study, I was continuously
aware that few men in Florida have been loved more than
Napoleon Broward was loved by his friends. There must have
been about him an indescribable, an almost incomprehensible,
charm. Certainly those who were admitted into the inner
circle of his warm regard considered his friendship a delight.
Broward's most impressive power lay in his moral force, and
his strongest leadership in high courage of the moral kind. His
character was founded upon a single rocklike faith—a belief
in the divine government of the universe and in the necessity
of making personal endeavor square with eternal principles.
As Samuel Butler once said, "Every man's work is always a
picture of himself." Thus, in this biography of Napoleon
Bonaparte Broward, Florida's Fighting Democrat, I have tried
not only to characterize the man and his time, but to portray
the work that he did.*

*Research into the life of any man necessarily obligates the
author to many people. I am particularly indebted to the
Broward family for making available valuable letters, manuscripts, and records from their family papers. They permitted
me to read and use what I wished, to quote what I pleased,
and to draw my own conclusions. They are in no way responsible for the mistakes which this volume may contain. Their
full understanding of the problems facing the biographer,
and their truly rare qualities of intellectual detachment and
sense of historical accuracy lightened my burden considerably.
I am deeply grateful to Mrs. Napoleon B. Broward and to
her daughter, Mrs. Josephine Broward Beckley, for their many
helpful suggestions, their kind cooperation, and their never-
failing courtesy and consideration. My informal conversations
in their home gave me an understanding of Broward's personality that has been of invaluable aid. I am also grateful to
Mrs. Dorcas Beckley Foster, Broward's granddaughter, who*

furnished most of the information relating to the filibustering expeditions; to Mr. Carlton Beckley, a grandson; and to Mr. and Mrs. Napoleon B. Broward, Jr. I am greatly indebted to Miss Hortense Broward, the governor's youngest sister, for information on the early history of her family, and to Mr. Harry Fozzard, Governor Broward's nephew, who cooperated in every way in locating and obtaining information of value to this study.

There are many who assisted generously and graciously in the writing of this book, and it is a pity that my indebtedness must be repaid chiefly in printer's ink. I am sincerely grateful for the helpful suggestions and invaluable aid given by Mr. and Mrs. M. A. Brown, and for the reminiscences and details of information supplied by Mrs. Maggie Kemps Jenkins, Dr. S. A. Morris, Judge Lonnie Howell, Mr. Burton K. Barrs, Sr., Mr. A. W. Cockrell, Mr. W. T. Cash, and Mrs. W. D. Vinzant. Mrs. Laura Buxton Hobbes, Judge Burton K. Barrs, Dr. J. E. Dovell, and Mr. Julien C. Yonge made available unpublished records, papers, and letters. Miss Alma Warren arranged a tour of the Executive Mansion in Tallahassee. The management of the Jacksonville Journal *allowed full access to its newspaper files. Mr. C. J. King, editor of the* Florida Times-Union, *not only made available his valuable newspaper file, but his suggestions and kind cooperation were of inestimable help.*

To Dr. James Miller Leake, of the University of Florida, who first suggested this biography, and who gave generously of his counsel, aid, and knowledge, in its original writing, I am profoundly grateful. I gladly acknowledge my indebtedness to Professors Rembert W. Patrick, William E. Baringer, Manning J. Dauer, William G. Carleton, Eugene A. Hammond, and Paul L. Hanna for their kindness in reading and criticizing all or parts of the manuscript. To the officials and employees of the following libraries I am indebted for every courteous assistance: the University of Florida Library;

the P. K. Yonge Library of Florida History, Gainesville; the University of Florida Law Library; the Florida State Library, Tallahassee; the Library of the Florida Historical Society, St. Augustine; the Jacksonville Public Library; the Library of the Jacksonville Historical Society; the Library of Congress, Washington; the New York Public Library; the Duke University Library; the University of North Carolina Library; the Emory University Library; and the Savannah Public Library.

I am also obligated to Dr. Lewis F. Haines, director of the University of Florida Press, who aided materially in the final revision and editing; to Helen S. Haines, who designed this book; to Mr. Howard L. Putnam, for reading and criticizing the manuscript in its final form; and particularly to Miss Rebecca Porter, assistant editor of the Press, whose careful editorial assistance and ready cooperation have proved invaluable. For checking the manuscript in its early stages of revision, I am indebted to Miss Bertha Mehlman and Mr. Lamar Gammon. Finally, I am deeply grateful to my wife, Bessie Rubin Proctor, for her considerable labors in reading and evaluating the manuscript, and for her wise counsel and long-suffering patience.

SAMUEL PROCTOR

Gainesville, Florida
July, 1950

∽ I ∽

Birthright of a Fighting Democrat

SINCE EARLY MORNING Napoleon had sensed that something was wrong. At breakfast his mother's hands had trembled and she had broken the little blue-figured cream pitcher which had been one of her wedding presents; and later, near the vegetable garden back of the house, he had seen some of the slaves talking excitedly in little groups.

It was hot, even for a March morning in Florida in that year of 1862. With his black puppy clutched in his arms, the child hurried along the dirt path to the river. There, near the bank, he released his dog Ring, breathed a sigh of relief at having escaped the troubles of grownups, and sat down on a blackened pine stump. Glancing idly across the water, he watched a crane and a pair of tufted kingfishers wading on the far side and listened to the noisy sparrows in the mimosas and glossy-leaved japonicas which shaded the riverbank. The boy threw a rock, hoping to disturb a clump of turtles sunning themselves in the shallow water. Just then he heard jumbled, excited noises behind him, in the clearing near the house. Instantly a woman's voice sounded, strained and urgent:

"Napoleon! Where are you? What are you doing?"

The boy did not answer, nor did he move. Only when she called a second time did he whistle for Ring and retrace his steps up the trail through the woods. When he reached the place where the heavy wood growth fell back and the clearing began, he saw half a dozen horses pawing the front lawn. A cluster of men in gray uniforms waited on the porch. His heart began pounding when he recognized his father, the tallest man in the group. The man's brown eyes softened momentarily as he stooped and hugged his son to him. He lifted the young-

[1]

ster high in the air, then turned back to the others and in a proud voice announced:

"This is my eldest son, Napoleon Bonaparte Broward."

Still holding the boy, the elder Napoleon continued the story which he had begun a few minutes before. The Federals, having captured Fernandina on March 4, 1862, were now headed toward Jacksonville and St. Augustine. Days before, word that the invaders were coming had spread along the Florida east coast like a prairie fire. Confederate headquarters in Jacksonville was alerted when, on the last day of February, Northern gunboats, under the command of Commodore Samuel F. DuPont, weighed anchor at Port Royal, South Carolina, and moved south toward Florida.[1] News relayed from one plantation to the other informed the Browards of the flotilla's progress as it wound its way slowly along the Georgia coast and past the Sea Islands.

Excitement in Fernandina, already high, rose to fever pitch. As the Federal fleet inched past St. Marys Entrance, and around the walls of Fort Clinch, the last of the city's inhabitants—women, children, and old men, black and white—hurried to the mainland and moved inland.[2] Former United States Senator David Levy Yulee was one of the last to leave.[3] His train pulled out of the railroad station as the gunboats approached.[4] Fernandina lay forlorn in the early spring sunshine; a white flag fluttered weakly from the most prominent pier as the Northern troops landed and occupied the town.

As Captain Napoleon Broward described the scene, his son noticed that the faces of the men on the porch were grave. Everyone listened intently as the captain told them that he had given his command to his brother, Lieutenant Montgomery L. Broward, so that he could ride across country to his plantation to warn his family that seven ships of war and a regiment of New Hampshire infantry were en route to Jacksonville.[5] Families along both sides of the St. Johns River would have to move out immediately.

Having finished his story, the captain ordered his slaves

to pile furniture and personal belongings in wagons and carriages, and then hurried over to the next plantation to confer with his father, Colonel John Broward. He found that his older brother Charles had just ridden in from Jacksonville and had already sounded the alarm. Standing on the wide veranda, unhurried and dignified, John Broward was ordering his slaves to chop down palmetto logs and blacken them with soot. Hoping that they would resemble a battery of cannon from the distance, he planned to have the logs placed on a promontory overlooking the river where the Federals were expected to sail. Any reasonable delay of the Union gunboats would enable the Browards to move their families, slaves, and personal property out of the area.[6]

Charles reported that scores of Jacksonville citizens were leaving the city. Most of them moved toward Baldwin, where the Confederate forces planned to establish and hold a line of defense. Jacksonville was a scene of dire confusion and complete disorder—a city of chaos, of movement with no purpose, of foul smells and choking clouds of dust. People with fear-blanched faces hauled furniture through the streets. Wagons and carts swamped the roads and trails through which army vehicles attempted to pass. Horses and people collided with each other as they tried to free themselves from the maze; master and slave—men, women, and children—sought refuge from the hated enemy.

Late on the afternoon of March 11, the Federal fleet arrived at the mouth of the St. Johns.[7] Soldiers were sent ashore in a small boat to reconnoiter. Officers questioned some Negroes about the extent and conditions of fortifications in Jacksonville and along the lower St. Johns. The invaders, assured that most of the fortified points were being either dismantled or entirely abandoned, crossed the Bar and proceeded cautiously up the muddy river.[8] Posted sentries broadcast this news to the planter families already clogging the highway. The Broward cavalcade moved west toward White Springs where John Broward owned property.

The trip was long and hot for the Browards. They moved slowly by back-country roads, because the Federals had fanned out into the woods around Jacksonville. The horses' hoofs threw up clouds of fine gray dust which flecked the sun-filled air and threw crazy shadows over the slow-moving wagon train. The Browards were not the only people moving into the interior. All along the road, wagons and carts, loaded with beds and mirrors, chairs and tables—antiques crowded in with trivia —rolled their slow way back from the coastal areas. To the children it seemed like a wild and fantastic outing to some far-off picnic grounds. The cavalcade traveled throughout the night, the children sleeping in the wagons on quilts spread by the slaves. Napoleon remembered being jolted awake when the wagon crossed open ditches. The sky was grayish red, lighted from fires in Jacksonville and the burning plantation houses. The smoke burned his nostrils and watered his eyes. He wanted to cry but his sister Josephine held his hand tightly and he fell asleep again. Once during the night the procession was halted for nearly an hour to allow some troops to pass. Napoleon heard a strange man talking with his father and grandfather. The man revealed that several hundred Confederate irregulars had arrived in Jacksonville on a railway train the afternoon before. They carried with them orders to burn property that might be of use to the enemy.[9] Throughout the area the torch had been laid to houses, barns, and sawmills by the fleeing Confederates. The few people who remained in Jacksonville, the stranger continued, were for the most part Union sympathizers who owned property in and about town.[10]

By early morning the Browards were near Baldwin. Refugees told them that in Jacksonville the steam mills, Moonet's foundry, over half a million board feet of lumber, and a Confederate gunboat marooned in the harbor had burned. The railway station, warehouses, all the hotels, and the business block were gutted by fire.[11] It was later reported in a Northern newspaper that a Mr. Remington, a Northern commission merchant, was "shot and left to die in the streets," because of "utterances of treasonable sentiments." The newspaper also told how two other Yankee residents were killed while trying to escape in boats.[12]

After their arrival in White Springs, the Browards heard a complete description of the capture of Jacksonville. When Union vessels nosed their way out of the gray dampness to the piers of the city, they were greeted by the charred ruins left by the Confederate "regulators." Some degree of order had been restored, however, and the city was taken with no show of resistance.[13] In fact, a deputation from Jacksonville came aboard the flagship to surrender the town, pledge the good behavior of its citizens, and pray for protection against further vandalism.[14]

In White Springs the family moved into the house which had formerly been their summer cottage. Too young to realize the tragedies and horrors of conflict, Napoleon lived there the well-rounded life of a healthy, wide-awake boy. Excursions with his sisters into the nearby woods to pick wild berries were pleasurable expeditions. With boyish enthusiasm he and his younger brother, Montcalm, raided the fields and groves of the neighborhood and secured watermelons, oranges, and pecans. Napoleon's life was full; he still had all the food he could eat and a bed to sleep in. Best of all, his grandfather told wonderful stories about the Indians and the fighting in the Seminole War, and how the people lived when Florida was still owned by Spain.

John Broward exerted great influence on Napoleon. During the war years when the boy's father was absent for long periods of time, the lad naturally turned to his grandfather for guidance. They hiked in the woods together and drove about the countryside in an old black-painted rig. In the evenings when it was cool enough for a fire in the living room, Napoleon and Montcalm begged their grandfather for stories. Relaxing into a comfortable position and drawing pleasantly on his pipe, the old man obliged by telling the history of his family.

It always thrilled Napoleon to hear about Francis, the first of the Browards to reach American shores.[15] Francis, a native of Provence, France, had sailed from Brest during the second half of the eighteenth century and settled in the Georgetown district of South Carolina. It is probable that he was a member of the group of three hundred seventy-one French Huguenots who arrived in South Carolina in 1764.[16] The political and religious persecution of French Protestants caused thousands to seek shelter in the New World. Hundreds of families settled at various convenient points along the Atlantic coast. South Carolina, one of their favorite retreats, became known as the home of the Huguenots in America.

According to Grandfather Broward, Francis had served under Count Pulaski in the fighting around Savannah during the American Revolution. The summer of 1779 saw Pulaski's forces suffering from fever and ague induced by constant exposure in the low, marshy sea-island country.[17] Young Napoleon knew by heart how Francis had made a successful raid through the English lines into Savannah and a secured a quantity of quinine for the hard-pressed American troops.[18] Prior to the war, Francis Broward had established a small mercantile business in Charleston, where he had met and married Sarah Bell of that city. When the conflict ended, Francis moved back to the Georgetown district, and there, on November 17, 1795, his fourth child, John, was born.[19] When the boy was five years old the family moved to Florida, where Spain, under the Royal Order of 1790, offered liberal land grants to settlers.[20] Francis Broward received a grant of three hundred acres near the Nassau River at a place called Doctor's Island, in the northern part of the East Florida territory.

At this time the Florida peninsula was sparsely settled and only a few dozen families lived in East Florida. The main arteries of travel were the St. Johns River and its tributaries. Land travelers used the King's Highway, which started at Colerain on the Georgia border and moved south across the St. Marys River through Cowford and St. Augustine to New Smyrna.[21] Another road, formerly used by the English, led

south from the entrance of the St. Johns, paralleling the sea-
shore to St. Augustine. As the new country opened, hardy
frontiersmen from Georgia and the Carolinas, among them the
Broward family, moved down to make their homes in Florida's
mild climate and on her fertile soil.

The Broward land was not patented to Francis by the Spanish Colonial government until many years after the family
had taken up residence. Writs were issued on February 13,
1816, and on August 16, 1816, by Governor José Coppinger.[22]
On April 29, 1825, the following grant was confirmed to
Francis' widow, Sarah Broward, by the United States Land
Commissioners: "Three hundred acres, situated, one hundred
sixty-two thereof on the waters of Nassau river, at the place
called Doctor's Island, and the three small neighboring islands
surrounded by marshes; thirty-eight acres situated near the
head of Pumpkin Hill creek, bounded on the north by Gilbert
McGlone, on the west by vacant lands, south by William Fitz-
patrick, and east by marshes; and one hundred acres at Pumpkin Hill swamp, bounded on the north by marsh, east by Gilbert McGlone, and south and west by vacant lands; which two
last tracts lie distant from each other about one and a half miles;
and on the Nassau river. . . ."[23]

John Broward spent most of his early youth on Doctor's
Island, and later, after his father's death, moved to Drum-
mond's Point on Cedar Creek.[24] The Spanish government in
Florida had been making "water sawmill" grants to any settler
who would build and operate a sawmill.[25] After applying to
Governor Coppinger for such a grant, John received the certification of his grant on April 24, 1816.[26] It consisted of "sixteen
thousand acres of land in different tracts, seven thousand of
which lie between Cedar creek and Dunn's creek, on the north
side of the St. Johns river; three thousand lie on the north
side of the St. Johns river, and on the east of the road to St.
Marys river; four thousand acres lie on the south side of
Dunn's creek, that connects Dunn's lake with the St. Johns
river at a place called Cabbage hammock; two thousand acres

lie at Sugartown, Cedar swamp, on the west of St. Johns river."[27]

Cutting enough pine lumber to fill his own schooner, John sailed his cargo to the island of St. Thomas, in the Virgin Islands, where he was cordially received by the governor and presented with a gold-headed cane.[28] John Broward was a man of considerable genius and versatility. Planter, soldier, politician—in each role he was successful. During the Cartagenian Rebellion of 1817 he was commissioned a captain by the royal Spanish governor, and he played an active part in the military expedition against the forces of Sir Gregor MacGregor that were holding Fernandina.[29] He married Margaret Tucker of Camden County, Georgia, on October 15, 1824, and their marriage license is the sixth on record in the probate court of Duval County, Florida.[30] Ten children were born of this union: five sons—Charles, Napoleon Bonaparte, Pulaski, Washington, and Montgomery; and five daughters—Maria, Caroline, Helen, Margaret, and Florida.

John Broward's plantation house was constructed on a site near the fork of Big and Little Cedar creeks. His slaves erected a small sawmill and built a dirt dam across the water to get the power to run his machines.[31] By 1835 John was already one of the large owners of land and slaves in north Florida. During the latter part of his life he was called Colonel, a title he acquired in the East Florida Regiment from Governor William P. DuVal.[32] In 1845 he represented Duval County in the first state Senate, and he was on the committee that returned a favorable report on draining the Everglades.[33] As chairman of several important legislative committees, John played an active part in organizing the government of the new state.

John Broward, in common with other members of his family, was a well-educated man. Always anxious that his children should have the finest education possible, he saw his oldest son, Charles, graduated from the Harvard School of Law. There is no way of determining the size of the Broward library, or of estimating the number of books it contained, for they were destroyed when the house was burned during the Civil War. But it is not likely that a man living in so isolated a territory, even though prosperous, would own a large library.

Colonel Broward's second son, Napoleon, Sr., was born in 1829 on the family homestead. His early life was similar to that of other young men of well-to-do Southern families in the nineteenth century. He received his education at home, in a private school which John Broward established on his plantation for the benefit of his own children and those of his friends. Teachers were brought from Charleston and from the North, and a full course of study was provided. Among the teachers were a Mr. Ochus, who taught music; Mr. and Mrs. Edward Augustus DeCottes from Charleston; James H. McRory, who later married a niece of Colonel Broward;[34] and Jefferson Plympton Belknap, a Harvard graduate. Belknap settled in Mandarin, Florida, and experimented in silkworm culture before becoming a teacher. Several children from Jacksonville attended the school. They were driven out to Trout Creek at the beginning of the week and were rowed across the river by a slave. After spending the week at the Broward home and school, they returned to town each Friday.[35]

The elder Napoleon, like his father, had considerable landholdings and was a large cattle owner in Duval County.[36] He loved the warm, rich life so closely associated with the planter class of the ante-bellum South and was recognized in Duval County as a hospitable and generous host. One of the amusing sights of Jacksonville was Napoleon Broward elegantly dressed in white linen, followed by a slave who held an umbrella over his master's head to shade him from the sun.[37] In 1851 Napoleon married Mary Dorcas Parsons, the only daughter of Amander and Elizabeth Burke Parsons, from Eaton, New Hampshire. Although they were from different sections of the country and differed greatly in background and political sentiment, the Browards and Parsons were close friends. There was little indication in 1851 of the bitter feelings that were to arise between the families in later years.

Mary Dorcas was in many ways like her husband in personality and disposition. She was vivacious, her movements were
quick, and she laughed often. Before her marriage she had
taught school for a few months at Mayport, and it was remembered that she dealt firmly with her students. Her family
knew her as a woman of high integrity—a person not likely
to compromise on ideals and principles which she thought just
and right.

After her marriage Mary Dorcas fell ill and was a semi-
invalid the rest of her life. Her helplessness changed her warm
personality and she became a quiet and retiring woman. Un-
pleasant clashes disrupted the family circle, and by 1856
Colonel Broward had become so incensed against his daughter-
in-law that because of her he disinherited his son. Part of his
will read: "In consequence of my son Napoleon B. Broward,
having married a woman (Mary Dorcas Parsons) of a bad
and in my estimation a tiranical disposition, rendering it un-
safe to put negroes slaves in her power, . . . I do hereby dis-
inherit him. . . . [38] Although this will was never changed, there
was a reconciliation between John Broward and his son and
daughter-in-law. In White Springs, Mary Dorcas and her family lived in John Broward's house. Napoleon Broward was
named in the will as an executor of his father's estate.

Napoleon and Montcalm learned the history of their ma-
ternal ancestors from their mother. She told them that Joseph
Parsons was the first of the family in America. He sailed from
Gravesend, England, in 1635, and settled near the present site
of Springfield, Massachusetts. An enterprising young man, he
secured a tract of land on both sides of the Connecticut River,
in the locality known then as Agawam. In 1646 Joseph was
town surveyor in Springfield, and during the next few years
secured monopoly rights of the beaver and fur trade of western
Massachusetts. When he died he was a large landholder and
was recognized as one of the wealthiest men in the colony.[39]

The generations of Parsons who followed played active
roles in the building of the social, educational, and political life

of New England.[40] One served as a judge and was a representative in General Court at Boston.[41] Another studied theology with Increase Mather at Harvard College and gained an outstanding reputation as a minister.[42] Still another Parsons was governor of New Hampshire during colonial days.[43]

William Parsons, great-grandfather of Napoleon and Montcalm, was a millwright by trade. He also acted for a time as adjutant in the New Hampshire militia. His oldest son, Amander, entranced by the fascinating stories of Florida printed in Northern newspapers, left his family in New England and moved to the Florida territory about 1840. At Mayport he bought a sawmill and hired Minorcans from St. Augustine as mill hands.[44] After purchasing a large house in Mayport he sent for his wife and his two sons, Joseph and William. His daughter, Mary Dorcas, born in 1835, either in Eaton or Effingham Falls, New Hampshire, stayed in the North for a short while to attend school. To celebrate the arrival of his family, Amander gave his workers a two-day holiday and invited all his friends throughout the county to a barbecue.

A few mornings after they arrived, the Parsons children were at the breakfast table when young Joseph asked his mother for permission to go fishing. In a reproving voice, Elizabeth Parsons said:

"Don't you know this is Sunday? You can't go fishing on the Lord's Day."

The boy was surprised. "Lord's Day? I didn't know God was in Florida."

"What do you mean, son? Of course he is in Florida. He's everywhere."

"Well, back home we had a church and we knew God was there," Joseph said. "There is no church here so I thought there was no God."

That same day Amander Parsons rode over the countryside announcing that church services were scheduled at his mill for the following Sunday morning. For years thereafter, church meetings were held there for the Parsons' family, millworkers, and friends.[45]

Later, during the 1850's, Amander purchased the point of
land at Newcastle on the St. Johns, and there on a high bluff
he built a fine plantation house. In this house his last son, Halstead, was born. The boy was named for Amander's partner
in the mill, Halstead H. Hoeg, who later became mayor of
Jacksonville.[46]

Mary Dorcas refused to be separated from her family, and
shortly after her mother and brothers moved to Florida, she
joined them at Mayport. In a letter written on December 12,
1849, to her uncle, Joseph Burke, she gave a picture of the
log schoolhouse which she attended: "The school room was
made of logs, no windows but very large cracks which give
plenty of light. And our hours of study from half past three
in the morning until half past eleven at night and of all cros
teachers ours was the crosest, he was Irish. . . ."[47] Obviously,
Mary Dorcas' young imagination was vivid.

Mary Dorcas was sixteen years old when she married Napoleon Bonaparte Broward at Mayport in December, 1851.[48]
John Broward gave his son, as a wedding gift, the piece of land
on Cedar Creek known as the Webb Place. Here, on a small
pine-covered ridge, close to where the creek flows into the St.
Johns River, Napoleon constructed a home for his new bride.
Their eight children—Josephine, Napoleon, Montcalm, Mary
Dorcas, Emily, Osceola, Hortense, and California—were born
in this house. The Browards liked historic and fancy names.

The couple's second child, and first son, was born on April
19, 1857, and named for his father. He passed the first five
years of his life on his family's plantation where the topography
and climate united to make an ideal place for a little boy to
swim and frolic. During these years Napoleon's great love for
nature and the outdoor world began to develop.

The family frequently went to the Boney Place, owned by
the elder Napoleon.[49] It lay about seven miles north of their
plantation, on the Nassau River, just across from Doctor's
Island. There, in the blue-bright days of summer, the Browards
held their picnics and barbecues. Sometimes they would camp

for several days on the river bank, a popular pastime called "marooning."[50] In the winter they dug oysters from the river and roasted them under giant live oaks which still stand.

Young Napoleon's parents and grandparents held a recognized social position in Duval County. They identified themselves with the professional men and the more prosperous planters in the area. Culture and refinement were dominant characteristics of this set; frequent entertainment and generous hospitality were the order of the day.[51] Chief amusements were dinner parties, cards, and dancing. Stately old Spanish dances, old-fashioned square dances, Southern reels, and lilting new Viennese waltzes were popular. The Broward home was often the scene of gay parties where Marcellini, an old Spanish Negro, with his "fiddle and bow," was the chief functionary. John Broward's plantation, conveniently located, was a rest-stop for friends traveling from Jacksonville to Fernandina and Savannah by stage. An old oystershell highway, crossing their land, ran past the rear of the house.[52] Seldom was there a meal in the Broward dining room without a guest.

Meanwhile, as storm clouds, so soon to break into civil war, began to loom menacingly on the horizon, a nervous tension became apparent in the daily lives of the people of the county. The public mind drifted into political channels. All during the spring and summer of 1860, groups of men collected in front of stores on Bay Street and on porches of the houses along Church and Duval to discuss excitedly the grave issues of the day. Heated discussions in the Broward home were frequent. Not since the political crisis of 1850 had such serious questions faced the South. The split in the Democratic convention at Charleston in May, 1860, was generally approved by the Democrats in the county, although the Whigs viewed the threat of secession with grave misgivings. The Browards were among those who joined a Jacksonville conclave on May 15 which declared that ". . . the rights of the citizens of Florida are no longer safe in the Union. . . . She should raise the banner of secession and invite her Southern sisters to join her."[53]

Reaction in Duval County to the election returns in November was immediate. Like secession factions all over the South, Florida Democrats regarded Lincoln's election as the beginning of the end of their struggle to safeguard Southern interests and institutions and to preserve what they considered their constitutional rights. It meant that the Republican party, holding strong abolitionist sentiments, was now in control in Washington, and that security, as the Southern planter had known it, was a thing of the past. Public meetings were held and passionate resolutions adopted, all fiercely pro-secession in tone. Typical of these petitions was that signed on November 6, 1860, by the "Ladies of Broward Neck," the Cedar Creek precinct. It was directed to the "Politicians of Florida" and asked if they would "remain in the Union and trust to the tender mercies of the Yankees . . . or . . . avail themselves of the means given them by God and nature and defend themselves?"[54]

On December 28, 1860, nearly two weeks before Florida's secession, Colonel John Broward's daughter, Helen, presented a new state flag to Governor Madison Starke Perry. Acknowledging its receipt, the governor, like other supporters of a Southern Confederacy, waxed enthusiastic and grandly proclaimed: ". . . You have only anticipated by a few days the proud position of our beloved commonwealth, by placing Florida under the symbol of a bright and effulgent star, by the side of South Carolina, on a field of azure which I devoutly pray God may fitly represent the future serenity and cloudless sky of Southern Nationality."[55]

It was a time of mad passions and wild excitement as the Articles of Secession were adopted in January, 1861, and Florida, along with South Carolina and Mississippi, left the Union. The die was cast and there was no turning back. The controversy between the North and the South was metamorphosing into bloody conflict. With secession, the South reached the brink of a gulf, and none of the commonwealths of the Confederacy approached its destiny with more shining gallantry and with more steadfast devotion than Florida. Hosannas greeted a future that was more uncertain than most Southerners believed. Years of waste and destruction, of misery and anguish, lay ahead. But the South moved forward unfearing, the hearts of her citizens filled with courage and hope, their spirits sturdy and unbending.

The Broward men responded eagerly to the call for volunteers. Pulaski Broward joined Marion's Light Artillery in 1861 and served as a private in Captain John M. Martin's company.[56] Marion's Light Artillery was organized in May, 1861, and saw its first service on Amelia Island near Fernandina. In the reorganization of the company the following year, Pulaski was made a corporal and served in this capacity until the end of the war.[57] Pulaski took part in the Battle of Chickamauga and was wounded in the Battle of Missionary Ridge.[58] Washington, another of Colonel Broward's sons, volunteered his services to the Confederate cause. He was captured by the Union forces and died in the Federal prison at Hilton Head, South Carolina, before he could be exchanged.[59] Montgomery L. Broward was seventeen years old when the Civil War began. He joined Captain Malitico's company, then commanded by his brother Napoleon. Montgomery was mustered into Marion's Light Artillery in 1862,[60] and later served in the Western Army, fighting under Bragg, Hood, and Johnston.[61]

Napoleon Broward hailed Florida's secession with great enthusiasm. Commissioned a captain, he organized a company, and by midsummer of 1861 was authorized to "repel invasion, suppress insurrection and take charge of all suspicious persons and also prevent every raid that may in your judgment be detrimental to the interests of Planters in your section. . . ."[62]

When news reached Florida that a Federal fleet was preparing to invade the state, Broward's company was alerted for immediate action. He marched his men north into the Fernandina area. The Confederate garrison at Fort Clinch was already removing guns and ammunition. Fernandina citizens were frantically piling furniture, trunks, and boxes into wagons and carriages to be moved into the interior. In numbers and equipment the scattered Confederate forces in east Florida were no match for their assailants, and there was little hope of repelling the invasion.

Broward's company was close enough to Fernandina on Sunday, March 2, 1862, to hear the tolling of the church bells and the agitation of the frightened people as they crossed over to the mainland. The following afternoon Captain Broward was notified that the advance squadron of the Federal forces had entered Fernandina Bay. His men remained hidden in the woods for six days, waiting to see whether the Union soldiers would stay in Fernandina or move down the coast.

When Napoleon heard that a Federal squadron loaded with troops had sailed south from Fernandina, he became convinced that the St. Johns River was a new target for assault. Remembering the many plantations that lay unprotected along both shores of the river, he rode to sound the alarm. His father's home would surely be attacked. His wife, babies, and slaves needed protection at his own plantation. They would have to be transferred as quickly as possible out of the danger area.

On the afternoon of March 10, the young captain turned his command over to his brother Montgomery and ordered his troops to Yellow Bluff Point to "fire into the first Yankee vessel that should come within range of their guns."[63] Napoleon rode through the night toward Duval County. By early dawn he had reached the first fringe of farmhouses, awakened the inhabitants, and notified them of the enemy's approach. Several soldiers on guard in the area rode with him to the St. Johns to help if the need arose. It was nearly noon when the men, worn and tired, turned off the shell road and galloped up the aisle of trees to the sun-splashed lawn before the house.

✷ 2 ✷

Winds of Adversity

PRIOR TO THE Federal invasion in 1862, Florida
had, for the most part, escaped any real fighting. Except
for the seizure of Federal property in St. Augustine,
Chattahoochee, and Pensacola, the burning of the Confederate
gunboat *Judah*, and the short-lived action at Fort Pickens, the
state was far removed from actual warfare. The invasion, however, left in its wake death and privation. Many were forced
to leave their homes and move inland for protection. The
Browards counted themselves fortunate to have a home in
White Springs.

The war continued until the Confederacy, overwhelmed, saw
its last gleam of hope fade. The conflict swept over the land
like some terrible flood, and the dream of independence, con-
ceived in the excitement of revolution, lay crushed in the disastrous denouement. The South was indeed broken. Defeat
brought humiliations, sacrifices, and dire poverty to her prostrate citizens. The war raged four long years on a scale unprecedented until that time. Its course had been run with heavy
costs in property, in human endeavor, in blood and tears, and
in mental anguish, and its aftermath bred bitter prejudices.

Everywhere in the South there were changes. Charred and
blasted towns, weed-choked fields, desolated gardens, ravaged
homes attested the reality of defeat. Now peace had its problems. Hunger and want were specters to be faced daily. Over-
burdened with taxes, their money worthless, their fields and
homes destroyed, many Southerners grew discouraged and dis-
illusioned. The fall of the Confederacy was a bitter potion to
swallow. Reconstructing a destroyed civilization would be a
long and difficult task.

Colonel John Broward and his family returned to Duval
County during the summer of 1865. Sick and old, bitterly disappointed over the results of the war, John died in November,
1865. He was deeply mourned by his family, and his death
was noted by many in the state. Obituaries appeared in several
Florida newspapers. His widow, his son Charles, and his daughters remained at their Duval County plantation. Two years
later Napoleon, Sr., brought his family back from White
Springs. The Browards were desperately poor. Their slaves had
been freed; their home, crops, and cattle, and most of their
personal possessions had been burned, destroyed, or stolen.
Unable to pay the heavy taxes levied by the "carpetbag" administration in Florida, they saw huge tracts of their land sacri-
ficed on the auction block in Jacksonville.

Napoleon Broward found his plantation greatly changed:
the house and the stables and fences had been burned; the high-
lands of the old farm had grown up in great clusters of chin-
quapin bushes and live-oak saplings; and the lowlands were
covered with a dense growth of high grass and weeds. Where
the house had stood, the undergrowth was so thick that traces
of the flowers and shrubs that once bloomed in the garden
could be found only with great difficulty.[1] The large oaks that
stood southeast of the house were burned on one side by the
fire which had destroyed the main buildings, and scarred on
the other by shot and shell from Federal gunboats. The riverbank was strewn with fragments of lumber that was once the
cabin work of Union vessels.[2]

Young Napoleon and Montcalm helped their father build a
single pen-log house to shelter the family against early spring
frosts and rains. They cut pine saplings and fenced in a field.
With no money to buy mules, horses, or farm implements, they
used the few tools they had brought with them from White
Springs to clear away weeds, bushes, and grass from the heavy
ground on the margin of the river. It was hard, back-breaking
labor far beyond the years of the two youngsters.

In the partly cleared field they planted Irish and sweet potatoes, sugar cane, beans, and English peas; and in a smaller garden they set out cabbage, turnips, beets, lettuce, asparagus, and onions.[3] The work around the fields was chiefly the responsibility of Napoleon and Montcalm, while their older sister, Josephine, did the lighter chores and helped her mother in the house. Their father secured whatever work was available in Jacksonville or in the county so that the family would have food until harvest time. Such was the postwar lot of many another once prosperous Southern family.

It was a dawn-to-dusk task helping to get something for the big family to eat, and Napoleon had to do a man's job. Although two schools opened in Duval County in 1868 and 1869, there is no record of the boy's attendance. During the evenings he received some instruction from his mother in reading and writing and in the fundamentals of arithmetic. This training, however, could only have been spasmodic and slight because of his mother's frequent illness.[4] It is likely, too, that days of hard labor in the fields and garden did not incline the lad toward books or schooling.

Many years later Napoleon recalled this first year of the return home and the disappointment he and Montcalm experienced when their crops failed. They planted four sacks of potatoes which yielded one. The English peas withered and died. Only the sugar cane promised a measure of success. As Broward later told the story, he and Montcalm "pulled the shucks off a stalk about one every day to see how many joints had ripened, until we had counted seven and eight joints to the stalk." Then one night, when the cane was almost ready for harvest, a tree blew down on the fence which protected the crop. The fence fell across a path and diverted a drove of hungry cattle into the sugarcane patch. Seeking pasture, the invaders trampled the stalks to shreds and ground them underfoot.[5]

In his *Autobiographical Sketch*, Broward describes how the children loved to hear their mother "tell of the delicious Florida-grown Irish potatoes, and the luxury of asparagus, which none, save the rich, enjoyed." Only he and his sister Josephine, of the Broward children, could remember "how lettuce tasted, fixed up with cream and sugar."

The spring of 1868 was cold and rainy and the whole family suffered from chills and fever. The Broward children were "dosed with tartar-emetic" and a "period of cholagogue followed, bitter enough to have cured, but it did not."[6] The elder Broward realized that his family suffered from these attacks because their log house, built too close to the creek, was continually damp. These conditions were even more acute during the spring months, when heavy rains caused the creek and river to swell and overflow their banks. Napoleon helped his father build a log cabin on higher ground, and during the summer the family moved. After taking liberal doses of quinine, a popular cure for fever and ague that was almost forgotten in the blockaded South during the war, the Browards began to improve generally in health.[7]

By fall the family's situation was less critical. The warm weather and the sun-bright days helped along a fine harvest. Napoleon and Montcalm used a drag seine in creeks and the river and caught fish to swell the family larder.[8] They earned a little money when their uncle, Joseph Parsons, paid them one cent each for water-oak pins, to be used for rafting logs.[9]

Just when things seemed to be going better for the family, tragedy struck. Napoleon's mother, in poor health for years, had been tried further by the sorrows of the war and its aftermath. Living in a log house in all kinds of weather, without proper food or medical care, Mary Dorcas failed gradually after the family had returned to Cedar Creek. Her death early in February, 1869, came as a painful shock to Napoleon. The mother and son, always close, had been drawn together during the dark days since 1865. The void brought by her passing was one that was never completely filled for the lad, and he, like the rest of the family, mourned her for many years.

Soon after the death of his mother, sorrow again came to young Napoleon. His grandmother, Margaret Tucker Broward,

died on her plantation on May 29, 1869, after a relatively
short illness.[10] On June 15, 1870, a listing of the debts of the
John Broward estate was made and filed in the office of the
county judge in Jacksonville. One item was the bill of thirty-
eight dollars owed the physician for services "during the last
illness of Margaret Broward."[11]

Unable to care for his children properly, Napoleon Broward
moved his family to the old John Broward homestead, which
had been partly restored after the war. The aunts welcomed the
opportunity to take care of Napoleon, his brother, and his sisters.
The old farm on Cedar Creek was abandoned, and soon the
fields and gardens were choked with grass and weeds and the
vacant house began to decay and fall apart. Pine and oak saplings took root, and in a few years were tall enough to hide
the remaining signs of human habitation. Today it is impossible
to determine exactly where the house stood.

Napoleon and Montcalm helped their Uncle Charles to plow
and replant the land that had been cleared and to do other
necessary tasks about the house and farm. Inexperienced as
they were, unable to secure any labor or to pay for it even if
such help had been available, they found that their efforts
were almost futile. Charles Broward, a Harvard graduate
trained for the practice of law, and a member of the planter
class, was hardly equipped to cultivate a farm that had once
required several Negro slaves to plow and plant and to harvest the crops.

Family records are incomplete on the activities of Napoleon's
father during this period. He worked at various jobs in Jacksonville, none of them important, trying to secure money to
help his family along. Deeply grieved by the loss of his wife,
he was unable to overcome the shock of her death. He spent
many hours brooding over her grave in the Parsons' family
cemetery. Sometimes he rowed to his old plantation, which
was only about two miles across the river from "Newcastle,"
and stayed there for days, alone in the desolate, weather-beaten
cabin, probably dreaming of the happier and more prosperous

days before the war. Keenly sensitive to the humiliations his
poverty brought, Napoleon, Sr., lamented the disastrous effect
of the South's defeat on his family's finances.

One rainy night, early in December, 1870, he made a trip
to "Newcastle." Grief-stricken, he spent the whole night in
the cemetery, oblivious of the weather, and caught a severe cold
which quickly developed into pneumonia. He sank rapidly and
in a few days was dead. Napoleon felt deep sorrow over his
father's death, but this loss did not seem to mean so much to
him as had his mother's death. He was too young before and
during the war to have had any deep appreciation for or close
understanding of his father. There was only the natural affec-
tion and admiration that a son has for his parent.

After their father's death Napoleon and Montcalm faced
new and complex problems. Their Uncle Charles had moved
to Jacksonville, where he had opened law offices and eventually
prospered.[12] Work in the fields and gardens of the Broward
plantation was now entirely in the hands of the two youngsters.
Before their uncle's departure, it had been a difficult task to
plant and harvest crops, but now the job was well-nigh impossible.

Napoleon's aunts—Colonel Broward's daughters, Helen,
Maria, and Florida—realized that under existing conditions the
farm could not be made to pay, and that they would have to
solve the problem of providing food for part of the family.
Consequently, in the early weeks of 1871 the Broward ladies
moved to Jacksonville, taking with them Napoleon's sisters,
Josephine, Mary Dorcas, Emily, and Hortense.[13] They lived
on Monroe Street between Pine (now Main) and Laura. Later
they moved to 48 East Bay Street on the corner of Market and
opened a boardinghouse.[14] The aunts enrolled their nieces as
day pupils in St. Joseph's Convent School, located on the corner of Pine and Duval streets.[15]

Napoleon and Montcalm lived alone on the Broward plantation for many months, trying to grow corn and potatoes and
fatten the few hogs that remained. They worked in the fields

until darkness drove them in, well past sunset. Their supper consisted of "hominy, peeled sweet potatoes, a piece of pork, all boiled together in the same pot."[16] There was little to do in the evenings and, as soon as supper was finished, they would "lean their guns against the wall near the head of the bed, . . . place a bowie knife in a crack of the log house within reach," and go to bed.[17]

During the long summer afternoons after the crops were in the boys swam in the river or fished off its banks. They were expert shots and liked to hunt with their dogs Ring and Lady.[18] In his later years, Napoleon remembered the Florida woods as "abounding in deer, turkeys and squirrels, the hunting of which furnished us a profitable and pleasing recreation."[19]

Life was lonely for the two lads, living by themselves on the deteriorating farm. Their nearest neighbor was two miles away, and contacts with the outside world were few. Occasionally Uncle Charles made the tiresome trip from Jacksonville to visit them, and sometimes on Sunday they would rise early and walk four miles to spend the day at the house of their Uncle Pulaski.[20] They went to church as often as possible since it was the most convenient place to meet their friends. On one occasion Napoleon planned to accompany his neighbors, Abram Geiger and his family, to church services. His Aunt Lizzie, Pulaski's wife, had promised to cut out new linen trousers for Napoleon and Montcalm. Montcalm's were completed, but the illness of one of the children prevented the finishing of the pair intended for Napoleon. Determined that he was going to wear these new trousers when he rode to church with Mr. Geiger's daughter, Eugenia, Napoleon sewed them himself.[21]

The boys lived on the farm until the fall of 1871. After they had harvested their crops, they moved to the home of Uncle Joe Parsons and worked for him in his lumber camp at Mill Cove. Napoleon's job was to raft logs after they had been cut by the loggers and brought to the river with horse teams. Both boys worked there for more than a year, but the spring rains of 1873 brought back their attacks of fever and ague. Unable to continue in the lumber camp, they moved to the plantation of Amander Parsons, their grandfather, on the south side of the St. Johns. A New Englander, and a comparative newcomer to Florida when the Civil War began, Amander had suffered the fate of many who had adhered to the Confederacy. He saw his mill at Mayport burned and his plantation at Newcastle destroyed. Although he had opposed slavery prior to the war and had used free labor in his mill, throughout the conflict he had remained loyal to the Southern cause. According to family story, the Federal officials in Jacksonville, suspecting Amander of being too strong a Southern sympathizer, had briefly imprisoned him. For a while the Parsons felt it necessary to leave Duval County and take refuge in central Florida. After the War Amander rebuilt his home and planted an orange grove, which by 1873 was thriving and productive.

Napoleon and his brother lived with their Parsons grandparents until Amander's death on August 30, 1873.[22] In the fall the boys moved to Mill Cove, farther down the river, to be close to the small country public school which had been established there. The lads boarded with a farmer of the neighborhood, Philip P. Lord. Montcalm's board had been provided for in his grandfather's will, but Napoleon, two years older, paid his own way by chopping wood, building rail fences, and doing other odd jobs and chores around Lord's farm.

Napoleon was tall for seventeen; his body was hard and swift. The boy's shoulders widened, his arms and legs lengthened, and his skin grew dark after daylong exertion in the hot sun. Throughout the summer of 1873, he and Montcalm worked on their grandmother's farm, helping to care for the orange grove. For his work Napoleon was paid seventy-five dollars. His brother received fifty.[23]

After another winter at Mill Cove, Napoleon left school in the spring of 1875 to work on Uncle Joe Parsons' steamboat. When he failed as a cook, he was made assistant fireman and then worked as a deck hand and wheelman.[24] It was a summer all green and golden for the boy, who could not remember when he had been so happy. He loved boats and he spent many years on them. The rest of his life was closely connected with ships and navigation.

The river to him was like an old friend. He learned to know every turn, every level, and every mark of the St. Johns from its source below Lake George to its mouth, where it entered the broad Atlantic. Napoleon found it exciting to sail between the banks of the river, and to watch the thickets of live oak and cypress and the sun-splashed pine barrens which cut across the hammocks and lay green to the river. In the jungle-like hammocks the thick muscadine and wild-grape vines climbed over the scrub and ascended the trees, winding round and round. Along the shore, clumps of cypress trees, with tangled masses of briars and vines around their trunks, were interspersed with lush prairies and low grassy marshes, where the water flowed torpidly and where large areas were paved with green lily pads. On many days the sun was so bright that Napoleon could hardly distinguish the purple and white violets and the thickets of azaleas blooming along the sides of the small streams that flowed lazily into the St. Johns. He liked to watch the white-eyed towhees, the yellowthroats, and the "piney-woods" sparrows fluttering among the palmetto scrub which echoed and re-echoed their high-pitched reedlike notes.

As the fall of 1875 approached, business declined for the Parsons' boat, and Napoleon returned to school. This time he went to New Berlin, Florida, attending the school there and living with an old lighthouse keeper, Captain Summers. The lighthouse, which was destroyed when the channel of the St. Johns River was deepened during the 1880's, stood out in the river about two hundred feet from Dame's Point. Captain Summers, living alone in his gray weather-beaten cabin, welcomed the boy, happy to have his company during the long winter months. Napoleon enjoyed this winter. His grandmother paid for his board,[25] so there was plenty of time free from study to fish in the river, watch the men build boats, and explore the

Confederate breastworks on the slopes of the bluff, which, manned and armed, had protected that area of the St. Johns.[26]

New Berlin was an active and thriving settlement. Formerly Yellow Bluff, it lay about twelve miles north of Jacksonville and was one of the larger shipbuilding centers of northeast Florida. Its harbor was usually filled with fishing smacks and ships waiting to be repaired. The town itself was built along the river's edge, its rutted roads winding past frame houses and stores at the foot of a steep bluff.

One of the prominent families of New Berlin was that of Captain David Kemps, who owned a fleet of fishing smacks and, at various times, several river boats as well. He built such vessels as the *Kate Spencer*[27] and other steamers, each of which played an important and interesting part in the history of navigation on the St. Johns River. The Kemps home, large enough for nine children, stood on a high, finger-like point of land overlooking the river. Since the township of New Berlin began almost at the line of the Broward holdings, the Kemps and Browards were friends and neighbors for many years. During his winter at New Berlin young Broward was a frequent visitor in the Kemps home. He and the captain's oldest daughter, Georgiana Carolina, began a friendship that deepened with the years.[28]

The following summer, after school closed, Napoleon shipped north on a lumber schooner. He drew his pay when the vessel docked in New York City, and traveled to Middletown, New York, to see his youngest sister, Hortense, who was living with Mr. and Mrs. Charles G. Dill.[29] Throughout the rest of the summer and fall of 1876 Napoleon worked at odd jobs along the New England coast. Early in December he arrived at Cape Cod, Massachusetts, where he hoped to secure a berth on a fishing vessel. He found, however, that because of the long-continued and excessive cold, the fishing season at this port had not begun. Snow, eighteen inches deep, covered the ground, and large, jagged blocks of ice lay along the shore or floated unevenly in the gray sea water.[30] Far from home, without money, shelter, or employment, Napoleon was faced with the immediate problem of getting a job. The *Emma Linwood*, a four-masted schooner and the only vessel in port at the time, was about to sail when Napoleon heard that there was still an unfilled berth aboard ship. Without knowing the destination of the vessel, he decided to try for the job. He had developed a bad case of whooping cough and was afraid that if he started coughing while being interviewed, the captain might think him consumptive and not hire him. He found Captain Newcomb of the *Emma* near one of the wharves, supervising the loading of supplies.

In the weak sunlight Napoleon looked pale. He swallowed a large glass of water to control his cough, walked quickly up to the officer and asked, "Captain, do you want to ship a man?" For a moment the captain seemed not to hear. He turned around slowly, shoved the pencil that he was using into his coat pocket, and scrutinized the lad from head to toe. Napoleon hardly dared breathe for fear of encouraging another coughing spell. After a moment the captain jerked his head and said, "O. K. You'll do. Get aboard."[31]

The schooner shipped to the Grand Banks of Newfoundland, where its crew spent the rest of the winter catching codfish. This was the first winter in the North for Napoleon, and he was totally unprepared for the frigid weather that he encountered in the Northern seas. Clad in Kentucky jeans and a gingham shirt, he would have frozen to death but for the generosity of other crew members, who lent him some warm woolens.[32] Napoleon remained in the North, following the sea, for almost two years. Leading a sailor's life, he worked on several different ships. After the winter in Newfoundland, he shipped out of New Gloucester on a vessel freighting lumber. Later, for a short time in 1878, he worked on an oyster boat, probably when he was making his way from New England to Florida.

There are only fragmentary records of his activities at this time. During the latter part of 1878, he worked as wheelman on a St. Johns River steamer. Probably he was in Jacksonville much of March and April, 1879, where his father's estate was being settled by the administrator.[33] Late in 1879 he moved to New Berlin, where he was employed by his old friend, David Kemps, on one of the captain's river boats. Here he worked for three years, first as a mate, then as captain of a vessel which plied between Jacksonville, Mayport, Palatka, Sanford, and Enterprise.

In the fall and winter months of 1882, he worked on a tug which brought huge clumps of brush, saplings, and tough wire grass from points up the river to Mayport, where Captain R. G. Ross was supervising the construction of the jetties. These brush *mattresses,* as they were called, were commonly used in the building of jetties. Chained together and submerged in the water, they served as bases upon which the huge boulders and broken stones, brought down from New York City by boat, could rest.[34]

A frequent traveler with Napoleon on the Kemps' boat was Georgiana Carolina Kemps, or Carrie, as she was called by her family and friends. Carrie, nineteen years old when Napoleon first began working for her father, often sailed on the steamer to Jacksonville, where she shopped. She liked to stand with Napoleon on the foredeck, the warm sun lighting her thick brown hair, and watch him as he skillfully maneuvered the vessel around the shoals and sand bars of the river and between the steep banks of summer green. Thin and lithe, and wearing the great belled skirts of the period, Carrie walked the decks and reveled in the sights and sounds of the river.

Napoleon was attracted. He admired Carrie's grace and her ease of manner; and in her eyes, set high in a long and rather thin face, he saw an open frankness which he liked.[35] And Carrie found in him those things which she desired in a husband. By December, 1882, Napoleon had saved enough money to become a partner in the boat business of Captain Kemps and the wedding date was set. A series of parties followed the announcement. One of the more resplendent was a reception and

dance given on New Year's night by Mr. and Mrs. John Mc-
Donald.[36] Napoleon and Carrie were married the first week
of January, 1883, in the old Methodist chapel at New Berlin.
Soon afterward they moved to Mayport, where they lived in
the home of Mrs. Arnau, who operated a boardinghouse for
men working on the jetties.[37]

In May, Broward gave up his work on the tug and applied
for a commission as pilot of the St. Johns River Bar. After
he had deposited the necessary bond of five hundred dollars,[38]
he received his license on May 12.[39] The rate of pilotage at the
St. Johns Bar, established by the Legislative Council while
Florida was still a territory, was two dollars for each foot of
water drawn by the vessel and two dollars for each day the
pilot was detained on board.[40] As more people began settling
in northeast Florida, and as its commercial enterprises became
more important, the value of the river and its harbors also
increased. The Territorial Act of 1839 had created a Board
of Port Wardens to regulate the anchorage, mooring, and
dockage of vessels at the port,[41] and successive legislation established controls over the pilots.[42] The large number of vessels crossing the Bar brought the pilots a lucrative income, and
commissions were much sought after.

During the summer of 1883, Napoleon's sister Josephine
died in Jacksonville. A few weeks later Napoleon and Carrie
moved from Mayport to live in his sister's house on East Duval
Street, across from the old St. Andrew's parish church, near
the corner of what is now Florida Avenue. The furniture in
the house cost Napoleon one hundred dollars.[43] The rooms
were large, with high ceilings, and the floors shone like sunshine on a late summer afternoon. Moss-bannered oaks shaded
the front of the two-story house, and the back yard was large
enough for a flower garden.

September in north Florida was a season of bright sunshine.
Great splashes of sunlight slanted through the trees, and everywhere the foliage was a rich summer green. Grass, weeds, and
flowers in the woods were thick and fresh. In the air was a

fragrance of clover hay, the first cutting. Carrie, big with child, was too sick to enjoy the warm autumn. She suffered from attacks of dengue fever, but the doctor, fearing that her heart might be weak, hesitated to give her his stronger medicines.[44] As the time for the birth of her child drew near, Carrie improved. Her face colored and her body grew stronger. A son was born on October 29, and the child was given his father's name.

It was a happy day for Napoleon. Captain Kemps, notified by messenger, started out from New Berlin immediately to see his grandson. Suddenly, in the midst of the excitement, Carrie's condition changed and became critical. A few hours after the birth of her baby, she suffered severe attacks of congestive chills and fever, brought on by the dengue. In her weakened condition she had little power of resistance. A strange quiet filled the house, broken only by the movements of the doctor and nurses, the baby's crying, and by occasional inquiries from kindly neighbors. Lamplights from the sickroom cut across the outside darkness with the color of a new moon. Carrie grew steadily worse during the night and in the early hours of the dawn of October 30, 1883, she sank into a state of unconsciousness from which she never rallied.[45] Her body was placed on the steamer *Mabey*[46] and carried back to New Berlin where she was buried in the Kemps family cemetery.[47]

Napoleon's world was filled with darkness. Grief-stricken, he could not work, and for weeks he lived with the Kemps family in New Berlin. Adding to his sorrow was the problem of his motherless child. Frantically he advertised for milk that would agree with the baby, and went into the woods among the Negro women, trying to find a wet nurse. But it was too late. The infant died on December 16, after a short life of six weeks, and was buried in the grave next to his mother's.[48] In less than five months Napoleon had lost his sister, his wife, and his child. He knew the fullness of sorrow.

∽ 3 ∾
River Runs and a Romance

THE WINTER OF 1883-1884 was a hard and bitter one for young Broward. After Carrie's death he continued to work as a pilot, directing the steamers over the treacherous St. Johns Bar, through the channel to Jacksonville, and then out again. Shocked by his tragic loss, he wanted to leave Florida and the scenes that reminded him of his wife. Upon the advice of Captain Kemps, he asked for and received an indefinite leave of absence, and early in June, 1884, took passage on a coastwise steamer headed north.[1] He planned to visit his mother's Northern relatives and his own Northern friends. Very little is known of Broward's activities during the next few months, but he probably traveled through the New England states, saw his Parsons aunts and uncles, and renewed old acquaintances at Cape Cod and New Gloucester. By late fall he was back in Florida.

At Jacksonville Broward boarded a down-river steamer. Although it was December, the air was like that of a warm April day. The trees on both banks cast long shadows on the river; moss scarves hung low from the branches and trailed in the water. A wind, redolent of the salt smell of the Atlantic, cut sharply across the vessel and lost itself in the woods.

The captain of the vessel was an old friend and Broward helped him collect tickets. Among the passengers was a young lady of seventeen, Annie Isabell Douglass,[2] who, with her mother, her brother Alexander, and her sister Elsie, was traveling from Sanford to Mayport, to meet her father, Captain Douglass. Annie had arrived from New York in October and had spent the past two months with relatives in Sanford. After meeting the captain in Mayport, the Douglass family

planned to go on to their new home at Mount Pleasant.³ The
paths of Napoleon Broward and Annie Douglass crossed for
the first time, but it is doubtful that the two young people
gave each other more than a casual glance during the entire trip.

Broward returned to New Berlin, where he worked for
Captain Kemps on the steamer *David Kemps,* recently purchased for twenty-eight hundred dollars from the Washington Steamboat Company.⁴ Later, he became a partner with
Kemps in the steamer *Kate Spencer,* which had been completed
in New Berlin.

The winter was a banner one for the river boats. The St.
Johns, like other rivers of northeast Florida during the 1880's,
swarmed with steamboats of every description, ranging from
small, odd-looking craft that ran to places far up the river,
to the fastest and most modern of passenger boats. Most of
these vessels were side-wheelers. With orange trees in full
bearing in the groves and plantations along the waterways,
and with few railroads south of Jacksonville to offer freight
competition, river-boat captains like Broward found the shipping of oranges a lucrative business.

The steamers played an important part in the development
of Jacksonville and the surrounding area. They transformed
the St. Johns River into a pulsating artery of trade that provided the major means of transportation of freight and passengers to a large portion of the peninsula. Moreover, they
helped northeast Florida remain a part of the social life of the
South. Coastwise steamers made it easy for the ladies of Jacksonville, St. Augustine, and Palatka to hear the latest up-
country gossip, to learn the intricate dance steps introduced
at the St. Cecilia cotillions in Charleston, and to receive the
new fashion books from New York and Boston. Broward's
cargo often included bolts of taffeta and silk, as well as boxes
that bulged with combs and pins and buttons, shipped from
the stores in Jacksonville to the farms and houses along the
river.

Captain Broward, as he was now called, was on the path to prosperity through the river trade. By June, 1885, the *Kate Spencer* made two trips daily to and from the St. Johns Bar, carrying both freight and passengers. The newspaper advertisements announced that the vessel loaded in Jacksonville from "Wightman's and Christopher's wharf, rear of the post-office," and promised "a glorious opportunity for sea air, fishing and bathing."[5]

The *Kate Spencer*, newest and fastest boat on the river, received a fair share of the tourist travel that constantly increased each year after the war. The journey by rail from the North was a tedious one, lasting two or three days. When the tired traveler had made the final change of cars at Live Oak and had finished the last lap over the Florida Central into Jacksonville, he breathed a sigh of relief. Jacksonville, in winter a city four times its summer size, was already known as "The Winter City in Summer Land."[6] The city offered few municipal attractions. Apparently Jacksonville appealed to the tourist because of its climate and because it was in Florida. The hotelkeepers and steamboat captains like Broward received the greater portion of tourist spending.

During the season of 1884-1885 approximately sixty thousand tourists arrived at Jacksonville's principal hotels and larger boardinghouses.[7] As the city could not accommodate them all, many were forced to go on to other towns. In the long summer months of 1885, when business was slack, the fashionable hotels—the Everett, Windsor, and Duval—spent considerable money for improvements and decorations.

Jacksonville in the 1880's was unimposing. On Bay Street the business buildings and hotels were interspersed between residences. Back from the river the streets, usually unpaved, outlined blocks of houses enclosed in trimly kept yards. During the winter season, tourists, dressed in the fashionable styles of the North, promenaded along the wooden sidewalks on Bay Street and watched the steamers as they passed up and down the waterway.

The announcement of a race between the *Kate Spencer* and a rival boat created considerable interest for the spectators. A billowing tide of parasols and bright dresses, of black vests and gold watch fobs, ebbed and flowed around the wharf from which the vessels were scheduled to leave. A band blared out the tunes of the day and added to the general clatter. The two boats, cutting cleanly from the brown water, throbbed while they awaited the starter's whistle. A great cheer went up as the steamships propelled themselves on the current for the race. There was furious betting, with the odds changing frequently. When the boats reached their destination, the name of the winner was hurriedly relayed back to Jacksonville. Many newspapers throughout the country described these races. One account reported: "A very hotly contested and exciting race occurred between the steamers *Kate Spencer* and *Seth Low*, Sunday afternoon while coming up from the Bar. There was but little difference in the time made by the two boats, the *Spencer* having gained in the entire distance several hundred yards."[8]

Broward arranged in July, 1885, to carry the daily mail by boat to individual families along the route to Mayport.[9] He tried to secure a mail contract from the government but was not successful.[10] Early in October, when the mail-carrying DeBary-Baya Steamers Company gave up its government contract, mail deliveries to Mayport were suspended. Living on his ship, Broward enjoyed an untrammeled, carefree life. He was, moreover, becoming prosperous through a growing amount of freight and passenger business. Besides her regular runs, the *Kate Spencer* catered to parties of fishermen and picnickers, and each Sunday made special excursions to Mayport, Fort George Island, or the Bar, all of which increased her earnings.

During the week, the Jacksonville paper published notices of the Sunday trips, which usually attracted capacity crowds. One such advertisement declared:

The newest and fastest steamer on the river, *Kate Spencer*, will leave Wightman's and Christopher's, rear of the post-office, for an Excursion to St. John's Bar and the Jetties. Sunday, July 5, 1885 at 10 a.m. Returning, leave Mayport at 4 p.m. Fare for Round Trip, 50 cents.[11]

Family groups often made a holiday of a river excursion on the St. Johns. They carried filled lunch baskets aboard, and throughout the voyage stuffed themselves with fried chicken, smoked ham, cold meat, biscuits, pickled watermelon rind, and a wide assortment of cakes and homemade candies. Other passengers ate the hot meals sold on the boat and served on deck by Negro waiters.

Many of the boats were elaborately fitted out. Their main parlors sparkled with cut-glass chandeliers; gilt and gold chairs lined the walls according to the latest fashion, adding more to display than comfort. Mahogany-framed mirrors decorated the ladies' salons, and carpets covered the floors. On the boats which served liquors and wines, glasses clinked continually in the smoking rooms. However, Captain Broward, a strong prohibitionist, refused to serve whisky aboard the *Kate Spencer*. At night the Negro hands assembled and sang spirituals and lullabies. Sometimes the passengers danced on the open decks, but more often, after a day of activity, they were content to sit and idly watch the dark-brown water flow quietly around the great bends of the river on its way to the sea.

Napoleon was every inch a prosperous river-boat captain. At twenty-nine he had developed into a large man, with his two hundred ten pounds well distributed over his six-foot two-inch frame. A mustache, thick and neatly trimmed in the fashion of the day, adorned his full face. Long hours in the sun had browned his complexion and had given a smouldering redness to his dark hair. He walked with an alert, almost military step, and usually wore a tailored, well-fitted coat of average length, open enough to allow a generous view of the white linen shirt front and the collar above it. Dark trousers, worn without cuffs, and a sash braid around his waist, completed his ship-captain's attire.[12]

In July, 1886, Broward went to Savannah to apply for an appointment as the United States Local Inspector of Hulls for the Savannah District, a job then unfilled. He was endorsed by Congressman Charles Dougherty and several prominent Jacksonville businessmen who wrote flattering letters of recommendation. One such letter described him as "a young man of great worth, and very superior intelligence. . . ."[13] Despite this support, Broward lost the appointment to a Georgia resident.

Several weeks later, on a clear bright morning early in September, Annie Douglass boarded the *Kate Spencer* when it made its regular run back from the Bar. She threaded her way through the crowds on the deck and found a seat on the awninged side of the boat. She sat alone, her gray cloak across the back of her chair, her dark hair thrown into strong relief. Idly Annie watched the green banks slip by. As the captain of the vessel approached her, she turned her head casually. He introduced himself and asked if she were the person who had made derogatory remarks about the service on his boat. A few days before, a friend of the Douglass family had tried to board the *Kate Spencer* at Fulton, but the ship had inadvertently passed him by. Annie had recounted the incident to another friend, who repeated the story to Napoleon. Since the young lady had been critical of the captain and the vessel, Napoleon was determined to talk to his censor, who had been aptly described to him.

With a flash of her dark-gray eyes, Miss Douglass admitted that she had made the remarks, and assured him that she considered them most fitting. Napoleon explained that on the day in question he had been on a holiday trip to New Berlin and had left a substitute captain in charge. She replied tartly, "If you want to take your holidays off the ship, you should choose someone to run the boat who knows how."[14] He flushed at her sharp words, and then noticed that she was smiling and that her eyes glowed warmly. They both laughed, and before the ship docked they had become good friends.

After their first meeting, Napoleon often saw Annie on the boat when she made trips to Jacksonville to shop and visit. During the voyages they talked politics and frequently compared the North with the South. Although they sometimes failed to agree, Napoleon always admired Annie's independent thought and the forceful way she presented her arguments. She never lacked spirit, and there was an innate charm and grace about her that fascinated him. She was a little shorter than middle height; yet when she stood next to the tall captain she gave the impression of being small. Her delicate eyebrows, finely etched nose, and precise little chin added distinction to her strong face. Her quick smile and her warm, gentle eyes charmed everyone.

In October, 1886, Annie's father, Captain Douglass, was injured when his ship was caught in a South Atlantic storm. After his vessel had docked in New York he was taken to a hospital, and Mrs. Douglass came up from the South to help nurse him. Since Annie and Elsie could not remain alone at Mount Pleasant, they moved to Jacksonville. Annie lived at the home of Captain M. C. Rice, an old friend of the Douglass family, and her sister boarded at the St. Joseph's Convent School.[15]

Before long, Napoleon was using a variety of excuses to visit the Rice home several times a week. In the evenings after his boat docked at Wightman's wharf, Napoleon, his shoulders sleek in his captain's coat, his face freshly shaved, walked the short blocks to the house. If he found other young men calling on Miss Douglass, he would swap stories with Captain Rice for a half hour or so; then if his rivals were still there, he would inform them that it would be better if they went home.[16] In spite of such presumptuous behavior, Annie always welcomed Napoleon's visits. During the early evening they walked with the smart crowds along Bay Street. On Saturday nights they either made excursions on the steamer or danced in the elegant parlors of the St. James Hotel.

One evening early in March, 1887, they returned to the

Rice house from a walk along the riverbank. Standing together on the porch they watched the new moon rise above the oak trees. The leaves of the columbine off the side porch murmured softly. The city was hushed. Napoleon reached out and covered Annie's hand with his own. In a quiet voice he asked her to marry him and she consented.

At nine o'clock on the morning of May 5, the Reverend W. H. Dodge performed the wedding ceremony in the Newnan Street Presbyterian Church. It was a day of glory for Napoleon. The flowers, the music, and the large gathering of relatives made the affair a social event in Jacksonville. One newspaper declared: "The groom is one of Jacksonville's strong and manly representative young men, and high character, joined to force and energy have given already influence and friends. The bride . . . is universally esteemed for graces of mind and person."[17]

Napoleon and his bride were escorted to the old "Augustine" ferry where they boarded a train for St. Augustine. After a three-day honeymoon, the couple returned to Jacksonville, visited for several days in the Rice home, and then moved temporarily into a small furnished apartment at the corner of Liberty and Bay streets.[18] Mrs. Broward owned some property on Church Street in East Jacksonville, then one of the fashionable suburbs, and there the couple built a home.[19] The two-story frame structure was completed in October and the Browards moved in immediately.[20] The furnishings for the house cost approximately one hundred eighty-five dollars.[21] Some of this furniture is in use in the Broward family today.

Broward was becoming increasingly popular in Jacksonville. His years on the river had made him a familiar figure to the people of the county, and his personable mien and affable good nature made him a favorite boat captain. He apparently showed only an average interest in politics at this time. In October, 1886, he transported his friend, Charles Dougherty, who was campaigning for re-election to Congress, to a po-

litical meeting at Mandarin.[22] There is no other record
of his participation in the fall elections of that year.

Broward continued to operate the *Kate Spencer*, which was
doing a thriving freight and passenger business up and down
the river. In continuous service throughout 1887, except during May, when Broward had her overhauled in Jacksonville,[23]
the vessel made her usual excursions all during the summer,
going as far as Palatka on many trips. On one of these voyages
a horse was carried to Mayport, for an army officer living
there.[24]

In October, 1887, Broward bought a small woodyard and
gristmill from George A. DeCottes.[25] The mill was used by
many people in the city to grind their feed and corn. The
captain hired a man to operate the business, while he continued
on the *Kate Spencer*. Nothing, it seemed, could wean him from
the river and his boat. However, events occurred during the
first two months of 1888 which greatly affected Napoleon
Broward and helped determine his future activities.

On the last Friday in January, 1888, a notorious forger
from New York, who had absconded with forty thousand dollars, was arrested in Jacksonville and lodged in the city jail.[26]
With the sheriff's approval, the prisoner was transferred to a
suite of rooms in the Tischler Building, where he was guarded
by two deputies. Late on the night of February 2, while the
guards slept, the prisoner escaped.[27] A great clamor arose all
over the state against the negligence of the sheriff, and Governor Perry asked for his resignation. The Democratic county
executive committee immediately called a meeting to consider
a nominee for the position and to make a recommendation to
the governor.[28]

Governor Perry explicitly demanded a man who was "thoroughly sober and of good moral character."[29] Many considered
Broward the best qualified person for the office. The *Florida
Times-Union* endorsed him as a "man possessed of four pre-
requisites . . . integrity, honesty, courage, and above all abso-
lute sobriety."[30]

At the meeting on Saturday morning, a majority of the executive committee voted for Broward on the first ballot, and unanimously recommended him to the governor. The county newspapers were enthusiastic over the committee's choice. Editorially the *Florida Times-Union* expressed the general sentiment of the voters when it declared the "nomination . . . one of the very best that has ever been made in Duval County."[31]

A letter from John L. Crawford, Florida's secretary of state, received by Broward on the evening of February 21, informed him that the governor had appointed him sheriff of Duval County.[32] Broward immediately subscribed to the oath of office and dispatched his letter of acceptance to Tallahassee. His official commission arrived at the end of the week, and on the following Monday, February 27, he took formal charge of the sheriff's office and entered upon its duties immediately. He appointed Ed Williams and W. D. Vinzant as deputies, and Pat Phelan as jailer.[33]

Some of Jacksonville's winter tourists, bored with Bay Street promenades and dances in the ballrooms of the Carlton and St. James hotels, demanded more excitement. As a result several gambling houses opened in the city. Gambling was not legal, but law enforcement was lax, and these luxuriously furnished establishments operated wide open. During his first week in office, Broward mapped out plans to clean the city of this vice.

The following Friday evening at nine-thirty, the sheriff, accompanied by regular and specially appointed deputies, left the county jail and approached the "West End" saloon. He posted his men in the shadows and then, with his slouch hat pulled low over his forehead, entered the building alone. No one recognized him at first, and he had time to survey the premises and secure sufficient evidence to justify his arrests. He took the proprietors into custody and his men hurried them off to jail. Broward and his deputies next raided a well-appointed gambling house on Newnan Street, and then went

on to a third establishment. There they found that the owners
in their hurried departure had forgotten to lock and shutter
the place. Here Broward seized "a roulette table, one stud
poker table, one faro table, and one draw poker table."[34]

Next morning when questioned by reporters, the new sheriff
declared in a voice strong with conviction, "The law against
gambling is complete and makes it my duty and not my privilege to break up such establishments. . . . I am under oath to
enforce it and I propose to do so."[35] A large number of Jacksonville citizens applauded the sheriff's actions, and he was
highly commended by both local and state papers. The *Florida
Times-Union* predicted that when "another raid becomes necessary . . . the fur will fly."[36]

On March 8, 1888, the case against the gamblers came to
trial with Sheriff Broward an important witness for the county.
The gambling interests, who were powerful in northeast Florida, had made several attempts to "buy" Broward. He later
told how one gambler came to his office to persuade him not
to introduce certain evidence. Broward refused the request.
When the gambler had gone, the sheriff discovered that a
large roll of bills, tied with a string, had been left as a bribe.
He promptly returned the money.[37] The gamblers were
eventually convicted and sentenced.

This first successful venture as a law enforcing agent helped
to build Broward's political reputation. Once again the *Florida
Times-Union* supported him with enthusiasm: "The wise and
politic course . . . is for Sheriff Broward to go straight forward
in the line which he has begun. He has only to listen to the
papers to see that he has already made the beginning of a
great reputation. A month ago he was a modest citizen, held
in high esteem by a reasonably large circle of personal friends,
but unknown to the state at large. Now he is known all over
the state, and his example is being commended to other officials
in like station."[38]

∾ 4 ∽

Politics and the Plague

B Y MID-APRIL OF 1888, summer heat, still and
heavy, blanketed Florida. The sun scorched the earth,
dried up small ponds, and threatened the crops. A
sour smell rose from the river and permeated Jacksonville.
The stench hung like a mist over the low places, penetrating
the houses until whatever was touched or eaten felt and tasted
like the river. Mosquitoes swarmed over green-scummed pools
of water. Many families moved to Pablo Beach or to resorts
in the North. Broward's wife and his sister, Hortense, left for
New York City in July. Hardly had they reached their destination when they read the news which shocked and horrified
the whole country—yellow fever had broken out in Jacksonville and a terrible epidemic was raging.

In the early spring of 1888, a peculiar fever, which somewhat baffled physicians, was prevalent in several sections of
Florida. Word spread that it was the dreaded yellow fever,
but this fact was denied. The people of Bartow, indignant
when the *Savannah Morning News* on April 22 reported that
there was fever in Bartow, Plant City, and Micanopy, urged
their city to sue the paper for libel.[1] The secretary of the Duval
County Board of Health investigated conditions in Gainesville,
Ocala, Dade City, Lakeland, Plant City, Seffner, and Tampa,
and found two cases of the fever in Plant City and a record of
twelve deaths there during the previous six months.

Vague rumors concerning the plague circulated in Jacksonville, and the Marine Hospital Bureau reported that yellow-
fever cases were being diagnosed as typhoid.[2] Jacksonville
physicians vigorously denied these charges.[3] There were scattered cases in the state during June, but none in Jacksonville,

and citizens there thought they were safe. If they could get through July, they imagined all would be well.[4]

During the last week of July the first case in the city was reported, but it caused only slight alarm. A man named R. D. McCormick, who had come into Jacksonville by way of Tampa, had registered at the Grand Union Hotel. He was ill and the local physicians who examined him diagnosed his case as yellow fever. On August 8 four more cases were found; and then, without further warning, new cases developed each hour. On August 10 the Board of Health issued its first proclamation, which admitted the fever was rapidly reaching the epidemic stage.[5] Panic and disorder swept the city.

When word of the fever reached Broward, he immediately placed his office at the disposal of the health authorities. With other officials, he worked endless hours through the close, windless night trying to keep some semblance of order in the maddened city. It was virtually impossible. Terror-stricken people waited hours for a train, filled the seats in the cars, and jammed the aisles. When the trains could carry no more, they pulled away from the station leaving hundreds behind. All the roads leading out from the city were congested with people, fleeing in every conceivable conveyance and on foot, scores of them uncertain where they might go. Their common purpose was to leave the plague-ridden city.

Intense excitement and great fear prevailed throughout the South. Nearly the whole state of Florida, as well as Savannah, Mobile, Charleston, and a number of Northern and Western cities, declared a rigid quarantine against Jacksonville.[6] The people of Waycross, Georgia, threatened to tear up the railroad tracks if any refugees traveled through from Jacksonville, even in locked cars and at a high rate of speed.[7] As a protective measure, the authorities at St. Augustine turned back all mail from Jacksonville, although it had undergone thorough fumigation. Other places in the state refused to allow merchandise of any description to come into their communities from the infected area. Some local boards of health placed restrictions on machinery, wagon wheels, railroad iron, ice, and even silver dollars.[8] The officials of the Clyde Steamship Line announced that their service to Jacksonville was stopped,[9] and this was followed by the discontinuance of all up-river boats.[10]

By the end of August, daily reports were being sent out so that relatives would know if any members of their family in the city were sick. As soon as she heard about the epidemic, Mrs. Broward wired her husband, asking if she should return to Florida. Broward answered immediately, cautioning her to remain in safety in New York. The sheriff could not leave, even had he wanted to, because several of his deputies were stricken and there were cases of the fever among the prisoners.[11] Trouble was expected from poor Negroes and whites. During the course of the epidemic, a bill was introduced in Congress to appropriate one hundred thousand dollars to assist in eradicating the fever.[12] Rumors had circulated that the money was sent for the needy. Although Federal funds had not arrived in Jacksonville, many people were determined to have money and rations. Scores of Negroes purportedly immune to the fever flocked to the city, drawn by the extravagant stories of free food and easy money.

Jacksonville became a place of despair and wretchedness. The dead were everywhere—in the houses and lying unburied in the cemetery on Union Street. Much of the white population had fled the city and those who remained burned trash and tried to disinfect their houses. Taking every suggested precaution, they tied handkerchiefs and scarves across their faces to keep fever germs out of their throats. The city's business slowed down and finally stopped. Deserted stores, shuttered houses, and empty streets told a disastrous story. Food ran short and coffin prices skyrocketed. Doctors and nurses worked endless hours under the direction of the Jacksonville Auxiliary Sanitary Association.

Many experiments were tried to check the plague. One of the more popular was the "concussion" treatment, the theory

being that the concussion caused by firing heavy cannon charges
would kill the yellow-fever "microbes." Four cannon and
quantities of powder and blank cartridges were brought in
from Tocoi, Florida, and on the evening of August 17 two
hundred shots were fired.[13] The only perceptible results from
this experiment were the noises of the cannonading and a number of broken windows in some nearby churches. One night
a detachment from Wilson's Battery placed one of its cannon
at the river's edge, pointing in the direction of Bay Street.
A Negro, hurrying along the sidewalk at the time, failed to
see the gun until it was fired within thirty feet of him. Thinking that the showers of sand thrown in his face were fever
"germs," he exclaimed: "Great Lord, how thick they falls."[14]
Bells were rung throughout the city "to keep the miasma
moving." Upon the suggestion of several doctors, weary citizens kindled huge fires of pine and tar each night in various
sections of Jacksonville to purify the air and prevent the spread
of the infection. Believing that night air encouraged the fever,
many people locked themselves in after dark. If they ventured
out at all they carried pieces of tarred rope as a disinfectant
and germicide.[15]

The weather continued hot, and by the middle of October
the fever had spread to Gainesville, Fernandina, Green Cove
Springs, Sanderson, Macclenny, and other communities. Past
experience indicated that the fever would abate with cold
weather, and church services were held to pray for frost. Then
suddenly the fever passed its peak. The epidemic was still
widespread in Jacksonville and elsewhere, but there was a
daily decline in the number of cases reported. On October 29
the temperature dropped to fifty-six degrees, the coolest
weather since the epidemic, and many persons hoped that the
end of the scourge was in sight.[16]

As soon as Mrs. Broward heard that there was a break in
the epidemic, she wired her husband from New York that she
was coming home. Despite his protests, Annie Broward took
passage on the steamer *Gulf Stream*.[17] The steamer's captain

refused to put in at Jacksonville, and Mrs. Broward left the vessel in Fernandina. She traveled overland by wagon to Mount Pleasant, her father's home, where her husband waited. Every evening after that Broward went to Mount Pleasant, returning to the city early the following morning. The family moved back to Jacksonville a few days before Christmas.[18]

Early in October, 1888, while the plague was still raging, the Democratic slate of candidates for the November county elections was announced. Broward was listed for the office of sheriff.[19] During the yellow-fever epidemic there had been little time for politics, and in the stricken city there was a decided lack of enthusiasm for the approaching election. So many of the white Democratic voters left the city that the Republicans, depending upon Negro support, became the major party in Duval County for the first time since the end of Reconstruction.

Election morning, November 6, broke dull and gloomy, with heavy clouds hanging overhead. Though the weather in the early part of the day threatened rain, none fell. The afternoon was oppressively sultry and sticky, and the occasional appearance of the sun made the heat almost unbearable.[20] Despite the large number of names on the registration lists, a light vote was cast in every precinct. Crowds of Negroes, voting the "straight Republican ticket," lolled about the polling places throughout the day. The Democratic vote was small, and the appearance at the polls of a white man—Democrat or Republican—was regarded with curiosity. The Republicans scored a great victory. Returns revealed that all the Democratic candidates had been defeated. Broward received 1,417 votes, whereas 2,573 were tabulated for his opponent, Roy P. Moody.[21]

While he was sheriff, Broward fortunately had not sold his woodyard on Bay Street. The yard was closed during the epidemic, but reopened in November with the first cold weather.[22] Earlier that year, Broward had given up his work on the *Kate Spencer*, although he retained his financial interest in the vessel. Captain Summers was in charge, and in December the *Spencer* resumed her regular river runs between Jacksonville and Mayport.[23]

Broward, however, was not finished with politics. On January 2, 1889, Moody presented his own bond as the new sheriff to the executive committee. While the bond was being considered, one of the sureties withdrew. Before this matter was settled, the time limit for the acceptance of the bond had expired, and the committee, strongly Democratic and arguing a technicality, declared Moody ineligible and disallowed his claim to office. The Florida Supreme Court, in its January term, reviewed the case and upheld this action.[24] In March, Governor Francis P. Fleming reappointed Broward to the vacancy. The governor's announcement delighted the public, and the county newspapers enthusiastically endorsed Broward. The *Florida Times-Union* called him a "brave resolute man," and declared the appointment "a most worthy one."[25]

Broward's distinctive qualities as a first-rate politician were recognized in all of his activities. His diplomacy and tact, and his scrupulous zeal in smoothing over incidents that could become embarrassing, were factors that helped him greatly throughout his public career. While Broward was sheriff, there was close cooperation between the county and city police agencies. A newspaper editorial complimented Broward and his deputies, declaring: ". . . They second each other in the utmost harmony and good faith, free from the petty jealousies, which often spring up between public officials. . . ."[26]

Jacksonville at this time had a Republican mayor, C. B. Smith, who had been elected in December of 1887. As an aftermath of the Reconstruction period, the Republican party, with strong Negro and conservative support, was still a factor in Florida politics. In the Smith administration five aldermen, the municipal judge, fifteen of the twenty-three policemen, two police sergeants, and the chairman of the Board of Police Commissioners were Negroes. The Democrats, dominated largely by a white supremacy philosophy, found this state of affairs distasteful and planned to change it. During the yellow-fever epidemic, only a portion of the white city and county officials, including Sheriff Broward, remained in Jacksonville, and much of the responsibility of administering affairs fell to the Negro officials. The Democrats, supported by some conservative Republicans, charged that the existing municipal government was not capable of performing the functions necessary for a judicious administration of the city's affairs, and that such a condition would destroy Jacksonville's standing and credit as a municipality. The Florida legislature, strongly Democratic, was asked to amend Jacksonville's charter so that Negroes could be excluded from public office.[27]

A legislative committee arrived from Tallahassee for a firsthand inspection of the situation, and Broward acted as their guide. Mayor Smith, notified of the visit, ordered white policemen to be on duty at the time. Hoping to thwart Smith's plan, Sheriff Broward, already important in county Democratic politics, suggested a ruse which the party leaders approved. He conducted the legislators on a lengthy and extensive tour of the city and its outlying areas. When they returned to City Hall in the afternoon, they found they had missed the train back to Tallahassee. As they were forced to stay overnight, Broward secured lodging for them at the St. James Hotel.

At breakfast the following morning the sheriff suggested that the committee make another inspection of the police force. Train time was several hours away and the investigators agreed. City officials, thinking the legislators had gone the evening before, ordered the Negro police to return to duty. Broward's scheme worked, and the committee returned to Tallahassee with the evidence it needed. The Florida legislature subsequently approved a major revision of Jacksonville's charter, House Bill No. 4, which empowered the governor to appoint an eighteen-man council that would in turn appoint the mayor. The Board of Police Commissioners and its chairman were to be elected by the city council.[28] Thus it was assured that in the future only white Democrats would be chosen as Jackson-

ville officials. House Bill No. 4, in the passage of which
Broward had played a vital part, became an issue in later city
and county elections, and eventually in the gubernatorial campaign of 1904.

While serving as sheriff, Broward continued his outside
business activities. In July, 1889, he sold his interest in the
Kate Spencer, at a profit, to George DeCottes. The woodyard
and gristmill were bringing in a small but steady income. In
both his political and business activities Broward prospered.

During the first week of January, 1890, Florida newspapers
were embellished with black headlines announcing the dis-
covery of phosphate in Marion, Citrus, and Hernando counties.
This news set Florida afire with excitement. Extravagant
stories were circulated about the untold wealth that was to
be had for the taking. Everyone would soon be rich. Sheriff
Broward heard that John F. Dunn had turned down an option
of two million dollars on his land, and that another man who
four years earlier had bought land at from fifty cents to a
dollar an acre had now sold his holdings for seventy-eight
thousand dollars.[29] The newspapers were filled with stories
about Dunnellon farmers, who six months before had been
worth only a few dollars each, and now were so well off "they
need not ever touch a plow again."[30] Albertus Voght, who discovered a phosphate bed while sinking a well on his small
farm at Dunnellon, acquired a fortune and became known as
the "Duke of Dunnellon," a title which he justified locally
by indulging in thoroughbred horses, half a hundred hounds,
handsome equipages, and lavish entertainments. The phosphate "boom" was underway.

Scores of prospectors poured into the Dunnellon area and
a typical boom burst into flower overnight. Gamblers, dia-
monds flashing on fingers and cravats, outlaws from as far
west as California and Mexico, and prostitutes suited for every
taste and pocketbook, flocked to the phosphate regions. Saloons
and brothels ran wide open. Only the primitive law of the
frontier held the rabble in check. Nearly everyone, black and

white, carried a pistol, the most effective variety of law. When Broward visited Dunnellon he watched the justice of the peace hold his Monday morning court session "under an oak tree with a bacon box for a desk, a nail keg for a bench, and a heavily armed constable nearby for emergencies."[31]

Businessmen all over the state were enthusiastic, some wildly so, and companies organized to mine phosphate sprang up overnight. Napoleon Broward and John N. C. Stockton leased land near Black Creek in Clay County and established the Black River Phosphate Company. Like many others, this mining company did not meet with the success that its organizers had hoped for. Land values were greatly inflated by the boom, land was frequently bought unwisely, and phosphate mining machinery was scarce and expensive. As there were few, if any, public roads or railroads to many of the deposits, they were difficult to mine and operate. Much land, boomed as containing "sure" deposits, was falsely advertised and sold to unwary buyers. Broward was disappointed but not discouraged with his phosphate company. During the two years following, he was associated with various mines near the head of Ichtucknee River and the Suwannee and Columbia County lines.[32] These mines were not successful, and Broward never recovered the full value of his investments in phosphate speculation.

Throughout this period Broward's interest in politics continued. In June, 1890, he announced himself as a candidate for the office of sheriff. As he was supported by most of the party, by many citizens of the county, and by local newspapers, there was little likelihood that he would fail to be elected.

Broward's popularity had grown tremendously. Numerous meetings held by his supporters during the early part of July were so well attended that the people overflowed the meeting halls and stood outside on the streets and sidewalks to hear him speak.[33] The campaign began to warm up when a rival candidate charged that sometime during election day, ballot boxes, stuffed with Broward votes, would be substituted for the regular boxes, and that occasion would be taken, during a

preconcerted rumpus at poll-closing time, to switch the boxes.³⁴
These charges were refuted in the newspapers and were denied vehemently both by Broward and his adherents, who took
the offensive and made political capital of the charges, winning votes as a result. The election held on July 24, 1890,
which named Broward delegates to the convention, was proclaimed as "a big victory for the Sheriff." One newspaper emphatically declared that "it means the nomination of Napoleon
B. Broward for Sheriff of Duval County and his triumphant
election at the polls in November."³⁵ The office of sheriff was
certainly not the most important one in a county election, yet
in this contest it seemed as though the vital issue was the
election of Broward. Heralded as the "uncompromising Democrat," he was declared the man who would "command the full
voting strength of his party."³⁶

A large crowd of delegates to the Democratic county convention streamed into the Park Opera House on the morning
of August 4. They filled the plush seats and stood against the
gas-yellowed walls. Curtains were pulled back from the windows and an unfamiliar light stirred in the corners of the
building. In an excited air of expectancy the delegates awaited
the business ahead. Broward's name was one of the first to be
placed before the convention, and when the vote was taken he
had 101½ votes to his rival's 12. When the nomination was
made unanimous, the convention was almost broken up by the
cheers and shouts from Broward delegates and from his supporters in the visitors' gallery.³⁷

Several large political meetings were held between the end
of the convention and the November election, at most of
which Broward was one of the principal speakers or the guest
of honor. At a rally in Jacksonville on the evening of October
16, two speakers extolled the virtues of Sheriff Broward.
They were Major Alexander St. Clair-Abrams and Colonel
Robert W. Davis, two men who later bitterly denounced and
fought the candidate they were now praising.³⁸ On October
24, with a group of supporters, Broward sailed on the steamer

Mary Draper to attend a meeting in Mandarin.[39] A final rally was staged in Jacksonville on the evening of October 29, one week before election day.[40] The Republican party was no longer a major threat in Duval County politics in 1890, and observers safely predicted that the Democrats would win. Of the 2,535 votes cast, Napoleon Broward received 1,756.[41] Because of the Republican success in Duval County in 1888, state Democratic leaders had been especially anxious for the party's triumph there in 1890. Along these lines John L. Crawford, secretary of state, wrote to Broward on November 11, 1890: "I congratulate you upon your triumphant election—upon the political redemption of Duval County and the State of Florida. Verily, the revolution very greatly exceeds my most sanguine expectations."[42] Immediately after the New Year, Governor Fleming forwarded Broward his official announcement of election and his commission. The sheriff's bond was renewed with the county commissioners on January 2, 1891, and his office settled down to the usual routine of business.

Though Broward's life after 1890 was conspicuously political, he was not completely occupied with politics. His correspondence shows that all his life he retained a love and admiration for the river and for boats. When he was not connected with boats in a business way, he constructed models of the vessels he dreamed of building some day. In keeping with this interest Broward, in the fall of 1891, formed a stock company and raised money to build a boat. Associated with him in this enterprise were his brother Montcalm, now the captain of the *Kate Spencer*, his brother-in-law, Captain Roberts, and Ed Williams and Henry Fritot.

During November, construction was begun in New Berlin on a thirty-foot yacht, which had a mast forty-two feet above the deck, a bowsprit twenty-eight feet over the bow, and an enormous canvas spread of three hundred and ninety yards.[43] The vessel, completed in January, 1892, was christened the *Annie Dorcas* by her namesake, Broward's young daughter. The *Dorcas* was a lovely sight on the river, standing with her

bow clear of the water and her sails spread to the wind. The
St. Johns Yacht Club regatta was scheduled for January 20,
and Broward entered the *Dorcas*. In her first race she made
a slow start, failed to pick up speed, and came across the finish
line far behind the other racers. Hoping to make a better
showing, Broward was determined to race the *Dorcas* the following day. It was a golden afternoon, calm and placid; a
brilliant sun gilded the wave caps and a salty breeze filled the
sails of the vessels. A large throng of spectators lined both
sides of the river shore along the scheduled route of the race.
The immense skirts of the ladies were vivid splashes in the
bright sunshine and their wide bonnets buckled in the playful
breeze. Broward, handsome in a shiny black coat, his face dark
from the sun and alive with excitement, captained the *Dorcas.*

The yacht made a fine start, taking the lead as she swept
out into the broad avenue of the river. Shielding his eyes from
the glinting brightness of the water, Broward worked mightily
to keep his boat ahead of the *Maud,* the entry from St. Augustine, which was moving up just behind. The *Dorcas* took too
wide a swing at the turn and in the homestretch fell into second
place behind the *Maud.* Just behind Broward's boat were the
Annie I. and the *Three Brothers,* Captain Kemps' vessels,
swaying in the afternoon haze like giant sea birds. The wind
freshened, and as the yachts approached the "Chaseville reach"
a stiff wind was blowing. Every boat had the last ounce of
ballast up to windward, and on either side of their bows a
white curling billow parted the water. Straining through the
mist, the *Annie Dorcas* crept up on the *Maud,* but just as she
crawled into first place she struck a submerged sand bar and
capsized. Some of the crew yelled for help, but Broward,
viewing the situation philosophically, climbed on the jutting
keel and watched the rest of the race in "water-soaked comfort."[44] The later record of the *Dorcas* belied her initial appearance.

By the end of 1891 Broward had become one of the popular
and prominent men in Florida. His exploits as sheriff were

frequently reported in state newspapers, and he was commended for his activities and cited as an example for other public officials. He was often invited to speak for civic and religious organizations, to appear at public receptions and social affairs, and to sign petitions to the governor and the legislature. Broward was developing a broad interest in civic affairs and in the social and business life of his community.

⟋ 5 ⟍

Breaking with Bourbonism

NAPOLEON BROWARD became involved in politics at a particularly propitious time. The Democratic party throughout the country was undergoing a transition and realignment, and liberals like Napoleon Broward forged to the front in party leadership. Aggressive, ambitious young Democrats marshaled their strength and moved inexorably toward a definite party split.

The period following the Civil War became one of glory for the powerful corporate and railroad interests. It was a "Gilded Era," when men like John D. Rockefeller, Commodore Vanderbilt, Jay Gould, and J. P. Morgan walked hand in hand with governors, Senators, and Cabinet members, and enjoyed lenient and gullible Congresses, and acquiescent Presidents. The tycoons, most of them staunch Republicans, maintained their power and influence in the North by means of consolidations and concentrations in syndicates, combines and trusts, and by a periodical waving of the "bloody shirt." In Florida, as in many other Southern states, political and economic supremacy was maintained to a great extent through subsidized legislatures, controlled elections, and political puppets as civil officers.

The Reconstruction era ended in Florida in 1876 with the election of George F. Drew to the governorship and the withdrawal of Federal troops from the state.[1] In succeeding years the corporate and railroad interests dominated state politics. Members of the great propertied group in the state—men like Henry Bradley Plant, Hamilton Disston, Henry Morrison Flagler, William D. Chipley, and James P. Taliaferro—had abundant influence with such governors as William D. Bloxham, Edward A. Perry, and Francis P. Fleming.

The need for reform throughout the United States had been apparent for many years. It had been recognized nationally in 1872 when Horace Greeley made his ill-fated excursion into politics. In each succeeding presidential campaign there had appeared one, and sometimes two or more, parties stressing issues that appealed mainly to wage earners and farmers. The aims and goals of each of these groups were similar, whether it called itself "Labor Reformer," "Greenbacker," or "Anti-monopolist" nationally; or "Straightout," "anti-corporation and anti-railroad," or "Independent," in the state of Florida.[2] Harsh and unsparing criticisms were voiced by these reformers, and they found sympathy and support for their cause among the farmers in the South and Middle West. Always active in politics, the farmers prior to the Civil War cast their votes, as a rule, with one or the other of the leading parties. Voters in Florida generally supported the Democratic ticket, although there was strong Whig strength in middle Florida counties during the 1840's and 1850's.[3]

After 1865 there swept across the nation movements which crusaded in behalf of a Utopia of social and economic equality. With strong support from the agrarian sections, these active and independent factions became the "Grangers," the "Greenback Party," and finally the sweeping Farmers' Alliance movement. These movements were also making themselves felt in Florida. But reform activities in the state, as in the rest of the South, were delayed by the Reconstruction era. William D. Bloxham entered upon his administration as governor in January, 1881—probably the most accurate date that can be given for the beginning of the split in the Florida Democratic party.[4]

The anti-corporate faction, which Broward was later to lead, received a tremendous acceleration because of the Disston land sale. Governor Bloxham and the Florida Internal Improvement Board sold four million acres of state land to Hamilton

Disston of Philadelphia and others for one million dollars.[5] The sale cleared the overdue indebtedness which had burdened the Internal Improvement Fund, and the board was able to grant land with undisputed title to encourage a much-needed transportation expansion.[6] The Disston purchase eventually became the target for much adverse criticism, when it was charged that top grade land was sold at too small a price.[7] In 1884, the transaction contributed largely to a threatened split in the Democratic party.[8] The issue was to continue even longer and was raised by the Populists against Governor Bloxham in the gubernatorial campaign of 1896, as evidence that he had sided with the vested interests. It also had repercussions in the Broward-Davis campaign in 1904.

The legislature of 1883 submitted the question of a constitutional convention to the people of the state, to be voted upon in the general election of the following year. The voters decided for the convention, 32,653 to 6,365.[9] The Disston land sale played a large role in the campaign of 1884. It was a major reason why the Florida voters predicted that this campaign would be heated, that it would "require hard work to heal disaffection in the Democratic ranks," and that, regardless of the "cause of the existing disaffection . . . whether it be the Disston land sale, the reputed fortunes that were accumulated in a few days by those who were permitted a knowledge of the contemplated sale, the feeling of antagonism against the so-called 'Tallahassee ring'; the virtual nullifying of the law permitting poor men to purchase homesteads at 25 cents an acre, or any other, disaffection is a reality, and it must be met in a conciliatory spirit or the Democracy will lose control of the government."[10]

The political crisis was real and the solution difficult. Until the adoption of the constitution of 1885, there was no statute or constitutional provision which prohibited a Florida governor from being immediately re-elected to office. In the election of 1884, both Bloxham and Drew, former governors, were candidates for the nomination.[11] Charges of speculation and fraud were brought against Bloxham by Drew supporters. In turn, Bloxham men charged Drew with land-sale corruption of his own.[12] Newspapers, like the voters, took sides in the conflict. However, there existed in Democratic ranks a strong element desiring party peace. Leaders of the harmony faction persuaded the convention that nominating either Bloxham or Drew would be unwise, and contended that a new man would be politically more desirable. The convention accepted this compromise proposal and thus postponed party schism. The convention was held in Pensacola, and General Edward A. Perry of Escambia County received the gubernatorial nomination.[13]

Meanwhile, an independent movement was organized by Democrats who opposed the Bloxham administration because of its pro-railroad policy and the Disston land sale, but this group refused to consider an alliance with the Republicans. Strengthened by a lack of unity among their opponents, the Independents held a state convention at Live Oak on June 18, 1884, and nominated Frank W. Pope, a brilliant young Madison County lawyer, for governor.[14] Indicting "Bourbon Democracy" and the disunity which had evolved from the Civil War, Pope campaigned on a platform which charged conservatism with holding "its corrupt tenure by the passions and prejudices born of that unhappy conflict."[15]

Had the general election come immediately after the adjournment of the Democratic convention, there is a chance that the Independents might have triumphed, but in the months before the balloting, the membership and strength of the movement gradually waned. This was the result of two things: a sober second thought about the risk in splitting the white vote, and the discretion that the older party had shown in nominating Perry. Nevertheless, the Independent vote cast in November was nearly 47 per cent of the total vote, and Pope carried Alachua, Duval, Madison, Jefferson, Leon, Marion, Nassau, and Washington counties.[16]

For the time being a break in the Democratic ranks was prevented. But the election had been more threatening to

Democratic supremacy in Florida than any other since Reconstruction. Had the Independents won that year, the future control of the Democratic party in Florida might have been seriously endangered. The election of 1884 marked the end of the Independents as a third party threat in Florida, but many of the progressive measures for which they stood became planks in the Populist platform and were later battle standards in the liberal crusade led by Napoleon Broward, Wilkinson Call, and William Jennings.

The disaffected element in and out of the Democratic party joined the Farmers' Alliance when it was introduced into Florida in 1887.[17] Membership in the Alliance spread rapidly, especially in the older and more densely populated farming sections in the northern part of the state. By April, 1890, Alliances flourished in all of the counties except Franklin, Lee, Dade, and Monroe, where the movement made little headway.[18]

The crest of Alliance activity in the state came when the National Farmers' Alliance met in Ocala in December, 1890.[19] In the fall elections of that year Alliance men and those who professed an adherence to Alliance philosophies and ideologies had won three-fifths of the seats in Congress, but an acute observer could already detect signs of defection.[20] Alliance leaders, in Florida and throughout the nation, had become more radical, and urged advanced legislation which the Democrats would almost all refuse to enact.

The Ocala convention was indisputably the most significant single event in the history of Florida's agrarian revolt. It had an important effect on Florida's political history, for out of this movement grew reform demands which would culminate in the election to the governorship of men like William S. Jennings, Napoleon B. Broward, Albert W. Gilchrist, and Park Trammell. Broward was not a Populist in the strict sense of the term, but in his gubernatorial campaign in 1904 he capitalized on Populist demands and agrarian discontent. A large part of the vote which elected him governor came from elements that figured prominently in the Alliance movement. And from the platform adopted by the Ocala convention delegates, the famous "Ocala Demands," Broward and other liberal Florida Democrats like the second Stephen R. Mallory, John N. C. Stockton, Frank W. Pope, John M. Barrs, and Wilkinson Call, received much of their political philosophy.

Immediately after the Ocala meeting the Florida Alliance began to weaken. Charges of radicalism were heard on every side. Its program of agricultural improvement was disappointing. The Florida Exchange, which opened in Jacksonville in 1888 to promote cooperative buying and selling, fell short of expectations and was finally closed four years later. Demoralization was accentuated by the inefficiency of the Florida legislature, which held its regular session in April and May of 1891. The majority of its members were Alliance men who showed no cohesion. The greater part of the session was consumed in an unsuccessful attempt to elect a successor to United States Senator Wilkinson Call.[21] When the end of the session came and Alliance men returned to dissatisfied constituencies, they could point to very few constructive measures. Conservative control was obvious when the legislators repealed the Railroad Commission Law, which had been one of the few reform measures inaugurated in 1887.[22] By 1890 discontent and the earnest desire to better the situation had accelerated the formation of an anti-corporation and anti-railroad faction. Under leaders like Napoleon Broward the young reformers demanded sweeping, even radical, changes.

A cleavage in the Democratic party appeared imminent in Duval County during 1891 and the first part of 1892. A liberal group of men, calling themselves "Straightouts," became the major political faction in Duval County and secured a number of important local offices. Growing in strength and influence, they attracted to their ranks many of the rising young men of Jacksonville. Such were Stockton, Barrs, and Broward. The Straightouts supported Populist principles as far as they affected the county. Holding anti-railroad and anti-corporation views,

the Duval County Straightouts became part of the liberal
Democratic movement and were in reality members of the
anti faction in state politics.

Opposed to the Duval Straightouts were the "Antis," who
protested the city "ring's" monopoly of key offices. In the ranks
of the Antis were men like W. McL. Dancy, Porcher L'Engle,
Fleming Bowden, J. E. Hartridge, and James P. Taliaferro.
Many of these Antis were closely connected with the Tallahassee administration, and their leanings were toward the railroad and corporate interests which exerted great influence on
the chief executives and legislatures of various state administrations. Although they were known as Antis within the
county, they were really the group that "stood in" with the
important vested interests in Florida. The term *Antis* meant
one thing in Duval County and another in state politics. The
rift, interesting in itself, was important also because it was part
of the larger break that was dividing the Democratic party
throughout the state and the nation.

The Republican vote became negligible in state elections
after 1888, and the Democratic party was firmly in the saddle,
although this did not always mean party accord. By 1892 there
were two conspicuous groups within the state party, each fighting the other. However, the Independent movement which
had developed in the 1880's as a result of conflict among the
Democrats lacked a cohesive force and seemed doomed to failure. The strength gained from the Independents' stand against
the Disston land sale was lost through their extreme anti-corporation attitude. This opposition to the corporations was too
radical for the time; the railroad interests were powerful in
Florida. Plant and Flagler spent millions of dollars in the
state, developing railroads, building lavish hotels such as the
Ponce de Leon in St. Augustine and the Tampa Bay Hotel in
Tampa, and advertising Florida as a great resort state. These
investments gave conservatism a strong influence in the Democratic party, and were stumbling blocks in the pathway of any
"politically immature hot-head" who dared protest corpora-

tion excesses and malpractices. In Florida the day for political reform had not yet arrived.

The conservatives, strongly entrenched, were led by men of wealth and political experience—William D. Chipley of Pensacola, W. Hunt Harris of Key West, James P. Taliaferro of Jacksonville, Ziba King of Arcadia, F. W. Sams of DeLand, John W. Watson of Kissimmee, Charles J. Perrenot of Milton, John E. Hartridge of Jacksonville, John A. Henderson of Tallahassee, and Tom Peter Chaires of Old Town. To dislodge them from the political supremacy they had enjoyed for so many years would be a hard and bitter fight.

Opposed to these conservative leaders were liberal Democrats whose party beliefs and aspirations conflicted with railroad and corporate interests and who demanded new party leadership. The anti-corporation Democrats suffered severe and heartbreaking setbacks, but instead of weakening they grew stronger in their determination to rid the state and party of corporation control. To them it was an evil to be eradicated.

In Duval County, Straightouts were aligned with the liberal forces of the state. Among no other Florida group was there more bitter opposition to the railroads and corporations. Broward, Barrs, and Stockton led the chorus of caustic criticism of the Tallahassee administration, launching vitriolic charges of corruption, malfeasance, and fraud against the corporations and their political supporters. To Broward and other liberals, the railroads had come to typify the chief political evils existing in the state and were the cause of corruption in the Democratic party. The anti-corporate forces felt that for the good of the commonwealth the alliance between the vested interests and politics should be broken and obliterated.

～6～
A Fight and a Riot

AT ITS MEETING early in March, 1892, the Duval
County executive committee set April 14 as the date
for the Democratic primaries which would name
delegates to the county convention. During the last week in
March, Broward announced his candidacy for re-election as
sheriff. On primary day large crowds gathered along Bay and
Forsyth streets, in front of the courthouse, and near every
polling place. Banners were jostled, men slapped each other
on the back, and there was much laughter. Caucuses were held
on almost every corner, and Broward and the other candidates,
together with their supporters, were busy all day persuading
voters to mark ballots one way or another. The Antis were
especially active. An opposition newspaper charged that "they
went into the highways and the byways, irrespective of party,
creed or previous condition, and invited all to come in and
vote early and often."[1]

Election returns showed a victory for the Antis, but evidences of fraud were many. Jacksonville would have needed
a population of nearly a hundred thousand to match the unprecedented vote cast.[2] It was later shown that men voted
several times and that many Republicans voted in this Democratic primary. Charges and countercharges of fraud, multiple
voting, bribery, and ballot-box stuffing circulated everywhere.
The *Florida Times-Union* maintained that "the management
of the Florida Central and Peninsular Railroad took an active
part in the primaries. . . . It colonized its employees here. It
sought to defeat the organized democracy of Duval County. . . .
It was determined to make its corporate influence felt on this
occasion."[3]

[63]

Excitement showed on the faces of the spectators, candidates, delegates, and party leaders who awaited the beginning of the Democratic county convention in Jacksonville on April 16. Since early morning scores of people, streaming in from all corners of the county, crowded the sidewalks on Laura Street in front of the Park Opera House and overflowed into the street. Groups of men collected in Hemming Park and along the wide porches of the St. James and Windsor hotels and talked about the impending political battle. In the convention hall every seat was filled and the aisles were jammed. From the oblong stage a military band blasted out marches and waltzes, but no one paid attention. The room was steaming hot. Men took off their coats and rolled up their sleeves; and women fanned themselves briskly with folded newspapers or palmetto fans.

From the beginning, the convention was divided over the eligibility of certain members who represented wards with questionable vote tabulations. At an earlier meeting, the executive committee, under the leadership of John M. Barrs, had compiled a list of delegates as reported by the poll inspectors. When Broward's faction submitted sworn protests and affidavits charging gross frauds that involved the rights of forty-three delegates to their seats, the committee refused to proceed further. A committee on credentials, "top-heavy with Antis," was instructed to investigate and report on the protests and fraud charges.

Evidences of fraud, especially in Wards Four and Five, were numerous. When affidavits were filed, proving that Republicans had voted, some of them several times, even the Antis on the committee admitted their guilt. This admission developed a crisis in the meeting, and when word reached Anti leaders of the decisions of the committee on credentials, they hurriedly pushed through a motion dissolving the committee, thus making its report invalid.

Immediately the convention became a bedlam. Hysterical shouts of delegates were engulfed in a pandemonium in which threats, curses, and protests occasionally were audible. The Antis, being in the majority, declared the convention sole judge of the eligibility of candidates and delegates, thereby discarding the accusations of the committee on credentials. A slate of delegates, headed by the convention chairman, was named, and an Anti ticket was selected for nomination to the legislature. Sheriff Broward was not included.

At this juncture the committee on credentials filed into the hall and demanded that its report be heard. The small but determined Straightout faction led by Broward insisted on hearing the report, and its demand was finally allowed. With the thunderous approval of Broward's liberal wing, it recommended a new election and a new convention, and demanded that the "election . . . be from registration lists and inspectors . . . be appointed satisfactory to the candidates and the convention now adjourn sine die."[4]

The lid blew off. Delegates stood on chairs and roared their approval or condemnation. The Antis succeeded in quieting the convention long enough to secure a majority vote to reject the committee report. As the convention chairman announced this vote, the Straightout faction, led by Broward, John N. C. Stockton, and John M. Barrs, left the hall. The threatened break in the county Democratic party had finally taken place.[5]

As the Straightouts walked out of the building and into the sun-filled park, they were greeted by cheers and shouts from men on the sidewalk and street. One of them, an owner of large lumber and turpentine properties in central Florida, congratulated Broward and offered him money for his coming political campaign.[6] After canvassing the primary returns in an empty room in the Park Opera House, the Straightouts called for a new primary election on May 19 and for a convention to be held two days later. They emphasized that "the convention will be a convention of democrats."[7] It was almost dark when the bolting Straightouts completed their work, ending a day that would long be remembered in county and state politics. These events, and their results, were destined to have an important and a far-reaching effect upon the future of the Democratic party in Florida. Meanwhile the Antis formed their convention into a permanent organization and named a slate of candidates. They offered Broward the nomination for the office of sheriff, but he remained faithful to his party and faction and refused this offer.

A week later some of the city records disappeared. Immediately the papers blamed the Antis. The *Florida Times-Union* implied that important Jacksonville officials were involved in the theft.[8] The stolen records contained an official census of the voters of the county, including those from disputed Wards Four, Five, Six, and Seven. Eventually the records were returned, but the persons allegedly involved were not apprehended.

On April 20, four days after the first convention, Broward again announced himself as a candidate for office for the May 19 election, promising to "abide the result of the said primary election and support the nominees thereof."[9] Broward, Stockton, and Barrs opened the Duval County Democratic Club at 5½ East Bay Street. This club was to exert a forceful influence in future city, county, and state elections. Broward, one of the principal speakers at a giant mass meeting held at this "headquarters" on the eve of the Straightout primaries, predicted "a success and victory" for the "genuine democrats of the county."[10]

The May 19 primary put Broward on the Straightout ticket as a candidate for sheriff. On election night a great victory rally was held in the auditorium of Metropolitan Hall, which was too small for the huge crowd. Broward, his dark eyes flashing with excitement, made a rousing speech. He complimented his party lieutenants for their labors and predicted that the day would be one to be looked back upon with pride because it would disgrace the "self-styled democrats who stood at the polls making a memorandum of democrats who were men enough to come out and vote, and trying to intimidate others who wanted to vote."[11]

The Straightout convention opened two days later in the Park Opera House. The meeting was orderly and the business of choosing delegates to the state convention at Tampa and the district convention at Gainesville was completed quickly. Broward was chosen to spearhead the Gainesville delegation, and other Straightout leaders were designated to go to Tampa.

Broward decided to accompany the Straightout delegation to Tampa. When the men arrived they eagerly joined the gay convention crowds flowing along the wide tree-bordered streets of the Gulf port. Bunting splashed across store fronts and hotels, and many private homes displayed American and Florida flags. Huge welcome signs greeted delegates at every corner in the downtown area. Firecrackers and band music added to the gaiety.

The convention opened in an atmosphere of expectancy and curiosity. Anything might happen. The conflict began immediately, for when the roll was read, only the names of the Anti delegates from Duval County were called. A roar of protest rose from the floor and from the visitors' gallery where Broward was seated. Broward and other Straightout leaders held a hurried caucus after the first district chairman, S. M. Sparkman, announced that seating the Anti delegation was the final decision of the state committee in charge. The Straightouts persuaded Major St. Clair-Abrams to protest the decision and to move that the case of Duval County be referred to the committee on credentials. This was allowed after both factions agreed not to participate until a decision was rendered.

At five o'clock in the morning, after an all-night session, the committee on credentials took a vote. Straightout leaders were waiting in Broward's room in the Tampa Bay Hotel for the decision of the committee. Upon learning that the Antis were to be seated, they planned a last-ditch stand that failed when the convention voted down St. Clair-Abrams' proposal that neither delegation be seated.[12]

The main business before the convention was the nomination of a Democrat for governor. On the evening of June 3, after the Alachua County delegate proposed Henry L. Mitchell of Hillsborough County, the newly installed electric lights began sputtering and then went out, plunging the hall into darkness. Lanterns were lit and the convention business resumed. Robert W. Davis seconded the Mitchell nomination, proposing that it be made unanimous. The roll call began and most of the county delegates climbed aboard the Mitchell band wagon. Mitchell received the nomination by acclamation.[13]

Broward and the Straightout delegation returned to Jacksonville disappointed but not completely crushed. Their defeat, they realized, was due to the strong corporation and railroad influences present in the convention, but their cause was growing in Duval County and throughout the state. Events in Jacksonville in the following weeks made Broward stronger politically and more popular than ever before.

Late on the hot afternoon of July 4, 1892, near a waterfront dock in Jacksonville, a fight began between a white man, Frank Burrows, and a Negro, Benjamin Reed. In the scuffle Reed crushed Burrows' skull with a heavy oak board. Reed tried to escape but was captured, placed in Broward's custody, and lodged in the jail at the foot of Liberty Street. When Burrows died during the night, an ominous undercurrent of lynch talk flowed throughout Jacksonville. Hoping to prevent such action, about five hundred Negroes quietly congregated in the area. Sentries, with guns beneath their coats, patrolled the streets leading to the jail, and controlled part of the East Jacksonville area. White pedestrians were surrounded and questioned, and only a whistled signal to watchers on the next corner allowed them to go through. When white men approached the jail, desperate Negroes closed in, covered them with guns, and refused to let them proceed.[14]

Although the excitement was intense, twenty of Broward's policemen arrived unmolested. A telegram from Adjutant General David Lang informed the sheriff that three local military companies—the Jacksonville Light Infantry, the Metropolitan Light Infantry, and Wilson's Battery—were mobilized in their armories and were ready to resist an attack upon the jail.[15] The evening passed without bloodshed. Sheriff Broward, expecting a hostile demonstration next day by Negroes, or an attack by whites, stationed his men with guns at all the prison windows and placed an extra guard outside Reed's cell. Hundreds of Negroes massed on porches, behind trees, and in streets and alleys around the jail, whispered among themselves, and waited for something to happen. Many were armed with muskets and rifles. Others carried clubs, knives, razors, and revolvers, "from the $2 pistols that shoot both ways to the improved self-cocker."[16]

A little after nine o'clock on the second evening, deputies came out of the main prison door and placed lanterns around the steps to light a makeshift platform. Mayor Robinson, Judge McLean, Sheriff Broward, and colored leaders talked to the crowd. The sheriff's voice had a confident ring as he explained that the armed militia gave no cause for a demonstration and that it was ordered out to protect the prisoner and to repress mob violence. About an hour later, the militia marched down Bay Street to Liberty and fanned out into the blocks around the prison building. A Gatling gun set up in front of the prison steps by a small detachment forced the crowd to move back. By midnight the marshes, shanties, yards, and trees within a three-block radius of the jail were filled with armed Negroes.[17] The atmosphere was electric with tension, but this second night passed without serious disturbance. The area around the jail turned into a tent city and there was a clatter all night as sentries changed and messengers hurried in and out. Broward slept only two hours in the forty-eight and his face was lined with worry and fatigue. Mrs. Broward sent him some fresh clothes and he shaved at his office. Broward was in constant communication with Tallahassee, and on the morning of July 6 he telegraphed Adjutant General Lang for more troops. Two companies—the St. Augustine

Rifles and the St. Augustine Guards—arrived during the afternoon and were immediately marched to Liberty Street where they were placed on duty before the jail. Adjutant General Lang, who had traveled from Tallahassee by train to take personal charge, ordered additional troops from Gainesville, Palatka, and Starke.

Meanwhile considerable desultory shooting by individuals, white and colored, kept the excitement at a high pitch. A fusillade of bullets ricocheted on the wall behind one of the policemen, and in the return fire a Negro was shot. A deputy was hit four times after he accidentally dropped his gun and it fired. About two hundred men were defending the prison, and many more from nearby Florida towns and from southern Georgia volunteered their services.[18] The Gainesville Guards, the Gem City Guards of Palatka, and the Bradford County Guards of Starke arrived by railroad on July 7. The entire city had assumed a martial appearance. Armed soldiers patrolled the streets, citizens were stopped and questioned, and those carrying guns were arrested. The sheriff heard rumors that Negro women were planning to fire the city, and with the city and military officials he tried vainly to ferret out the facts.[19] On the afternoon of July 7, the military companies stationed in Jacksonville staged a battalion drill and a parade on Bay Street, both as reassurance and warning to the populace. The weather was oppressively hot and tempers were short. In the evening, storm clouds began piling and a downpour helped disperse the mob. Negro citizens, in a meeting held that afternoon, had denounced the mob leaders and asked the people to return home. There was no outbreak during the night and by the next day the city was quiet. The military companies departed after holding a dress parade on Bay Street in front of the Carlton Hotel.[20]

Jacksonville settled back into its normal routine, although its citizens realized that they had had a close call. For three days and nights the tension had been so great that the slightest untoward incident might have touched off a catastrophe.

Sheriff Broward was the recipient of much well-deserved praise; his tact, levelheadedness, and sense of fairness contributed largely to the protection of his prisoner, to the holding in check of incendiary elements among both white and colored, and to the preservation of law and order. Throughout the crisis Jacksonville was the news center of the nation. Newspapers in Eastern and Northern cities published stories of the "race riot" on their front pages.

The excitement gradually died down and the public returned to the political situation. On July 20, 1892, a newspaper notice invited the young men of Duval County to meet the following Friday night and form an organization to back Broward in the approaching election.[21] The sheriff's popularity was strongly evidenced by the many Democrats who gathered in Metropolitan Hall to form the Young Men's Broward Club, and to hear Major St. Clair-Abrams speak in Broward's behalf. Broward already was probably the strongest man in Duval County politics, and his influence in state politics was rapidly becoming more apparent. The club became the most talked-of organization in the city, and its membership soon rose to over seven hundred; by election day it was even larger. Smaller "Broward" clubs were organized throughout the county.[22]

Broward was one of the principal speakers at the meeting which formed the Young Men's Broward Club, and during his campaign he made many political talks. Never a great orator, Broward was a clear, honest speaker who possessed a novel technique. With his clothes neatly pressed and his dark hair well brushed, he made an impressive appearance on the speaker's platform. There was something winning in his modest demeanor, he was direct and forceful as his arguments developed, and he always spoke in language that his hearers could understand.

During the afternoon of August 2, Broward and other members of the Straightout delegation boarded a dusty day coach and traveled to Gainesville for the second district Congressional convention, which was to meet in the Alachua County Court House. As Duval County was represented by two delegations, the convention faced the same seating problem that had affected the Tampa meeting. The question was immediately referred to the committee on credentials, and Duncan U. Fletcher[23] argued the cause of the Straightouts. The committee recommended by a vote of 10 to 8 that the Straightouts be seated.

Charles M. Cooper of Duval County, General Robert Bullock, D. H. Young, E. M. Hammond, and E. C. Sanchez were candidates for the Congressional nomination. After the first few ballots the contest narrowed to Bullock and Cooper. Twenty-nine votes were taken on August 4, Cooper leading General Bullock on every count. After a supper intermission, the delegates reconvened and balloting was resumed. Ninety ballots were tabulated before adjournment, and there was no prospect of an immediate nomination. Broward and the Duval delegation, who supported Cooper, hoped to break the deadlock. Political caucuses ran far into the night. Broward went from one to another, "buttonholing" party leaders and persuading delegates to support Cooper. When the convention reassembled the next morning, Cooper's prospects were brighter. On the one hundred and sixth ballot Sumter County voted for Cooper, bringing his total to 113 votes. On each succeeding count Cooper grew stronger and the one hundred thirty-ninth ballot gave him the necessary majority and the nomination.[24] The convention adjourned and the Duval delegation returned to Jacksonville.

The sheriff attended a huge rally and barbecue the following day at Plummer's Grove in Mandarin. Speaking for his faction, Broward presented an intimate analysis of the records of several of his political foes and admonished his listeners to stick by the "true Democratic party," assuring them that "all good and pure people would stand by the Straightouts."[25] The Broward Club was in session almost nightly during all of August and September. The club now had a membership of over one thousand, a substantial part of the voting population in Jacksonville, which could prove a formidable weapon in any election.

On the evening of September 30 the Straightout campaign came to a close with a huge torchlight procession. Precincts all over the county sent representatives to march in the parade, and many of them carried signs and banners which read: "Help, Holler, We feel Good. Our Candidate is Napoleon B. Broward for Sheriff." The streets were filled with flags and faces; bunting and gaudy crepe paper fluttered from windows, housetops, and storefronts. Several precinct delegations brought bands with them, and as the music from one blared into the bannered distance, the sounds were picked up by another band marching past. The crowds flowed across the sidewalk into the streets and pressed against the marchers who went their slow way up Bay Street, and then down Duval to Laura Street and the Park Opera House, where a giant political rally was held. The crowd was so huge that almost three thousand people stood outside. The speakers that night included many of the state's political leaders, who lauded Broward for his past accomplishments and made generous predictions concerning his political future.

Election day was filled with sunshine and triumph for Broward and his Straightout faction. They were successful at the polls, and Broward won by a vote of 1,406 to 564. One newspaper's headlines proclaimed: "Broward leads the ticket and beats Fleming Bowden in the latter's own precinct—wild enthusiasm all over the city."[26] The Straightout victory was not the only triumph. As the returns from all over the nation flashed over the wires, they told of Cleveland's election with a Congress that was Democratic in both branches. Democratic hopes of a jubilant victory were a reality.

The year 1893 was uneventful for Sheriff Broward until November. Early in that month a group of Jacksonville businessmen and sport enthusiasts formed the Duval Athletic Club and announced that a boxing match for the heavyweight championship of the world would be fought in the city. The fight between James J. Corbett and Charles Mitchell of England was scheduled for the following January 25.[27] Opposition to the project was immediate and wrathful. Mayor Fletcher of Jacksonville compared prizefighters with "pickpockets, thieves, thugs and blacklegs";[28] the rector of St. John's Church felt that the fight would injure and shock "the best and purest element" of the community.[29] Governor Mitchell, opposed to any "prize fight, boxing or sparring contest,"[30] issued a special message "directing every sheriff to do his utmost to prevent the fight coming off. . . ."[31]

Preparations for the exhibition continued. During December, Corbett trained in Mayport and Mitchell in St. Augustine. The Athletic Club leased the site of the old Fair Grounds, which lay within the city limits,[32] and advertised the fight as a "boxing match with five ounce gloves."[33] Sheriff Broward, instructed by the governor to prevent the fight, was promised "all the assistance you really require in upholding the laws of this State."[34] He conferred with the state adjutant general, and, as a result, four companies of troops were detailed to Duval County to aid in keeping "the peace of the State."[35] On January 17 the Gate City Rifles Company from Sanford was en route to Jacksonville and the second battalion of state militia was under orders to march.

Broward was called to Tallahassee on January 19 for a meeting with Mitchell. On his return, when he was asked by a newspaper reporter whether the governor was unalterably determined in his stand against the fight, Broward answered with great vehemence: "Determined? Humph. I should say so! You let anybody go up there and talk fight to the Governor and he'll hop on 'em as quick as a lark on a grasshopper."[36]

State militia marched into the city two days before the fight. As the troops paraded through the crowded streets, the people who were interested in the fight hissed and booed, and many hurled rocks and paper bags filled with sand.[37] The military activities were of no avail. The Athletic Club's attorney, A. W.

Cockrell, secured from Circuit Judge Rhydon M. Call a permanent injunction against Broward, forbidding him to interfere with the boxing match in any way.[38]

By eight o'clock on the morning of the fight dense crowds jammed the streets. A glittering mob—gamblers, sports writers and enthusiasts, roustabouts, promoters, and prostitutes—flocked to the city for the event. Jacksonville had never before seen a day like this. The bannered sidewalks vibrated with the noise of hawkers shrieking their wares, bawdy songs, gamblers taking bets, shrill laughter, raucous band music, profanity, and fine talk.

The fight was to begin at two o'clock, but the crowds started moving to the Fair Grounds by eleven. Every hack and rattletrap conveyance in the city was pressed into service and "hitched behind nags, horses, and mules of every description." Streetcars were jammed, excursion boats plied back and forth, and fight enthusiasts rode on horseback or walked. By noon the seats in the Fair Grounds were filling rapidly, at ten to twenty-five dollars each, and a full crowd was there an hour before the fight. The fight promoters sent Sheriff Broward a twenty-five dollar seat ticket, but it was not used.[39]

By fight time the sky was bright and warm sunshine filled the grounds. The ladies' gaily-hued dresses and the loud-checked vests of the gamblers were bright splashes of color on the tiered seats. "Sportingmen" gathered in the ringside seats, and there were "few present who did not have something in the shape of a flask in their hip pockets, or a basket of beer within easy reach."[40] Among the celebrities were New York's Steve Brodie, wearing a silk shirt and a derby hat, Lillian Lewis, the Manhattan actress who bet twelve hundred dollars on Mitchell, and Clara Desplaines, who owned the most famous brothel in Kansas City, and who came dressed in shoes, suit, and hat like a man.[41]

The fight was short. Corbett knocked Mitchell out in the third round and retained his title as world's heavyweight champion. After the fight, Broward's deputies stopped the boxers and served them with warrants ordering them to appear in court the following morning. Charged with assault and battery, each man posted a five thousand dollar bond. Corbett went on trial in February and a jury of six men brought in a verdict of not guilty. The case against Mitchell was dropped.

After this excitement wore off, Broward resumed his usual business activities. He and Montcalm worked, that spring, on a small river tug they hoped to complete by fall.[42] There was every reason for Broward to be content. His political star was growing brighter and the liberal cause he espoused was gaining popularity and support. Napoleon Broward was now the avowed "strong man" in Duval County and was a recognized party leader in Florida. The names of Broward, Barrs, and Stockton were revered by Straightout adherents throughout the state. When this trio spoke politically, they spoke for the liberal Democrats of the largest and richest county in Florida.

ᗣ 7 ᗒ

'Iniquity of the Corporation People"

HE COUNTY EXECUTIVE COMMITTEE of
which Broward was a member met in Jacksonville
early in July, 1894. Duval County was split into two
political factions which seemed irreconcilable. Two executive
committees functioned and, later, separate primaries were held.
Rumors during the first week in July indicated that the Antis
were planning to call a "snap-election" to name delegates to
the party convention. Denouncing such a move in a heated
talk before the executive committee, Broward declared: "If
the other side tries to take snap judgment by calling primaries
on twenty-four hours' notice, it will show that they do not
intend to have a fair election. Nothing but a fair count can be
had. The people are not going to stand fraud."[1] The
Straightout committee decided that should this snap-election
materialize, they would find some way of naming delegates
to their own county convention.

The question of election inspectors was also heatedly discussed by the Straightouts. Florida law provided that inspectors
would supervise elections to assure an honest ballot-count. In
past elections these inspectors had usually been Antis; consequently, the tabulations were often questioned by Straightouts,
who made frequent charges of fraud, and who were now determined to help supervise vote tabulations. "The votes are
going to be counted," they insisted. "We will see that they are
counted, whether we are given an inspector or not."[2]

W. McL. Dancy, an avowed Anti and a delegate to the
Tampa convention of 1892, announced himself as a candidate
for the nomination for state senator. During the campaign the
Florida Times-Union usually classified the Antis as *Dancyites*.

[77]

To Straightouts, Dancy's candidacy and the question of election inspectors were all part of the same issue. They were willing to "go into the primaries with the Dancy contingent, provided they will be fair enough to agree to the 'straightouts' having one inspector out of the three, and using the registration list to vote from. . . ."[3]

The campaign began on July 9 with a large political rally at Gravely Hill; Straightouts and Antis attended. Broward, one of the principal speakers, was loudly cheered by the crowd when he scathingly denounced corporation control in the state, and lashed at ". . . Chipley in the West . . . Plant in the South and . . . Flagler in the East, all protesting and fighting to maintain the rates. . . ."[4] The sheriff charged that "the great wealth of Florida is so bottled up by the railroads as to pay tribute to Georgia ports, to the detriment of those of Florida. . . ."[5] These frank statements were amply substantiated by facts and figures produced by the liberals. Georgia cities were receiving more favorable rates in the shipping of citrus and phosphate than Florida cities, although the latter were really closer to the groves and mines.

In an open letter to the press, on July 20, 1894, Broward revealed how four railroads—two in Florida[6] and two outside[7]—had established an interstate transportation monopoly which was costing Florida approximately four hundred thousand dollars a year. The companies manipulated local rates on oranges so as to receive an additional twenty-four dollars per carload, or about eight cents per box.[8] Rate discriminations for phosphate shipments from mine to port were flagrant, and Broward, in his open letter, harshly arraigned the railroads for their practices.[9]

The corporation forces in the state denied the charges and pointed to the vast revenues brought to Florida by the railroads. They argued that new roads were the primary factor in opening the southern part of the state to settlers, and that Northern capital had developed and populated frontier sections of Florida. The philosophy of the railroad adherents was expressed in a newspaper statement of Henry B. Plant: "... It seemed to me that about all South Florida needed for a successful future was a little spirit and energy which could be fostered by transportation facilities."[10] In trying to rebut Broward's charges, the railroad forces circumvented the real issues. Without denying the benefits which railroads brought to Florida, the liberals complained against abuses practiced by the transportation interests.

W. McL. Dancy and E. J. Triay headed the Anti delegation to the Gravely Hill rally. They rode up in an elegantly decorated rig, "... the finest on the grounds, drawn by two high-stepping thoroughbreds, and maneuvered by a liveried footman." Tables were placed beneath the widespread branches of the trees, and after the meeting there was a barbecue. One newspaper reported that the Antis ate apart from the crowds and that "they had sandwiches made of costly canned meats and chicken and golden pheasant, with jellies, and wines and ginger pop with ice to wash it down, and a box of fine cigars to smoke after their banquet was finished. . . ." According to the newspaper's story, Dancy sensed that this aloofness was resented and helped himself to "the largest and best pickled cow rib he could find. Selecting a conspicuous place against the side of the schoolhouse, and brandishing the rib like a broadsword, he nibbled at it."[11]

A few days later the Antis met in Jacksonville and announced that the Duval primaries were scheduled for July 24 and that elected delegates would assemble in convention two days later. There were loud protests from the members of the Anti executive committee when Dancy stated that he was withdrawing as a candidate for state senator. Broward's uncle, Captain Joseph Parsons, who was an Anti leader, arose to speak against Dancy's decision. In his excitement he put his lighted cigar on the seat of his chair. The captain introduced a resolution which asked Dancy to reconsider his decision, and then, having forgotten his cigar, he sat down. The meeting was almost broken up by Parsons' loud yell of pain. He quieted down after someone sloshed a bucket of water on the seat of his trousers. Helped from the meeting room, Captain Parsons stood up in his carriage all the way home.[12] Dancy reconsidered and decided to run after all.

A Straightout committee, invited to the meeting by the Antis, proposed that for party amity both factions agree upon the election date. They also asked for representation on the board of election inspectors. The Antis denied both requests and suggested that an Anti-Straightout committee meet and appoint the inspectors.[13] Refusing this, the Straightouts met the following Saturday morning, July 14, to map their campaign tactics. Broward headed the committee which named July 24 for the primaries and July 26 for the convention. After the meeting, the sheriff traveled to Mayport by steamer and spoke at an evening political rally. It was a hot night and Broward's linen suit was streaked with perspiration, but his talk was calm and to the point. He accused the railroads and corporations of "trying to get possession of the state," and detailed "facts and figures that surprised many who had not given the matter much consideration."[14]

On the evening of July 18 a large rally was scheduled for Mandarin, and both Duval County factions sent speakers. The Antis arrived about an hour before the Straightouts and walked to the meeting place near the school a mile from the river. They erected a crude platform and waited for the crowd to assemble. By six o'clock the schoolyard was filled; men sat under the trees, on the ground, and on the school steps, and some of the boys perched on the tree branches. Just before the Straightouts came into sight, Joe Akorn, an Anti leader, climbed onto the platform, called the meeting to order, and introduced Dancy. When the opposing faction arrived, Dancy was speaking, and he was immediately followed by E. J. Triay and Judge Christie. Apparently the Straightouts were to be muzzled. The crowd started calling for Duncan U. Fletcher, Dancy's opponent, but the Anti chairman ignored the demands. During Christie's address, Anti men quietly circulated the story that, as soon as the judge was finished, beer and whisky would be served on a boat anchored in the nearby St. Johns. By this means the Antis hoped to break up the meeting before the Straightouts could participate. A man interrupted Christie to ask about Straightout speakers, but the judge took no notice of him. Akorn, aware of growing excitement among the spectators, suddenly turned down the lantern used to light the platform and loudly announced that the meeting was adjourned. In the darkness, Anti men tried unsuccessfully to start a rush through the woods to the river. Thereupon the Straightouts hurriedly took over the platform; and as soon as they turned up the lantern, Fletcher began his talk. When Broward spoke, Akorn and his men stood on the outskirts of the crowd, cat-calling and insulting him. A fight began when a Straightout called Akorn a traitor, and the latter struck at his insulter. In the general brawl, a rock shattered the lamp on the platform, and men hit each other with bottles, sticks, and fists. The rally ended in an uproar and the Straightouts started back to Jacksonville, but not before the sheriff arrested Akorn for disturbing the peace and wearing "brass knuckles" in the fight.[15]

Jacksonville's citizens daily grew more excited about the campaign. The Straightouts suspected that people were being registered illegally, and asked that two of their men "be allowed to stand within the room and note who were being registered, so that those who had not, might be sought out and impressed with the duty of qualifying themselves to vote."[16] E. J. E. McLaurin, the supervisor of registration and a strong Anti supporter, denied the request. When the Straightouts refused to leave his office, the supervisor declared he could register no one. It was evident from the wild rumors circulating throughout the city that trouble was expected. Crowds of rowdies from both factions collected before the courthouse. Inside the building, the halls were filled with men who talked in loud, agitated voices. Curses, threats, and oaths stirred the air. At this moment, Broward, followed by a squad of deputies, arrived and entered the building. Slowly they marched up the steps and through the main corridor, carrying their guns, but saying nothing. The brawlers, quelled at this show of force, quickly dispersed.[17] Again the sheriff's prompt action and levelheaded tact had helped to mitigate a situation that might have developed into something serious.

Meanwhile, McLaurin moved his office from its regular place in the courthouse to a new location across the street. The Straightouts protested this move and *Florida Times-Union* editorials denounced the supervisor. On July 19 a petition which demanded that McLaurin be removed from office on charges of misfeasance was forwarded to Governor Mitchell, who refused to act.[18] Although Mitchell had been elected by liberal and conservative voters, the latter group was the more influential. Attempts were made to secure a compromise on the issue of the election inspectors when the Straightouts submitted their list. The Antis, however, objected to most of the nominees and proposed that only eight inspectors be Straightouts. This arrangement would give the Antis a majority of the inspectors. When the Straightouts rejected the proposal, negotiations failed.

Turmoil filled Jacksonville on the day the two rival primaries were held. A hot July sun poured over the city. Crowds of people gathered in front of every polling place, rode in buggies along Bay, Forsyth, and Adams streets, filled up the green benches in Hemming Park, and lolled on the open porches of the St. James and Windsor hotels. Everybody talked about the election and its outcome.

After the Anti votes were tabulated and published, the Straightouts protested the results and violently denounced their opponents. Broward's group charged that "men who had not resided in the city two weeks were marched to the polls and made to vote the railroad ticket; railroad men . . . away on the trains in other parts of the state, were voted by proxy; boys of 16 and 17 were induced to vote in as many wards as they could . . . ; sailors from vessels which had been in port

two days were enthused with free booze and marched up to
the ballot boxes . . . ; dead men's names were raked up from
graves and the shroud and used to swell the majority. . . ."
One report said that men "came from Callahan, Gainesville,
Ocala, Fernandina, and points within 100 miles of Duval
County to participate in the travesty of a primary."[19]

Two conventions were held on July 26. The Antis met in
the Park Opera House, and the Straightouts in Metropolitan
Hall. John E. Hartridge won the Anti nomination to the
Florida Senate, and W. McL. Dancy and Edward Plummer
were nominated to the Florida House of Representatives. The
Straightouts nominated Duncan U. Fletcher for the Florida
Senate. In the balloting for nominees for the legislature, J. E.
Pickett defeated Broward's uncle, Pulaski Broward. Pickett
and Benjamin R. Powell became Straightout candidates.

When the state convention met in Jacksonville five days
later, there were two delegations from Duval County. The
committee on credentials settled the seating question, and
accepted the Antis by a vote of 28 to 12. The *Florida Times-
Union* reported that William D. Chipley, while not a member
of the committee, had "set in" on its sessions, and influenced
its decisions in favor of the conservatives.[20] The convention
named Benjamin S. Liddon as Democratic nominee for Florida
supreme court justice and Stephen M. Sparkman from the
First Congressional District to succeed Stephen R. Mallory.
Representative Charles M. Cooper was renominated from the
Second District.

During the campaign, Broward became convinced that the
establishing of a railroad commission would help to eliminate
railroad abuses and to diminish unfair corporation influence
and control. At a large political rally on September 21, he
sharply reiterated his advocacy of the legislation suggested
in his widely quoted open letter of July, 1894.[21] Broward was
particularly interested in laws which would forbid rate discriminations between long and short hauls.[22]

As election day drew nearer, the Straightouts, holding a

tenuous political position, were determined that they would help supervise the election. Though many voters in Duval County gave them sympathetic support, in other sections of the state their policies and actions were curtailed by the railroad-corporate forces. Broward's faction, given no voice in the state convention and little voice in the legislature, now seemed destined to play a minor role in the local election. Straightout leaders advocated immediate action to cope with this situation.

During the last week in September, Mayor Fletcher wrote a letter to John M. Barrs, Jacksonville's city attorney, and asked whether there were powers under the city charter to intervene in a state election, provided illegal interference at the polls was suspected. Barrs informed the mayor that it was legal for city police to keep polling places under surveillance on election day if there was strong evidence that balloting would be obstructed by persons employing such "weapons as guns, clubs, and brass knuckles. . . ." Barrs' letter was so worded as to give county authorities the same rights as those delegated to city police.[23] The Antis immediately protested and telegraphed a copy of Barrs' letter to Governor Mitchell. Even before the letter was published, the Antis surmised what Barrs' opinion would be. Conservative leaders apprised the governor daily of political developments in Jacksonville.

On the morning of September 30, Broward received a telegram from the governor, summoning him to Tallahassee: "Come here by first train. Business very important. Answer time of arrival here."[24] When the sheriff did not answer this message, Mitchell wired again the next morning: "I sent letter last night. Comply with instructions therein."[25] Broward probably received a letter from Mitchell about the same time that he received this second telegram. Mitchell wrote:

It is reported to me that many Conservative Citizens of Duval County are apprehensive that breaches of the peace and rioting will occur at the General Election which is to take place in Duval County on Tuesday, next, the 2nd. Inst., and you are hereby instructed, *1st.* It is your duty to preserve the peace during said Election. *2nd.* That under the law you can have but *one* Deputy at each polling place, and that Deputy is to act strictly under the direction of the Inspectors at said Election, and said Deputies are under no circumstances to enter the polling places unless instructed to do so by the Inspectors, or to vote themselves. *3rd.* You will be held to a strict account for the conduct of yourself and Deputies at said Election.[26]

Governor Mitchell thus made Sheriff Broward responsible for good order, but deprived him and the other county police officers of the power to carry out the law. By existing state law and by the governor's instructions, Broward's course of action should have been clear. Regardless of Barrs' letter, it was Broward's duty as county sheriff to comply with state law, and to carry out the orders from Mitchell. He knew that if he refused to comply with the instructions, the governor had the legal right to remove him from office. The sheriff, in addition, had every reason to know that his removal would please the Antis. He weighed the facts very carefully, and in the end decided to follow the course he thought right, namely, to stand by his faction. To Broward, his decision to contravene the governor's instructions meant intervention in behalf of honesty in the election.

So far, neither the two telegrams nor the letter from Mitchell had been answered. The sheriff was sitting on his front porch on the afternoon of October 1 when a third telegram was delivered. He opened the envelope and read: "Unless you reply to my telegram of this afternoon that you can and will prevent the threatened interference with tomorrows election I shall suspend you from office at once."[27] Broward answered immediately, assuring the governor that he would uphold state law to the best of his ability, although this was clearly not his intention.

Earlier that morning the sheriff had talked with a group

of newspaper reporters in his office in the courthouse. He refused to divulge how many deputies were detailed for each polling place, but said that he would give the men no definite instructions. Their duty was simple; if they saw "anything going on inside, which they think is wrong, they will go in to prevent it. They . . . will go in anywhere and everywhere they think the law is being violated."[28]

About the time the sheriff was meeting the reporters, Adjutant General Patrick Houstoun arrived from Tallahassee with specific instructions from the governor to prevent a possible riot and to see that the ordinances of the state were upheld.[29] Throughout the morning Houstoun conferred with Fletcher in the mayor's office. Fletcher's instructions to the chief of police concerning the specially appointed deputies stipulated that they would be present to ". . . maintain order, and . . . to take orders from the regular officers at each polling place, and . . . from the deputy sheriff on duty, and that the police . . . were not to enter the polling places unless called on by the deputies to prevent or suppress a breach of the peace."[30] The governor instructed Charles M. Cooper to deliver a special proclamation to Fletcher on the eve of the election. The proclamation called Barrs' letter revolutionary, maintained that both the deputies and special police had no right in the polling places, and ordered those officers to stay outside.[31]

The situation was becoming hourly more serious. Fletcher induced Cooper to interview James P. Taliaferro, leader of the Antis, and secure his consent to admit "one citizen of probity and integrity, not allied with either side, in each polling place."[32] Taliaferro refused, saying that such action would cast a reflection upon the integrity of the inspectors. Many believed that Adjutant General Houstoun endorsed Fletcher's plan, but Houstoun knew that without complete cooperation from both factions it could not succeed.[33] The Straightouts were convinced that unless they were represented in the election and in the counting of votes, they would certainly lose. The *Florida Times-Union* predicted that "on a full vote, a free ballot and a fair count, Duval County today will go for the straightouts by a majority of 500." With so narrow a margin, liberal leaders were determined that there would be no tampering with ballots, and they approved Fletcher's "200 special policemen" and Broward's "100 deputies," who were to "preserve peace and order" and "quell the turbulent spirits, if there should be any."[34]

Election day in Jacksonville was bright and hot, and throngs of people, pouring in from every part of the county, stirred up confusion and turbulence. While shirt-sleeved crowds stood outside the polling places and waited to see what would happen, the Antis and Straightouts continued negotiations. Refusing to consider the list of observers suggested by Mayor Fletcher, the Antis submitted their own slate. Though the mayor, who was in conference with Cooper and General Houstoun, approved this list, the compromise failed when the inspectors refused to give their approval.[35] When Houstoun telegraphed for further instructions the governor ordered out the militia. As the troops could not be used legally for quelling riots until the civil authorities had exhausted all other resources, they merely held a dress parade along Bay Street.[36] People swarmed on the sidewalks to watch the soldiers pass, and the hubbub and disorder added to the general agitation.

Meanwhile, tension increased throughout the city and an outbreak of violence seemed imminent. The inspectors closed Wards Three, Four, Five, Six and Eight, after Broward's deputies had refused to leave. The voters at Ward Four objected to the poll closing and were lined up for half a block, waiting for the balloting to be resumed. Men sat on the ground or on borrowed chairs, and many marked their places in line while they slept in the shade of the trees. At lunch time housewives in the neighborhood brought out steaming plates of food, and nearly everyone had an iced bucket of beer. Rioting, which many had feared, did not occur. However, fights between individual Antis and Straightouts were reported throughout the city.

The Straightouts violently protested application of the "Gag Law," and charged that the Anti inspectors denied "2,300 qualified voters—more than one half of those of the county . . . the privilege of exercising the elective franchise."[37] The *Florida Times-Union,* calling the election a "Carnival of Fraud," declared that "the darkest page of reconstruction times is bright as the noonday sun, compared with the action of Triay and his co-conspirators. . . . The old carpet-baggers— Conover, Littlefield, Stearns, Putnam, and others—can rest easy now. Their sins are as white as snow compared with the fraud perpetrated by white Southern Democrats in the city of Jacksonville. . . ."[38]

Liberals denounced a system of "White and Blue tickets" used at the polls to facilitate a dishonest vote. One Jacksonville newspaper reported that "heelers of the railroad crowd" approached voters who waited in line and offered to buy their votes. Should the voter consent to sell out, he was given a "White ticket" with a "private mark on it," which he carried into the polls with him. He gave this ticket to the election inspector, voted the "railroad ballot," and received a "Blue ticket" in return. Outside, the "heeler" paid the venal voter two or three dollars, according to the terms of sale.[39]

Ballot tabulations revealed that the Antis won, although their majority was not so large as they had expected. The Straightouts claimed that the Antis closed those wards in which the voters were known generally to be supporting the Straight-out ticket.[40] The presence of county deputies and city police in the voting places was clearly a violation of state law. The Straightouts showed, however, that the police had been distributed in all wards, and they felt that if their presence necessitated the closing of some polls, then all of them should have been closed. Any other course was unreasonable and discriminatory.

John E. Hartridge defeated Duncan U. Fletcher for the office of state senator by a little more than a hundred votes; Dancy and Plummer, the two Anti candidates, beat Pickett and Powell by about the same margin. In areas other than Duval County, sizable gains were tabulated for the liberal forces. Anti-railroad and anti-corporation strength in Baker and Calhoun counties was such as to leave the race between the two candidates for the state legislature in doubt for a time. In Osceola County, anti-corporation candidates received a majority of the votes cast, and in Sumter and Washington counties the liberal vote was substantial. Such results clearly foreshadowed the approaching schism in Florida's party ranks.[41]

Broward's political future hung in the balance. His "interference" in the state election gave the Antis evidence for his indictment, something for which they had long been waiting. They realized that if Broward were removed as sheriff they would rid themselves of one of their chief political opponents and would injure the anti-railroad cause in Florida. The anti-Broward group, led by T. L. Allen, George W. Wilson, Edward Gillen, and Fleming Bowden, was indicted by the *Florida Times-Union*, which claimed that the "whole pack of antis, in their war-paint, with their tomahawks and knives out, are on the trail of Broward, all eager for his scalp."[42]

On October 9 the following petition, signed by forty-seven prominent Duval citizens, was forwarded to Governor Mitchell:[43]

We charge N. B. Broward, sheriff of Duval county, Florida, with malfeasance, misfeasance and neglect of duty in office, as shown by the sworn statements of the inspectors of election and other affidavits herewith inclosed, whereby it appears that he appointed a number of deputies to serve at each of certain of the polling places in Duval county, in some instances four or five, whereas the law authorizes the appointment of but one at each polling place.

The said deputies, under instructions from said sheriff, forcibly entered the polling places, and refused to vacate the same when ordered to do so by the inspectors, thereby, instead of maintaining the peace and good order at the polls, and obeying the lawful orders of the inspectors, as required by law, themselves became violators of the law and inciters of disorder and riot and prevented an election in certain of the election districts.

That instead of remaining where he could be communicated with to properly instruct his deputies if necessary, and to assist in maintaining the peace and good order, the said sheriff absented himself or kept in hiding on election day so that he could not be found after diligent search, notwithstanding the fact that he well knew that there were grave apprehensions of disorder and riot on election day, made all the more probable by his instructions to his deputies.[44]

Accompanying the petition were affidavits from the election inspectors, detailing the extent and degree to which Broward's deputies had interfered in the polling places and with ballot boxes. Such interference, it was charged, was specifically against the law. One of the affidavits stated that in Ward One, George A. DeCottes, the first voter, deposited his ballot, showed his special deputy badge, and refused to leave the polling place. After a heated discussion he agreed to leave the room, but posted himself in a chair outside the building so that he could watch everything that went on inside. The inspectors forcibly barred A. F. Boyce, another deputy sheriff, from entering the room.[45]

In Ward Four, an affidavit stated, the inspectors were faced with another problem. John M. Barrs and J. S. Maxwell showed their deputy sheriff badges and refused to leave the polls when ordered. Barrs upset a pile of ballots lying on the railing in front of the ballot boxes; and when one of the inspectors threatened him, he clenched his fists and yelled: "Come on, I am ready for you." When the inspectors asked Deputy Sheriff Maxwell to put Barrs out, he refused, as did Deputy Sheriff William H. Padelford. In desperation, the inspectors "dispatched a messenger to find Sheriff Broward to report the situation to him and ask his assistance. But the said sheriff, after diligent search, could not be found. . . . No election was held therein."[46]

These and other charges were placed in Governor Mitchell's hand. A. G. Hartridge, an Anti leader, declared that Adjutant General Houstoun, on election day, had instructed him to deliver a letter to the sheriff as quickly as possible. Hartridge took a carriage to Ward Two. Unable to secure any information from Chief Deputy Ed Williams, he went to Broward's home, and was informed by Mrs. Broward that her husband had left early that morning and she did not know where he was. Hartridge went from ward to ward, looking for Broward, but he could find no one who had seen the sheriff for several hours.[47]

Faced with these affidavits and statements, the governor asked Broward to answer before he decided whether he should be removed from office. On October 13 Broward received the following dispatch from the governor's secretary: "I am directed by the governor to send you the enclosed impressions made against you by prominent citizens of Jacksonville for malfeasance, misfeasance and neglect of duty in office, supported by affidavits of inspectors and clerks of the election held in Jacksonville, Fla., on the 2nd inst., and by other citizens and to cite you to show cause on or before Wednesday next, the 17th inst., why the suspension therein suggested should not be made, in accordance with the provisions of Art. IV. Sec. 15, of the Constitution of Florida."[48]

Broward succeeded in obtaining an extension of time until October 22, and in the meantime the Straightouts gathered evidence for his defense. The Straightouts claimed that "the effort to remove Sheriff Broward is partly inspired by a desire on the part of the railroad faction to have everything their own way, and partly from a desire on the part of certain of the railroad followers for a large-sized plum in the shape of the sheriffalty of Duval county."[49] Strongly supporting Broward, a *Florida Times-Union* editorial stated emphatically: "There are few Floridians, from governor or senator or constable, who are Sheriff Broward's equal in ability. There are none who have a greater hold on the confidence of their constituents. None are more popular, more faithful, more honest in the discharge of duty. No official in Florida has made a cleaner record."[50]

The Straightouts were active in securing signatures to a petition to send to Governor Mitchell. Defending Broward, they reiterated that he was attacked by "politicians because he was not in accord with them, and because they could not use him to their ends and purposes." Liberals supported him for doing "all in his power, within the law, to see that . . . rights as Citizens were not trampled upon, and that . . . votes . . . cast . . . be counted fairly and honestly." The Straightouts indicted the "scheming Politicians, who were bold enough to say that 'they would carry the election if they had to steal it,' which they prepared themselves to do. . . ."[51]

Sheriff Broward sent the governor his answer. Reviewing all the facts of the case, he admitted that deputies had been ordered for duty at the polling places on election day. This practice, however, had been used for nearly seven years while he was sheriff, and he was merely following precedent. The appointment of deputies, while not in strict conformity with state statutes, had never before been probed. The questionable side of the case, Broward contended, was whether he had the right to ask the county to pay for the services of more than one man in each ward. He had no intention, he said, of making such a request.[52]

This political campaign heightened to an almost unprecedented pitch the feeling among the people of Duval County. According to the sheriff, the Antis controlled the entire election machinery, the supervisor of registration, all the members of the board of county commissioners, many of the election inspectors, and the clerks in almost every election district. The Broward-Barrs-Stockton group accepted the fact that the railroads, the express companies, and other corporations, which believed that the establishment of a state railroad commission would be injurious to their interests, were out to win the election, and would use any means to elect conservative candidates. The Straightouts had heard that the corporations had compelled their employees to join an organization which pledged them to vote for legislative candidates who opposed the commission. Such was the Anti program for the campaign and election in the county.

Throughout the latter part of September, many supporters of the Hartridge ticket boasted that they intended to carry "the election by perpetration of such frauds as might be necessary."[53] It was also reported that J. B. Christie, then solicitor of Duval County, allegedly stated during an afternoon recess of the criminal court in Jacksonville, in the presence of the judge, clerk, attorneys, and spectators of the Court of Records, "that it did not make any difference how many votes were polled for either of said tickets, because a majority would be counted for the ticket of his faction."[54]

Thus Broward reasoned that there was a real basis for his belief that fraud would take place at the polls. Moreover, it was stated that the citizens of Duval County, who in the main supported Broward, were incensed by the loose talk of fraud, and threatened to employ force, if necessary, to "secure a fair election." Under the circumstances, Broward presumably felt that in order to secure peace and order in the election districts, he had to assign several deputies to the various voting precincts.

Governor Mitchell had ample authority under the Florida constitution to remove Broward immediately. The sheriff had known this before election day, and he could have followed the easier course and the more strictly legal one, that of nonintervention and noninterference at the polls. His zeal for firmness and honesty, however, had prompted him to exceed his authority; consequently, he was formally removed from office on December 22, 1894. A bitter political enemy, Fleming Bowden, was appointed by the governor to fill the office until the next election.[55]

In the days which followed, Broward received scores of

letters and telegrams from citizens all over the state and the nation who pledged their support and bitterly denounced Fleming Bowden, the machinations of the Antis in Duval County politics, and Governor Mitchell's actions in removing Broward from office. The message which more than any other reflected the strong feelings of Broward's supporters in Florida was that penned by United States Senator Wilkinson Call:

Dear Napoleon:

I see that you have been removed without cause or rather because you are a good officer and an honest man, a genuine Democrat and a true friend of the people. It is a great honor to you that you should be condemned by the enemies of the people for these qualities.

It is said in the Litany of the Christian churches that "the blood of the martyrs is the seed of the church." So it will be with you and the people. Your removal will bring strong light to bear on the iniquitous proceedings of the corporation rule party and their servants. Their purpose to disfranchise the entire white people of the State has been manifest for a long time. It is rendered more conspicuous by your removal.

I regret the pecuniary loss you sustain, but otherwise am gratified at the fact, in as much as I think it will benefit you and the people by exposing the iniquity of the corporation people.[56]

On April 24, 1895, the state Senate ratified the action of Governor Mitchell in removing Broward. The *Florida Times-Union*, the Straightout organ in Duval County, thus stoutly defended the sheriff: "He was suspended for attempting to secure a fair election. . . . This was his crime. It was a work of patriotism. Patriots have been punished before, but the world honors them just the same. Sheriff Broward's removal and the cause of it, will be worth more to him than the cross of the Legion of Honor. It decorates him as a man who gave up his official position in an effort to preserve the liberties of his people. . . ."[57]

Napoleon Broward's removal from office, although apparently a heavy blow to the anti-railroad faction, actually strengthened Florida's liberal cause. The strong man of Duval County had become a political martyr, personifying to the common folk their dissatisfaction with the state government and their avid desire for reform. Broward's political reputation did not suffer. He emerged as the leader of the independent Democrats, standing against the forces of corruption, dishonesty, fraud, and evil which he believed had so long characterized the corporate interests in his state.

∽ 8 ∾

Bearding the Spanish Lion

IN THE CITY ELECTION of June, 1895, Broward again entered politics, this time in a minor way. Endorsed by the Straightouts as a candidate for councilman from Ward Two, he won easily. The *Florida Times-Union* acted as though Broward were the only man in the race, and the morning after the election hailed his triumph with an exultant headline: WELL! BROWARD WAS ELECTED AT ANY RATE AND HE IS A HOLY TERROR.[1]

During this time Broward was also busy with his family. His house had become too small now that there were three daughters—Dorcas, Josephine, and Enid Lyle. He and Mrs. Broward had long considered building a fine new home on their vacant lot, next to the house in which they were living. Construction began in November of 1894, and the house was ready for occupancy the first week of March, 1895. The two-story white frame dwelling covered a large part of the lot. Across the front and on either side were long piazzas, enclosed by solid railings "so that the children would not fall over into the yard."[2] Dividing the lower floor, a deep hall ran from front to back. On one side were the kitchen, the dining room, and the parlor; on the other, the drawing room and the library. The ceilings were high, and the woodwork and floors were of Honduras mahogany, which had been salvaged from a wrecked steamer. The house was one of the first in Jacksonville to have electric lights in every room.[3] A large yard in the back provided a play area for the Broward girls.

Broward had again become interested in new business enterprises and, with his brother Montcalm and George DeCottes, he raised forty thousand dollars to design and build a "powerful seagoing tug" to be used principally for towing and wrecking along the south Florida reefs.⁴ The partners also planned to carry freight and passengers between Jacksonville and Nassau in the Bahamas.

Finding it difficult to choose a name, the owners decided to sell the privilege of naming the boat to the highest bidder. Charles M. Ellis acted as auctioneer. The bidding was spirited, but finally DeCottes won the contest with an offer of eighty dollars, and he decided to name the vessel the *Three Friends*, in honor of her triple ownership.⁵ Identified by many Jacksonville people as the "Queen of the Southern Waters," the boat was expected to be even faster than the *Dauntless*, then reputed locally to be the "fastest tug in the South."⁶

On christening day, February 2, 1895, a gay, well-dressed crowd of people gathered to witness the launching. Captain Broward, his brushed black coat glinting in the sun and a white yachting cap shading his dark eyes, gave the order to take away the chocks which held the boat in place. As the vessel slid gently into the shining river, Hortense Broward smashed a bottle of wine over the bow. Shrill whistles from river craft and nearby sawmills blasted the air. The *Three Friends* was on the threshold of a place in history.

Already in motion were world events that would vitally affect Napoleon Broward and his *Three Friends*. Early in the damp gray dawn of February 28, 1895, newsboys shrilly announced that an insurrection against the decaying authority of royal Spain had broken out in Cuba. Spanish officials hastily assured the world that the incident was unimportant, and Spain's minister in Washington haughtily proclaimed the collapse of the movement. However, Cubans in communities along the Atlantic coast received the news with great interest. They considered the revolt war in earnest, opened upon a prearranged schedule of "which every detail had been prepared with the most minute attention."⁷

News that the independence movement had not collapsed but was spreading came with dramatic suddenness; already the provinces of Matanzas and Santiago de Cuba were under martial law. American newspapers filled their front pages with startling headlines.[8] A new chapter in the history of the American people was opening; these events presaged war with Spain.

Cuban revolutionists capitalized on American sympathy. Their propaganda, disseminated by Cuban expatriates, glossed over the seamy side of the rebel cause and portrayed the Spanish "butchers" in the blackest hues. America, traditionally friendly to the ideals of liberty and democracy, thrilled to the cry, *Cuba Libre!*

In dire need of military supplies, revolutionists used the shores of the United States as a base for filibustering expeditions to smuggle contraband to the Cuban armies. The vigilance of the United States authorities prevented about two-thirds of these enterprises from reaching their destination. The Spaniards were bitterly unappreciative of these efforts, and repeatedly charged, with a considerable measure of truth, that the revolt was kept alive only by aid from the United States.[9] However, as long as Grover Cleveland was President, any such aid came from private capital, not from the government.

Florida, because of her proximity to Cuba, her long seacoast, and the ease with which a vessel could slip out from any one of a thousand inlets, bays, and rivers, afforded the best facilities for filibustering. The mainland of south Florida and the Florida Keys lay about a hundred miles north across the open sea from the island of Cuba. The Keys—numerous small, wooded islands, sand bars, and rocks extending fingerlike into the Gulf of Mexico—were a filibuster's haven. Narrow, crooked channels running into innumerable sand bars and treacherous, jagged reefs made it difficult for revenue cutters to catch the small, swift vessels carrying guns and ammunition to the revolutionists.

Many of the islands were inhabited by Conchs, an English-speaking people from the Bahamas, who helped the insurgents whenever they could.¹⁰ The other Keys were inhabited largely by Cubans. The population of Key West, the southernmost island, consisted almost wholly of Cubans, who strongly sympathized with the *insurrectos,* and were anxious to aid the filibusters financially and in other ways.

The large Cuban colony in Jacksonville had been organized into a *junta* by J. A. Huau, a successful cigar manufacturer of the city and one of Broward's close friends. Huau's cigar store served as a secret meeting place for the Cubans and their supporters. The Jacksonville *junta* planned to raise funds to buy arms, ammunition, and other military supplies for Cuba, and to ship war matériel and recruits to the insurrectionists on the island.

In the spring of 1895, several expeditions were fitted out and some of them reached Cuba safely. Broward knew that the Spanish minister in Washington was demanding that official action be taken to stop these expeditions. Moreover, in June, 1895, he read Cleveland's presidential proclamation which promised prompt arrest for those ". . . accepting or exercising commissions for warlike service against it [Spain], by enlistment or procuring others to enlist for such service, by fitting out, or arming, or procuring to be fitted out any armed ships of war for such service, by augmenting the force of any ship of war engaged in such service in a port of the United States. . . ."¹¹

During the summer, while the *Three Friends* was still under construction, several members of the *junta* approached Broward at various times concerning the possibility of employing his vessel to carry them to Cuba.¹² Regarding the Cuban insurrection simply as a case of an oppressed people rising spontaneously to free itself from alien tyranny, Broward hoped that Congress would grant formal recognition to the freedom movement. Like many other Floridians, spurred on by patriotism, sympathy, thrill of adventure, and yellow journalism, he wanted to help the Cubans. Nevertheless, if he did sign a contract with the *junta,* Broward was determined to stay within the law. He would agree to transport patriots only if they would sign the ship's log as passengers. He would not take munitions unless they were carried beyond the three-mile limit by another vessel and then loaded on the *Three Friends*. He felt that technically such transactions would not violate the law.[13]

The remaining months of 1895 passed quickly for the captain. Besides his political activities, he was completing the *Three Friends* for her maiden voyage. On the afternoon of January 14, 1896, she was ready to sail to Nassau. She was fueled, and loaded with a cargo of flour and fertilizer; additional cargo was to be picked up at Miami and Key West. With Broward as captain and John Dunn as chief engineer, the *Three Friends* pulled away from her dock and out into the swirling brightness of the St. Johns, "amid the blowing of whistles from the river craft and the waving of the handkerchiefs of well-wishers on shore. . . . The steamer had a large American flag . . . flying from her flagstaff. A union jack was flung to the breeze from her jack staff."[14] The vessel crossed the St. Johns Bar at five o'clock, after a quick run of two hours and fifteen minutes.

In a few days, the *Three Friends* returned to Jacksonville. When additional freight contracts did not materialize and when it appeared that there would be no immediate towing or wrecking jobs, Captain Broward became discouraged. Naturally he and his partners were concerned over whether the boat could be put on a sound paying basis. After serious consideration, the owners of the *Three Friends* decided to negotiate a formal contract with the Cubans.

One rainy afternoon late in February, 1896, two Cubans, Hernandez and Freeman, accompanied by C. B. Barnard of Tampa, met in Huau's cigar factory with Broward, Huau, and John M. Barrs. The owners of the *Three Friends* signed a contract in which they agreed to transport a company of Cuban patriots, under the command of General Enrique Colasso, and to tow war supplies which were loaded on the schooner *Stephen R. Mallory* of Cedar Key.[15] Meanwhile, General Colasso and his staff were hiding in the home of a friend in Tampa and sixty-five of his men were on the little schooner *Ardell,* which lay somewhere behind the Florida Keys, probably near Hawk Channel.[16] A messenger was sent at once to Cape Sable to locate the *Ardell* and to advise her men that the *Three Friends* would pick them up shortly and carry them to Cuba. The *Stephen R. Mallory* was loaded with munitions that had been stored in a warehouse at Cedar Key.[17] While a fierce tropical storm raged in the Gulf, the *Mallory* sailed from Cedar Key for Caesar's Creek where she was supposed to meet the *Three Friends.*

Near Tampa, the *Mallory* was chased by a United States revenue cutter, the *McLane,* but escaped. The following day the cutter sighted another small vessel and, suspecting that it was a filibuster, fired a warning shot and forced the boat to head into Tampa. An inspection of the vessel's cargo revealed heavy packing cases marked "groceries." Lacking authority to pry open the boxes, the inspectors ordered them shipped to their consignee, John G. Christopher, a wholesale merchant in Jacksonville, and a Cuban sympathizer. The "groceries" were actually guns and ammunition that would have been added to the *Mallory's* cargo had not the cutter interfered. They were sealed in a Florida Central and Peninsular Railroad car, with instructions that the car was not to be opened until it was claimed by Christopher and the railroad was assured that all demurrage would be paid.[18] However, a Cuban working in the Jacksonville railroad yards notified the *junta* when the car arrived, and that night the cases were quietly unloaded and hidden in the Christopher warehouse at the foot of Newnan Street.[19]

After the guns had arrived, Huau notified General Colasso in Tampa to come to Jacksonville. As the general was being closely watched by United States government agents and by private detectives in the pay of Spain, it would be hazardous to spirit him out of Tampa. Despite the danger, an attempt was made on March 2, and it was successful because of its very daring. There have been controversial accounts concerning the exact nature of the plan. The newspapers reported that late one afternoon the general and a companion went out for a stroll in the suburbs. Eluding detectives, they entered a carriage which was waiting at a prearranged spot, and were driven rapidly to Plant City where they boarded a train for Jacksonville.[20]

According to Broward's own account, a closed carriage, late one moonless night, drew up to the house in Tampa where the general and his staff were hiding. Colasso and his men quickly entered the vehicle and were driven toward Port Tampa. At a point previously agreed upon, the carriage stopped in the shadows of an old building and the whole party, except one, alighted. The lone occupant drove on to Port Tampa, and there, disguised as Colasso, boarded a ship which was just sailing for Key West. The detectives following him also came aboard and the vessel sailed out into the Gulf. Confident that they had at last trapped the wily Cuban revolutionist, the detectives congratulated themselves on the ease with which they had outwitted him. Meanwhile, the general and his followers were driven through the night to Plant City, where they boarded the Florida Central. Before daylight next morning they left the train at Orange Park, twelve miles out of Jacksonville. They were met by Huau's nephew, Alfonso Fritot, an ardent worker in the *junta*, who took them in a launch to Clark's Mill near the city. Just before dawn on the following day, after hiding in the mill nearly twenty-four hours, they drove in a closed carriage into the city to the house of John M. Barrs, where they remained hidden in his attic for a week.[21]

In Key West, detectives were carefully searching the ship and the docks for General Colasso. After fruitless hours, they realized that they had been outwitted, and wired the Spanish consuls in Tampa and Jacksonville, asking that the homes of known Cuban sympathizers be watched. Although Huau's home in Jacksonville was under constant surveillance, no one yet suspected the Barrs brothers, John M. and A. W., of Cuban activity, and no guard was placed at their home.

Throughout the morning and afternoon of March 11, the *Three Friends* was lying at her dock being rapidly overhauled and readied for a long voyage. A hundred tons of coal, sixty barrels of water, and a huge store of provisions were quickly loaded. The Spanish vice-consul of Jacksonville, Señor de Mariteague, whose suspicions had been aroused several weeks before when he heard rumors that the *Three Friends* was a filibuster, kept a close watch on the loading activities. He became concerned when he saw two pairs of davits erected on deck, but he accepted Broward's explanation that the boat was sailing to Palm Beach, where the equipment would be used on a towing job.

That evening about seven o'clock, the *Three Friends*, with a full crew aboard, hoisted on a naphtha launch and two large yawls. Rain was falling as she pulled away from her dock and moved rapidly to the Christopher warehouse to load the "groceries," which Broward had originally planned to pick up beyond the three-mile limit. These stores consisted of two rapid-fire field cannon, five hundred Remington rifles, three thousand Winchester rifles, five hundred machetes, three hundred thousand rounds each of Winchester, Remington, and Spanish caliber cartridges, and one million repriming caps, in addition to five hundred pounds of dynamite, five hundred pounds of sulphur, five hundred pounds of miscellaneous equipment, and a large quantity of clothing and medicine.[22]

There was little secrecy about the loading, and only one guard was on duty. Loud blasts of steam from the funnels of the *Three Friends* awakened occupants of a houseboat anchored nearby.[23] To divert suspicion, Broward repeated the story he had told Mariteague, and insisted that the *Three Friends* was sailing only to Palm Beach.[24] Instead, she moved down the river past the *Boutwell*, a revenue cutter which had inspected the Jacksonville port several times in January and February while looking for filibusters. The cutter was in dry dock for repairs and her guns were dismantled and useless. Even had Captain Kilgore of the *Boutwell* known of the illicit expedition, he would have been helpless to prevent it.

At DeCottes' Mill, three miles from Jacksonville, General Colasso, Colonel Hernandez, Duke Estrada, and A. W. Barrs were waiting impatiently for the *Three Friends*. Afraid to light a fire, they sat huddled together in the dark, with blankets held tightly around their shoulders. Water from the branches of the trees dripped noisily against the sides of the building. The dark shadow of the boat finally slipped into view. Several of the crew stowed on deck another large launch and two iron surfboats, to be used later in unloading the cargo. A. W. Barrs and John Dunn helped the Cubans aboard. Then Captain Broward quietly ordered the crew to "cast off your lines" and instructed John Dunn to "give her full speed ahead." The *Three Friends* sailed down the river under rainy skies toward the sea. A fisherman near the St. Johns Bar later reported the *Three Friends* moved with such speed that "small fishing boats along the river were thrown violently upon the platform, or else high up on the banks."[25]

When Captain Kilgore of the revenue cutter *Boutwell* learned of the expedition and questioned fishermen near New Berlin, one of them informed him that "some darned boat passed here, throwing my boat up on the platform; and if she kept on at the same rate of speed she will by now have reached a place too hot for you to catch her in."[26] The pilot boat keeper at the mouth of the river told Kilgore: "God knows what passed here; something the color of blue dawn, with her forward deck piled high with boats, and her afterdeck filled with boxes, or something of the kind. The swell she made in passing washed our decks and floated our boats."[27]

By dawn the *Three Friends* was fully fifty miles southeast of the Bar. A new coat of steel-gray had replaced her usual white, and she now bore the name *The Ox*.[28] The rain stopped about five o'clock, but the ocean was rough. Waves dashed against the sides of the vessel; sea spray washed over her deck. Captain Broward and John Dunn carefully adjusted the caps on the engine journals and on the crank brasses of the main engine, leaving the slightest bit of slack, to avoid overheating the bearings in the event they should meet a Spanish gunboat or a United States cruiser, and should have to drive the *Three Friends* hard to prevent capture.

The captain ordered his crew to keep a steady lookout from the top of the pilot house for "anything with a smoke stack in her."[29] Dunn, gibing the lookouts, shouted: "Better make those glasses fast to your hands, for if you should sight a Spanish cruiser, they'll look so small you'll be wanting a megaphone to look through instead. Some of you will be speaking through spy glasses and looking through megaphones."[30]

The Cubans walked restlessly about the deck but finally settled themselves on the mahogany bitts in the bow of the vessel and watched a school of porpoises playing in the spray and waves. One of the men saw a "sun-rainbow" in the water spray, and Colasso considered this a good omen. Deeply religious, the general fingered the beads on his rosary, and then turning toward his staff he asked God's blessing in the battle ". . . for political liberty and the right to worship God as we please."[31] All was quiet on board the vessel until about nine that evening. As the steamer was rounding Cape Canaveral, the lookout, posted toward the port bow, hurriedly beckoned the captain and reported the lights of three approaching vessels. Broward alerted the crew to battle stations, but the lights proved to be those of a tugboat towing a large "derrickbarge."[32]

Toward morning on Friday, March 13, a northeast wind sprang up. With it came a sharp sea, upon which the boat rolled and tossed. By midafternoon it was calm again, and around four o'clock the *Three Friends* entered Hawk Channel off Cape Florida. Sighting the *Stephen R. Mallory* anchored near Elliot's Key at the point where Caesar's Creek flows into the channel, Broward sent a messenger in a small boat to inform the captain of the *Mallory* that the *Three Friends* would sail south at daylight, and to suggest a rendezvous at Indian Key.

While waiting for an answer, Broward noted that the wind was changing and was blowing stronger. By night it would be of gale force, and the waves would be running high. Just after sunset, near Turtle Harbor, Broward's lookout spied a suspicious-looking vessel putting out to sea in the face of the storm. Reaching open water, the strange craft headed on a course outside the reef, parallel with that of the *Three Friends*. Closer scrutiny revealed that the boat was the *Commodore*, another Cuban filibuster. Mistaking the *Three Friends* for a revenue cutter and trying to outrun her, the *Commodore's* captain ordered his vessel to turn and head toward the "Bahama Banks."

The next day at dawn the *Three Friends* moved down the coast, and by ten o'clock had rounded the treacherous reefs and anchored near Indian Key. An hour later the *Mallory* arrived, and both vessels awaited the arrival of the schooner *Ardell* with the sixty-five Cuban patriots aboard. According to plan, these men were to be transferred to the *Three Friends*. A launch was lowered from the davits, and Barrs, Colonel Hernandez, and Lewis roared off to look for the *Ardell*. They hoped to find her at anchor in the Gulf of Mexico, just on the other side of the crooked channel and innumerable sand bars. Unable to find her, the men returned to the *Three Friends* in the late afternoon and resumed their search the next morning. The sun was low on the western horizon when a lookout announced that the *Ardell* was approaching. When Broward went aboard the *Mallory*, he found that Captain Elliot had been stricken with paralysis and had to leave immediately for Key West to secure medical aid. Although this upset Broward's plans, he ordered the *Mallory* cargo loaded on his own vessel. The transfer was accomplished with the utmost difficulty as the vessels rolled and pitched in the choppy sea. Everybody, including the Cubans, worked all night, and by four o'clock the next morning the job was completed. Captain Elliot's condition was critical, and he died that evening, just as his vessel sighted the lights of Key West.[33]

After the *Mallory* had departed, the *Three Friends* steamed out into the channel alongside the *Ardell*. The Cubans were quickly transferred, and Broward ordered his vessel to get underway. He set a course due south, heading past Alligator Reef into the open ocean. Gray dawn filled the sea and sky when the last rocks of the reef faded into the distance.

About eleven o'clock that morning, Captain Broward sighted the Double-Headed Shot Keys, and informed Colasso that they would reach Cuba in a few hours. He advised the patriots to keep out of sight until dark, when the landing could be made.

Unable to find the small schooner near Salt Key which usually escorted filibusters to shore, Broward set his course toward the lighthouse at Cardenas on Key Pedro. Under a prearranged agreement, Santos, the Cuban pilot, was to take charge at this point and steer the vessel to its landing place. Rain was falling, and a strong wind blowing out of the northeast roughed the ocean. The whole sky was flecked with light from the burning cane fields on the Cuban mainland. When Santos turned the *Three Friends* south, Broward insisted that southwest was the right direction and ordered him to change his course. Although Santos objected, he obeyed the captain's insistent orders. Thirty minutes later, the pilot turned the boat south again, contending that they must be about twenty miles west of the Pedro lighthouse since they could not see its flare. The captain disagreed, and argued that the heavy rain obscured the lighthouse lamps. He finally yielded to the pilot, but first he had the engines stopped and ordered the first mate to "throw the lead." The first time the lead showed "no bottom," but on the next trial it registered "twenty-four feet." Broward sprang to action and rang "full speed astern." Before the headway of the vessel could be checked, her bow was in the shallow breakers. It was not grounded, however, and the boat was moved until the lead again showed twenty-four feet and Santos announced, "This is the place . . . to land."[34] The anchor was lowered, and the *Three Friends* swung around into position.

Although he was still hesitant, Broward gave the signal to unload. A lifeboat was speedily lowered, and General Vasques, Charles Silva, and five other Cubans started for the beach on a reconnoitering expedition. Instead of waiting for the return of the scout boat, Santos ordered other boats loaded and launched. Fifteen Cubans were packed between cases of arms and ammunition in each large boat and were rowed to shore. A few minutes later, lookouts excitedly reported that the *Three Friends* was anchored near a Spanish town and that there was a fort about a hundred yards off the starboard side. Santos had miscalculated and had missed the designated landing place by over two miles.

Meanwhile, General Vasques and four of his men were hiding in the brush around the front of the fort, covering the door with their guns. Three lifeboats were swamped with water when they struck the beach, and one was wrecked on a coral reef. Fearing an attack from the fort, the Cubans on shore tried to bury the munitions in the soft beach sand. General Colasso ordered Colonel Hernandez to go ashore with one of the remaining lifeboats and bring back the patriots. Colasso wanted to wait until the following night to try another landing, but Broward feared the Spaniards would find the munitions, spread a general alarm, and prevent a landing anywhere in the area. He convinced Colasso that the nearby Spanish town could be surprised and taken by the patriots before morning. The general declared, "We will go ashore."[35]

When Broward was unable to recruit volunteers from his crew members to row the revolutionists to shore again, he offered to give the Cubans two boats. Duke Estrada, noting the name *Three Friends* on the craft, refused the proposal. "That will not do, Captain," he said, "the Spaniards will apprise your government, when the boats are found, and it will give you away. Your steamer will be seized and this fact will be used as evidence against you."

With excitement edging his voice, Broward announced: "I will row you ashore myself." Immediately Patterson, the second engineer, spoke up, "If you are going, I will go with you." With that, half a dozen crew members volunteered to row two boats.[36] As the last launch pushed through the waves, searchlights from a small Spanish gunboat beamed out over the white beach and silhouetted the startled Cubans, burying their ammunition boxes. Immediately Spanish bullets ricocheted along the ground, hurling up showers of coral shell and rock. Cuban guns aimed toward the searchlight, and in a few seconds it was dark. Rifle clicks sounded hollow against the roar of the surf. Sand and smoke spurted into giant puffs and sprays, enveloping cursing, sweating men. Shells exploded over the black water into sudden fountains of light. One landed close to the *Three Friends* and fiercely rocked the vessel. Whining bullets strafed the Cubans on the beach and those still in the boats. Flares lit up the blackness. Broward stood in the bow of the vessel, directing his crew to gun stations. Powder grime burned his eyes; smoke and salt-water spray nearly stifled him. Searching the sea with his spyglass, he discovered a large gunboat off the port bow, about a mile away. He scaled a ship's ladder, rushed onto the upper decks, and shouted to his men below: "Do not use your guns! The fire will attract the attention of a large gunboat on our port side. Get your axes and lie under the bulwarks. If this small gunboat attempts to board us, use them!" John Dunn was standing close by and Broward told him: "I promised the sailors that we would not leave them on the beach. Rather than do it, if capture is imminent, I will beach the boat and we will all fight together."[37]

Two landing-boats raced back through the tide. A water fountain nearly swamped them when a shell exploded only fifty feet away. Sweating and straining, the sailors pulled the boats alongside and were hoisted aboard. The captain shouted orders to make fast the boats to davits, and then cried out, "Lewis, cut your anchor cable! Dunn, go ahead full speed!"[38] The race was on. Every crew member knew the story of Captain Fry and his men on the ill-fated filibuster, *Virginius*. Captured by Spaniards in the early seventies, they were stood up against a slaughterhouse wall in Santiago and riddled with rifle bullets.[39] A similar fate threatened Broward and his men should they fall into the hands of Weyler or his forces.

The *Three Friends*, traveling slightly northeast, ran parallel to the coast line, holding her course on the inside rim of the bay. The Spanish vessel headed east, just across the bow of the *Three Friends*, and sailed along the outer edge. The wind was blowing hard, and a rainlike mist fell. A. W. Barrs hid the binnacle light with his overcoat, leaving visible a spot about the size of a silver dollar by which to steer the boat.[40] In a moment the Spanish would be close enough to fire point blank on the *Three Friends*. Realizing this, Broward called out to his first mate: "Line all the men on the port side and have them ready to get in the boats. I shall run into him as we head, and I believe that both boats will be sunk in the collision."

"What then, Captain?" the mate asked.

Broward answered sharply, "We will have the advantage . . . of having our boats overboard and our men ready. He will have to lower his, and I believe we can get the start and beat them back to the Cubans we have just landed."[41]

The crew huddled near the boats, none daring to talk above the wind's screams. Suddenly remembering the fat pine-wood knots piled on deck, Broward ordered his crew to fill the furnace with them as quickly as possible. The wood burned like paper, and the engines became a huge glow in the night. Black clouds belched from the smokestack. Broward put his wheel hard astarboard, changed his course sharply, and headed west. The wind blew heavy smoke back into the bay, and the Spaniards, believing the *Three Friends* had doubled on her track, turned their own bow toward the bay. Broward veered northward, and the *Three Friends* headed out to sea. In another moment, she had disappeared in darkness and rain. By morning the crew had berthed her safely in Key West harbor.

Shortly after noon on Sunday, March 22, the *Three Friends* sailed across St. Johns Bar, through the swirling brown river-water, to Jacksonville.[42] White from bow to stern, and with cargo stowed in the hold below, decks washed and brass shining, and name letters back in place, she showed no evidence of having just returned from a voyage of adventure and peril. Captain Broward, wearing an immaculate white uniform, walked briskly down his gangplank and onto Wightman's wharf. Awaiting him in a black-painted surrey was Mrs. Broward, and together they drove home through the bright afternoon sunshine.

Detailed accounts of the voyage filled newspapers throughout the country. Angry and protesting, the Spanish inadvertently supplied much of the information. Broward, when questioned, jovially denied knowing about any filibustering voyage, and claimed he was busy in south Florida towing the steamer *Scotia* to port. He explained that armaments were aboard because "certain parties in the city, hearing we were going to Key West, got us to carry the arms and ammunitions there. When we got there the party refused to take them. I understand the reason is that the vessel for which they were intended had already sailed."[43] The newspapers repeated Captain Broward's explanations, and his crew related a similar story. But neither port authorities nor the Spanish consul were so naïve as to believe them.

Many people surmised that government action against the *Three Friends* and Broward was imminent. There were also rumors that Spanish spies, disguised as Cubans, had been aboard the vessel and had secured evidence against her,[44] and that a Philadelphia lawyer had arrived in Jacksonville to help the Federal government prosecute its case.[45] These rumors were not substantiated by fact. Newspapers, for the most part, discounted the stories, for they knew that "no penalties can be imposed . . . unless it can be proved that the *Three Friends* carried an armed expedition by having both men and arms on board. . . ."[46] Definite proof was not likely to be forthcoming. The *Daily Florida Citizen* suggested that "the trip was carefully planned and carefully executed and this means that everything has been done to prevent the law from holding them for wrong-doing in any way."[47] No action was taken, at the time, against the *Three Friends* or her owners.

In May, the arrival of arms and ammunition from Tampa started a rumor that Broward planned a second trip to Cuba. Hurried orders brought the cutter *Boutwell* from Savannah to the mouth of the St. Johns to "watch for any attempted filibustering expedition in general, and the steamer *Three Friends* in particular."[48] Shortly thereafter the people on Fort George Island and in Mayport became alarmed when they noticed near the St. Johns Bar a large steamer which at first they thought to be a Spanish man-of-war. Closer scrutiny, however, revealed it to be the *Laurada*, a filibuster from New London, Connecticut. She was waiting to accompany the *Three Friends* on the next trip to Cuba. Now sure of himself and his plans, Broward invited Captain Kilgore of the *Boutwell* to escort him as far as Key West, his purported destination.[49]

On the evening of May 21, Collector of Customs Bisbee received a telegram from Washington with instructions for the United States Marshal at Jacksonville to "require the master of the *Three Friends* . . . to give a bond that he will not engage in any enterprise in contravention of international law. The Department is of the opinion that the facts in the case do not warrant the seizure or libeling of the vessel. . . ."[50] Later that night Bisbee received another wire, this time from the Secretary of the Treasury, forbidding the *Three Friends* to clear the Jacksonville port or even to leave the St. Johns River until further notice. These orders were immediately transmitted to Captain Kilgore, who moved his vessel close to the *Three Friends* and trained his guns upon her.[51]

At daybreak the following morning, Broward ordered his vessel out into the channel and headed toward the Atlantic.

The *Boutwell,* anchored nearby with her fires banked, quickly got up steam and followed. The *Three Friends* sailed to "Woodlawn," the country home of Alexander Merrill, part owner of the Merrill-Stevens Engineering Company. Without any attempt at secrecy, the crew began loading arms and ammunition that had been stored at "Woodlawn" earlier that week. Merrill's steam launch, the *Lillian,* transferred guns from shore to Broward's boat, which was anchored in midstream.[52] Carrying her cargo, the *Three Friends,* with the revenue cutter close behind, sailed back to Jacksonville and anchored at her dock at the foot of Washington Street.

Broward, learning of the Washington orders, protested. He argued that he was making a peaceful trip to Key West to tow back a boat, and that he was not filibustering. Bisbee explained that his instructions were to restrain the vessel if "she were going on a military mission," or if "a military expedition were on board."[53] After agreeing to check the vessel he drove in Broward's carriage to the dock where the *Three Friends* was anchored. Examining the ship's hold, Bisbee found scores of crates neatly piled from floor to ceiling and plainly marked "ship stores." Without opening the cases the collector decided that "ships stores" would not make or constitute a "military expedition." He telegraphed these findings to Washington, and the *Three Friends* was free to embark on any peaceful voyage.

After their inspection tour, Broward and Bisbee returned to the collector's office, where they found J. M. Barrs and J. A. Huau. A few minutes later the Spanish consul, Señor de Mariteague, came in, hoping Bisbee would reveal the nature of Broward's cargo. Recognizing Broward, Barrs, and Huau, he flushed slightly but said nothing until the collector good-naturedly invited him over and introduced him to the group. After an exchange of pleasantries, Mariteague abruptly asked Broward about his cargo.

"Well," replied Broward, slouching into a more comfortable position in his chair and thoughtfully puffing on his black

Cuban cigar, "I've got one hundred twenty tons of coal and a whole boatload of arms and ammunition for Key West."

The Spaniard's eyes narrowed quizzically at this unexpected frankness, and he asked, "What for do you have so much coal, Captain?"

Barrs, breaking into the conversation, explained that coal was high in Key West and that Captain Broward would realize a great profit in selling it there.

"Humph!" retorted the consul, "I did not hear he sold coal when he go to Key West before."

Convinced that Broward's real cargo was a secret neither to Bisbee nor to Captain Kilgore, Mariteague shrugged his shoulders and remarked glumly, "Queer country. Everybody know where you go, but nobody can testify."

Broward enjoyed this colloquy, and when Mariteague was leaving, he cordially invited him to be his guest on the next voyage of the *Three Friends*.[54]

Early the following morning, additional guns and ammunition were loaded aboard the *Three Friends*. Many of these boxes and crates, plainly marked "J. A. Huau, Jacksonville, Florida," had arrived from Philadelphia several days before.[55] Everyone, including Bisbee, suspected that the boxes contained guns. Nevertheless, Broward insisted that his vessel was headed for Key West, where his cargo would be unloaded. When Bisbee telegraphed Washington again to inquire whether he should hold Broward's vessel, he was instructed that he could not detain the *Three Friends*.[56]

With this assurance, the *Three Friends* got underway, followed by the *Boutwell*, with a United States marshal aboard. Kilgore's instructions were to sail only as far as the three-mile limit. Broward reached the St. Johns Bar after midnight and anchored near the mouth of the river to await a change of tide. A half moon rode the clouds and cast sharp shadows across the water. Two hours later, when the *Kate Spencer* sailed in across the Bar, the only sign of life aboard the *Three Friends* was a single lantern which glowed from her poop.

The special train which brought Cuban patriots from Tampa to north Jacksonville had traveled a circuitous route through Baldwin, Callahan, and Yulee. At Panama Park, the Cubans had left the train and transferred to a small boat, on which they sailed up the narrow steep-banked river until they reached the waiting *Kate Spencer*. En route to the Bar, the *Spencer* disposed of her passengers either by transferring them to the *Laurada* or landing them on the deserted sand dunes south of Pablo Beach, to be picked up by Broward's boat. Forty additional Cubans, who had been hidden at "Woodlawn," were carried by the *Lillian* to the Atlantic, to be transferred to the *Three Friends*.[57]

Next morning Broward's vessel, followed by the cutter, crossed the Bar into the ocean. During the night Captain Kilgore lost sight of the *Three Friends* and turned back to Jacksonville. The *Three Friends* was off on a carefully planned venture, and it was not until the early morning of June 3 that she stole back into port. When news of Broward's arrival spread, scores of people hurried to the dock to see the celebrated little steamer. Crew members were peppered with questions about their trip, but the men guarded their answers, and refused to say where the steamer had been, admitting only that the "mission had been successful."[58]

Broward, in announcing that his vessel had never reached Key West, said that after she had been blocked by a storm, she had unloaded her cargo on one of the Keys and had proceeded to Biscayne Bay to pick up two barges belonging to Henry M. Flagler. He did not explain why the barges were not in tow, nor did he indicate what happened to them.[59] Great risks seem to have shaken Broward's sense of security but little.

The *Three Friends* had been in port only a week when a story published in a Northern newspaper, and reprinted in Jacksonville, stated that arms and ammunition had been shipped from the North and unloaded at a deserted point near Punta

Gorda. The news items revealed that the *Three Friends* was to reload and run the guns into Cuban waters and that the expedition would be commanded by Colonels Vidal, Nuñez, and Arteago.[60] Captain Broward denied that he was sailing on another expedition, and asserted that when his boat was ready to leave, he would "have no hesitancy about informing the Spanish consul."[61] Despite Broward's denial, Colonel Vidal, on Wednesday, June 17, took the *Three Friends* to "Woodlawn," where he loaded several small surfboats and a quantity of ammunition.

When Mariteague heard that the *Three Friends* was at Merrill's plantation to pick up a new war cargo, he immediately chartered a small fishing smack. Following the course of the river he came upon the *Three Friends,* boldly loading in broad daylight. He returned to Jacksonville and hurried before United States Commissioner Locke to swear an affidavit that Colonel Vidal was forming "an armed expedition against the peace of Spain."[62] He charged that Vidal was at that moment loading the *Three Friends* at "Woodlawn" and preparing to sail for Cuba.

The consul found Marshal McKay and Collector Bisbee at supper, and although it was after dark, he persuaded them to sail with him to "Woodlawn" to ascertain the facts. Arriving at the wharf, they found Mariteague's boat gone. The consul, in his rush and excitement, had neglected to leave a deposit for the launch, and it had been rented to someone else. The consul was infuriated, and as Bisbee later said, his exclamations were "more forcible than beautiful."

The three men hurried along the water front until they found Captain Beerbower of the *Ida B,* who agreed to carry them down the river. It was nearly three o'clock in the morning before they were finally under way. Then, about two miles from the city, around a sweeping bend of the St. Johns, they met the *Three Friends* chugging up the river toward Jacksonville, and not toward open sea as Señor Mariteague had suspected. The consul's plan to catch Broward had failed again.[63]

Spanish authorities in Washington secured warrants for the arrest of Colonel Vidal and Colonel Nuñez, based on their alleged activities against Spain. Colonel Arteago was not included. Newspapers and considerable Jacksonville opinion agreed immediately that both Vidal and Nuñez were beyond the jurisdiction of the United States and that nothing could be done. According to Judge James W. Locke, there was "no law to prevent a vessel from loading arms and taking them to Cuba. They could come in to the city and advertise and nothing could be done."[64] Newspapers, public opinion, and Judge Locke, however, were wrong in their opinion. Such activity was a violation of American neutrality, as defined by United States statutes. Cuban leaders, and the filibusters who assisted them, were seldom convicted by United States courts and imprisoned because substantial evidence, or witnesses who were willing to testify against them, could never be found.

Despite Broward's filibustering record, the guard was relaxed when he insisted that he was not planning a new voyage. Shortly thereafter, on June 18, the *Three Friends* was loaded with little fanfare and sailed for south Florida waters. Her hold was only partly filled with munitions; a full cargo was to be transferred from the steamer, *City of Key West,* at a barren point off the Florida Keys.[65] Three days later, the revenue cutter *Winona,* under orders of the deputy collector at Key West, left port to follow the *City of Key West,* which had sailed before dawn. The cutter scouted through coral reefs and sand bars all morning. About two o'clock that afternoon a lookout discovered the *Key West* anchored near Alligator Light and half hidden by projecting rocks. Recognizing the cutter, the filibustering vessel fled. The *Winona* chased the little steamer until night, and then, rather than risk being wrecked upon treacherous reefs, she anchored until morning.

At dawn the *Winona* was again under way, and after an all-day search, found the *Key West* putting into a small cove. She was stopped and boarded by Navy officers, who examined her ship's papers and found that she lacked a wrecking license, that her passenger list was obviously wrong, and that there were four hundred forty-nine cases of ammunition aboard. A prize crew from the *Winona* manned the steamer, which was turned back to Key West.[66]

About noon the next day, when the captured craft was sailing near Alligator Light, lookouts discovered a steamer lying near Knight's Key. As the *Key West* approached, a small boat was lowered from the anchored vessel, but quickly turned back when a warning was flashed by a regular crew member of the *Key West*. Unable to escape, the steamer was boarded by a *Winona* officer. A search of her ship's log showed her to be the *Three Friends*. Though Captain Broward hotly protested orders to proceed to Key West, there was little he could do but obey. Registered as a passenger aboard the *Three Friends* was Dr. Joaquin Castillo, secretary of the *junta* and long identified with Cuba's cause. A search of Broward's cargo revealed a few boxes of ammunition, which were not sufficient to call the voyage an "armed expedition." Next day, when Broward appeared before Key West government officials, his vessel was released from custody.[67]

Captain Broward left Key West immediately and set his course for a Florida Key where he took aboard forty-five patriots and a large cache of military stores. On the night of June 22 he landed at Juan Clara, on the south coast of Pinar del Rio, and delivered three hundred Mauser rifles, three hundred fifty thousand rounds of ammunition, two hundred seventy machetes, one thousand pounds of dynamite, and a quantity of electric batteries, wires, and fuses.[68]

The *Three Friends*, a few hours out of Key West, noticed a three-masted warship on the horizon. Believing it to be a Spanish vessel, the filibuster tried to escape, and raced across the water, hotly pursued by the *U. S. S. Raleigh*. Moving in close to shore, the *Three Friends* held a steady course while the *Raleigh* sailed farther out in the Gulf. Nearing American territorial waters, the *Raleigh* attempted to signal the *U. S. S. Maine*, anchored near Key West. The *Maine* did not notice the signals, however, and made no attempt to help. When the filibuster turned sharply left and entered the narrow reefs, the warship, knowing that it would be impossible to follow, gave up the chase.[69]

On July 10 the *Three Friends* arrived in Fernandina, and when Broward refused to reveal the ports which he had visited, the officials of the State Board of Health ordered his vessel quarantined until it could be steam sterilized. Ship captains who could prove they had sailed from ports declared free of disease by American health officials were exempt from such restrictions. It was obvious that Broward was in no position to offer any kind of proof.

Three days later, the *Three Friends* sailed across St. Johns Bar toward Jacksonville. Riotously welcomed up the river, she might have been a hero-ship returning from the wars rather than a filibuster breaking her country's laws. Flags were "flying proudly in the breeze. . . . Every craft that can whistle, from a naphtha up to a Clyde line, and every mill along the shore from Mayport to the city welcomed the boat." Above the bedlam, the whistle of the *Three Friends* was shrilly audible, "sounding like a Cunarder."[70]

The *Dauntless,* the *Kate Spencer,* and the *Martha Helen* escorted the now-famous vessel as she sailed between the river's green-walled shores. Almost a thousand people filled the wharf and the nearby streets. River breezes buckled the ladies' bonnets and whipped the flags to brilliant splashes of color. Captain Broward, bowing and waving, stepped briskly down his gangplank to be greeted by a committee of city officials, all of them Cuban sympathizers. Huau escorted him to Mrs. Broward's carriage, which had been decorated with red, white, and blue bunting. Preceded by a hastily assembled band, the Broward buggy, drawn by a pair of white horses, started toward Market Street. The procession moved along Forsyth Street to Bridge, then to Bay Street, and finally to Broward's home in East Jacksonville. Scores of people crowded the flag-filled sidewalks and streets to watch the impromptu parade pass and to cheer the captain. Enthusiastic spectators waved American and Cuban flags. Shouts of welcome greeted Broward as he rode triumphantly through the golden afternoon.[71]

During the following week Broward's family closed their home and traveled by train to Smyrna, Georgia, for the summer. Atlanta was only fifteen miles from Smyrna, and the captain spent several days there. When an *Atlanta Journal* reporter asked him if he planned any more filibustering voyages, Broward "closed his weather eye and glancing at the clouds," remarked, "Do you think it will rain?"[72]

⁓ 9 ⟲
"A Price on His Head"

THE UNITED STATES rushed toward war with Spain. Each day the Hearst and Pulitzer newspapers vied in reporting gruesome and bloody exploits of "Butcher" Weyler, Spain's military commander in Cuba. So real did front-page stories make the acrid smell from the burning cane fields and the nauseating stench of rotting human bodies, and so detailed were their pictures of starving children, mutilated women, ravaged homes, and gutted churches that many people in the United States argued that a holy crusade was needed. Captain Broward and the other filibusters became the renowned heroes of the American public, and their exploits were heralded by a press whose circulation leaped as its stories became more violent. Most Floridians, ignoring the fact that Federal laws were violated on every filibustering expedition, did not condemn men like Broward. Rather they looked on them almost as saviors of civilization. Whatever sympathy there might have been before 1895 for the Spanish government in Cuba was swept away by a wave of indignation against Weyler and his activities and was replaced by solicitude for the patriot cause.

Answering Grover Cleveland's neutrality legislation with defiance the Cuban *junta* laughed at the President's insistent determination to enforce American laws, and dismissed his proclamation of June, 1895, as a "scrap of paper." Public clamor for a declaration of war against Spain became increasingly louder and reverberated in Congress. Cleveland's efforts to stem the rising tide with another stern anti-filibuster order issued on July 27, 1896, were not successful.

Meanwhile, in a proclamation issued from his headquarters in Cuba, General Weyler bitterly protested the filibustering expeditions from the United States. Like the Spanish Minister in Washington, he charged that without American aid, Cuba's insurrection would be easily crushed. He announced that the Spanish government would pay twenty-five thousand dollars for the capture of any filibustering captain, dead or alive; or for any ships engaged in transporting men or arms to the island rebels. Captain Broward now had a price on his head.

During July, 1896, when the *Three Friends* was in dry dock having her hull sheathed with copper, Colonel Emilio Nuñez arrived in Jacksonville. His presence in the city started rumors that Broward planned a new filibustering trip. When questioned, Captain Broward offered vague explanations about his business activities and refused to divulge his actual plans. Engineer John Dunn explained that the *Three Friends* was sailing first to Key West and then would proceed to another key, where the crew hoped to raise and salvage a large Mexican tug which had been sunk several months earlier.[1] A story was told in Jacksonville that Broward's family objected strenuously to his previous filibustering voyages to Cuba and that he had promised that he would not command any more of them.[2] Whether this had anything to do with the projected plans for raising the tug, no one knew.

Early in August, Horatio Rubens, the *junta's* attorney general, arrived in Jacksonville and it seemed more certain than ever that some filibustering trip was planned. A newspaper story reported that arms and ammunition had been shipped into Florida from the North and were stored at an isolated spot about a hundred miles south of Jacksonville. The *Boutwell* was ordered into Jacksonville from patrol duty to watch the *Three Friends*, the *Laurada*, and the *Commodore*, all of which were suspect as filibusters. In the meantime, orders from Washington, dated August 10, instructed Collector of Customs Bisbee to be on the lookout for any filibustering activity in the Jacksonville area.[3]

By the middle of August the hull of the *Three Friends* was completed, her engines were tested, and her chief engineer announced that she was ready to sail "through hell and high water." Late on the evening of August 13, Broward supervised the loading of a cargo of coal that would "last a month." Work continued all night, and interested spectators who had foregone their sleep to watch the proceedings reported that "hundreds of square and long wooden boxes were loaded and stored in the coal bunkers."⁴ This report was later proved false.

The following afternoon Broward's crew put aboard four new surfboats which had been stored in a small shed on the grounds of the Florida Yacht Club. The captain had told a newspaper reporter that he needed the surfboats to help raise the Mexican tug, but later he announced that his steamer was going on a fishing trip to Snapper Banks and that the boats would be used by fishermen.

After the loading was completed, the *Three Friends* sailed to Mayport, where the *Boutwell* was waiting. Before Broward could cross St. Johns Bar, he was stopped and boarded by her officers. Irritated at this interruption, Captain Broward informed the officers of the *Boutwell* that he was sailing on a peaceful voyage and that his ship held nothing except her regular crew, a supply of coal, and the necessary cargo. Nevertheless, Captain Kilgore stubbornly insisted that the *Three Friends* move back up the river to Jacksonville to be searched. Broward lifted his head angrily as if to continue his protest, and then in a tense voice ordered his ship back into port. At the Jacksonville dock, Collector Bisbee supervised the search, which revealed a store of regular supplies, three medicine chests, an extra amount of coal, and the surfboats. Bisbee wired a report of his findings to the Secretary of the Treasury. Although the actions of the *Three Friends* had been somewhat suspicious, there was no evidence that she was preparing to set out on another filibustering voyage, and the Treasury Department ordered the vessel released from custody. However,

Captain Kilgore was instructed to follow the *Three Friends* whenever she sailed.

To avoid further suspicion, Captain Broward for a time went about his everyday business in Jacksonville. Late in August, he was reported in New York City buying nautical instruments.[5] Broward returned to Jacksonville, and on the morning of September 2, advised newspaper reporters that his vessel was sailing immediately to Key West. The Spanish consul, suspecting that the real destination was Cuba, persuaded Collector Bisbee to search the *Three Friends* once more. Bisbee's routine investigation revealed only one hundred and fifty bags of coal; no arms nor men, other than the regular crew, were aboard. The *Three Friends* could not be held and at midnight she left port. About three hours earlier, the *Martha Helen* had tied up at a nearby dock to load boxes of arms from a freight car, which had been moved in earlier in the day. The launch *R. L. Mabey* was also docked at the foot of Main Street, and throughout the night small groups of men dressed as fishermen boarded her. After eluding the revenue cutter, these two vessels cautiously moved out into the Atlantic and transferred their cargoes to the *Three Friends,* which was already at sea.

Broward remained in Jacksonville and Captain William Lewis, a seasoned tow boat skipper, was in command of the *Three Friends.* The expedition landed successfully at Pinar del Rio, within a few hundred yards of General Maceo's forces. The filibuster delivered seventy-five Cuban patriots, a small group of American and Russian soldiers of fortune, a thousand rifles, four hundred sixty thousand rounds of ammunition, one pneumatic dynamite gun, two thousand pounds of dynamite, a thousand machetes, and a large supply of medical stores and clothing.[6]

Returning to Key West on September 9, the *Three Friends* was quarantined for a week. Spanish authorities, furious when they learned of the landing, demanded that the United States officials take action at once to stop further filibustering expeditions. Receiving a new complaint from the Spanish embassy in Washington, the Secretary of the Treasury instructed Frank Clark, United States District Attorney in Jacksonville, to institute legal proceedings against Broward, Captain Lewis, J. A. Huau, and A. W. Barrs for an alleged violation of the neutrality laws in sending to Cuba a steamer loaded with arms. It was reported in Jacksonville that Spanish authorities were bringing witnesses from Cuba to testify against the *Three Friends*. Released from quarantine in Key West, the *Three Friends* proceeded to Fernandina, where she was placed under new restrictions. Washington ordered officers of the revenue cutter *Colfax* to detain the vessel "until an investigation is made as to whether she has not been recently on a filibustering expedition."[7]

During the next four days the United States Marshal and the port collector at Fernandina questioned Broward's crew and searched his vessel, hoping to secure enough evidence to prosecute him. When Frank Clark questioned a sailor about the large crew on the small boat, he was told that the men had been hired to measure up to the resonant "Rocked in the Cradle of the Deep" whistle of the *Three Friends*. Captain Broward's crew stood behind him to a man, but the extensive investigation revealed that many who had signed as crew members were not sailors, and, indeed, had never been to sea. Some members of the crew testified that the *Three Friends*, so far as they knew, had never been out of sight of land. Others agreed they could have been sleeping when the vessel was at sea, but they added that they "didn't sleep much." Libeled in the United States Court, Southern District of Florida, on September 22, Broward's vessel was charged with having loaded on September 2 a large amount of coal and stores, with taking aboard an additional cargo of arms and ammunition, and with transporting them to "some foreign port."[8]

From the start it was apparent that the government would try to make an object lesson of Captain Broward and his steamer. Action was necessary, for although public opinion,

many congressmen, and a majority of the country's newspapers
sympathized with the filibustering expeditions, both citizens
and the press had to admit that Federal neutrality laws had
been violated. The *New York Herald* condemned the port
officials of Jacksonville for allowing filibustering expeditions
to clear.[9] Meanwhile, Dr. Castillo, a suspected revolutionist,
was arrested in Key West on a perjury charge. When port officials asked him where he had sailed from, and the name of
the vessel in which he traveled, he testified that he had sailed
from Cape Sable in an open boat, and he emphatically denied
having been aboard the *Three Friends*. Castillo was released
on one thousand dollar bond and his case was set for hearing
before Judge James W. Locke on September 28.

At the hearing, the nineteen officers and crew members of
the *Three Friends* were subpoenaed as government witnesses
against Dr. Castillo. Captain Lewis was the first witness to
testify, but he volunteered little information. He refused to
identify the vessel he had commanded or to say whether Dr.
Castillo had been a passenger. John McDonald, another witness, acknowledged that he had been aboard, but insisted that
he "didn't know where the ship went, or how long she was
out." He was unable to identify Dr. Castillo, and he added
that he "didn't think any passengers were taken on board the
Three Friends while that vessel was at sea." The court learned
little from McDonald because, according to his testimony, "he
didn't know whether or not the *Three Friends* went near Key
West, but he might have been asleep. He didn't know who
employed him to go on board the *Three Friends*, he just went
aboard when he heard the steamer was going near Miami to
help raise a wreck. He didn't see any wreck, and didn't know
if any effort was made to raise a wreck. Didn't know of any
person coming aboard in a small boat near Miami, such might
have been the case, but he might have been asleep."[10] Other
witnesses gave similar answers to all of the questions. For example, when Frank Kirksey, a crew member from Jacksonville,
was asked if he had been to sea, he answered, "I am not in

the habit of going, as an occupation." The court, unable to produce enough evidence against Dr. Castillo, was compelled to dismiss the case.

Meanwhile, Broward's vessel, released on seven thousand dollar bond, was free to sail anywhere, so long as she obeyed the laws of the United States. Montcalm Broward repainted her white and announced that he was sailing for Key Largo to search for wrecks among the reefs. He invited a government agent to go along wherever and whenever the *Three Friends* sailed.[11] This invitation was not accepted, and late in October the *Three Friends*, without a government watcher, went on a wrecking trip to Wilmington, Delaware. A few days later on November 8, the *Three Friends* attempted another filibustering voyage, but quick action on the part of the Spanish stopped the venture.[12]

In Washington, Spanish officials were rapidly building a case against the *Three Friends*. Spanish spies, disguised as Cuban patriots, were supposed to have traveled on the filibustering voyage of the *Three Friends* in May, 1896. Their hidden cameras allegedly photographed illegal cargo being unloaded in Cuban waters. When the Spanish Minister presented this new evidence to Treasury Secretary Carlisle, the latter, on November 12, ordered a marshal in Jacksonville to seize Broward's vessel again. New libel papers, charging the steamer with a violation of Section 5283, *United States Revised Statutes*, declared: ". . . The *Three Friends* was on the 23rd day of May, A.D. 1896, furnished, fitted out and armed, with intent that she should be employed in the service of certain people, to wit, certain people then engaged in armed resistance to the government of the King of Spain, in the island of Cuba, to cruise and commit hostilities against the subjects, citizens and property of the King of Spain in the island of Cuba, with whom the United States are and were at peace. . . ."[13] Two days after the seizure of the *Three Friends*, Napoleon and Montcalm Broward, as principal owners of the vessel, filed their claims with the clerk of the United States

Court in Jacksonville, and asked that they be allowed to defend their suits.[14] Although Judge Locke was in Key West at this time, the libel papers were delivered to him there. The Browards and Barrs were making every effort to secure their boat's release on bond, but the future was not promising. Jacksonville newspapers predicted that Judge Locke would set a bond for at least sixty thousand dollars, or twice the vessel's value.[15]

Immediately after the second seizing of the *Three Friends*, Montcalm Broward chartered the *Martha Helen*, to use in towing vessels to and from St. Johns Bar. After a week of this work the steamer became disabled, and there was no other boat available which could be used for such river work. Earlier, Montcalm had towed several schooners up the St. Johns to Jacksonville, but now that they were loaded and ready to leave he had no boat to take them back to St. Johns Bar. Learning of these circumstances, the United States Marshal allowed the *Three Friends* to resume towing activities until the *Martha Helen* was back in operation.[16]

Judge Locke, in the meantime, returned to Jacksonville, and on December 1, A. W. Cockrell and John M. Barrs, the attorneys representing the owners of the *Three Friends*, applied for the release of the steamer. District Attorney Clark contested the application, contending that a court could not accept bond in a case where the penalty could be forfeiture of the vessel.[17] Judge Locke ruled otherwise, and the following morning he announced that "the case does not present such unusual features as to call for an exceptional ruling upon the question of admitting to bail, and it is ordered that upon an appraisement being had, said claimants be permitted bond . . . for the release of vessels under attachment."[18]

Broward's appraisers fixed bond at four thousand dollars, but when Clark protested their low valuation, the court raised it to ten thousand dollars. This amount was secured, with the Fidelity and Casualty Deposit Company of Baltimore acting as surety, and after the bond was paid the court ordered the release of the *Three Friends.*

The government's position was directed by international law and by its own neutrality legislation. A note, dated July 15, 1896, from Secretary of State Olney to the Spanish government definitely stated that "citizens of the United States have a right to sell arms and munitions of war to all comers— neither the sale nor the transportation of such merchandise, except in connection with and in furtherance of a military expedition prosecuted from our shores, are a breach of international duty. . . ."[19] On December 10, Attorney General Harmon issued a similar statement, declaring that "the mere sale or shipment of arms and munitions of war by persons in the United States to persons in Cuba is not a violation of international law, however strong a suspicion there may be that they are to be used in an insurrection against the Spanish Government. Nor does the sale or the shipment of such articles become a violation of international law merely because they are not destined to a port recognized by Spain as being open to commerce or because they are to be landed by stealth."[20]

In the light of such declarations, which were based on sound legal interpretation, Broward was not guilty of violating international law. Nothing in his filibustering activities contravened accepted principles of the law of nations. However, the violation of the United States neutrality laws presented another side to the question. Broward was charged with violating Section 5283 of the *Revised Statutes,* which stated that "every person who, within the limits of the United States, fits out and arms or attempts to fit out and arm . . . with intent that such vessel shall be employed in the service of any foreign prince or State, or of any colony, district, or people, to cruise or commit hostilities against the subjects, citizens, or property of any foreign prince or State, or any colony, district, or people, with whom the United States are at peace . . . shall be deemed guilty of a high misdemeanor, and shall be fined not more than ten thousand dollars, and imprisoned not more than three years. And every such vessel . . . shall be forfeited. . . ."[21]

This Federal statute, supplemented by President Cleveland's two proclamations, constituted the basis for the government's neutrality policy toward the Cuban insurrection. Although the Browards and the Barrs must have been aware of these neutrality laws and of Cleveland's proclamations, they remained strangely defiant. Their filibustering activities were apparently not curtailed by threats of heavy fines and possible prison sentences, and they continued to defy the law. Rumors in Jacksonville, early in December, told of plans for a new filibustering expedition, but from all indications it appeared that the *Commodore* and not the *Three Friends* would sail. The *Boutwell* relaxed her guard over Broward's boat and watched the new suspect. The plan that Broward had carefully formulated began to unfold.[22]

Late on the afternoon of December 13, at the dock where the *Commodore* was tied, a watchman placed near the ship's gangplank a sign reading "POSITIVELY NO ADMITTANCE." A few minutes later, the captain came out of his pilothouse and ordered a passageway on the dock cleared of the crossties lying there, presumably to facilitate the loading of arms and munitions. Earlier, two freight cars loaded with war supplies had been moved near the *Commodore* and had remained there until evening. Spanish spies, watching the *Commodore*, became convinced that she would sail that night. The arrival of a group of seventy-two Cubans from Tampa confirmed these suspicions. These Cubans, when questioned, explained that they were cigar workers, en route to Thomasville, Georgia, to work in a cigar factory. In Jacksonville, they were met by representatives of the *junta*.

After dark the "cigar workers" gathered before the El Modelo building and began dispersing in groups of two or three. Later they reassembled in the Florida Central and Peninsular Railroad yards, where a Pullman car was waiting to take them to Fernandina. Meanwhile the *Three Friends* had cleared port quietly and had sailed for Fernandina that morning. There she took aboard the Cubans and loaded a cargo of twenty-five hundred Winchester and Mauser rifles, fifty thousand rounds of cartridges, five thousand pounds of dynamite, five thousand machetes, and a large quantity of medicine, stores, and provisions.[23] Then she put out to sea.

The startling newspaper reports that the *Three Friends* was en route to Cuba stirred the United States Government into action. Washington immediately telegraphed orders to all revenue cutters in Southern waters to intercept the steamer. The *Newark, Raleigh, McLane, Winona,* and *Forward* began combing the South Atlantic and the Caribbean area for the filibuster.

The weather was cold and rainy throughout her voyage along the Florida coast, and as the *Three Friends* approached Cuba, it became worse. Thick gray fog blanketed the sea. The shore was a dim shadow in the distance, and it became impossible to obtain accurate bearings. For over thirty hours the vessel cautiously felt her way through the fog. Deciding against an immediate landing near Bahia Honda, Captain Johnny O'Brien, who was in command, changed his course and headed toward the western shore of the island. The boat rounded Cape San Antonio and Cape Corrientes, and approached a point near the mouth of the San Juan River. The fog had thinned somewhat, but the hard rain made it difficult to see land. Units of the Spanish blockading fleet might be lurking anywhere, hidden by darkness and fog. Nevertheless, Captain O'Brien decided that he would be forced to unload his cargo because it was risky to keep it aboard. The engines of the *Three Friends* were quieted and she was run in close to shore.

Night settled over the sea. A steady splash of rain and the wailing of the winds through the palm fronds were the only sounds Captain O'Brien could detect. The *Three Friends* moved parallel to the coastline, threading her way carefully across jagged coral reefs to the river's mouth. Just then a small Spanish coast-patrol boat hove into sight over the port bow and approached the steamer. Cloaked by the fog, the Spaniards moved within six hundred yards of the filibuster and suddenly began firing. The first shot fell short of the *Three Friends*, but a second landed so close that giant waves crashed against her deck. Sharp orders turned the filibuster out toward open sea. A twelve-pound rapid-firing Hotchkiss gun, mounted on the bow of the *Three Friends*, was fired as the distance between the vessels shortened. The first shot fizzled because of a poor cap, but the second landed nearer its target. The next shell hit the Spanish boat with a loud explosion. It was impossible to determine the damage.[24]

It was raining harder and a brisk wind whipped sheets of salt spray across the deck. The Spaniards began sending up rockets, to signal other ships for aid. Vivid blue-white streaks lighted the sky and the surrounding sea. When a large gunboat emerged from the fog, veering toward the *Three Friends*, Captain O'Brien decided to try to outrun his pursuers. Quickly rounding the two capes he set a course for the Keys, a few miles away.

The Spanish patrol boat limped along, and the gunboat found it difficult to follow the zigzag trail set by the nimble filibustering steamer which was running for its life. Aboard the *Three Friends* was a barrel of bacon rinds, which the crew quickly hoisted to the stern and set afire. In a moment, a great black cloud of smoke bloomed out over the water, hiding the filibusters. Rain, fog, darkness, and bacon smoke favored the little American boat, and before an hour had passed she slipped away to safety among the reefs of the Keys.[25] This adventure caused a sensation in newspapers throughout the United States and among government officials in Washington. Spain, more vehement than ever, denounced filibustering. A point was made of the firing between the *Three Friends* and the Spanish vessels, and this exchange of shots has sometimes been called "Cuba's first naval battle."[26]

With a large number of United States cutters patrolling the waters, it was impossible to land either cargo or "passengers" in Cuba, and hazardous to keep either on board. Captain O'Brien decided, therefore, to unload his cargo without delay on No-Name Key.[27] There Cubans and munitions remained on a deserted key, forty miles east of Key West, until they were taken off by the *Dauntless* a few days later. When the customs officers in Key West questioned Captain O'Brien and the crew of the *Three Friends* about their voyage, they were unable to secure any reliable information. Captain O'Brien insisted that his vessel was returning from a wrecking trip to the Keys and not from a filibustering voyage. John M. Barrs told a similar story in Jacksonville.

Three days after Christmas, a new hearing of the libel case against the *Three Friends* was opened in the United States Court, with Judge James W. Locke presiding. A. W. Cockrell and J. M. Barrs were Broward's lawyers, and Frank Clark and Cromwell Gibbons argued the government's case. Interest in the case was widespread because it would test the government's power to prevent aid being sent to persons or groups not recognized as belligerents. Section 5283 used the words "colony, district or people," a phrase of primary concern in this dispute. Were Cuba's insurgents a "colony, district or people," even though recognition was not yet accorded? The libel charged that the *Three Friends* had been fitted out to be used by the Cubans in their rebellion against Spain, a nation with which the United States was at peace. Broward's attorneys argued that the *Three Friends* had not been armed, fitted out, or furnished for the service "of any body politic recognized or known to the United States as a body politic."[28] Government attorneys countered this argument by declaring, "There is nothing in section 5283, *Revised Statutes,* which requires that the vessel subject to condemnation should be employed in the service of any body politic recognized to the United States as a body politic."[29]

A decision favoring Broward was announced by Judge Locke on January 18, 1897. This opinion, based on the nonbelligerent status of the Cuban insurgents, stated that if they had not

134 Napoleon Bonaparte Broward

been granted recognition, then Broward was not in "the service of a foreign prince or state, or of any colony, district or people recognized. . . ."³⁰

A new libel was filed, charging J. M. Barrs, J. A. Huau, Henry P. Fritot, Captain John O'Brien, Captain W. T. Lewis, and John Dunn with having "fitted out and expedited a ship to Cuba, in violation of Federal neutrality laws." The libel charged that a gun was mounted on the bow of the *Three Friends* and that there were intentions of engaging in hostilities with Spain.³¹ Neither Napoleon nor Montcalm Broward was named in this libel, possibly because they were not aboard their ship at the time of the alleged violations.

Immediately after the filing of the libel, Attorney General Harmon instructed Frank Clark in Jacksonville to bring piracy charges against the *Three Friends.* Lurid stories in the nation's press served as a basis for this indictment, which was directed against the steamer and not against her officers or owners. The *Three Friends* was seized again on February 6, 1897. The government charged that on December 14 a steamer was loaded by John O'Brien, W. T. Lewis, John Dunn, Henry P. Fritot, Augusta Arnoa, Michael Walsh, and Ralph Paine "with supplies, rifles, cartridges, machetes, dynamite, and other munitions of war, including one large, twelve-pound Hotchkiss gun or cannon and a large quantity of shot, shell and powder . . . with intent that said vessel should be furnished, fitted out and armed for the purpose of being employed in the commission of piratical aggression, search, restraint, and depressions upon the high seas, on the subject, citizens and property of the King of Spain in the island of Cuba. . . ."³²

Two days later the *Three Friends,* again released on bond, began making regular runs to and from St. Johns Bar. Schooners, loaded with supplies from New York, Philadelphia, and Baltimore, and consigned to Jacksonville merchants, were guided up the St. Johns to river-front wharfs by small steamers like the *Three Friends.* Then with new cargoes of citrus, lumber, or phosphate, the large vessels were returned to the Bar.

A United States marshal traveled aboard the *Three Friends* wherever she voyaged.

Government officials in Washington, prodded by the Spanish Minister, and not content with Judge Locke's decision, petitioned the Supreme Court for a writ of *certiorari* to review the case. The case was docketed for February 15. Broward, accompanied by his attorney, A. W. Cockrell, went to Washington to present his defense. William Hallett Phillips was also retained as a defense attorney. E. B. Whitney, United States Assistant Attorney General, based the government's demand for forfeiture upon President Cleveland's proclamations. He argued: "When a vessel, belonging to citizens of the United States, commits hostilities upon the high seas against a friendly power, her act is *prima facie* piratical. She is forfeit and her owners, officers and crew are liable to be hanged."[33] Broward's attorneys reviewed the points which had been thrashed over in the original hearing. How could the vessel be employed by a "colony, district or people" if there were no American recognition of Cuban belligerency? Without such recognition, Cockrell and Phillips contended, the insurgents were not a "colony, district or people," and there was no violation within the libel's meaning. They did not deny the vessel had been fitted out or that it had sailed; they did deny the alleged violation of Section 5283 by the *Three Friends*. The United States Supreme Court, in delivering its opinion on March 1, decided against the steamer, and reversed Judge Locke's decision. The court ruled that "belligerency is recognized when a political struggle has attained a certain magnitude and affects the interest of the recognizing power; and in the instance of maritime operations, recognition may be compelled, or the vessels of the insurgents, if molesting their parties, may be pursued as pirates."[34] A majority of the justices felt that there was "no justification for importing into section 5283 words which it does not contain and which would make its operation depend upon the recognition of belligerency; and while the libel might have been drawn with somewhat greater precision, we are of the opinion that it should not have been dismissed."[35]

Justice Harlan's dissenting opinion upheld Judge Locke's decision as a correct interpretation of the statute, and described Cuba's insurgent government as existing only "on paper, with no power of administration." Harlan argued that "the words 'of any colony, district or people' should be interpreted as applying only to a colony, district or people that have 'subjects, citizens or property.' "[36]

An order issued by the United States Supreme Court was received on March 17 in Jacksonville by Cromwell Gibbons, United States Assistant District Attorney, and was delivered to Judge Locke. Captain Broward, who had asked Locke to call him immediately upon receipt of news from Washington, was reading in his living room when the judge's shiny black buggy stopped before his door. Locke's serious expression foretold his news: Bond for the *Three Friends* would have to be cancelled, and the steamer seized and placed in the custody of United States authorities. The situation facing Napoleon Broward and his business associates was critical. It seemed for a time that they could not escape punishment for violating American neutrality laws.

But 1897 was a propitious year for Captain Broward and the other filibusters. William McKinley was now in the White House and was strongly influenced by a group of bellicose young Republicans, led by Theodore Roosevelt, Assistant Secretary of the Navy, who vociferously demanded war with Spain. The American people, moreover, were ripe for a war, and their mood was not to be denied. Many felt that only by a baptism of blood could the country prove its greatness to itself and to the rest of the world. The tempo toward war increased measurably after publication of Minister de Lome's famous letter in which he described McKinley as a "spineless politician." Although Theodore Roosevelt once asserted that President McKinley had "no more backbone than a chocolate éclair," Americans were not going to tolerate a foreigner's criticism of their Chief Executive. Filibustering would hardly be condemned at such a time nor men like Captain Broward prosecuted. In the eyes of the public they were not criminals but shining American heroes.

Judge Locke, aware of this sentiment, ignored the Supreme Court ruling. After talking with the Browards, the Barrs, and members of the Cuban *junta,* he decided to postpone taking any immediate action against the *Three Friends.* If the war with Spain materialized, there would be no necessity for enforcing the court's decision; if conflict were averted, action could be taken at a later date.

The *Three Friends* continued to ply to and from St. Johns Bar, and to travel up and down the coast looking for wrecks. A United States marshal was placed aboard the steamer, and port authorities decided that this was sufficient precaution. As freight and passenger business thrived on the St. Johns, Broward's investment in his vessel was becoming increasingly valuable.

The case of the *Three Friends* was not finally disposed of until after the outbreak of hostilities against Spain. War finally came in the spring of 1898, after hectic weeks in which the battle cry "Remember the Maine!" rent the air. On May 10, a few days after Admiral Dewey's leisurely capture of Manila, the piracy charge against Broward's boat was dismissed in the Circuit Court of Appeals, Fifth Circuit, on the ground that there was not sufficient evidence to determine whether the *Three Friends* was equipped or armed within the limits of the United States.[37] The Supreme Court ruling was never enforced.

◈ 10 ◈

Fireworks in Florida

THE SUMMER OF 1896 marked an important turning point in Broward's political career. The Antis
and the Straightouts in Jacksonville were cementing
their differences, and an "era of good feeling," born of a
common concern over current economic problems, seemed to
be setting in. This change was especially noticeable in the
Democratic primaries in Jacksonville on June 3, 1896, when
the Antis scored a victory. In the local convention which followed there were no contesting delegates even though some
Straightout candidates had been defeated by only a few votes.
Broward, a delegate to the convention from Ward Two, was
appointed to the important committee on resolutions.

Broward and the other leading Democratic liberals of
Florida were strongly pro-silver by 1896. During the preceding years they had been bitterly anti-railroad and anti-
corporation. This opposition had not abated; Broward, Pope,
Fletcher, Stockton, Barrs, and their supporters continued to
denounce the abuses and the political practices of the "interests." Silver had become an additional and a burning issue.
Many men who earlier had separated on the railroad-corporation question now united in a "white-metal" crusade which
swept through the South and West like a prairie fire. The
issues in the campaign of 1896 aroused more interest than
those of any since the triumph of Abraham Lincoln and the
Republican party in the elections of November, 1860.[1] A
correspondent of the *London Daily Mail*, who arrived in
America when the national campaign was beginning, wrote
rhetorically: "Night and day, in every newspaper, in every

[138]

cafe, in every streetcar, it is the dollar, and the dollar alone, whose fate is discussed."[2]

When the state convention met in Ocala on June 16, 1896, a majority of the delegates were silver men. In speeches and in statements to the press, they expressed the hope that the Democratic party in Florida would unify to support the stand of the national party on currency. Broward attended silver caucuses each night and helped plan party strategy. General Robert Bullock, chairman of the caucuses, openly reported that only silver adherents would be nominated for the governorship and for the senatorial seats then held by Senators Wilkinson Call and Samuel Pasco.[3] The convention adopted by a large majority a strong resolution which indicted "the single gold standard, brought about by the crime of 1873," and asked that silver "be made a lawful and legal tender of payment of all debts...."[4]

For weeks prior to the state convention, former Governor William Bloxham was loudly proclaimed by the conservatives as a likely candidate for the gubernatorial nomination. Assured of railroad and corporation support, Bloxham had not yet declared himself on the silver question. Broward suspected that Bloxham was planning a straddle, hoping to secure votes from both sound-money and free-silver advocates. This equivocation cost Bloxham the support of Broward and other "silverites" who desired a candidate more directly in accord with their views.

As he stood on the Ocala House porch one evening during the convention, Frank W. Pope, the renowned Florida liberal, delivered an impromptu speech in which he condemned Bloxham's candidacy. Pope looked at the large crowd which overflowed the widespread porch and filled the sidewalk and street. Then he asked defiantly: "Are you silver men on principle [or] as a mere matter of expediency? Will you stultify yourselves to vote for a gold bug for governor? Do you know what it means?" Stubborn determination underscored Pope's words as he continued: "They tell you that the financial views of the governor make no difference, but he appoints the *ad interim* United States Senator; he can use his influence, his dispositions of patronage to make his choice of United States Senator, and in many other ways can show his hand as a gold advocate."[5]

Although the silverites claimed a majority of the convention delegates, the two-thirds rule for nominations was adopted. They were thus compelled to seek support outside their own ranks in their attempt to nominate a silver man for the governorship. The silver forces were strong, but Bloxham's support was stronger, and the silverites failed in their efforts to present a more acceptable nominee.

B. H. Palmer, a staunch silverite, tried unsuccessfully to unleash a dark horse. He bitterly charged that the Alachua County delegates were bargaining with the conservatives and that they had agreed to support Bloxham if W. N. Sheats of Alachua was nominated for state superintendent of public instruction.[6] On the night of the nomination for governor, Robert W. Davis rose, looked about at his fellow delegates, and almost casually nominated Bloxham. No other candidate was presented, and Bloxham was named by acclamation.

When the Democrats met in Chicago in July, silver advocates won control of the National Convention. By a vote of 628 to 301, they adopted the "sixteen to one" plank in the platform, and found a suitable presidential candidate in William Jennings Bryan of Nebraska, a young man only thirty-six years of age, who was already well known because of his persuasive oratory. Broward was early attracted to him by his eloquent speeches. He was stirred by Bryan's powerful stand on tariff, and he endorsed his acceptance of Populist doctrines as a cure for the depression.

During the months preceding the Democratic convention, Bryan spoke often on free silver to Western audiences, rehearsing many times the ringing phrases that were to bring him fame at Chicago. Political adherents like Broward could easily perceive that it was the emotional rather than the economic aspect of the irrepressible conflict impending in 1896 which William Jennings Bryan represented, and to which he gave voice. Well aware of the political value of an appeal to the masses, Broward could easily understand why Bryan appeared to the humble and inarticulate as almost a Messiah. He did not wonder at these country people, riding in their creaky farm wagons or walking for dozens of miles to hear Bryan's political gospel of "equal rights to all; special privileges to none."

Florida liberals were prepared for Bryan's nomination by reading in their newspapers the "magic words" of his "cross of gold" speech. Broward anxiously followed each ballot at the convention hall and was elated when on the fiftieth ballot, Bryan secured the nomination. In July, 1896, Broward helped to organize a large Bryan-Sewall Democratic Club in Jacksonville, with Frank W. Pope as its president. Florida's Democrats, both liberals and conservatives, enthusiastically joined the silver crusade. At a meeting held on July 23 in the Park Opera House, Broward discussed the issues and predicted that victory in November would insure "honesty, economy, courage and fidelity" for the country. Robert W. Davis, another speaker, extolled Bryan's virtues by likening him to Old Testament patriarchs and calling him the "Moses of the Masses."[7]

Meanwhile, the "era of good feeling" in Jacksonville was nearing an end. During the last week of July, the executive committee of Duval County announced that primaries would be held on July 30 to choose delegates to a convention which would nominate a slate for the county offices. After the city primaries in June, in which the Antis won by a few votes, the Straightouts began clamoring that nominations for the county offices should be made in a direct primary. Many citizens supported this suggestion, and several likely candidates for nomination openly approved the idea. The executive committee, strongly Anti, called a special meeting on July 29 to consider this proposal, but after listening to arguments from both sides, it voted against the primary and announced that the regular convention would be held. The *Florida Times-Union,* expressing Straightout sympathy, denounced this decision in an editorial entitled "Democracy in Danger."[8]

Another major grievance voiced by the Straightouts was the fact that the convention was being called upon such short notice. In addition, the executive committee, according to the Straightouts, had postponed selection of inspectors until three days before the scheduled primary, thus "keeping them in the dark" as long as possible. Ward representation, the Straightouts felt, was unfair, for in two of the largest city wards there were no Straightout inspectors representing their faction. Straightouts, however, were represented in some of the smaller wards.

After the executive committee scheduled the snap-primary, the officers of the Bryan-Sewall Democratic Club, all of whom were Straightouts, called a mass meeting to air their grievances. Although Broward was not an officer of the club, his position in local and state politics caused him to play an important part in its proceedings. In leading the discussion, at this meeting, he charged the Antis with trying to establish oligarchic rule in Duval County, and admonished his listeners to follow the dictates of their consciences which, he hoped, were all "straightout consciences."[9]

The club decided that if the Antis persisted in their stand, Straightouts would take no part in the primary elections.[10] The "era of good feeling" was thus abruptly ended. The factional fight had once more become bitter; city and county were again politically divided; and almost immediately there were repercussions on the state level.

The Antis' primary day, July 30, was orderly and quiet. The convention, two days later, assembled at the Park Opera House, where the business of naming a political slate was completed in short order. J. E. T. Bowden and W. S. Pickett were candidates for the state legislature; Fleming Bowden became a candidate for county sheriff.[11]

On August 12, the Straightouts met in their respective wards and elected delegates to a convention, which was to meet three days later.[12] The convention assembled in Metropolitan Hall at 11:30 A.M. on the scheduled date. Broward, busy with activities concerning the *Three Friends*, was not present. One delegate proposed that the Straightouts fuse with Republicans and Populists in Duval County to assure victory at the polls. After heated argument, the convention overwhelmingly voted this motion down. Nominations for county offices were next on the agenda. When the convention chairman announced that nominations for the office of sheriff were in order, the convention suddenly became a bedlam. Men throughout the hall began shouting Napoleon Broward's name. Yells, whistles, stamping of feet, and rapping of canes upon chairs seemed to shake Metropolitan Hall from floor to rafters. Another ovation rose when Broward's name was placed in nomination. At that point, H. W. Clark, a county representative, rushed into the hall waving a piece of paper. It was a message from Broward announcing that under no consideration would he accept the nomination for sheriff. The delegates were momentarily stunned. Then a few began shouting: "Broward! Broward! We want Napoleon B. Broward!" Immediately the hall was in another uproar. Others joined the chant while convention leaders held a hurried caucus in one corner of the large room. Broward enthusiasts paraded up and down the aisles, swinging banners and signs upon which his name had been hastily and crudely scrawled.

Tom Boyd, on the speakers' platform, quieted the delegates long enough to protest Broward's decision. "I tell you gentlemen of the convention," he shouted, "Mr. Broward cannot refuse to bow to the will of this convention when it calls upon him to be its standard bearer." Telfair Stockton then moved that Broward be nominated by acclamation, but since no one was sure he would accept, a delegate hurriedly nominated John Price. When W. McQueen's name was also put before the delegates, Stockton withdrew his motion.

A few minutes later, W. N. Conoley received a second note

from Broward, reaffirming his decision not to accept the nomination. Conoley, his face flushed with excitement, announced: "Gentlemen of the convention, we have received a message from Napoleon B. Broward in which he says that he cannot accept the nomination for sheriff of Duval County. I move that we send back a message to Mr. Broward saying that when he needed friends the straightouts and democrats stood by him; they are now sore oppressed and want him as a leader and appeal to his loyalty and fidelity to accept the nomination of sheriff."

The delegates roared their approval, and both Price and McQueen offered to withdraw should Broward accept. Stockton's motion was reintroduced and without waiting for Broward's approval or disapproval the convention nominated him by acclamation. The cries and cheers from the crowd drowned out the chairman's voice and the insistent banging of his gavel. A delegation was chosen to go to Broward's home in East Jacksonville and escort him to Metropolitan Hall. While waiting for their hero to appear, the delegates quieted somewhat and nominations continued.

As candidates for the state legislature were being presented, the delegates heard a great clamor outside. A band played discordantly, and voices shouted, "Broward! Broward!" The noise grew louder and reached a crescendo when Broward walked up the stairs leading into Metropolitan Hall. A large crowd escorted him toward the rostrum. Delegates yelled hysterically, stamped their feet, and threw their hats into the air as Broward proceeded slowly down the main aisle. Scores of hands were thrust out to grasp him. He was clapped on the back and pummelled. His hat was knocked awry, and his coat was nearly ripped off. A few enthusiasts began a snake dance on one side of the room, and others milled around waving signs and banners. Never before had there been such a demonstration at a Duval County convention.

Telfair Stockton introduced Broward as "the standard bearer of the straightout democratic party." Shaken by this great manifestation of popularity, Broward straightened his tie and coat, tugged at his black mustache, and grinned broadly at the delegates. He made a short speech in which he thanked the convention for his nomination and explained that his many business activities had made him reluctant to take on added duties. His voice trembled as he spoke: "There is not one of you that, in the matter of appreciation, excels me. I will stand by you in politics and in every other way. If it is possible for me to lead you to victory, I will do so. If I lead you to defeat, don't jump on me too hard."[13]

Thus Broward made a spectacular return to active politics. Even though he had not held a high public office since his removal as sheriff, he had remained a top strategist in Duval Straightout circles, and was prominently identified with the growing liberal faction in state politics. The enthusiasm at the convention left little doubt in Broward's mind of his popularity and power among county Straightouts. He was their accepted leader, and his position in state politics was, consequently, advanced immeasurably.

Meanwhile the state campaign was under way. At a political rally in Jacksonville on August 4, Bloxham announced that he was standing squarely behind the Chicago platform and strongly supporting Bryan and Sewall. Throughout most of his campaign, he continued his equivocal tactics by generally denouncing the Republican party instead of clarifying his own position on questions and policies affecting Florida. In his Jacksonville talk, the former governor revived memories of Republican extravagance and misrule during the Reconstruction era and promised "an economical but progressive administration."[14]

While Bloxham flogged the dead horse of old Reconstruction issues, he evaded the live one of currency. When questioned about his stand on silver, he said: "The great democratic host of Americans, through their representatives recently in convention assembled at Chicago, proclaimed themselves in favor of the free coinage of both gold and silver and, to lead the hosts, called upon Nebraska's young statesman, William Jennings Bryan, and placed him at the head of the ticket. I give my hearty support to the leader selected."[15]

An old bugaboo, the Disston land sale of 1881, was resurrected to become a major campaign issue. Edward R. Gunby, Republican candidate for the governorship, and A. W. Weeks, Populist candidate, bluntly charged in their political speeches that the Disston land sale had been a grave error and a detriment to Florida.

Bloxham answered these charges on August 23 at Chipley, Florida. He defended the sale, declaring that it was an emergency measure, necessary at that time to free the hands of the Trustees of the Internal Improvement Fund. According to Bloxham's figures, sixteen million additional acres of land and twenty million dollars of railroad property became available for taxing purposes because of the sale which, he contended, had "enabled the Democratic party of the state to reduce taxes to its [sic] present point."[16] Whether the Disston sale was responsible for all those good things was open to question as far as Broward was concerned.

Bloxham, Davis, Sheats, Collins, and other leading Democrats made an extended trip through Florida, before the general election. Speaking in each hamlet and town, they tried to rally lukewarm Democrats to their ranks. Bloxham persistently denounced Republicans and Populists, and cleverly skirted the real issues that faced Florida Democracy. When specifically asked at Ocala to declare himself upon the question of a railroad commission, all that he would promise was "no veto of a railroad commission."[17] He was obviously trying to keep a foot in each opposing Democratic camp and to secure support wherever it could be found.

The political cauldron boiled furiously in Jacksonville, and interest heightened as election day approached. On October 2, Pleasant A. Holt, executive committee chairman of the Straightouts, secured an injunction against the members of the Board of County Commissioners—Charles Marvin, Walter F. Coachman, J. D. Kelly, E. A. DeCottes, and W. S. Pickett.[18]

Holt's purpose was to assure a public counting and canvassing of the vote.

At its September meeting the board authorized the printing of paper circulars entitled "Notice to Voters," which contained instructions on how to use an Australian ballot. The last paragraph of the "Notice" read: "Only officers of the election are allowed within 15 feet of the polling place during the conduct of the election and the canvass of the returns." This ruling accorded with the Antis' interpretation of Section 39 of the State Election Law. Meanwhile, Judge Rhydon M. Call of the Circuit Court issued an injunction interpreting Section 39 to be applicable during voting hours, but not while ballots were being counted. He emphasized that Section 60 clearly meant "that the public shall be present and see the canvass made. . . . Everything must be done openly and in the eye of the public so long as the public obey the law themselves and do not interfere with the inspectors or the clerk."[19] The attempt by the commissioners to forestall a public counting of ballots, and the actions of Supervisor of Registration E. J. E. McLaurin, which were aired in the local newspapers the following day, convinced the Straightouts that the Antis and the interests supporting them were determined to win a political victory at any cost.

Accordingly, they charged before Judge Call that McLaurin had fraudulently struck from the records almost four hundred names of registered voters, a majority of whom were allegedly Straightouts and Straightout followers. These omissions were discovered after the list of voters was published in the *Jacksonville Metropolis* on October 1. When John N. C. Stockton questioned them, he was told by McLaurin that their absence was accidental and that the voters could restore their names to the registration lists by appearing personally to request a correction.[20] In a day when a few votes might determine a close election, purging the list of four hundred voters, especially if they belonged to one faction, could well be the deciding factor.

Judge Call issued a mandamus on October 3 ordering Mc-

Laurin to restore "the names of those persons as set forth in the certified lists of those who have paid their poll taxes, duly certified and delivered to said supervisor by the tax collector of said county in accordance with law...."[21] The supervisor of registration was thus forced to restore the names, and the mandamus against him was dismissed on October 5.[22]

The race between Napoleon Broward and Fleming Bowden for sheriff of Duval County aroused great interest throughout the state. Although the office of county sheriff was not considered overly important, the political battle between the two candidates was viewed by the voters and the newspapers as a clear-cut contest between the conservatives and the liberals. It was rumored that if all the wagers and bets made on the outcome of this race were added together, "the sum would be well up in the thousands." Broward, busy evading the clutches of the United States Marshal, had little time to campaign; and he depended on his wide personal popularity, the support of the anti-corporation group, and his own strength to elect him.

Straightout leaders, confident they would carry the election, agreed to make a strong plea for peace within the state's Democratic ranks. Thus, on election day, October 6, the leading editorial in the *Florida Times-Union* strongly advocated an end to the bitter factional quarreling which had been characteristic of politics in Duval County for a number of years. "There is no reason," it asserted, "why this bitter warfare should be waged between men advocating a common policy."[23] The confidence and optimism which had been expressed so frequently by the Straightout leaders prior to the election seemed justified by the results at the polls. The tabulation of votes showed that the Straightouts had scored an overwhelming victory and had replaced the Antis in the public offices of Duval County. Republican and Populist candidates had received an inconsequential vote.

The official canvass, which was announced three days after the election, formally named Broward as sheriff of Duval County. He had defeated Fleming Bowden by a vote of 1,633 to 1,439.[24] Although Broward's majority was small, he was sheriff, and his victory must have been sweet. He had defeated his old political rival and had been returned to the same office from which he had been removed two years earlier. He was now stronger than ever in Duval County politics.

Early in November the newly elected county officers registered their bonds with the county commissioners pursuant to law. Broward's bond for ten thousand dollars was quickly guaranteed by five of his friends.[25] On December 1, 1896, he received his notification and commission from Governor Mitchell,[26] and on January 5, 1897, he formally assumed office.[27] He appointed R. H. McMillan chief deputy.

Having won his own battle, Broward campaigned in Florida for William Jennings Bryan. The Bryan-Sewall Democratic Club of Jacksonville tried unsuccessfully to attract the presidential candidate to the city. Two huge Democratic rallies were held in Jacksonville on October 27; Robert W. Davis was principal speaker at one rally, and Senator Wilkinson Call and Broward spoke at the other. The Democrats employed Davis, probably to please the Antis, and used Call and Broward to stimulate Straightout interest. There was no doubt that Florida would vote for William Jennings Bryan. Nationally, the Republican party was confident of electing William McKinley. Final election returns showed that McKinley had received 7,035,638 votes to 6,467,946 cast for Bryan. In the electoral college McKinley's vote was 271; Bryan's, 176. Bryan carried nearly all the South and much of the West. The Democratic victory in Florida was overwhelming—Bloxham became the new governor, and Davis and Sparkman were sent to Congress.[28]

In Jacksonville and in Duval County, after 1896, the Straightouts had a firm hold on political affairs and were preparing to strengthen their control. Broward was generally recognized as one of their leading spokesmen. Popular and picturesque, he possessed great appeal for the average voter. His exploits as a filibuster had popularized him throughout the state, especially after the United States had declared war against Spain. Many national and Florida newspapers, including some of those opposing Broward's political views, commended him and other filibusters for their courage in aiding the oppressed Cubans. Broward was never entirely divorced from Duval County politics, but he was now recognized as a state leader; his counsel was sought and his suggestions were followed.

After the election excitement had subsided, Florida's Democratic leaders began planning strategy for the approaching session of the legislature. Liberals girded themselves for battle against the railroad and corporation forces that controlled the state government. Throughout March, Sheriff Broward conferred frequently with Straightout leaders in Duval County and with liberals throughout the state. For Broward's career the state legislature of April and May, 1897, had special significance. Its activities and proceedings set in motion forces that were to develop the primary issues of the gubernatorial campaign in 1904. The newly elected sheriff headed an unofficial delegation from Duval County. Leaving an assistant in charge of his office, the sheriff and Mrs. Broward, their family, and Mrs. Broward's sister, Elsie Douglass, traveled to Tallahassee. Lodged at the Hotel Leon, they planned to remain two months. A nurse was hired to attend the children.

Every morning Mrs. Broward and Miss Douglass drove in their buggy to the capitol. Seated in the visitors' gallery in the House of Representatives, they watched activities on the floor. Broward kept his eye on the Senate, occasionally entering the Senate chamber to advise his delegation. Sometimes he joined liberal caucuses in the corridors and meeting rooms of the capitol to plan strategy and to line up votes for measures which he considered favorable to his anti-corporation cause.

Mrs. Broward and Miss Douglass met the sheriff for lunch nearly every day and they compared notes. In the afternoon they exchanged places, Broward going to the House gallery, and Mrs. Broward and her sister to the Senate gallery. During the evening the three conferred again.[29] Broward thus received a detailed report on daily legislative proceedings; and when he attended the caucuses held each evening in the rooms of Tallahassee hotels, he was equipped with a wealth of valuable information. One obvious reason for Broward's political success was that he usually had at his fingertips pertinent points of an issue under discussion, and could readily present them to his audience in an authoritative manner. Much of this knowledge came from his system of legislative observation.

Broward and other leading Democratic liberals had long since become convinced that a principal objective in their crusade against the corporations and the railroads must be the restoration of state railroad regulation. Such regulatory measures were not new to Florida.

In 1855 the General Assembly of Florida had enacted a law whereby Florida railroads already completed and those still under construction would be tax-exempt for a period of thirty-five years.[30] Although this exemption was limited to specific roads, transportation companies as late as 1880 were trying to take advantage of the situation, and the state was thereby losing large revenues. Finally, in 1881, the legislature adopted a resolution which declared that the special exemptions applied only to "the original Companies owning said roads and did not pass with the roads into the hands of the present owners."[31] This legislative resolution was later upheld by the state courts.

During the 1880's railroads "over-built" in Florida. Neither the state's population nor its commercial activity warranted this mushroom growth, and almost one-third of the railways in Florida were quickly thrown into receivership. Such conditions necessitated, in 1887, a second step in railroad regulation—the establishment of a state railroad commission.[32] Florida transportation and corporation interests, wielding a strong hand in state politics, marshaled their forces in an effort to abolish the railroad commission. These interests had grown increasingly powerful and influential in politics since the Reconstruction era. Their activities substantiated the bitter charges made by Broward, Barrs, and Stockton, namely, that corporations and railroads had controlled the legislatures and the governors of Florida since 1876. There was a real basis for Broward's anti-corporation campaign. He realized that the railroads did not favor regulation, and were opposed to the commission; and he knew that corporation influence was mainly responsible for the repeal of the Railroad Commission Act in 1891.

Florida liberals worked hard to restore this act or to replace it with a similar law. During the legislative session of 1893, Broward joined a group of merchants and brokers who appeared before a joint House-Senate committee in Tallahassee to argue for restoration of the state Railroad Commission. Interested in the production and shipment of phosphate, Broward urged legislative correction of railroad abuses, which were caused chiefly by the rebate system and discriminatory freight rates.[33] This committee reported favorably on plans to re-establish the commission, but the measure was blocked in the legislature and it did not become law.

Throughout the remaining years of the 1890's Broward continued his fight for a new commission. In 1894 he wrote: "I don't blame the railroads for taking all they can get, and making the long haul every time, if the people will stand heedlessly by, with their mouths open, and be treated this way. I believe that nothing short of just and proper legislation will do us any good."[34] In an attempt to secure such legislation, Broward and other liberal leaders persuaded Duncan U. Fletcher, a Duval Straightout, to run for state senator on a railroad commission platform. Fletcher failed to win a seat. Broward later charged that Fletcher was defeated by "railroad money and their [sic] manipulations, they, at that time, having with them the Governor and the Chairman of the State Democratic Executive Committee."[35]

Two liberal leaders, Frank W. Pope and John N. C. Stockton, were elected in the fall of 1896 to represent Duval County in the Florida House of Representatives. Immediately after their election, they began planning their anti-railroad strategy for the coming legislative meeting, and devoted long hours to writing proposed bills, lining up support, and publicizing throughout Florida the necessity for railroad regulation. Two days after the legislature assembled in Tallahassee, Stockton introduced two bills. His first measure, House Bill No. 9, provided for a commission authorized to regulate railroad schedules, freights, and passenger depots "to prevent unjust discrimination in the rates charged for the transportation of passengers and freights, and to prohibit railroad companies, corporations, persons and all common carriers . . . from charging other than just and reasonable rates. . . ."[36] His second measure, House Bill No. 10, was designed to prohibit "any railroad or other transportation company or any officer or official thereto from contributing any money or free transportation to persons or political parties for political purposes. . . ."[37]

The first bill was referred to the Judiciary Committee, of which Pope was a member. The Railroads and Telegraph Committee, of which Stockton was a member, received the second measure. Each committee reported favorably. Railroad commission advocates had spent many hours in securing support for the bills, and, as a result, they triumphed over the strong corporation forces. When the proposed acts were read in the House and Senate there was a minimum of debate and both bills were passed. They were signed into law by Governor Bloxham on May 8.[38]

Governor Bloxham appointed R. H. M. Davidson, Henry E. Day, and John L. Morgan as commissioners for two-year terms. Succeeding commissioners were to be elected for terms of four years at an annual salary of twenty-five hundred dollars.[39] Anyone holding railroad stocks or bonds, or employed by a railroad, could not be a commissioner.[40] Extensive powers were vested in the body. Not only could it "investigate thoroughly all through rates from points out of Florida to points in Florida" and adjust "excessive, unreasonable or discriminating" claims of overcharge, but it had authority to make "reasonable and just rates of freight and passenger tariff." It could, in addition, "prevent the giving or paying of any bonus or rebate, or devices of any description used . . . directly or indirectly, for the purpose of deceiving or misleading the public as to the actual rates charged."[41] The new commission law was a determined and sincere effort to establish a competent agency for remedying railroad and transportation abuses and to place the agency under control of the voters. The Railroad Commission law was the major progressive measure of the second Bloxham administration, but Bloxham could claim little credit, as his attitude toward it seems to have been largely negative.

The essential soundness of the law was borne out by the performance of the Railroad Commission. Broward, in the campaign of 1904, thus summarized its effect: "Passenger rates have been reduced from four and five cents per mile on the main lines to three cents per mile, the freight rates on staples have been very much reduced as have also the rates on vegetables and oranges, to the great benefit of the people, and recently, the matter having been brought to the attention of the Commission that the railroads of the State are discriminating against Florida ports in favor of ports beyond the limits of the State, a phosphate rate of one cent per ton per mile has been ordered put into effect. It has been estimated that the saving to phosphate shipped alone by this will amount to TWO HUNDRED THOUSAND DOLLARS PER ANNUM, enough to pay the maximum expenses allowed to the Railroad Commission for over thirteen years."[42]

By 1897, a majority of the citizens of Florida generally accepted the fact that some sort of law was needed to regulate county elections. Abuses had developed and prevailed in many areas for a number of years. Persons whose poll taxes were in arrears voted, and teen-age boys were often allowed to cast ballots. Over-ambitious or unscrupulous candidates for county offices encouraged and profited by these election abuses.[43] During the early 1890's, in Duval County's factional battles, the *Florida Times-Union* had frequently charged Antis with perpetrating such frauds. Similar charges were made throughout Florida during this period.

Governor Bloxham did not refer to the primary question in his legislative message of April 6, 1897. State agitation, however, encouraged the introduction of a primary bill during this session. A bitter fight developed between liberal Democrats, who supported the measure, and conservatives, who opposed any act that would deprive corporation interests of their power in directing elections. The measure finally enacted as Florida's first state primary-control law required voters in county and state primaries to be members of that party holding the election. It further stipulated that the voters in a state election must have the same qualifications as the voters in a general election.[44] The primary law, while not very strong, was a progressive measure, and foreshadowed later legislation.

Sheriff Broward did not expect these reform efforts within the party to continue without resistance and opposition from the corporations and the railroads. Broward and his supporters had good reason to believe that their conservative political opponents were working hand in glove with the corporate interests. They were convinced that the protests and denunciations constantly leveled at their program were, in reality, inspired by those interests. Conservatives, on the other hand, claimed that the welfare and progress of Florida were being jeopardized by this "up-start element" in the Democratic party with its anti-railroad legislation. The corporate-owned newspapers in the state joined in this denunciation. One critic called the Railroad Commission an affront to civilization, because "security in holding and freedom in using property is what chiefly distinguished civilization from barbarism."[45]

The developing trend toward liberal reform was obvious to the conservative Democrats of Florida. Liberals were gaining rapidly in strength and numbers all over the state. Many rising political leaders, following in the footsteps of Broward, Pope, Stockton, Barrs, and Jennings, adhered to the independent wing and brought in their train a large part of the agrarian vote. To this liberal group belonged such older political figures as Senators Wilkinson Call and Stephen R. Mallory, whose experience and training proved valuable.

Conservatives marshaled their strength for a fight to retain control of state government. Many Florida newspapers were already under their jurisdiction, and they began widening their influence with the press by purchasing other newspapers throughout the state. An important acquisition by the Flagler interests was the *Florida Times-Union*, which changed hands on September 9, 1897. It was merged with the *Daily Florida Citizen*, and until 1903 the consolidated journal was known as the *Times-Union and Citizen*. Assuming a pro-railroad and pro-corporation bias, the newspaper opposed Broward on almost every issue throughout the rest of his political career.[46]

Liberals closed their ranks and prepared for the fray. Those taking an anti-corporation stand received their greatest support from the small businessman, the farmer, and others in the rural sections of Florida. Voters in these areas and in small towns were inevitably aware of the benefits Florida derived from its railroads. Nevertheless, the liberals willingly assumed the responsibility of revealing to their supporters the obvious abuses and the rank discrimination practiced by the transportation companies in the state. A farmer could easily appreciate the fact that he received less profit from his products if railroad rates were too high. Businessmen realized that their profits were lessened by excessive freight rates.

In Governor Bloxham's administration, the political event of greatest significance for Broward and his cause was the battle between conservatives and liberals, occasioned by the expiration of Senator Wilkinson Call's term on March 3, 1897. Governor Bloxham, no admirer of Senator Call, refused to reappoint him, and named John A. Henderson, of Tallahassee, to serve until the Florida legislature elected Call's successor.[47] The United States Senate, in refusing to seat Henderson, charged that Governor Bloxham was authorized to appoint a Senator to office only until the state legislature had convened. While the controversy was being argued in Tallahassee and Washington, Florida was represented by only one Senator in Congress.[48]

When the state legislature assembled, it was obvious that a large number of the legislators were controlled by the avowed political enemies of Senator Call.[49] Broward, as head of the important unofficial Duval County delegation to Tallahassee, was active in trying to secure support for Call. Both Charles J. Perrenot of Santa Rosa County, president of the Senate, and D. H. Mays, of Jefferson County, speaker of the House, opposed Call. William Dudley Chipley, a state senator and an influential leader of the conservative railroad faction, was also a candidate for the vacant office.[50] Chipley hoped that the anti-Call men would support him, but many of the legislators who opposed Call disliked Chipley even more. Perrenot and Mays were anti-Call, but they were not pro-Chipley.[51]

In addition to the two leading candidates, William A. Hocker and Robert A. Burford, both of Ocala, and George P. Raney, of Tallahassee, were in the race. Hocker, Burford, and Raney offered no real competition, and they received only scattered votes. Balloting began on April 20. On the first ballot, Call received 33 votes; Chipley, 24.[52] Many legislators were obviously not voting. Successive ballots were taken during the afternoon, at a special evening session, and on the following day. Though a few votes were traded back and forth between the supporters of Chipley and Call, they were not enough to break the deadlock. The anti-Call men, who stubbornly refused to give Chipley their votes, held the balance of power. Dozens of ballots were marked and counted during the succeeding April days, but neither candidate received the requisite number of votes for election.[53] Then, on May 7, the liberal forces persuaded Senator Call to withdraw from the contest, and entered John N. C. Stockton in the race.[54]

Call was dissatisfied with the situation, but agreed to swing whatever support he had among the legislators to Stockton. The first written ballot, taken on May 7, tallied 37 votes for Chipley and 33 votes for Stockton.[55] Although the liberals tried desperately to force a break, the weary legislators continued to be divided for still another week. Finally, on May 13, Senator T. A. Darby introduced a resolution which asked that in "the present interest of the State and the future interest of the Democratic party . . . W. D. Chipley and John N. C. Stockton withdraw from the Senatorial contest. By their doing so there would cease to be factions, and the efforts made and time now given to serve individuals would be devoted to serving the entire people."[56]

Chipley refused to withdraw, but the following day Stockton dropped out and Stephen R. Mallory was nominated as a candidate.[57] Mallory and Chipley, both residents of Pensacola, were bitter political enemies. Mallory leaned toward Florida's liberal cause; Chipley was recognized as one of its leading political foes. A key member of the railroad-corporation faction, Chipley was often a target of Broward's attacks, and, in turn, Chipley indicted Broward and his supporters. Under the circumstances, Mallory—never so liberal as Broward, Call, or Stockton—was acceptable to the liberal forces as a compromise candidate. On a voice vote, Chipley was declared the winner, but on the written ballot, Mallory received the necessary majority by a 53 to 44 vote. Chipley had lost the treasured prize; Mallory was declared United States Senator from Florida; and the liberal cause had chalked up another important victory.[58]

Florida liberals took a long stride toward state-wide political success with the defeat of William Dudley Chipley. They were building a sound structure for their political future.

⌒ II ⌒

Liberalism Comes to Power

THROUGHOUT THE REST OF 1897 and during
1898 Broward was actively occupied with politics. His
interest in the *Three Friends* continued, but he left the
immediate supervision of the vessel to his brother Montcalm,
who also directed the *Florida*, a nine hundred forty-three ton
vessel owned by John N. C. Stockton, John M. Barrs, and the
two Broward brothers.[1] Broward's other business enterprises
were operated by foremen and supervisors. Politics had become the prime interest in his life.

Demands for reforms were developing clear-cut trends
throughout the nation. The old familiar issues—internal improvements, cheap money, railroad controls, an income tax,
protection and free trade, elimination of waste and corruption
in the government's machinery—were debated continually in
Congress and in state legislatures. Out of the interminable
speeches came antitrust legislation, railroad regulatory commissions, primary laws, and election-spending laws, in response
to the nation's demands. Withal, the United States continued
building immense fortunes for a few men; railroads multi-
plied, crisscrossing the land like gray-brown serpents; and
immigrant millions touched the golden shores, filled up tene-
ment blocks in Eastern cities, or moved across the Mississippi
to plant grain on the Western prairies.

The closing years of the 1890's brought Florida a large
measure of prosperity and a growing demand that railroad-
corporation influences in politics be curtailed. The state's proximity to Cuba made it a logical embarkation point for thousands
of soldiers on their way to fight the war with Spain. Millions
of dollars were spent in Florida by the military personnel, by

their families who came to see them off, and by the Federal government. A sprawling training camp, *Cuba Libre,* was constructed near Jacksonville,[2] and huge amounts of money were spent in the Tampa area to deepen the harbor and to build warehouses, docks, wharfs, and camps.[3] Much of this money remained in the state and gave an increasing prosperity to farmers and small businessmen.

Foremost among the crusaders against railroad-corporation control and influence in Florida was Napoleon Broward. After 1898 there was hardly a political action taken in the state in which his recommendations or reactions were not considered. During the legislature of 1897 he had played a vital role in the passage of the Railroad Commission Act, the Primary Law, and in the Call-Chipley fight. As early as the summer of 1898 he and other liberals met often to plan the election campaign of 1900. Lists of possible candidates were compiled, and scores of men were questioned about their political views and their availability for public office.

Political reconnoitering continued for many months. By the end of 1899 a likely candidate for the gubernatorial nomination was found in William Sherman Jennings of Brooksville.[4] Jennings was a cousin of William Jennings Bryan and, at the time, this relationship was recognized by Broward as an important political asset in Florida. Although Jennings had never openly declared himself a liberal, he was known to be inclined favorably toward progressive principles and the platform which Broward supported.

In the Duval County primaries of May 17, 1900, Broward was elected to the county convention as a delegate from Ward Two. In the convention two days later, Broward and John C. L'Engle were named Democratic candidates to the state House of Representatives. There was little dissension during the primaries or the convention; Broward and L'Engle were nominated without opposition. Broward was also chosen as a delegate to the state convention, scheduled to meet in Jacksonville on June 19.[5]

The state convention assembled in a large new hall, Emory Auditorium, which had been gaily decorated for the meeting. Workmen, supervised by a committee of ladies, had hammered flags into place, draped doorways, windows, and the stage with red, white, and blue bunting, and rolled huge tubs of palms onto the speaker's platform. A giant portrait of William Jennings Bryan gazed benignly from the back wall of the rostrum, and gaudily tinted pictures of Thomas Jefferson, Andrew Jackson, Robert E. Lee, and Grover Cleveland bedecked the side walls.

Scores of people arrived from every county in the state for the meeting. It was a hot, dry summer in Jacksonville, and the heat spiralled up from the bricked streets and sidewalks as simmering alpaca-coated citizens and their summer-gowned wives promenaded in Hemming Park, along the river's shore, and peered into the decorated shopwindows. Livery stables carried on a brisk business. Buggies were hired for drives to Springfield, along Riverside Avenue, and out to Fairfield. The Florida East Coast Railway provided ten cars to carry delegates on an all-day outing to Pablo Beach and Mayport.[6] Each afternoon a band played in the park, and at night there were dances and balls in the St. James and Windsor hotels. Crowds packed the Park Opera House each evening for a special show, and returned home along streets brightened by lighted colored lanterns.

The convention opened with band music: the "Star Spangled Banner" and "Dixie." The mayor of Jacksonville welcomed delegates and visitors, photographers snapped pictures, and then the real work began. Thomas M. Palmer, of Hillsborough County, was made permanent chairman; a state platform was drawn up and the Chicago platform of 1896 was enthusiastically endorsed. The Democratic party of Florida declared for tariff reductions, a graduated income tax, "free, unlimited and independent coinage of both silver and gold at a ratio of 16 to 1," government control of corporations, primary elections, continuance of the state Railroad Commission, and "the stand taken by that great, true and brave leader and friend of the people, Colonel William Jennings Bryan."[7] Broward's faction was mainly responsible for the liberal planks in the platform which was adopted. On the third morning of the convention, the gubernatorial contest began. According to plan, C. M. Brown of Marion County nominated William S. Jennings with a rousing speech.[8] Dannitte H. Mays was nominated by C. B. Parkhill; William Hall Milton, by Judge B. S. Liddon; Frederick Myers, by Judge G. P. Raney; and Judge James D. Beggs, by C. A. Carson. The liberals at the convention regarded Frederick Myers as the candidate of railroad and corporation interests.

The first ballot, counted at 3:30 P.M., showed Jennings in the lead with 78½ votes; 68½ votes were tabulated for Myers; 47½ for Beggs; 50 for Mays; and 37½ for Milton. During the succeeding tabulations Broward, heading the delegation from Duval County, purposely tried to split the county's vote among all the candidates except Myers in order to convince the delegates from small counties that Duval County was not dominating voting activities. Broward's design was to channel as much support as possible away from Myers. During the first eight ballots little change developed, and when the convention adjourned at six o'clock, there was slight hope for an early nomination. Under the two-thirds rule, a candidate had to have 188 votes to win.[9]

The thunderstorm which broke over Jacksonville early next morning did not prevent scores of spectators from packing the visitors' gallery to watch the proceedings. Men with gold watch fobs and heavy canes pushed and shoved each other in their hurry to find seats. A sprinkling of women, their bonnets awry and their clothes raindamp, pushed into Emory Auditorium when the doors opened.

The delegates resumed their work, and on the ninth ballot tallied 79½ votes for Jennings; 74½ for Myers; 50½ for Beggs; 51 for Mays; and 26½ for Milton. A slight break appeared on the eleventh tally when Columbia County threw its block to Jennings. Duval County followed with 22 more votes, and Hillsborough County strengthened this lead. Jennings had 123½ votes on the twenty-first ballot.

There was little change until the thirtieth count, when the DeSoto County delegation switched to Mays, and he became a leading threat. The delegates had been waiting tensely for a break, which now seemed imminent. The convention fell into wild confusion. County representatives called hurried caucuses on the assembly floor, delegates ran to and fro about the hall, and visitors cheered as the candidates tried to marshal available support. The convention chairman rapped for order, but the pounding of his gavel could not be heard above the din.[10]

The threatened landslide for Mays proved a false alarm and another deadlock ensued. After Myers withdrew on the thirty-fifth ballot, Mays lost votes and quickly dropped to third place. When the latter withdrew from the race after the forty-first ballot, the liberals became jubilant over Jennings' strength. Broward worked feverishly with county delegates, trying to swing their support to his candidate. Conservatives tried in vain to make a last-ditch stand for Milton, but on the forty-third ballot Jennings had a 59 vote lead over his opponent. On the next ballot the break came. Leon County swung her 14 votes to Jennings and ended the long contest. Jennings received 192 votes and the Democratic gubernatorial nomination.[11] Mrs. Mays, sitting in the visitors' gallery, viewed the outcome of the contest with disappointment. She was overheard remarking: "Anybody can be governor of Florida these days, even a jack rabbit. All you have to do is wag your ears and you are chosen."[12]

The completed slate of Democratic nominees included: John L. Crawford, secretary of state; W. B. Lamar, attorney general; W. H. Reynolds, comptroller; James B. Whitfield, treasurer; W. N. Sheats, superintendent of public instruction; B. E. McLin, commissioner of agriculture; and John L. Morgan, railroad commissioner. Stephen M. Sparkman and Robert W. Davis were nominated for Congress.[13]

The question of removing the capital from Tallahassee was

debated. This old issue, with which Broward was now closely identified, had reappeared from time to time since territorial days. Prior to the state convention of 1900, several Florida cities had announced themselves superior to Tallahassee as the seat of government. St. Augustine based her claim on her historical importance; Jacksonville, on the fact that she was the largest city in Florida; and Ocala, on her central location in the state. In the state convention, Broward argued Jacksonville's cause with great fervor, and revealed that the city was ready to float a bond issue to help construct a new capitol. Many delegates insisted that the question should be placed before the citizens in the coming election. Voters would have no power to designate the seat of government; they could, however, suggest on their ballots a location for the state capital. Should any place other than Tallahassee receive a majority of votes, the legislature would consider itself instructed to submit a constitutional amendment to voters in 1902.

When the convention adjourned, the candidates announced their campaign itinerary. The Republican party, by 1900, was of negligible importance in Florida, and a Democratic nomination was tantamount to election. It was important, however, for the electorate to meet and hear William S. Jennings and the other Democratic nominees and determine their stand on issues like the convict lease system, reapportionment, taxation, public lands claimed by the railroads, and the general trend toward increased government control and regulation.

Although prior to 1900 Jennings had not been recognized in Florida as strongly anti-corporation and anti-railroad, he directed his campaign along liberal lines, and there was growing evidence that he would be Florida's most progressive governor since the Reconstruction period. In a speech at Jasper, Florida, September 13, 1900, Jennings denounced the trusts, claiming they were "sapping the lifeblood of the country and should be speedily suppressed or controlled by the Government."[14] Jennings favored free textbooks for school children,[15] as well as the leasing-out of convicts, but in Palatka he argued that profits from the latter should go into state coffers, and

not into the pockets of individuals.[16] To the interests that
wanted to amend the constitution so that Florida could issue
state bonds, he declared that such indebtedness brought only
a "fictitious prosperity, which is sure to react to the disadvantage
of the people."[17]

In addition to stumping the state for Jennings, Broward
campaigned strenuously in Duval County for his own election
to the legislature. Promising to support forcefully all legislation aimed at reform and corporation-railroad control, he outlined the bills he proposed to introduce in the legislature.
Meanwhile, another party split appeared to be developing in
Duval County, for a "Citizen's Party," led by T. J. Boyd
and J. E. T. Bowden, announced an incomplete slate of candidates for county offices. Despite the party's appeal to the
labor vote, poor organization and a lack of adequate financing
weakened it. The *Florida Times-Union,* now opposed to the
Straightouts, also strongly denounced the adherents of the
"Citizen's Party" as egoists "falling prostrate before false
gods," and suggested that its leaders were victims of "political hallucinations."[18]

On election day, November 6, there were few disturbances
at the polls, and election activities were generally quiet and
orderly. A canvass of votes revealed Broward and L'Engle
easy winners over Boyd and Bowden of the "Citizen's Party."
Broward received 1,695 votes; L'Engle, 1,591; Boyd, 1,053;
and Bowden, 1,133.[19]

William S. Jennings became the new governor. The vote
was surprisingly small in view of the pre-election excitement
aroused by the possibility of removing the state capital. Jacksonville, eager to become the capital of Florida, had named a
campaign committee, led by Judge John L. Doggett, which
had traveled all over Florida in search of support. Because of
the large amount of money invested in government buildings
in Tallahassee, however, voters opposed the removal of the
capital. The vote was Tallahassee 16,742; Jacksonville 7,675;
Ocala 4,917; and St. Augustine 2,881.[20]

Broward, during the next few months, conferred with state

Democratic leaders in Jacksonville, Orlando, Tallahassee, and Brooksville concerning plans and strategy for the coming legislature. With a liberal governor and substantial liberal majorities in the state Senate and House, Broward and his followers were confident of success for most of their proposed antirailroad and anti-corporation legislation.[21]

The legislature assembled in Tallahassee at noon on April 2. When the standing committees were announced, Broward found himself on the Commerce and Navigation Committee, the Education Committee, and the Public Roads and Highways Committee.[22] On April 4 Broward introduced his first measure, House Bill No. 14, which authorized a redistricting of the state.[23] The Federal census of 1900 had revealed that because of an increase in Florida's population, she was entitled to an additional representative in Congress. The state constitution vested redistricting power in the legislature, and Governor Jennings, in his first message, suggested immediate action.

The bill drawn up by Broward embodied a plan whereby Florida would be divided into three districts, each having a total population in excess of 170,000. The First District would include the west Florida counties;[24] the Second District, east Florida;[25] and the Third District, the middle and south Florida counties.[26] Broward was appointed to a special eight-man legislative committee to study his bill and the other questions relating to reapportionment.[27] Dissension over the size of the electoral districts developed in the committee, and both a majority and a minority report were returned. Broward, siding with the other two minority committeemen, C. M. Jones, of Escambia County, and E. W. Russell, of Monroe County, charged that the opposing report was a "plain and unmistakable violation of the provisions of the Act of Congress."[28] The Redistricting Act, as finally adopted, was a compromise measure which included many of Broward's original proposals. It was signed by Governor Jennings on May 22, 1901.[29]

The legislature of 1901 was long remembered for the bill

introduced on April 9 by W. L. Palmer, the representative from Orange County. House Bill No. 135, which made "incurable insanity a ground for divorce of husband and wife," was destined to become one of the most notorious bills ever introduced into a Florida legislature.[30]

The bill, referred to the Judiciary Committee for consideration, was reported favorably to the House, and a similar measure, introduced in the Senate, was given favorable consideration. Both measures were pushed to a speedy passage.[31] The act, signed by Jennings on April 25, declared that "incurable insanity in either husband or wife shall be a ground for the dissolution of, and divorce from, the bonds of matrimony upon the application of the other party to the marriage...."[32] The enactment of the divorce law stirred up a great furore throughout the state. Newspapers and citizens openly charged that the act was for the express purpose and interest of Henry Morrison Flagler, the builder of the Florida East Coast Railroad and a chain of lavish Florida hotels. The measure was immediately dubbed "Flagler's Divorce Law." Flagler's second wife was hopelessly insane and in a sanitorium.[33] When he changed his residence from New York to Florida in 1899, Flagler explained that his business interests could better be served in the South. It was believed that he was already planning a Florida divorce, although the state, at the time, did not recognize insanity as a legal cause for such action.[34]

There were numerous charges that members of the Senate and the House had been bought, and newspapers like the *Pensacola Journal* indicted "Flagler's influence in state affairs."[35] Probably these accusations were only partly true. Many supporters of the measure doubtless voted from honest conviction and without undue influence. Broward voted for the divorce bill, although he received no money for his vote and was not classed as one of Flagler's supporters. Asked about his vote, he declared that he thought the law just and that he voted as his conscience directed.[36] Frank Harris, editor of

the *Ocala Banner*, argued, like Broward, that the law was
just.[37] Unlike Broward, he was charged with receiving part of
the twenty thousand dollars which Flagler allegedly spent
in getting the bill passed.[38] The wealthy railroad magnate,
an immediate beneficiary of the new law, filed a plea for
divorce on June 3, 1901, in the Circuit Court, Seventh Judicial Circuit of Florida, and on August 13 received a favorable award. On August 24 he married Mary Lily Kenan,
a socially prominent North Carolina woman.[39] For the third
Mrs. Flagler he built, at Palm Beach, a magnificent marble
palace, Whitehall, which cost two and a half million dollars.[40]

Another important bill, the effects of which were echoed
in the 1904 campaign, was introduced into the legislature
by Representative John P. Wall of Putnam County. The act
was designed to "prohibit the manufacture and sale of intoxicating liquors as a beverage within this State . . . ," except
through state-owned and operated "dispensaries."[41] Broward,
a lifelong advocate of prohibition, heartily supported Wall's
bill. Like many others, he reasoned that it was a wise step in
the direction of temperance, and "towards the rescue of the
youth . . . from the evils that now surround them on every
side from the liquor traffic, by abolishing completely the
'social life' and 'social glass' of the barroom."[42] The wholesale and retail liquor interests in Florida exerted their strength
to defeat the prohibition bill in the legislature. An active
lobby operated in Tallahassee; and there were rumors that
tremendous sums of money were being spent in entertaining
legislators, purchasing space in newspapers, and "buying-up"
representatives and senators. With Broward's support, the
bill passed the House.[43] An amendment striking out the enacting clause and making the act ineffective was introduced by
Senator W. A. MacWilliams and was adopted on May 23.[44]

In commenting on MacWilliams' opposition, the editor of
the *Daily Capital* in Tallahassee wrote:

Not Humpty Dumpty, not Mr. Wall
None of these received a fall.
It was only the Dispensary Bill
In the Senate, that was all.
The Dispensary Bill, that was laid to rest,
Is only temporary at the best;
You may watch us boys in 1902
And see what us voters are going to do.
Then just wait until 1903
And then see what the verdict will be.
The Barroom must go.
As we all well know
For the voters of Florida all say so.
Mr. Mac and his little chicks
Will be left at home in a devil of a fix,
And that's no joke
For the man who supports the Dispensary.[45]

Despite the defeat of this measure, Broward, like many others in Florida and throughout the nation, felt that more adequate regulation of the liquor traffic was necessary, and he hoped that future bills would be enacted into law.

May 3 was a sunny, blue day in Tallahassee. When the House adjourned for lunch, Broward, L'Engle, and M. A. Brown[46] walked together toward town. Broward decided to stop at the post office and pick up his mail. Just as he passed in front of the Western Union office, the telegraph operator, his face pinched with excitement, rushed out.

"Mr. Broward, have you heard the latest news?" he asked. "Jacksonville's burning up!"

"How do you know?"

"The news is coming in over the wires right now. Come on in and listen."

People crowded into the little office and jammed the street and sidewalk outside, trying to read bulletins as they were typed out and pasted on the window. It was clear that no one knew yet how serious the fire was, nor what damage it was

doing. The first reports announced that it had started about
12:30 P.M. in the Cleaveland Fiber Factory on the corner of
Beaver and West Davis streets.[47] Sparks from a nearby wooden
shanty had ignited pieces of fiber on a loading platform, and
the factory had burst into flames. While firemen tried to ex-
tinguish the blaze, the wind, rising in gusts, carried sparks
to nearby frame cottages.

The weather in Jacksonville had been dry and hot for several days, and the houses burned like matchboxes. The dry
moss in the oak trees ignited and helped to spread the fire.
The reports arriving in Tallahassee were confused and con-
tradictory. Some said the fire was under control; others, that
it was spreading and that all Jacksonville was burning. After
about an hour, Broward shoved through the crowd and hurried to Mrs. Long's boardinghouse to tell his wife and family
about the fire.[48] The news had preceded him, and when he
arrived at his house, he was greeted at the door by his daughter Josephine, who shouted: "Papa, do you know Jacksonville
is burning up?"[49]

In a few minutes Broward was back again at Western Union
to read more bulletins. They were coming in fast now and
they contained more information. They revealed that the fire
was heading straight east, toward the center of town, and
razing scores of houses, churches, stores, and buildings. Hundreds of refugees were moving out of the city to escape the
flames. Broward, hearing that Governor Jennings was sending
a company of troops by special train to help keep order, aid
in rescue work, and stop pilfering, asked permission to go
along, and was on the train when it pulled out late that
afternoon.[50]

Whenever the train stopped at a depot for water, Broward
jumped out to inquire for news. In Madison, an excited telegraph operator handed him a bulletin which stated that fire-
fighting units from St. Augustine and Fernandina were helping Jacksonville firemen, and that more help was on the way
from Savannah, Brunswick, and Waycross. There was no halt-

ing the flames, and already a wide path had burned as far as the Windsor Hotel.

In Live Oak, telegraph keys nervously chattered out a report that both the Windsor and St. James hotels had been destroyed and that the fire had swept across Hemming Park and had burned the piles of household goods stacked around the base of the monument. As the train carried Broward across the darkening land, he heard other stories and read more reports. At a stop outside Lake City late that night, a railroad employee gave him a newspaper which described the scene of the fire: streets crowded with throngs of hysterical people running toward the river with their personal belongings clutched in their arms; carts loaded with baggage; wagons hauling household goods; wildly rearing horses adding to the confusion. The newspaper account told of one man who had stood in the middle of Adams Street, near Laura, and had rolled his goods downhill to supposed safety. A little old lady, in an effort to save her rosewood piano, had tied a rope around her mule and tried to make him pull the piano along Bay Street.

From Lake City, Broward could see a red glow in the sky to the east. In Baldwin there was a long delay, and he talked with refugees from Jacksonville. They were dripping sweat, dirty, and unkempt. They told him how the fire had bypassed the post office, then split in two—one section burning toward the river, and the other rapidly moving west. The courthouse, the Law Exchange, the Armory, St. John's Episcopal Church, the Catholic Church, St. Joseph's Orphanage, and hundreds of homes had been consumed. Flames had roared along Bay Street, burning Emory Auditorium, the Board of Trade building, the Seminole Club, the Metropolis Publication building, the city market, the Hubbard building, and Furchgott's store. Supplies of dynamite, powder, and ammunition in the Hubbard building had exploded and added to the confusion and noise.

The highway paralleling the railroad into Jacksonville was

jammed with people leaving the city and with additional fire-
fighting units that were coming in from other Florida cities.
Special trains with more troops inched along. Smoke and choking clouds of dust hung like a thick fog above the trees. Late
in the afternoon, weary from sleeplessness and lack of food,
Broward arrived in the blackened city. A scene of waste, horror,
and devastation stretched before him wherever he looked. The
wide area between the St. Johns River and Hogan's Creek
had been completely destroyed. The houses, stores, and buildings which had formerly filled one hundred and forty-six city
blocks had burned. In a matter of a few hours, some twenty-
three hundred and sixty-eight buildings, valued at fifteen million dollars, had been consumed by the fire.[51]

Broward was unable to hire a buggy, so he walked from the
train toward East Jacksonville, where he hardly expected to
find his home still standing. The fire, however, had not burned
past Hogan's Creek, a body of water four blocks west of the
Broward property. Mrs. Broward's father, old Captain Douglass, who was living in the house while the family was in
Tallahassee, had saved the house by using wet blankets and
quilts to beat out falling sparks and cinders carried by the
wind.[52]

Late that evening Broward conferred with city officials and
was informed that seven persons had lost their lives and that
nearly ten thousand people had been left homeless and without food; many of them had saved nothing except the clothing
they wore. All city records, except a few tax reports, marriage licenses, and wills were destroyed. Broward knew that
Dr. L'Engle's bank had been in the path of the fire, and he
heard how two cashiers had taken the money from the vaults
and loaded it in a rowboat. They had rowed out into the river
and guarded the craft with their shotguns.[53]

Broward remained in Jacksonville for two days helping to
organize the Citizens' Relief Association, a civic group which
distributed food and clothing to the destitute. He donated
many of Mrs. Broward's sheets and linens to the association.

As important bills were pending in the legislature, Broward felt compelled to return to Tallahassee. He was present for roll call on May 7.[54]

Late in May, Broward introduced in the House a memorial to Congress requesting "an appropriation for the refunding to the County of Duval . . . the sum of three hundred thousand dollars, the amount expended by said County in the improvement of the navigable waters of the St. Johns River and for which bonds of said County are now outstanding, said moneys so appropriated to be used for the purpose of supplying free public school buildings in place of those destroyed by fire May 3, 1901."[55] This proposal was heartily endorsed by Jacksonville's hard-pressed citizens, and Broward was warmly praised in an editorial printed in the *Jacksonville Metropolis*.[56] The memorial received a favorable vote in both Houses and was approved by Governor Jennings on May 31.[57]

Of the many measures passed during the legislative session of 1901, few were more important or had more repercussions in Florida politics than the Primary Election Law.[58] Since the end of Reconstruction in 1876, a growing sentiment had demanded laws which would establish a general primary system in Florida. Probably the greatest complaint against conventions which determined the party's candidates grew out of a belief that they were controlled by political cliques and rings. The basis for this grievance became apparent to Broward when he reviewed proceedings of the state conventions in which former Governors Edward Perry, Francis Fleming, Henry Mitchell, and William Bloxham had received the Democratic nomination.

Another strong argument for the primary involved opposition to voting by Negroes. In such counties as Monroe, where primaries were already being used, Democratic committees formulated the rules governing elections. They were always careful to include a provision generally limiting the qualified voters to "whites only." The advocates of the primary election system, including Napoleon Broward, argued that with Negroes excluded by party rule from the primaries, nominations would be practically tantamount to election. Party statistics had revealed that many Negro voters did not ordinarily participate in the general elections. Conservatives and liberals throughout the South opposed each other on many political issues, but they joined hands in trying to preserve white supremacy and Democratic rule. When Florida liberals thundered for railroad-corporation regulation, antitrust legislation, and a wider participation in government by the common people, their program did not envision racial tolerance or political equality for the Negro in the state. The gifts of Jeffersonian democracy were to be accorded only to the white population.

The Florida Democratic platform of 1900 had pledged that all state, county, and Congressional candidates would be nominated in white Democratic primaries.[59] Subsequently J. Emmett Wolfe, of Escambia County, introduced into the House of Representatives on April 19, 1901, House Bill No. 262, which was "an act to provide for and regulate the holding of Primary Elections."[60] A similar measure was introduced into the Senate. The speaker of the House and the president of the Senate appointed a joint committee, with Wolfe as its chairman, to consider the measure. When a weak substitute was reported to the House,[61] a bitter debate referred the measure back to the joint committee.[62] Reintroduced on May 17, it was still only a shadow of the original Wolfe bill. Broward, actively involved in debate over the measure, argued and voted against the amended bill because of its limitations and obvious bias. His efforts failed, and the substitute bill passed both Houses[63] and was signed into law by Governor Jennings on May 31.[64]

Broward later explained his stand on this substitute bill. To him it was an attenuated version of the original, cleverly designed to advance the interests opposed to an effective primary system. Broward wrote: "I was a member of that Legislature, and I was one of those who contended for the adoption of the primary election law as prepared by the committee ap-

pointed by the State Convention, but notwithstanding that
every member of that Legislature was elected as a Democrat,
and was bound by the platform, which pledged the honor of
the party 'to the carrying out of the same to the full extent that
the united strength of the party in the State may render possible,' sufficient influence was brought to bear upon the
Legislature of 1901, by men styling themselves Democrats, together with some other members who object to some of the
features of the bill, to compass the defeat of the bill presented
by the committee; which provided against fraud, bribery and
intimidation and other vicious influences, and the primary law
finally adopted was the most that could be obtained at that
time."[65]

The law, though far from perfect, set up the primary election system. Its main defect was that it failed to prevent many
corrupt voting practices. The earlier Primary Act of 1897 had
provided only for nomination by a plurality; the new law
required that a second primary be held for those offices in
which candidates had not received a majority. The Act of
1901 also authorized the nomination in Democratic primaries
of state officers, congressmen, and all elective officials in the
counties.[66]

The first state-wide primary in Florida was held in 1902.
Despite Broward's disappointment in the law, the system
worked well in its first trial. Nevertheless, there were certain
obvious defects that would have to be remedied. During the
legislative session of 1903, those opposing the primary tried
to nullify its results, but their efforts failed. In fact, the act
was strengthened by new legislation regulating the method of
registration.[67] Broward, an active and able supporter of the
primary system, later indicted the legislators who had opposed
the law after 1903 and the corporation and railroad interests
which had fostered antagonism toward the act. His courageous
and outspoken support of a strong primary became a principal
factor after 1901 in bringing him prominently before the
people of Florida.

When the legislature adjourned on May 31, 1901, Broward and his family returned to Jacksonville. A week later, Governor Jennings announced that he had appointed Broward a member of the State Board of Health, and he signed an Executive Department Commission which he forwarded to Jacksonville on June 10, 1901.[68] Broward held this office until 1904.

After he returned from the legislature in 1901, Broward became more active in the Jacksonville Towing and Wrecking Company which he, his brother Montcalm, George DeCottes, and Harry Fozzard had organized during the latter part of 1897.[69] In September, 1901, the company decided to salvage the schooner *Biscayne*, which had been wrecked months before near the French Reefs, midway between Key West and Miami. In November Broward ordered the *Salvo* loaded with heavy wrecking equipment and proceeded with her down the coast. He remained only a few days, leaving operations temporarily in charge of Alex Douglass, Mrs. Broward's brother. In February, 1902, Broward moved his family and Mrs. Broward's sister, Elsie, to south Florida so that he would not be separated from them while he worked at French Reefs. Closing their Jacksonville home, the Browards sailed on the *Admiral Dewey*. After two weeks in Miami, the family moved to Key West. They thought it would be a matter of only a few weeks before they would return to Jacksonville, so they lived in the Jefferson Hotel, the "only clean hotel in town." The hotel did not serve meals, and the Browards ate in a restaurant across the street. This proved inconvenient, and Mrs. Broward rented the Pendleton house, a large, sprawling structure at "Barracks Beach."[70]

The only furniture that the family had brought to Key West was Mrs. Broward's sewing machine, so they purchased beds, chairs, a stove, and a huge dining table from a local merchant. After Mrs. Broward had rented a piano for the cavernous room on the lower floor, the girls immediately dubbed it "the ballroom." On rainy days the girls played there, and frequently Elsie Douglass and Dorcas invited their friends over in the evening for informal dances and parties. A huge old barn located in the back yard became a pirate's cove for the little girls. They swam and fished, and when old Beauregard, a Negro who worked on the *Three Friends,* was around the place, he took them rowing.[71] During the winter months the children were enrolled in the Convent school. In addition, Dorcas and Josephine attended special art classes supervised by the nuns.[72] There was little social activity in Key West at that time, but the Browards made friends with most of the American families and with many of the Cubans, who regarded Napoleon Broward, the filibuster, as a heroic figure.

These were busy months for Broward. He had intended to move his family back to Jacksonville as soon as the *Biscayne* was salvaged, but he postponed their departure so that he could supervise the raising of a French bark loaded with mahogany, which had sunk during a storm near Alligator Key.[73] The Browards finally returned to Jacksonville late in August, 1903. The house was reopened, and the following month the children were registered in school. Thereafter, Jacksonville was home to the family of the rising liberal Democrat.

⌒I2⌒

The Battle of the Giants

PRECISELY HOW AND WHEN the ambition to attain high political office became a self-admitted aim of Broward cannot be stated definitely. He was obviously political-minded, and although he devoted himself extensively to business activities, a desire for public office was evident throughout his later life.

His decision to enter the race for the governorship was probably reached in the early spring of 1903. Shortly after he had moved his family back to Jacksonville from Key West, Broward informed his wife that several politically important persons in Florida were urging him to announce his candidacy. He realized that to do so would require a long and hard campaign which would keep him away from home for weeks at a time. There was also the problem of financial backing. Broward was far from wealthy, and demands for money came often, for his family was large and his generosity well known. His papers reveal that he was frequently hard pressed for funds and that sometimes he found it difficult to repay even small loans when they fell due, though they were always finally paid. A gubernatorial campaign would be expensive, and Broward carefully considered his financial situation before making a decision.

He talked with Mrs. Broward several times about the advantages and disadvantages of being a candidate. One morning, seated at the breakfast table, he noted something in his morning newspaper that recalled his conference of the previous evening with a group of Democratic leaders from Tallahassee. Suddenly pushing back his chair, he walked over to the window and watched his daughters as they played with their dolls on the side porch. He began speaking quietly, and for a moment Mrs. Broward thought he was talking to himself.

"I am comparatively unknown in the state. I will have to travel up and down, to city, town, and village, to acquaint the people with the issues for which I stand."

Mrs. Broward realized then that her husband's decision was made; he would be a candidate; nevertheless, he wanted her reassurance. Many times Annie Broward had rehearsed this scene in her mind. Now the moment was here. She walked over and took his hand.

"Do you think you can win, Napoleon?" she asked. "The forces fighting you will be great. The cities, Flagler's papers, railroad money—all will be thrown in the race against you. Those are tremendous odds."

Broward's answer was confident: "I don't intend to go after the cities. Their newspapers are against me and they don't take me seriously. But I'm going to stump every crossroads village between Fernandina and Pensacola and talk to the farmers and the crackers and show them their top ends were meant to be used for something better than hatracks. I'm going to make 'em sit up and think. They won't mind mistakes in grammar if they find I'm talking horse sense."[1]

Before finally becoming a candidate, Broward suggested the names of other Florida liberals whom he thought qualified. He traveled through the state interviewing many of these men himself and looking for a leader in the battle against the railroads and corporations. During his campaign, he said: "Many people, including myself, tried industriously to persuade to become a candidate for Governor some one of the many whom we thought could and would define the issues, and whom we believed would make an active campaign; but failing in this, it was concluded that I should make the effort, hence my candidacy."[2]

The issues of the campaign of 1904 had been developing for several years, and had finally become clearly defined in the fierce party skirmishes during the administrations of Blox-

ham and Jennings. Skirmishing was now over; a bitter political battle was beginning. The time was ripe for a "Broward"
in Florida. Governor Jennings, by his middle-of-the-road
liberalism, set the stage for this chief actor. The role of Napoleon Broward was an all-important one in Florida's liberal
movement; he gave it direction, leadership, and a name—
"The Broward Era."

Broward made a series of speeches throughout the state during the latter part of 1903, and while he talked as though he
were already in the race, he refused to announce his candidacy
officially. As a result, the newspapers continued to speculate
up to the time of his announcement. Early in December, 1903,
the following headline appeared in the *Jacksonville Metropolis*:
NAPOLEON B. BROWARD MAY RUN FOR GOV-
ERNOR. The news story stated emphatically that Broward
had "no superior as a campaigner. He is one of the 'wool hat
boys,' and when he takes to the woods he usually does most
effective work. He is not one of the high-faluting spread eagle
kind of orators but he is an entertaining talker on the stump.
Broward is a Florida 'Cracker.' "[3]

Continuing the speculation about Broward's candidacy, the
editor of the *Tampa Herald* wrote: "Mr. Broward is a strong,
forcible man and is well and favorably known in all sections
of the State. This fact makes talk of his candidacy of the
deepest moment. Few men possess his ability and qualifications for campaigning, together with the very best of executive and business ability. From Key West to the Georgia line
there is a strong pressure being brought to bear upon him to
enter the race, and much interest will be manifested until he
gives a definite answer, one way or another. Mr. Broward, it
would appear, still remains a quantity that must be reckoned
with, if public sentiment counts for anything, and it generally
does in a State campaign."[4]

By December, 1903, Congressman Robert W. Davis, C. M.
Brown, and Dannitte H. Mays had entered the gubernatorial
contest, but Broward was still waiting for the propitious

moment before making his formal announcement. It was a
certainty that he would be a candidate, particularly after his
friends and political allies—John N. C. Stockton and John M.
Barrs—revealed that they were candidates for seats in the
United States Senate and the House of Representatives, respectively.

On December 22, 1903, the following news items was
printed in the *Ocala Banner*:

A prominent citizen of Putnam county, in conversation with
some friends at a Jacksonville hotel a few evenings ago, related the substance of a colloquy which occurred during Mr.
J. N. C. Stockton's recent visit to the county. That gentleman
was inquiring of citizens whom he met there how many votes
he would probably get in a county. In reply he was told that
he might have got a good many, perhaps, if he had not been
instrumental in bringing out Mr. Broward as a candidate for
governor against Mr. Davis of Putnam county. Mr. Stockton
immediately made a most emphatic and vehement denial that
he or his friends had had anything to do with bringing Mr.
Broward out as a candidate for governor, and positively
asserted that it was done by Governor Jennings or his friends
as a movement against himself—Stockton—so that they might
say in the campaign that the Jacksonville "Three Friends"—
meaning Stockton, Broward and Barrs—were seeking to corral
all of the choice offices in sight.[5]

Liberals throughout Florida could not help questioning the
accuracy of this alleged Stockton statement. It appeared obvious that it was an early thrust at Broward and a definite
attempt to split his support by diverting public attention away
from the real issues. It is unlikely that John N. C. Stockton
would have cherished such feelings against Broward, and it
is certain that he would not have voiced them in public. As
a candidate for office, he was running on a progressive platform and was continuing his strong fight against the corporations and the railroads.

On January 4, 1904, Broward issued a statement to the press

in which he officially announced that he was in the race.[6] The lines were already drawn for a long, hard, and bitter campaign—one of the most heated gubernatorial contests in Florida's political history, and certainly one of the most picturesque. Broward depended for his support largely upon the farmer and cattleman in the rural areas, and the small businessman and laborer in the cities. These groups, however, did not comprise all his supporters: in his campaign he planned to stand firmly on those principles which would appeal to all the common people of Florida. For them he would lead a fight against the forces of corporate wealth and influence, so strongly entrenched in the state. He would crusade against the railroads and the political abuses which he believed they fostered. Broward became the pivotal figure in Florida's liberal movement and his battle for the people's cause was to be a long and fearful ordeal.

On the national political scene in 1904, the militant forces of Wall Street and Tammany Hall cooperated in wresting Democratic party leadership from William Jennings Bryan and succeeded in nominating Judge Alton B. Parker for the presidency. On the other hand, the Republican party bosses had accepted Theodore Roosevelt, who seemed to be willing to compromise his progressivism with the aspirations and wishes of Penrose, Platt, Crane, Harriman, and their associates. Although the nation seemed to be swinging back to conservatism, in Florida the groups who demanded reform were mobilizing and were preparing for a real offensive against the vested interests. The Broward Era was swinging into full action.

Broward was almost forty-seven years old when he began his campaign for the governorship. The years had dealt kindly with him, and he had developed into a striking and powerful figure, well over six feet in height. His dark face was full, and free of lines and wrinkles. Though there were traces of gray at his temples, the glints of red in his hair were as noticeable as ever. He wore a heavy and thick mustache, of the "walrus type" still fashionable in the early 1900's. Dressed in a dark mohair suit and wearing plain black shoes, Broward presented a dignified appearance on the speaker's platform. During the hot summer months he often wore a suit of white linen, but his shoes were usually black. A small white or black tie, and a wide-brimmed felt slouch hat, gray, tan, or black in color, completed his dress.[7]

On October 20, 1903, several months before he was officially in the gubernatorial race, Broward had announced in a speech at Fort Pierce that if he were ever elected governor, he would be the representative of all the people and not of the privileged few. He appealed to the small independent retailer when he said that "a hundred stores are better than one. If trusts are permitted to control we shall become a country of paupers and beggars."[8] In all his talks he reaffirmed his unequivocal support of the Railroad Commission and the primary election law. Closing his Fort Pierce speech dramatically, he declared that "the ballots should be as pure as snow-flakes; they must fall quietly and silently, until they represent the sovereign will of the great majority."[9] He spoke in Clearwater on November 14, and in Tampa two days later. The *Florida Times-Union* reported that in Tampa he was "not impassioned and he talks in a quiet unassuming manner."[10] In Plant City, on November 17, he made his first attack on Robert W. Davis, whom he recognized as the railroad-corporation candidate. Broward accused the railroads of backing Davis because the latter promised to repeal the primary law.[11]

Although Davis, Mays, and Brown were in the race, it was generally conceded that the battle was between Davis and Broward. Davis felt that his background and his professional and political experience had ably equipped him for the high office of governor which he sought. A native of Lee County, Georgia, he had moved to Florida with his family in 1879, and had settled in Green Cove Springs. In 1884 he had been elected to the state legislature, and the following year he had become speaker of the House.[12] During the campaign of 1904, Broward consistently reviewed the past railroad affiliations

Napoleon Bonaparte Broward

and activities of his opponent. In his "Open Letter as Candidate for Governor," Broward wrote:

During that session of the Legislature [1885] he [Davis] so impressed himself upon the representatives of the Railroad Corporation that immediately after its adjournment, he . . . located at Palatka, the headquarters of the Florida Southern Railroad Co., to be the general counsel of that company under the presidency of Sherman Conant. He appeared at the St. Augustine Democratic State Convention, three years after, as the pronounced choice for Governor of the land grant railroads of the State, which had obtained land grants aggregating many millions of acres of the State's best lands. . . . I remember that a special train load of his shouters were brought to that convention, but that fact injured his chances. He subsequently appeared before the Trustees of the Internal Improvement Fund as counsel for the railroads and obtained for them large amounts of land. From that time, until his election to Congress he was never out of their employ, and ever their faithful attorney, appearing one day . . . in Tallahassee before one State Board to urge the conveyance of lands to the railroads on the grounds that the railroad[s] had cost the stockholders a vast amount of money and were very valuable, and later the same day, appeared before another Board in the same Capitol building to urge a reduction of the tax assessments on the ground that the railroad was not so very valuable after all.[13]

Broward further claimed that the activities of Davis in Congress had been influenced by his railroad connections ever since he had been elected in 1896 to represent the Second District.[14] Broward and his supporters frequently called Davis "Our Bob" to illustrate the alleged control that the railroads exerted over the congressman.

In this same open letter, Broward reviewed the political record of Dannitte H. Mays and pointed out that in the legislative session of 1891 Mays had represented Jefferson County. Broward argued that when the legislators were bitterly disputing the issue of Wilkinson Call's re-election to the United

States Senate during that session in 1891, "Mr. Mays voted once for Senator Call, then permitted the railroad forces to use his name as a candidate, to prevent Senator Call's election. He continued to do this for several weeks, until Senator Call was elected without his vote. . . ." Broward reminded the voters of Florida that during the Call-Chipley fight in 1897, Mays was speaker of the house, and "did not vote for Senator Call, but for a gentleman who was the Vice-President of the Louisville and Nashville Railroad. He continued to vote for him against Hon. J. N. C. Stockton and Hon. S. R. Mallory, both of whom were candidates of the people. . . ."[15] Thus did Broward dispose of D. H. Mays and his candidacy. Throughout his campaign Broward paid relatively little attention to Mays, and did not consider him a dangerous contender. His fight was with Robert W. Davis and the interests that Davis represented.

The threat of C. M. Brown's candidacy was smaller still. His campaign tactics developed into a mere presentation of his Confederate army record. After reading the platform which Brown issued, both Broward and Davis decided he was a weak opponent and a negligible threat. In evolving a platform, Brown obviously sought votes from the economic and social groups in Florida that were supporting Broward. A typical campaign poster issued by Brown read:

C. M. Brown
The People's Candidate
—For—
Governor of Florida
56 years a citizen of this State
A soldier under General R. E. Lee from the
First to Last
A Friend to the People
HIS PLATFORM

The farming and laboring men his first consideration. Liberal Pensions, Liberal School Policy, the Primary, the Railroad

Commission, Hard Road, Economical Administration, Payment of State Debts. Regulation of Criminals, Corporations and Trusts.[16]

During the campaign, Broward and Davis worked hard for the rural vote, each boasting of the years he had spent on the farm in his youth. Broward, as part of his campaign literature, published his *Autobiographical Sketch*. The conservatives immediately recognized the readable pamphlet as a shrewd political device aimed at securing the "backwoods" vote. Hoping to curtail its effect on the voters, Davis often dealt satirically with Broward's description of the hard times that he and his family had suffered after the Civil War when they returned to Duval County from White Springs.

Davis told a large audience in Lake City how Broward "planted four sacks of Irish potatoes, which produced one," and jeeringly remarked, "Think of it, that big, strapping Napoleon Broward planting four sacks of potatoes and only getting back one. Why, when I was a farmer's lad, I planted four sacks of potatoes and they produced twenty. See how much smarter I was."[17] A few weeks later in Gainesville, Davis tried to convince his listeners that Broward was a poor farmer if he allowed a fallen tree to destroy part of his fence and let the cattle come in and eat his sugar cane. "I'll tell you, boys, a fellow who would lie in bed when he knows his fence is down and the cows are eating his cane is too lazy to be Governor of such a grand State as Florida."[18]

Broward continued his active campaign throughout the state, speaking at least once every day and on some days two or three times. He shook hands with hundreds of farmers, listened to songs by crowds of school children, and met and greeted the many "forgotten men" of Florida who gathered to hail him as the emerging man of the hour.[19] He spoke in St. Petersburg on November 20, and in Newberry three days later. After spending the Thanksgiving holiday in Jacksonville, Broward resumed his strenuous campaign. He traveled into every Florida county, speaking at political rallies, before civic groups, and to individual farmers, lumbermen, and fishermen. He traveled in dusty day coaches and rickety buggies, rode on horseback, and, when necessary, walked to the more isolated communities.

During the campaign, Broward's supporters praised him as an anti-corporate crusader; his enemies damned him as a demagogue, a radical, and a hothead. He had no greater foes than the railroad-owned and controlled Florida newspapers in which he was frequently satirized in biting cartoons, ridiculed in news articles, and denounced in editorials. In December, 1903, the "Three Friends"—Broward, Barrs, and Stockton—were cartooned in the *Florida Times-Union* in a drawing which depicted a large blazing yuletide fireplace. Three shafts of light from the fire lay across the floor and were labeled "early primary," "demagogism," and "campaign chestnuts."[20] After Broward, Barrs, and Stockton had thrown their hats into the political ring, the conservative press, in reporting news of the campaign, caustically referred to them as the "Three Friends."

By January, 1904, John N. C. Stockton, William S. Jennings, and James P. Taliaferro, the incumbent, had announced that they were candidates for the nomination for United States Senator. For the Second District Congressional nomination, John M. Barrs opposed Frank Clark, and the two men launched a campaign in which insulting accusations became common.[21] In one speech, Barrs told Clark: "While you were in Oklahoma [Clark lived in the Oklahoma Territory for a time between 1901 and 1904] you wrote J. R. Parrott, vice-president of the Florida East Coast Railway, and told him that if his road did not put up your campaign expenses for the Congressional race of 1904, you were going to expose some things you knew about the road and its methods."[22] Clark answered these statements with a stinging indictment of the dealings that Barrs supposedly had with certain corporations. He claimed that Barrs, while city attorney in Jacksonville, had signed an agreement on March 16, 1900, with the Atlantic, Valdosta and Western Railroad, which gave the railroad a municipal franchise to operate a city transportation system in the area south of Bay Street and on other Jacksonville streets. In return, Barrs allegedly received 25 per cent of the stock in the new company.[23]

Claude L'Engle, then the editor of the *Florida Sun and Labor Journal*,[24] published these verses denouncing Barrs for signing this contract:

There was a young attorney, and his name was J. M. Barrs;
He had a rank aversion to the railroads and the cars,
He was the city's lawyer, and he ran the whole machine
In the interest of the people (?) Did he think the people green?

He advised the city council and the board of public works,
He got on to their secrets and he knew their little quirks.
They found him indispensable and they kept him in his place;
And he ran the whole department with an air of careless grace.

It was easy—oh, so easy!
The job was not enough to fill his day,
It looked easy—oh, so easy!
When everything seemed coming Murdoch's way.

Then came a Georgia railroad that was engineered by Long,
Who wanted all the city for the singing of a song.
So he sized the situation, and he called on Mr. Barrs,
The man who hated railroads and the running of the cars.

It was easy . . . for Long and Barrs to make their deal;
It was a secret . . . the whole of which they would not reveal.

Said Long, "We'll run down through the streets and parallel
the bay.
We'll take what is least valuable (?) and be out of the way.
And just to satisfy you, Barrs, that railroads are no sin;
We'll give you twenty-five percent of all that we take in."

. . . Oh, it was easy!
For twenty-five percent seemed lots of tin;

It looked easy—oh, so easy!
And Long smiled to see the railroads win.

It had seemed easy—oh, so easy!
But Barrs says he never got the mon,
Oh, the pity! Ah, the pity,
Say, Murdoch, did you do it just for fun?[25]

When Clark was bluntly accused of being a drunkard, his friends defended him. They admitted that at one time in his life he might have imbibed too freely, but they pointed out that he had overcome his weakness. Self-mastery, they claimed, was an invaluable qualification for a congressman.[26]

The senatorial race was as heated as were the Congressional and gubernatorial contests. Violent charges were hurled back and forth, past records of candidates were denounced, and muckraking became the order of the day. James P. Taliaferro had wealth, prestige, influence, and a record of having already served five years in the Senate. Supported by Florida's leading newspapers—the *Florida Times-Union*, the *Tampa Tribune*, the *Miami Metropolis*, and the *Pensacola News*—he had a great advantage over Jennings and Stockton and looked unbeatable.[27]

Jennings depended upon his record as governor to win the nomination. He had been an able governor and his record appeared to be clean, but as a vote-getter he lacked the necessary magnetism and personality. His success in 1900 was based chiefly on the desire of the people for a reform leader, and on the fact that he more nearly met the qualification than any other candidate in the race. Stockton, well educated and well liked, had many years of political experience. He, too, lacked personal magnetism, but he had ability as a rough-and-tumble political fighter and was known as a "vote-go-getter." The voters were inclined to regard Stockton as a more sincere liberal than Jennings, and in an era of revolt and reform this was considered a definite advantage. Regardless of their platforms and their party affiliations, none of the candidates possessed a personality so warm and so appealing to the "common folk" of Florida as did Napoleon Broward.

Surveying the field of candidates, the *Florida Times-Union* editorialized on "The Campaign in Florida" as follows: "Whether Messrs. Stockton and Jennings and Broward and Barrs are still running for their money or not, the tide sets away from them, and their sands of ambition and aspiration grow dry and white under the fierce blaze of truth. Their charges have been commended to their own lips and turn into Dead Sea fruits to the taste—to ashes and wormwood."[28]

These denunciations and incriminations were brushed off by Broward as he continued his campaign. Unhesitatingly he preached his doctrine of government to men and women— young and old—at every crossroad and in every hamlet and backwoods village he could reach. In words that his audiences could easily understand, he urged a "pure State government, freed from the seductive and enslaving power of corporate interests," and he advised the people "to take advantage of the opportunity offered by the primary, and place power in themselves instead of in the corporations."[29] He charged that "the railroads are draining the people instead of the swamps and the representatives of the people in [the] halls of Congress and Tallahassee are responsible for such conditions."[30]

A vital issue in the campaign was Everglades drainage, which had come to the forefront during the administration of Governor Jennings. Broward inherited this issue at the outset of his contest for the governorship and made its endorsement a major plank in his platform. The railroad and canal companies bitterly fought the drainage program, and Broward, standing squarely against the corporate interests, naturally encountered their animosity. From the beginning of his campaign, Broward fearlessly met the well-planned attacks which the railroads and corporations made on drainage. Armed with graphs, pictures, and a large map of the Everglades area, he spoke throughout Florida about drainage. His map explained in detail the basic features of the reclamation

program. Known as "Broward's map," it was often referred
to humorously in newspapers supporting him, particularly
those published in the rural areas. The opposition was out-
raged over the map, and it became an object of severe satire
and sarcasm in the "Davis" press. Broward visualized great
public benefits to be derived from the drainage of the Everglades—"lands salvaged to men who wanted to build homes,
plant crops and tap the wealth of the fabulous muck."[31]
Sometimes when Broward became hard pressed in a drainage
argument, he took refuge in one of his famous phrases—
"Water will run down hill!" Broward argued that the people
of Florida should "knock a hole in a wall of coral and let a
body of water obey a natural law and seek the level of the
sea. . . ." His favorable attitude toward Everglades drainage
was a principal reason why Governor Jennings supported him
during the political campaign. Jennings knew that Broward
would continue the gigantic task laid out in the drainage program.

Davis and his supporters did not limit their ridicule to
"Broward's map," but included all his activities and much of
his program. For instance, after Broward had issued his
Autobiographical Sketch, the *Florida Times-Union* described
its author as "a man who can write history as intelligently with
his toes as he can with both hands and Barrs' assistance."[32]
A cartoon in the same paper depicted Broward as a huge goose
walking through a lane of signs which read "Our Bob for
the Governorship." Underneath the cartoon appeared these
verses:

> *Goosey Goosey Gander,*
> *Where do you wander?*
> *In fact, where are you at?*
> *If you can't see the "signs of the times,"*
> *You are certainly as*
> *"Blind as a Bat."*[33]

Jacksonville's other newspaper, the *Jacksonville Metropolis*,
remained neutral on the gubernatorial race during the early

part of the campaign. Prior to the first primary, the editorial policy of the *Metropolis* was announced: "We are not the party, neither the head nor the tail of the party. We are simply Democrats and we do not believe we have a right, as a rule, at any rate, to decide between Democrats who shall or shall not hold office."[34] The attitude of this paper changed drastically before the second primary, when William Ringwood Carter, editor in chief, openly began to oppose Broward and to support Davis. William Wallace Douglass, city editor, supported Broward privately, but there was little that he could do for his candidate in the columns of the *Metropolis* against the expressed orders of Editor Carter.[35]

Many Florida newspapers treated Broward's candidacy as more or less a joke until they realized how strong his support was in the rural areas of the state. They could not disregard Broward, but in their opinion, Davis was too strong an opponent to be defeated. Despite the popular appeal of Broward's platform, many Jacksonville citizens refused to take his chances of success seriously. They had frequently supported him in city politics, but now that he was seeking the highest state office, they felt that a former "farm boy and deck hand with no schooling" could not represent them ably as governor.[36] Many people who liked Broward's platform voted for Davis because they were so sure Broward could not be elected.

In appearance and personality, Broward was unlike his opponent. He always dressed well and presented a dignified appearance, but he lacked Davis' suavity. Hoping to secure a major share of the rural vote, Broward accentuated the belief that he was a "man of the people," in political ideas as well as in dress and habit. It was said that Davis, a smooth politician, "could fit into any group at any time and would always be welcome." An eloquent and entertaining speaker, he carried his audiences with him. Nevertheless, when Davis tried to channel the farm vote away from his opponent he was not successful.

Broward continued energetically on his way. In March he

spoke before dozens of groups all through west Florida, and
returned to the central part of the state to make talks in Sanford, Orlando, and Kissimmee. By the middle of April he
had appeared at meetings in Leesburg, Ocala, Gainesville,
Starke, Lake Butler, Jasper, Inverness, and Bartow. As he
was well-nigh exhausted from waging such a strenuous campaign, his doctor persuaded him to rest for several days at his
home in Jacksonville.[37] On April 25 he was about again,
stumping south Florida and the Gulf Coast area. In Tampa
on May 5, before a crowd of five thousand, he charged that
Davis was planning to give away more state lands to railroads if he were elected governor.[38] Two days later, in Orlando, he announced that "it is not enough to say of a candidate
for Governor that he was honest. He must be one of the
people."[39] He tried to prove that the conservative faction in
the Democratic party in the state was in reality a division of
the Republican party. He hoped to forewarn his listeners when
he recalled the following plank which had been written into
the Democratic platform in 1900:

We warn the people that an attempt is being systematically
made by avowed Republicans, through the connivance and cooperation of persons claiming to be Democrats, to subsidize
the press of Florida for the purpose of teaching Democrats
false doctrines, and of keeping at the front, under the guise
of Democracy, men as leaders of Democracy who will be sub-
servient to trust magnates, and who will, under the pretense
of conservatism, attempt to instill Republican doctrines and
oppose the principles of true Democracy. Such newspapers
should, under no circumstances, be given any patronage controlled by officers elected by the Democratic party. This insidious attempt to corrupt the Democracy through the medium
of newspapers claiming to be Democratic must be thwarted
in every way. Subserviency to Republican influences of any
sort is incompatible with true Democracy, and should receive
no encouragement from Democrats. Avowed Republicanism is
infinitely more tolerable to true Democrats.[40]

On some issues Broward and Davis agreed. When Broward announced that he believed "in a longer school term for the children attending our free schools, and . . . liberal appropriations for our colleges," he received no protest from the conservatives. Davis endorsed Broward when the latter declared that "the patriotic service and self-sacrifice of our soldiers and sailors in the Civil War, should guarantee to the deserving needy ones, or their widows, such reasonable pensions as an appreciative people are ever ready to pay."[41] Conservatives, as well as liberals, saw the worth of the plank in Broward's platform which asked for the "passage of such laws as will best tend to the improvement of our system of public roads, hard surface or otherwise, as may be most practicable. As automobiles cost little more now than a good horse and buggy, or horse and wagon, it is to be hoped that our people in the country, will, in the near future, find it easier to cover distances to the school houses, and make near neighbors, in point of time, even of those living many miles apart."[42]

Broward found the larger cities of Florida, including Jacksonville, generally cold to his candidacy. But the small-town folk and country people were enthusiastic, and accepted him as their leader and spokesman. The prediction of a Madison newspaper was typical: "We are not a prophet nor the son of a prophet, but when the count of the ballots on May 10th is completed, we predict that it will be found that Broward has received a few."[43] A report from Brooksville was similar: "It can be truthfully said that while Mr. Broward is practically a stranger here, he left a splendid impression on the minds of the people and no doubt made many friends, if not several votes."[44] And again from Brooksville: ". . . his straightforward talk, convinced a great many that he was the man who should be Governor. Where he had none, he now has enthusiastic supporters, and we would not be surprised if he carried Hernando County."[45]

A rally in Jacksonville on May 9, the evening before the first primary, climaxed the campaign. The meeting was

scheduled to be held on Laura Street near the river, and the
high point of the program would be the talks by Davis and
Broward. About six o'clock in the evening, the river shore and
surrounding streets began filling up with men, women, and
children. They sat on curbstones and on crude wooden benches
under trees scarred by the great fire. A large wooden platform, decorated with American and state flags, awaited the
speakers. Strings of electric lights crisscrossed the area, flicker-
ing feebly in the gathering dusk.

As the people assembled, the Davis supporters conducted
a spirited demonstration. A loosely organized group, mainly
composed of teen-age boys carrying placards and banners,
marched up and down the streets. Pushing through the crowd,
they sang popular campaign songs, hallooed to friends they
recognized, and demanded that everybody vote for their candidate. There were several small bands, each playing a different song, which added to the noise and turmoil.

By eight o'clock Davis, his campaign managers, and some
of the other candidates were seated on the platform. Broward,
who had not arrived, was in East Jacksonville with his supporters, who were holding a mammoth torchlight parade.
The cadenced notes of music mingled with shouts as they
marched down Bay Street, and in a few minutes solid ranks
of men, chanting Broward's praises, joined the large throng.
Dressed in a cream-colored linen suit, and a wide-brimmed
tan hat, Broward rode in the first carriage. Alighting briskly,
he walked onto the platform, shook hands with everybody,
and held his right hand up to the crowd. Waiting to be introduced, he stood facing the noisy audience. At first his voice
was quiet, but it had a confident ring as he reviewed his stand
on the Railroad Commission, the primary election law, Everglades drainage, and public schools. As he began to sense that
many in the audience liked what he was saying, his voice became louder, and in strong tones he reiterated his determination to thwart railroad-corporation influence in Florida, and
outlined his plans for instituting a series of reforms that would

make government more democratic. Throughout his talk, his supporters punctuated his remarks with claps, yells, and howls. There were loud cheers when he dramatically warned the audience to beware of his opponent's alliance with "land pirates and purchased newspapers." Several fights broke out in the crowd as Davis and Broward men taunted each other, and when Broward at last sat down, thunderous applause vied with resounding jeers. Cowbells clanked, whistles shrieked, and the bands played louder than ever.

When Davis was introduced, the clamor became even louder and more discordant, and seemed to churn up the whole river area with its fury. When huge banners carrying Davis' picture were hoisted above the crowd, his adherents shouted their approval. Davis quieted his audience, and had just begun outlining his program when the raucous whistle of a boat on the river drowned out his voice. It was the whistle of the *Three Friends*, which had moved unnoticed to the Laura Street dock and tied up. Her captain was primed to start blowing the whistle when Davis began talking. The blasts continued. Realizing that he was talking to people who could not hear him, Davis waved his great arms, and his face reddened with anger as he tried to shout above the confusion. His efforts failed, and the meeting broke up. Followers of Davis and Broward moved among the crowd and passed out cigars, political cards, and campaign literature. A great cheer greeted the promises of both factions that they would distribute beer on election night.[46]

Voting was quiet on election day. All day large groups of voters lined up outside polling places throughout the state, and a record vote was predicted. Everybody waited impatiently for an announcement of the outcome of the election, but it was two days before a substantial number of election returns were tabulated. By May 12 incomplete returns were in from twenty-five counties. Davis led, with Broward running a close second. Then the rural vote was counted, and it put Broward ahead by a small margin. The *Jacksonville Metropolis* car-

The Battle of the Giants 197

ried these large headlines: BROWARD'S RACE PROVES A SURPRISE TO EVERYBODY. SECURES GREAT STRENGTH FROM UNEXPECTED S O U R C E S THROUGHOUT THE STATE.[47] Davis carried Duval County with a total of 2,058 votes to the 1,065 for Broward. Broward lost his own ward in Jacksonville by a vote of 121 to 91. In the official canvass for the state, 13,247 votes were tabulated for Broward and 13,020 for Davis. Brown and Mays received a light vote in comparison with that of the two leading contenders.[48]

Broward carried eighteen counties—Calhoun, Clay, Columbia, Hamilton, Hernando, Hillsborough, Holmes, Jackson, Lafayette, Levy, Liberty, Madison, Manatee, Monroe, Pasco, Santa Rosa, Taylor, and Washington. These west- and middle-Florida counties contained a substantial rural and small-town vote. Davis captured eleven counties—Alachua, Dade, Duval, Franklin, Nassau, Orange, Osceola, Putnam, St. Johns, Sumter, and Volusia. Brown carried Baker, Bradford, Brevard, Gadsden, Lake, Lee, Marion, Wakulla, and Walton counties. Mays was successful in Citrus, DeSoto, Escambia, Jefferson, Leon, Polk, and Suwannee counties.[49]

Davis and Broward were scheduled to battle again in the runoff primary. Stockton and Taliaferro in the race for United States Senator, and Barrs and Clark for nomination to Congress also went into the second primary. This campaign brought several changes in political alignment. After his defeat for the Senate nomination, Governor Jennings supported Broward even more strongly, much to the chagrin of many conservative newspapers backing Davis. On the other hand, both Brown and Mays asked their supporters to vote for Davis in the runoff.

There was also a change in the attitude of some Florida newspapers. The *Belleville News Letter*, which had supported Brown, became a Davis paper. The *DeSoto County Advertiser*, the *DeSoto County News*, and the *Palmetto News*, which formerly endorsed Mays, came out for Davis. The *Pensacola*

Journal, the *Polk County Advocate,* and the *Lakeland News,* which had supported Mays, endorsed Broward in the second primary.[50]

Davis' campaign managers, J. S. Hilburn, E. J. Fearnside, and E. S. Crill,[51] had not expected so close a race, and were greatly disturbed when the results were announced. They realized that it would be an arduous task to beat Broward, but they relied upon the fact that they had the money to defray campaign expenses, the support of Florida corporate and railroad interests, and the backing by most of the large state newspapers. With these weapons they were confident of final success.

~ 13 ~

A Crusader Becomes Governor

A S THE SPRING DAYS lengthened into summer, the gubernatorial campaign in Florida became more heated and bitter, and the mudslinging became increasingly violent. The opposing candidates and their supporters leveled ridiculous accusations and frantic denunciations at each other. The libels and insinuations were circulated on both sides and invited immediate retaliation. The newspapers throughout the state watched their circulation figures rise as they devoted their front-page columns to the impossible charges and countercharges.

Robert W. Davis and his campaign workers turned the whole force of their formidable attack upon Napoleon Broward, and everything out of the ordinary that he had ever done was hauled to the surface to be examined and disparaged. The *Punta Gorda Herald* bluntly described Broward as "a man without consistency, [and] without steadfastness."[1] The complaints which this newspaper detailed were frequently elaborated upon by Davis during the runoff campaign:

Mr. Broward is a man of but little ability and no intellectual brilliance whatever. . . . He was once sheriff of Duval County and his management of the office was so culpable that he was summarily removed by the Governor. In violation of the laws of the land, he ran filibustering expeditions to Cuba, and now has the assurance to boast of his lawlessness in the hope it will gain him voters. . . . He was sent to the Legislature from Duval County, and while there, was one of the most active advocates of the insanity divorce bill, whose passage a member of the Legislature openly charged was bought for $20,000. . . . Broward's activity in getting the bill passed helped to bring a great scandal upon the State. He denounces the trusts; and yet as a member of the Legislature, he secured the enactment of the Jacksonville Ferry Bill, which established the worst trust known in the State of Florida.[2]

The *Daily Tallahassean* also remembered Broward as sheriff of Duval County, and warned voters not to elect a man who "pulled off prize fights and overrode the law as Sheriff until Governor Mitchell had to remove him."[3] The editor of the *Tallahassean* declared emphatically that Broward dyed his mustache daily; a Pensacola paper boldly stated that he was an Apache Indian; and one of the south Florida newspapers said that he was a Catholic. Despite his long avowed advocacy of temperance, he was accused of being a "whiskeyhead" because he had voted for the dispensary bill when he was in the legislature in 1901. In a speech in Jacksonville, Broward answered these accusations and declared that the "whiskey-vote" had been cast for his opponent in the May primary. In his "Open Letter to Democratic Voters of Florida," published May 18, 1904, he reminded his accusers that he had never denied supporting the dispensary measure. He showed them, however, that the original bill had been "introduced by Hon. John P. Wall of Putnam County, a close friend and ardent supporter of and enthusiastic speechmaker for Hon. Robert W. Davis." Broward promised that if elected he "would not inspire, instigate, aid or counsel the passage of a dispensary bill" and he insisted that the "liquor question should be left to the several counties to settle themselves. Let each one decide whether it wants local option, temperance, open saloon, high license or what not."[4]

Not only was Broward accused of being intemperate and opposed to prohibition, but one newspaper charged, with strange logic, that he really favored railroads and corporations because, while in the legislature, he had voted to extend the charters of two Florida railroads.[5] To the liberals this was a curious indictment in view of the united stand that the railroad interests of Florida were making in their bitter fight to defeat Broward.

Meanwhile, Broward and his followers were not idle. In their speeches and statements to the newspapers they were equally vehement in their political and personal attacks on Davis. A major issue of which Broward made capital during the runoff concerned the use of "free passes" on railroads, an abuse long fostered by the carriers of the state. It was a common practice, usually after election time, for the transportation companies to extend free riding privileges to public officials on the several railroads running in and out of Florida. In 1904 Broward announced that Davis had received passes annually, while he was a member of Congress, because he allegedly supported the legislation which the carriers favored. Broward asked, "Why does he still receive free annual passes from the railroads? Is it for legal services, or is it because he is a member of Congress? If only as a Congressman, then what consideration does he give them as a Congressman?"[6]

When Davis failed to answer these inquiries, Broward stated that while his opponent was in Congress he had been specifically instructed "to work for passage of an act giving to the Inter-State Commerce Commission power to control inter-state freight rates and passenger fares."[7] He also asserted that if Davis had "ever introduced a bill, or made a speech, or been in any way active in advancing this measure so much antagonized by the great railroad corporations of this country, I have not heard of it. He at least has not antagonized them enough to prevent them from furnishing him with annual free passes, on which he rides free, while drawing from the United States Treasury twenty cents per mile for traveling between Palatka and Washington."[8]

Two vital issues—the Railroad Commission and the State Primary Law—had been widely discussed and debated in the first primary campaign and were argued still more bitterly in the runoff. Broward, who favored both agencies, fully explained his partisanship to the Florida voters. He wanted the powers of the Railroad Commission increased and strengthened, and he demanded that the state constitution be amended "so as to make our Railroad Commission a permanent part of our governmental system." He claimed that the carriers were not paying their just share of taxes and he promised the voters that he would "bring some mode of valuating the property of the transportation companies," so that "reasonable dividends," based "upon the value of the property," could be levied.[9] Broward tried to arouse the public mind to the fact that, in order to escape taxes, railroad officials had frequently falsified, in affidavits and under oath, the value of their roads. In a speech, made a few days before the election, he related how one "official swears that the railroad of his company is worth $1,300,000, then when he desires to get an injunction to prevent the Railroad Commission from managering a 3-cent per mile passenger rate, he swears that the railroad is worth $5,000,000. . . ."[10]

Meanwhile, the Davis forces used every political weapon available to secure additional support. Money to purchase space in daily and weekly newspapers and to print and distribute large quantities of campaign signs, handbills, and posters poured in a steady stream from their party coffers. A majority of the Florida papers, particularly those in the larger cities where there was wide circulation, supported the conservative candidate and his platform. These journals searched every activity in Broward's political career for campaign ammunition. Broward's family and friends, his removal as sheriff of Duval County, his filibustering activities, and his vote in favor of the "Flagler Divorce Bill" were publicized and castigated.

Broward's political associates, John N. C. Stockton and John M. Barrs, also came in for their share of abuse. The *Miami Metropolis* reasoned that the "Three Friends" had forced "the people into a second primary, just to prove to them that they are not 'it' but 'nit,' and it is to be hoped that the proof will be both satisfactory and sufficient."[11] A *Florida Times-Union* editorial insisted that the three candidates were "a personal and political trust, formed principally for the purpose of seeking to control the politics of a faction and to boost themselves in office. They make a common destiny of their political ambitions—endeavoring to use the people for their personal aggrandizement. They plan together, scheme together and work together, using the same purse for the same purpose—a political trust for the benefit only of the 'Three Friends.' "[12]

Broward's campaign managers, William James Bryan and Nathan P. Bryan, were often hard pushed to answer these thrusts and attacks that came from every direction. They were skilled politicians, however, and they turned many of the assaults to their own advantage. For instance, when the conservative forces organized a Davis-For-Governor Club in the Tampa area and sought to enlist as members those Spaniards who resented Broward because of his filibustering activities prior to the Spanish-American War, the Bryan brothers hastily formed a much stronger and more vocal Broward Club with Cubans from Ybor City as members. Similar tactics and countermaneuvers were brilliantly employed by the Bryans throughout the campaign.[13] They planned strategy, wrote speeches, supervised public relations, and in general contributed invaluable aid to the liberal cause of Florida. When funds were low, as they often were, they gave generously of their own money. Once they collected a legal fee of three thousand dollars from a case involving the Jacksonville Electric Company and spent all of it on Broward's campaign.[14]

Although his campaign was not so expensive as that of Davis, Broward spent a large amount of money. A moderate estimate placed his costs between ten and fifteen thousand dollars, most of which came either from his personal resources or from his friends, none of whom were wealthy.[15] Broward went into every county in Florida at least once, and in some instances several times, to present his program; consequently, his traveling expenses were considerable. In addition, he spent a considerable sum of money on campaign literature which he distributed generously wherever he spoke. His *Autobiograph-*

ical Sketch, which was printed in huge quantities, was widely read throughout the state, and helped to persuade many people that its author was a "real man of the people." By emphasizing his hard struggle after the Civil War, and omitting any mention of his planter background, Broward cleverly convinced the voters in 1904 that his origin was humble and that he could rightfully assume his place as a "dyed-in-the-wool Florida cracker." This belief, still held by many people today, was based entirely on Broward's *Autobiographical Sketch* and upon his campaign speeches. Fully realizing the influence that the booklet might have in the rural areas, the Davis press went to great lengths to ridicule it and insisted that Davis had not given away "tons of literature throughout the State as did his opponents."[16] One day, as Broward was riding on a train in south Florida, he noticed an elderly gentleman, seated across the aisle, reading the *Autobiographical Sketch*. The man seemed highly amused, and when Broward asked him why he was laughing, he pointed out several passages which he considered ludicrous. Broward's wry comment was, "Laugh at the book if you like, but that book is a vote maker. The part that you are laughing at was put in there to laugh at. That is all right. See if the book doesn't have its weight in the result."[17]

The campaigning continued with full force until the very day of the second primary. The Davis and Broward supporters berated each other in the last party rallies, and the newspapers on election day carried the final insults and smears. Denunciations and incriminations, promises and pledges rang in the ears of the voters as they trooped to the polls all over the state.

It was several days before the votes were tabulated. Early returns seemed to indicate a victory for Davis, but Broward gained steadily as votes from the smaller counties and the farming districts were reported. The executive committee met to canvass the returns on June 17, ten days after the election. The next day it announced that Napoleon B. Broward was the Democratic candidate for governor of Florida. He had re-

ceived 22,979 votes; and Davis, 22,265.[18] Broward's majority
was small, but the second primary victory was tantamount to
election. Thus a majority of 714 votes had won the election
for the liberals. Broward was successful in twenty-seven of
the forty-five counties—Baker, Citrus, Clay, Columbia, De-
Soto, Escambia, Gadsden, Hamilton, Hernando, Holmes,
Jackson, Jefferson, Lafayette, Lake, Levy, Liberty, Madison,
Marion, Nassau, Orange, Pasco, Polk, Santa Rosa, Sumter,
Taylor, Wakulla, and Washington.[19] Davis won in Alachua,
Bradford, Brevard, Calhoun, Dade, Duval, Franklin, Hillsborough, Lee, Leon, Manatee, Monroe, Osceola, Putnam,
St. Johns, Suwannee, Volusia, and Walton counties.[20] Mays
and Brown had tried to throw their first primary votes to
Davis. However, of the sixteen counties which supported them,
ten went for Broward and only six for Davis.[21] Broward lost
his home county of Duval again, and Hillsborough, which
voted for him in the first primary, switched to his rival in
the second.

In conceding defeat, Davis issued a statement to the press
in which he urged cooperation: "Let all dissatisfaction cease.
Let us now get together."[22] Newspapers that had bitterly opposed Broward during his campaign now came forward and
congratulated him. The *Florida Times-Union* was one of the
first to announce: "From this writing the *Times-Union* is
with the nominee of the Democratic party in his trials, trust-
ing all, believing all, hoping with the strength that is born
of utter faith in its party and the future of the State."[23] The
liberals did not take the pledge of the *Times-Union* seriously.
The editorial policy of the paper remained generally conservative, and within a few weeks after the inauguration the
editors were opposing Broward and his policies as vehemently
as ever.

The *Tallahassean*, accepting the inevitable but still bitter,
declared editorially: "Individual Democrats may deplore the
use of methods to bring about this result [Broward's election]
which were the direct result of glaring defects in the funda-

mental law governing primary elections, but no advantage can be gained by further resistance to a condition which will require some legislation and the holding of another primary or a convention to cure."[24] Earlier in the political battle, the *Jacksonville Metropolis* had printed a cartoon showing Broward as a little boy sitting on his nurse's lap, the nurse being William James Bryan, one of his campaign managers. Broward was crying for the moon, which was labeled "The Governorship," while Nurse Bryan soothed him and said, "All right, I'll try and get it for you, Tootsy Wootsy."[25] On June 18, when the results of the election were announced, the *Metropolis* printed another cartoon, depicting Broward as the same little boy, sitting on his nurse's lap and holding the "moon." The picture was captioned: "He Cried For the Moon and B'Gosh He Got It."[26]

Broward received hundreds of letters and telegrams from all parts of the state, many congratulatory, some denunciatory, and a great many from persons asking for favors or political appointments. One letter bluntly stated that its writer knew that "just a very small quantity of whiskey would make Davis drunk but Broward could take whiskey by the tumblerfull and one could not tell he'd taken any and that Broward keeps full of whiskey all the time."[27] A man who claimed he had succeeded in garnering for Broward all the votes in his community wrote and asked for a jug of corn liquor. He said, "I have promised all your friends to have it for them and I don't want to disappoint them. You know they will think you stingy if you don't send it. . . . Don't fail to send me about a gallon. A box of cigars would help along also."[28]

Neither M. B. Macfarlane, the Republican party's gubernatorial candidate, nor W. R. Healey, the Socialist party's nominee, constituted a serious threat to the Democrats. Nevertheless, Broward, through the office of the Democratic executive committee, announced a state-wide campaign tour before the November election. He planned talks in Daytona, Titusville, Fort Pierce, West Palm Beach, Miami, Key West, Tampa,

Fort Myers, Bartow, Lakeland, Kissimmee, and Orlando.[29] In addition, during October he spoke in Mayo and Madison, as well as in Monticello, where United States Senator Samuel Pasco entertained him in his home.[30] Broward's itinerary also took him to DeFuniak Springs, Milton, Pensacola, Apalachicola, Fernandina, Green Cove Springs, Palatka, and St. Augustine. He closed his tour in Jacksonville on November 7 with a big political rally in the Duval Theater.[31]

Broward's talks were devoted mainly to the broad state and national issues confronting Florida. He championed Everglades drainage and strongly supported increased expenditures and a sounder policy for Florida public schools. He consistently maintained that "education is a matter of the first importance to the people, more so now than in former times, because the opportunities for making a living are becoming more and more restricted. . . . Education is needed as much on the farm as in the counting room."[32]

Traveling and speaking with Broward were Stephen R. Mallory, Frank Clark, William B. Lamar, and Robert W. Davis. In Kissimmee, Davis described his former opponent as "a clean and able man, in whose keeping the ship of state will be safe";[33] and at Palatka, he introduced the Democratic nominee at a political meeting by explaining that "the recent campaign was only a Democratic family tilt; two good men were in the race, with the difference that my opponent proved the stronger in the second heat."[34] This reconciliation between Broward and Davis was short-lived and never really extended to the factions which supported them. After the general election the temporary era of good feeling ended, and Florida's conservatives and liberals continued to oppose each other on most issues.

In the November election Broward received 28,971 votes; Macfarlane, 6,357; and Healy, 1,270. A total of 36,598 ballots was counted, 8,646 fewer than were cast in the runoff.[35] In addition to Broward, the newly elected administrative officers of Florida were H. Clay Crawford, secretary of state;

W. H. Ellis, attorney general; A. C. Croom, comptroller;
W. V. Knott, state treasurer; B. E. McLin, commissioner of
agriculture; and W. M. Holloway, superintendent of public
instruction.

Inauguration Day was Tuesday, January 3. In Tallahassee
the weather was bright, but there was enough of winter's
crispness in the air to make it bracing, and women wore wool
coats and jackets over their dark skirts and white shirtwaists.
Warm sunshine flooded the tree-lined streets, and the smell
of flowers and clover was sweet in the air. People from every
county in Florida thronged the flag-filled city. Store fronts
were gay with bunting, firecrackers burst, and crowds flowed
along the streets and sidewalks, shoving, pushing, and jostling.

It was a busy morning in the house of the governor-elect.
The family had moved to Tallahassee the week before and
were living in their new home. As there was no Executive
Mansion, the Browards had rented a large rambling two-story
house on North Monroe Street, formerly a convent, "the
only house in town large enough to hold the Broward family."[36] Sophie, the nurse Mrs. Broward had hired when she
arrived in Tallahassee, scrubbed and dressed the Broward
children—Annie Dorcas, Josephine, Enid, Elsie, Ella, Agnes,
and Florida—and had them ready long before eleven o'clock
when the inaugural parade was scheduled to begin.

Monroe Street was jammed. Carriages, soldiers, bands,
caissons, and floats assembled, preparing for the march to the
capitol. Polished metal, gaudy uniforms, and fluttering flags
turned the busy streets into an array of color and light. Troops
from Jacksonville, Fernandina, Lake City, and Marianna,
each with a regimental band, joined the procession. The state's
supreme court justices, the cabinet members, Florida's Congressional delegation, and the governor-elect's staff and aides
rode in freshly painted buggies. Broward rode with Governor
Jennings, Mrs. Broward was seated with Mrs. Jennings, and
two surreys conveyed Broward's daughters.[37]

Bugle blasts halted the procession at the capitol's front en-

*Portrait of Mrs. Broward
as the First Lady of Florida*

*Broward in 1910; one of the last
pictures taken before his death*

Chief Justice Whitfield administering the oath of office to Broward at Tallahassee in January, 1905

The Broward family on the porch of the Executive Mansion at Tallahassee in 1908

The Three Friends on the St. Johns River

trance, and a band played as members of the official party left their carriages and walked up the capitol steps. Amidst resounding applause, Florida's new chief justice, James B. Whitfield, administered the oath of office, and Governor Jennings handed the great seal of Florida to the new governor.[38] A hush came over the crowd as Broward began his inaugural address. Reading from a prepared manuscript and speaking slowly, he restated the strong convictions that he had staunchly supported throughout his public career, and his words rang with sincerity and determination:

Governments are created by the people for the protection and benefit of the people who created them and those who are to come after them. How to keep a Government in touch with the people at all times, has been the burden of the most devoted statesmen of our country. How to make the Government do that work which is best for the great majority of the people is the work that we have to do, as the tendency of most Governments of the world is to drift away from the people, and to develop into a machine that oppresses them. . . .

Our Government is the outgrowth of public opinion. This Government was established by and must be administered for the good of the people regardless of personal and local surroundings. The policy of the Government is your creation and your dictates must be obeyed. It cannot be perfect, but it will be just what its citizens make it. Its excellencies and the efficiency of those you elect to administer its affairs will always depend upon the virtue and good sense of the people who make it and uphold it. This emphasizes the importance of education and of a general interest in affairs of State. Our continued success, our prosperity, our power rests on the intelligence of the people. . . .

I cannot do better than close with the words of the immortal Jefferson, "I shall often go wrong through defect of judgment. When right I shall often be thought wrong by those whose position will not command a view of the whole ground, I will ask your indulgence for my errors, which will never be intentional, and your support against the errors of others, who may condemn what they would not if seen in all its parts. The approbation implied by your suffrage is a great consolation to me and my future solicitude will be to retain the good opinion of those who have bestowed it in advance, to conciliate that of others by doing them all the good in my power, and to be instrumental to the happiness and freedom of all."[39]

As Governor Broward looked into the upturned faces of the people, who had gathered to hear his inaugural address and watch him take his oath of office, his thoughts may have run backward to the many years of struggle. He had traveled a long road of trial and hardship. Denounced as a demagogue, cursed as a radical, and threatened as a visionary Populist crusader, he had come through it all, valiant and undaunted, with high hopes and deep devotion to service. The phrases of his address, which had become household words through months of reiteration in the campaign, were unchanged: "I favor the primary election system. . . . Make the Railroad Commission a constitutional part of the Government. . . . The common school is the cornerstone of our political structure. . . . The Everglades of Florida should be saved . . . , and they should be drained and made fit for cultivation. . . . Economical administration of our state government. . . . The law must be equally enforced." The promises of a candidate had become the objectives of a governor.[40]

That evening a brilliant reception and inaugural ball were held in the capitol. Mrs. Broward, wearing "a directoire gown of silk brocade with chiffon and turquoise velvet" was a center of attraction. Newspapers reported that "Mrs. Broward has made a most favorable impression upon the rather critical Tallahassee society. She appears so thoroughly sincere and womanly and bears herself with such graceful dignity."[41] Standing in the receiving line with Mrs. Broward was her sister, Elsie Douglass, who planned to live with the family in Tallahassee and work as the governor's secretary. Dorcas and Josephine Broward, wearing white silk gowns, were belles of the ball, and danced with their father's new aides and the handsome officers of the military companies. Governor Broward's sister, Hortense, came from Jacksonville to attend the inauguration and reception.[42] The governor's old aunts, Maggie and Florida, refused to come to Tallahassee. They were humiliated by Broward's *Autobiographical Sketch*. It gave an impression, purposely exaggerated for political capital, that the Broward family were "piney-wood crackers," and the aunts feared that Tallahassee society would look down on them.[43]

Of the many things Broward supported in his administration, Everglades drainage became the project he hoped most ardently to bring to a successful conclusion. Anxious to get as much firsthand information as he could, he left Tallahassee on February 1, 1905, to inspect the Glades. Earlier he had explored them with William M. Bostwick, Jr. and B. H. Barnett, of Jacksonville.[44] On this second expedition Attorney General Ellis, State Treasurer Knott, former Governor Jennings, Captain R. E. Rose, and the Trustees of the Internal Improvement Fund accompanied the governor. Hiring a launch in Fort Myers, the inspectors began their journey up the muddy Caloosahatchee River. Early on the morning of February 4, they traveled across Lake Flirt and along the upper waters of the river to a drainage canal, opened years before by Hamilton Disston's company. Next day they passed through this narrow canal to Lake Okeechobee to check the drainage work at the southern end of an inlet called South Bay. On February 6 the party sailed past dense cypress swamps up Rita River and into a drainage canal that was open for several miles. Although this canal ended in the Everglades, it did not connect with any body of water other than the river, and Broward quickly realized that it had little drainage value.

As the party returned to Lake Okeechobee the next day, the men inspected all neighboring canals to decide if they could be adapted to the new program. The explorers then crossed the vast expanse of saw grass to the lake's northeastern shore. Slowly their boat moved up the Kissimmee River to Lake

Kissimmee and toward Lake Hutchincha, and passed through another weed-choked canal leading into Lake Cypress. They reached Lake Tohopekaliga the following morning and continued their journey into the city of Kissimmee. Soundings had been taken every few miles through the Everglades and careful records kept. The data on elevation, topography, and geography supplied Governor Broward with the detailed information on the drainage problem that he needed when he presented his plan to the legislature.[45]

After his return to Tallahassee, the governor immediately began compiling the necessary facts for a draft of his legislative message. With his secretaries, C. H. Dickerson and Elsie Douglass, he spent long hours in the capitol library.[46] State life insurance was a new idea Broward planned to outline in his message. He made an exhaustive study of the subject and wrote to the governor general of New Zealand asking for information about the plan in use there. Enthusiastic over the Australian program, Broward hoped to use it as a model for Florida.[47]

In March Governor Broward appointed James P. Taliaferro as interim Senator from the state, until the legislature could elect a Senator.[48] Earlier the *Florida Times-Union* had prophesied: "If there be any politician with gray matter so limited as to suppose that N. B. Broward will be the factional Governor of which they have dreamed, what a cold thud they will experience, for as surely as the bright sun shines above us today, he will rise above the schemes of politicians and small intriguers. He will be master of himself and Governor of all the people."[49] Although apparently the *Times-Union* soon changed its opinion, the citizens of the state found no better proof of the truth of this prophecy than in Broward's action when he appointed Taliaferro, the avowed leader of the conservatives, to the United States Senate.

The Florida legislature met on Tuesday, April 4, 1905. Members assembled at noon to listen to Governor Broward's first message—one of the most progressive messages ever delivered to a body of Florida lawmakers. Its various divisions, which were planned to inspire and focus attention on legislation designed to benefit the common people, included these clear-cut proposals:

1. "Every encouragement should be extended to enterprise and capital to assist in developing the vast resources of our State, according to everyone equal protection of the law and requiring of all an equitable contribution to the expense of government, honestly, fairly and economically administered."

2. A State Board of Equalization of Assessments should be created.

. 3. There should be "strictest economy in your appropriations and expenditures" of state funds.

4. A thorough and systematic reorganization of the schools of higher learning should be undertaken, providing for their economical and efficient maintenance and for extensions and improvement in their teaching force, buildings, and equipment, as the growing population of the state and the increasing interest in educational matters demand.

5. Florida's public schools should receive the greatest possible consideration from educational boards and officers; efficient and talented teachers should be provided even in the smallest country schools, and their salaries increased to meet their increased efficiency; and a conservative outline or course of study should be devised and prepared for the guidance of teachers and school officers.

6. Florida should adopt a uniform system of textbooks and appoint a competent committee to choose these books.

7. Florida should increase its appropriations to the common schools.

8. Every necessary precaution should be taken to secure humane treatment of state convicts.

9. A constitutional amendment which would make the Railroad Commission a constitutional branch of state government should be submitted to the people.

10. The primary law should be amended so that primaries would be mandatory rather than optional, and all candidates should be required to submit a sworn itemized statement of

expenses incurred in a political campaign and a list of contributions they received.

11. Laws should be enacted providing severe penalties for miscounting of votes by inspectors and for bribery or intimidation of voters in any election.

12. State pensioners should be paid from funds appropriated by their county of residence.

13. A compulsory life insurance program should be enacted with the state operating the insurance company.

14. Members of the judiciary should be paid better salaries.

15. Fish, oyster, game and forest conservation laws should be passed.

16. Laws promoting efficiency of Florida State Troops should be enacted.[50]

The governor's message was printed in most of the Florida newspapers, and reaction to it was immediate and enthusiastic. Nevertheless, many Florida citizens considered the suggested state life insurance too advanced for the times and felt that several other proposals were unwise. They argued that pensions paid by counties would be unfair, as many of the more populous and wealthy counties had few pensioners while some poorer counties had a great many.[51] Governor Broward had not mentioned his greatest project, Everglades drainage; he planned to deal with that in a special message.

Years were to pass before men and women were ready to accept some of Broward's aspirations and ideas. But his message, expressed in clear and unequivocal words, was the most constructive and farsighted that had ever been placed before a Florida legislature. Governor Broward, realizing that social change could be achieved only by bold and courageous experimentation, based his program on the needs of his state. Refusing to deal in glittering generalities, he presented cold facts and figures to substantiate his arguments; and yet, throughout the message, his warm regard for the welfare of the individual was apparent. His message showed an intimate acquaintance with every department of state government; it reflected his firm belief that government should serve the public good. It was a document that marked the opinions of a humanitarian who believed in the common people and in the soundness of basic American institutions. The enactment of the new governor's program launched in Florida a great era of progress and liberalism—the Broward Era.

⟋ 14 ⟍
The Broward Era Begins

ON MAY 3, 1905, Governor Broward sent the legislature a special message outlining his program for
Everglades drainage and reclamation.[1] This report,
the product of careful study, included vast and minute data
accumulated over a long period of time. It summarized the
activities of the Trustees of the Internal Improvement Fund,
and it reviewed the history of drainage proceedings from territorial days until 1905.

The governor revealed that as early as 1845 the General
Assembly of Florida had discussed Everglades drainage and
had decided that "at a comparatively small expense the . . .
region can be entirely reclaimed, thus opening to the habitation
of man an immense and hitherto unexplored domain perhaps
not surpassed in fertility and every natural advantage by any
other on the globe.[2] John Broward, the grandfather of the
governor, represented Duval County in the first legislative
meeting, and was a member of a state senate committee which
returned this favorable report on drainage. As little was known
of south Florida, the proposal aroused no interest. To most
Floridians it was an uninhabited, wild, unexplored country,
and of little value. Nevertheless, a few individuals, like General Thomas A. Jesup, realized in 1848 that if the lands were
reclaimed they "would soon be converted into valuable sugar
plantations, as rich as any in the world."[3] The United States
Senate on June 1, 1848, received a report written by Buckingham Smith which also acknowledged the feasibility of Everglades drainage.[4] Governor Broward's message in 1905 repeated Smith's words: "That such work would reclaim millions
of acres of highly valuable lands, I have no doubt. . . . It is

my opinion that it would be the best sugar land in the South, and also excellent for rice and corn. It could, in that latitude, be made valuable for raising tropical fruits—and it is the only region of the present Southern States in which they can be raised. . . . I do not know of a project that I would regard as more calculated to benefit than this."[5]

There was no drainage activity, however, until Governor Bloxham's first administration. Shortly after Bloxham's inauguration in January, 1881, the Atlantic and Gulf Coast Canal and Okeechobee Land Company was incorporated in Florida by Isaac Coryell and Hamilton Disston. A few days later Disston signed a contract with the state, agreeing to drain and reclaim the overflowed lands "south of Township 23 East and east of Peach Creek." In return his company would receive alternate sections of the reclaimed tracts.[6] When it was discovered that a court order prevented the trustees from further involving the lands belonging to the Internal Improvement Fund without the approval of its creditors, Bloxham was determined that he would clear the obligations of the fund. As a result of the governor's persuasion, Disston, on May 30, purchased four million acres from Florida at a cost of twenty-five cents an acre, and thus became for a time the largest landholder in the state. Reclamation operations began on a small scale, and in 1883 Governor Bloxham announced that twelve miles of drainage canal had been constructed. Nothing further was done on a major drainage project for almost twenty years.

As Florida developed southward during the latter part of the 1890's, and as the agricultural production of the state expanded, interest in the Everglades area was revived. Drainage and reclamation plans received new consideration, but this time as a public work, state-controlled and financed. Governor Broward, in his message of 1905, explained that when Florida was admitted as a state in 1845, she had received from the Federal government 500,000 acres of land for internal improvements. Five years later additional sections of swamp and overflowed lands were transferred to the state for drainage and reclamation and by 1904 Florida had received a total of 20,133,837.42 acres.[7] In accepting these huge grants the state legislature evolved the Internal Improvement Fund and gave the trustees of the fund jurisdiction over the lands. Nevertheless, no major drainage project was started by the state prior to the Broward administration.[8] After the Reconstruction era there began a scramble for Florida land and, between 1879 and 1901, almost 15,000,000 acres of swamp and overflowed sections were granted to railroads. Under legislative grants approximately 9,100,000 acres were actually deeded to them by the trustees.[9]

Governor Broward, in his drainage message, applauded the stubborn determination of Governor Jennings in trying to save the remaining public lands for the people. Broward recalled how Jennings, in his legislative message of April 7, 1903, had revealed that a patent for much of the Everglades had never been issued by the Federal government.[10] This situation was finally remedied by a deed, issued on April 29, 1903, for 2,862,880 acres,[11] and as a result Florida, in August of the following year, held a total of 3,076,904.68 acres.[12] The railroads of the state became infuriated when the trustees finally decided not to issue certificates for additional lands. Claiming these tracts under legislative grants, the railroads began litigation, and years elapsed before the claims were adjusted.

Governor Jennings, in 1903, had insisted that the swamplands must be dedicated to drainage and in the following year he announced that as a trustee "his first and chief duty in handling the swamp and overflowed lands was to have these lands drained and reclaimed."[13] The collected data, which described the rainfall, altitude, outlets, and topography of the Everglades, revealed, according to Jennings, the possibility and practicability of the program. He referred to the profile drawings, made in 1901, which had established the altitude of Lake Okeechobee and measured the elevation above tidewater of the Kissimmee River and adjacent lakes.[14] The normal elevation of Lake Okeechobee was 20.42 feet above the level of the Gulf of Mexico; and it was practically the same above the level of the Atlantic Ocean. Governor Jennings, in his message of 1903, explained that the drainage outlets would have to be deepened by cutting canals from Lake Okeechobee to the Gulf and to the Atlantic so that the level of water could be lowered. This condition provided the basis for Broward's drainage program and suggested his famous slogan: "Water will run downhill."

Governor Jennings asked further that the legislature in 1903 memorialize Congress for an appropriation of one million dollars to begin "energetically and determinedly to reclaim territory."[15] Broward in 1905 told the Florida legislature that the policy of his predecessor had been directed toward a fixed drainage program, as revealed by the minutes of the Trustees of the Internal Improvement Fund[16] and by the testimony that Jennings gave on November 24, 1904, in a suit between the Louisville and Nashville Railroad Company and the trustees.[17] A few days after the inauguration of Governor Broward in January, 1905, Jennings was employed as general counsel for the Trustees of the Internal Improvement Fund.[18] Broward's special message on drainage referred to the letter written by Jennings on January 21, which called particular attention to the issues involved in the Louisville and Nashville Railroad suit and explained Jennings' earlier testimony in that case. The letter urged the immediate launching of a dredge and the beginning of the actual drainage operations in the Miami River or at any other point chosen by the trustees.[19]

Governor Broward continued his message by reviewing various legislative enactments and the expressions and messages of former Florida governors which had a bearing upon the drainage project. He emphasized judicial interpretations on various phases of these laws and declared further that "from these reports [of] the action of both the Congress of the United States and the Legislature of Florida . . . it is clear that the very great value of these lands to the State were fully appreciated, and the possibilities of their future development and reclamation realized."[20]

Much of Broward's message dealt with the fierce battle between the Trustees of the Internal Improvement Fund and the railroads claiming vast grants of swamp and overflowed lands. In the following tabular material, Broward showed the status of the lands under the jurisdiction of the fund at the beginning of his administration:[21]

Number of acres swamp and overflowed lands patented to the State to August 6, 1904	20,133,837.42
Number of acres deeded and conveyed under legislative enactments	8,242,317.69
Number of acres deeded to canal and drainage companies	2,252,816.96
Number of acres deeded (E. N. Dickerson in 1867 for coupons on Florida R. R. bonds, which fell due prior to 1866)	248,602.98
Number of acres deeded (Wm. E. Jackson in 1866 for coupons on Florida, Atlantic & Gulf Cen. R. R.)	113,064.80
Number of acres deeded in Disston sale	4,000,000.00
Number of acres deeded other than under legislative enactment as above stated	2,200,130.31
Total disposed of prior to August 6, 1904	17,056,932.74
Balance on hand August 6, 1904	3,076,904.68

According to Broward, the more than three million acres of land still held by the fund were involved in litigation. At the time Broward made his report to the legislature, there were six suits pending, with the trustees as either complainants or defendants against the Louisville and Nashville Railroad Company,[22] the Florida East Coast Railway Company,[23] the Florida Coast Line Canal and Transportation Company,[24] and Matilde C. Kittel.[25]

The governor offered the legislature the following proposal for digging the drainage canals: "By digging 22 miles into the St. Lucie a navigable canal, which can be quickly done, then by digging 10 miles from Tomoka River into Haw Creek . . . or by digging from the head of North River into Julington Creek, a distance of 8 or 10 miles, we can open for transportation and connect through St. Johns River with North and Matanzas Rivers, with the Halifax and Indian Rivers, St. Lucie River with Lake Okeechobee, which has a coast line of 130 miles, and 309 miles of the Kissimmee and Caloosahatchee Rivers, and into the Gulf of Mexico at Fort Myers. Thus by digging 30 miles of canal we will prevent Okeechobee overflowing its banks, and at once make 'lowlands' instead of 'overflowed lands' of the Everglades, and connect by this 30 miles of cutting all of the above waterways, which would become by this means a waterway across the State from Fort Myers to Indian River, and would also connect Indian River with the St. Johns River, so that freight steamers from Jacksonville and Indian River, as well as steamers from the Gulf of Mexico via Fort Myers and Caloosahatchee River, and also steamers from Kissimmee via Kissimmee River, could all pass through Lake Okeechobee and do business throughout the 740 miles of inland waterways that would by this 30 miles of cutting be connected together. . . ."[26] The governor explained that his suggestions were based, in part, on a report which J. H. Kreamer, chief engineer of the Okeechobee Drainage Company, had submitted in 1886 to Hamilton Disston.[27]

Broward continued with the information that reclaimed lands were favorable for growing sugar cane and, in this connection, he quoted a letter from Claus Spreckles, the authority on sugar production, written to Hamilton Disston on March 22, 1890: ". . . My surprise was great at finding such a country for the growth of sugar cane. The soil is as rich as any that I have ever seen, and, with proper cultivation, the yield should be equal to that of any other country on the face of the globe."[28] Governor Broward predicted that the reclaimed areas would be dotted with "hundreds of fertile farms within ten years, and will by degrees develop into one of the most productive tracts of land in the world."[29] Broward closed his lengthy message by asking for a constitutional amendment "creating a drainage district, embracing the Everglades, and the adjacent swamp and overflowed lands, including the Kissimmee Valley, and the right to establish other drainage districts, authorizing a drainage commission to levy an acreage tax for a reasonable amount, to be levied and collected annually, to be used in the drainage and reclamation of said territory, and in the aid of the great purposes and the trusts accepted by the State of Florida in its acceptance of the magnificent domain, patented to her by the United States government."[30]

Florida's reaction to the program was immediate and surprisingly favorable. Even the railroad-controlled *Florida Times-Union* at first called it "a great and far-reaching plan," and the editors of the paper applauded Broward's sincere "desire to serve his state by adding to its resources a vast body of land which is believed to be rich in the elements necessary for agricultural success. . . . He has outlined a great proposition and essayed a great task."[31] The people and newspapers of south Florida enthusiastically endorsed the program. Resolutions adopted by communities, hundreds of telegrams from Florida citizens, and dozens of newspaper editorials convinced legislators in Tallahassee that the plan was supported by a majority of the population. One Miami newspaper stated: "No greater scheme for the benefit of the whole State has ever been devised. . . . Beside this great enterprise all other plans for improvement pale into insignificance, when the number of people to be directly benefitted is taken into consideration. An empire, now a wilderness, is to be brought into cultivation and thousands of families will find homes and farms where now is nothing but a vast waste. . . . Broward's name and fame are secure in this State for generations to come."[32]

The legislature took prompt action and on May 11, 1905, bills were introduced concurrently in the House and Senate which provided the necessary legislation for making the drainage program effective. Senate Bill 281, introduced by Thomas

F. West, was referred to the Committee on Drainage and Reclamation of Lands for further study.[33] The House measure, proposed by J. P. Wall, was sent to the Committee on Canals and Drainage.[34] Both bills asked that a board of drainage commissioners be created, that drainage districts be established, and that "the building of canals, levees, dikes and reservoirs for the purpose of drainage, irrigation and commerce," begin.[35] The two committees were immediately faced with the problem of financing so vast a project. They reviewed the legislative act of January 6, 1855, which had authorized the Trustees of the Internal Improvement Fund to apply all proceeds from the sale of swamp and overflowed lands to drainage and reclamation.[36] The committees also studied the proposed drainage tax law which had been drawn up by former Governor Jennings in January, 1905, and which had been adopted by Governor Broward as an integral part of his program. The tax measure defined the drainage district embraced in the Everglades and provided for an acreage tax of five cents per acre per annum, to be assessed against lands in this district. The legislators estimated that the annual revenue from this tax would be approximately two hundred thousand dollars.[37]

Although Governor Broward had hoped to have his project underwritten by a constitutional amendment, he was not successful. There was little debate about the proposed statutes, and both houses adopted a resolution to amend Article 16 of the Constitution, but this was as far as they were ready to go at the moment.[38] Governor Broward seemed content, and he signed the measure on May 29, 1905.[39]

The newly created Board of Drainage Commissioners included the governor, treasurer, attorney general, and the commissioner of agriculture. Later, severe criticism of the board came from land companies who objected because they were not represented. The commissioners were "empowered to establish drainage districts . . . prepare lists of all alluvial or swamp and overflowed taxable lands within such drainage . . . districts, and levy thereon an acreage tax not exceeding ten

224   Napoleon Bonaparte Broward

cents per acre per annum. . . ."⁴⁰ The governor hoped that most lands would be taxed only five cents an acre.

Eventually, land companies brought lawsuits which tried to prove that the taxing power as a whole was unconstitutionally delegated. These companies owned Florida newspapers and used them to sway public opinion to their side. The conservative press denounced the tax and, as the months passed, their opposition enveloped the entire drainage program. Several journals that had opposed Broward when he ran for governor now delighted in daily criticizing his leadership of the Everglades project. Broward was unperturbed, and remained throughout his administration the moving spirit behind Everglades drainage. C. G. Elliott, an engineer from the United States Department of Agriculture, wrote: "While the Governor is aided by other members of the Board it is evident that he is carrying this matter forward in a very energetic and possibly arbitrary manner. . . . He has a sort of plan of his own and is evidently the engineer as well as the promoter and pusher of the whole drainage scheme.⁴¹

Meanwhile, Florida legislators debated and enacted other legislation. A bill introduced into the House of Representatives by J. R. Johnston of Dade City asked that a state school book commission be created "to procure for use in the public schools . . . a uniform series of text books."⁴² H. H. McCreary, of Alachua County, introduced a similar bill in the Senate.⁴³ This was not the first legislature to be concerned with setting up a school textbook commission and enacting a uniform school textbook law. In the 1903 session Senator McCreary had asked for such a measure, but no action had been taken.⁴⁴ In 1905, the Senate and House committees reported the measures favorably, and many members of the legislature optimistically believed that a commission would finally be established.⁴⁵ The Senate passed the bill, but opposition developed in the House. After a second reading a vote was postponed, and no further action was taken during the session.⁴⁶

Among the notable achievements of Governor Broward's

administration was the passage of the Buckman Act in 1905. In his first legislative message, Broward, after describing the seminaries and colleges in Florida, had declared: "The business of educating the youth of our State . . . should proceed along lines of definite purpose, and the only way to secure the best results from these institutions is to establish some definite plan for their work and progress and adhere strictly to it. . . . In my judgment, the needs and requirements of these institutions can never be intelligently and properly considered until an efficient system of management, control and supervision over them is provided. . . . I therefore recommend that such a .thorough and systematic reorganization of these schools be provided for. . . ."[47] The institutions referred to by the governor included the University of Florida at Lake City, the East Florida Seminary at Gainesville, the West Florida Seminary at Tallahassee, the South Florida Military Institute at Bartow, the State Normal (for whites) at DeFuniak Springs, the State Normal (for colored) at Tallahassee, the Osceola County Agricultural Institute, and the St. Petersburg Industrial and Normal Institute. The last-named school received only incidental aid from the state.

During the weeks prior to the meeting of the legislature of 1905, Governor Broward, Representative H. H. Buckman, Senator Frank Adams, and others met often to discuss the problem of the colleges in Florida. The governor was convinced that these schools had failed to offer instruction above the high-school level and that, in competing with each other for students, they had lowered educational standards. Broward realized also that the critical problem of financing schools must be solved. The income from Florida taxes was small; as a result, there was little money available for educational purposes. The budgets of all the schools were inadequate and, at each legislative session, lobbyists from the institutions had appeared in Tallahassee to badger representatives and senators into voting appropriations for their particular schools. Broward stated emphatically that he did not believe "that the management of these colleges and seminaries should be put in the attitude of beggars before the legislature for the means of existence."⁴⁸ It was with this knowledge that the governor had recommended the sweeping reorganization of the college system in the state.

On April 12, 1905, Representative J. P. Wall introduced a bill which proposed "to control, manage and maintain certain educational institutions in the State of Florida." The Special Committee on State Institutions began considering the measure and on April 27 offered an addition to the bill which would provide for a "board of uniformity." Before either bill could be acted upon, Representative Buckman asked that the vote be postponed. On May 9 he introduced a third education bill; it was long, and its reading consumed almost an hour. Besides completely reorganizing the colleges and seminaries, it stipulated that the governor appoint a board of control, which would be empowered to choose sites for the Deaf, Dumb and Blind Institute, the colored normal school, and two colleges, one east and the other west of the Suwannee River.⁴⁹

On May 15 the Special Committee on State Institutions reported the first two measures unfavorably to the House. They announced that the Buckman Bill had been rewritten to conform to suggestions offered by Representative W. A. Rawls and that it would be ready for House action on May 18.⁵⁰ This compromise bill was educationally sound, and had the endorsement of Buckman, but it was obvious to Broward and the legislators that the measure was loaded with political dynamite. The governor knew that the counties in which the various institutions were located would resent any attempt to have their schools removed and that the institutions themselves would fight "tooth and nail" any threat of their abolishment.

Almost the entire morning of May 18 was taken up with the reading of the Buckman Bill, and debate was postponed until the afternoon session. The representatives opposing the measure attempted to forestall debate and a final vote, but they were not successful. The arguments began with Buckman's firm statement that "the time has come when we must prune out some of the sprouts which have grown up in the educational institutions of Florida, since the appropriations required for their maintenance and support have grown beyond the resources of the State to supply." Among other things, he criticized the laxity in presenting and publishing institutional reports, and showed that in one report to the governor, a school principal had listed the cost of his personal horse and surrey. Buckman, fully aware of the political implications in the compromise measure which carried his name, felt that it was "time to use the knife and cut this sore from the body politic."[51]

In opposing the measure, A. J. P. Julian, of Lake City, claimed that the political clique controlling Florida school affairs would establish the university at Jacksonville. Julian admitted that "our colleges are not what they ought to be. Dr. Buckman has carefully examined the diseased conditions. . . . He may have private convictions that there has been mismanagement, blunders and graft, and now this kindhearted physician, instead of suggesting a treatment that will eradicate these diseases partially, says that you shall take this instrument and stab them to death."[52] Another strong opponent, William A. Bryan, of Chipley, described the provisions of the bill as "cruel as hell and as wicked as the iniquity of Satan's own heart."[53]

Interest in the measure was widespread throughout the state, and people everywhere anxiously followed the legislative debate as it was reported in the newspapers. In Tallahassee, interest was particularly intense and the visitors' gallery in the House was jammed on May 18 with men and women who wanted to watch the proceedings. The evening before, delegations from the East Florida Seminary and the University of Florida had arrived in Tallahassee, and now these people also crowded into the gallery. Mrs. Broward and her four oldest daughters had come to the capitol early and were seated in the front row. On the floor of the House the legislators busily tried to round up support either for or against the proposed

law. The arguments continued throughout the afternoon of
May 18, and all of May 19. It was not until the morning
of May 20 that the House was ready to vote. The room was
suddenly hushed as the clerk rose to announce the results;
then a great cheer burst from the legislators who were clustered
around the desk of Representative Buckman. The bill had
passed by a vote of 34 to 22.[54] Noise and confusion swept
through the House as a dozen legislators, hoping to be recognized by Speaker Gilchrist, jumped to their feet. Laughter
greeted the explanation given by Representative J. L. Robison
that he had voted against the measure because "I heartily
endorse co-education which the bill prohibits."[55] The uproar
continued until the House adjourned for the day.

In the Senate, the opposition to educational reform was also
strong. Senate President Park M. Trammell, a liberal, and
generally considered a consistent Broward supporter, so strongly opposed the bill that he left his chair as presiding officer
in order to speak and vote against the measure. He felt that
the Senate had not had sufficient time to examine the contents
of the bill and he argued that "the special plan of consolidation
proposed is not what will meet the demand. The appropriation
it carries shows it is not economical. South Florida and the South
Middle Florida, paying more than half the taxes, with more
than half the population, under the measure get neither of
the two schools. If it is right to have only two, is it not wrong
to place them in the same section of the State?"[56] After heated
debate the bill finally passed on May 26 by a vote of 16 to 5,[57]
and Governor Broward signed it into law on June 5, 1905.[58]
Later in the month, when he appointed the first Board of
Control, the Governor named his cousin and long-time friend,
Nathan P. Bryan, as chairman. Other members were Philip K.
Yonge, of Pensacola; Nathaniel Adams, of White Springs;
Dr. A. L. Brown, of Eustis; and T. B. King, of Arcadia.[59]
Governor Broward refused to be swayed by political prejudices
in these appointments; he chose men because of their ability
and qualifications.

The legislature of 1905 appropriated funds to build a badly needed Executive Mansion in Tallahassee and appointed a committee to obtain a suitable site and contract for the building.[60] George W. Saxon, a Tallahassee banker, contributed four city lots and four more were purchased.[61] After plans were drawn by H. J. Klutho, a Jacksonville architect, the contract was given to O. C. Parker, of Tallahassee. Meanwhile, the legislators raised Governor Broward's salary from thirty-five hundred dollars to five thousand dollars a year.[62] An important action repealed the famous insanity divorce law. There had been so much furore in the state about the law since it was enacted in 1901, that in the debate repealing the measure, one representative enthusiastically proposed that all Florida divorce laws be revised and that only adultery be recognized in the future as grounds for divorce.[63] This proposal was voted down, but since 1905 Florida has refused to accept insanity as a cause for divorce.

The legislature showed relatively little interest in the governor's proposal on life insurance. A bill, introduced into the House on May 4, was entitled "An act to provide for life insurance by the State of Florida, and for the appointment of insurance commissioners."[64] The measure passed the House, but was rejected by the Senate. In reporting the Senate debate, the *Suwannee Democrat* wrote: "Governor Broward's famous suggestion . . . that the State go into the life insurance, was bold and brilliant, but we hazard the opinion that the solons will let it severely alone for the reason it is too bold and too brilliant. The proposition is of an epochal character, and this Legislature is not in the epoch-making business."[65]

One of the most popular actions taken by the legislature in 1905 was the passage of the joint resolution which acknowledged the return to Florida of the Confederate battle flags captured by the Union forces during the Civil War. On March 25, 1905, William Howard Taft, the Secretary of War, had informed Governor Broward that a joint Congressional resolution allowed him to return the flags and that they had

already been shipped.[66] A few days later Adjutant General
J. Clifford R. Foster advised the governor that the flags had
arrived.[67] In a special ceremony at the capitol on the morning
of May 2, the battle standards were formally accepted by
the state. Governor Broward, R. H. M. Davidson, of Quincy,
and former Governor Francis P. Fleming, of Jacksonville,
had been invited to address the legislators and the invited
guests on this gala occasion.[68]

For many weeks prior to the legislative session of 1905,
there had been rumors circulating around Tallahassee that
certain members of the Board of State Institutions, which
included Governor Broward, Secretary of State Crawford,
Attorney General Ellis, Comptroller Croom, State Treasurer
Knott, Commissioner of Agriculture McLin, and State Superintendent of Public Instruction Holloway, owned stock in the
Capital Publishing Company and were "contracting with themselves, purchasing supplies, goods and material from themselves
as such stockholders."[69] After this charge was formally made
in the Senate it was decided to investigate the situation. As a
result, a special committee was set up and hearings were held
in the comptroller's office in the capitol. On May 26 Broward,
the other members of the board, and several leading members
of the Broward administration were closely questioned about
their alleged affiliations with the company. After the testimony
was studied, the investigating committee submitted the following report on May 30 to the legislature: "Your Committee
appointed in compliance with Senate Resolution No. 46, as
amended, relative to the alleged rumors that members of the
Board of State Institutions were interested in the Capital
Publishing Company, and with the State Printer in his contract
with the State, beg leave to report that the said Committee
has taken the testimony of all witnesses suggested and made
a thorough examination and find that while there were rumors
to the effect that members of the Board of State Institutions
were interested in the printing contract, we find that there
is absolutely no foundation for said rumors and nothing in
the testimony to indicate that any member or members of

said Board are now, or have heretofore been interested in said
printing concern or any other printing business."[70]
    During the last weeks of the session, the legislators heard
in detail about the situation at the Hospital for the Insane in
Chattahoochee, which had threatened for months to erupt
into a major scandal. Reports that the patients had been starved,
beaten, and forced to live in decrepit, unsanitary buildings
had appeared occasionally in the past in the newspapers, and
had aroused the people. In order to check these rumors, the
legislature in 1901 had appointed F. W. Sams, Joseph Y.
Porter, and Frank McRae as a joint investigating committee.[71]
This group filed a report which was considered generally
favorable and upon their recommendation a recess committee
had been set up. The legislature in 1903 heard the findings
of the recess committee and their specific recommendations
for improving the asylum.[72] Broward, after he became governor, recalled that the legislators in 1903 had "failed to adopt
a single one of the many recommendations made by the
Committee for the comfort, scientific and humane treatment
of the inmates. . . ."[73]
    During 1904 the scandalous reports about the hospital be-
came more frequent, and it was obvious that some of the
conservative newspapers in the state were trying to blame the
Jennings administration for the condition. Broward was very
much concerned about the situation, not only for humanitarian
reasons, but because the charge had been made that some of
the dissension among the hospital supervisors had been caused
by differences of political opinion during the gubernatorial
campaign in 1904. Apparently some of the employees, including Superintendent V. H. Gwynn, had supported Broward,
while others had voted for Davis. It was alleged that Gwynn
had discharged his chief bookkeeper because the latter had
refused to come out for Broward.[74] Hoping to remedy conditions in the institution, Broward, in March, 1905, accepted
the resignation of Dr. Gwynn and appointed B. F. Whitner
superintendent.
    In his first message, the governor reviewed the new super-

intendent's report, and recommended substantial appropriations for the hospital. When appropriation bills were introduced in the House and Senate they caused so much controversy that a special legislative committee, headed by W. K. Jackson, was appointed to "visit, inspect, investigate, and report its findings of the condition, needs and affairs of the Hospital for the Insane of the State."[75] After the committee had held brief hearings at the hospital and questioned Superintendent Whitner, two hospital physicians, and a few of the employees, it returned a report to the legislature on May 17, 1905.[76] The report created a sensation; it was a complete indictment of the institution. It criticized the supervisors, the general care of the patients, the lack of sanitation in the wards and buildings, and the dire shortage of trained personnel. The report announced that "the institution is not a Hospital for the Insane, but is more of a dumping place for all sorts of people, where they are maintained after a fashion at an enormous expense to the State. . . . The institution has been more of a prison than an asylum. . . . Those poor helpless unfortunate inmates . . . have been caused to suffer the pangs of hunger, the humiliation and pain of the keen cut of the lash, the thud of the fist, the stamp of the foot. . . . The management has been cruel, negligent, and heartless in some instances. . . . Attendants and nurses have been drunk while on duty. . . . The very atmosphere of the institution has been scented with vice and immorality to the extent that even inmates have begged and plead for release on account of it."[77]

Governor Broward, the newspapers, and the citizens of Florida were greatly disturbed over the report and the fact that it had been adopted by the legislators. Twenty nurses from the hospital signed a formal protest and dispatched it to Tallahassee. There were conflicting opinions about the committee. Some people felt that the investigation had been thorough and that the findings were valid; others, like Broward, charged that the committee had been prejudiced and that there was no truth to its disclosures. As a result, a second committee was appointed to investigate the report of the first committee.[78] This second group met in Chattahoochee and in Tallahassee and questioned dozens of witnesses, including doctors, nurses, ward attendants, orderlies, office employees, the former superintendents, Chattahoochee residents, the state purchasing agent, Governor Jennings, W. N. Sheats, and members of the Board of State Institutions. The report of this committee, which filled two hundred seventy-six printed pages, revealed that there was an immediate need for new buildings, more doctors and nurses, an improved diet, and more supplies, but it refuted most of the charges of immorality, mismanagement, and cruelty. It showed that the few instances of gross abuses in the asylum were not condoned by the officials of the hospital.[79]

Governor Broward was so incensed over the first report that he felt impelled to send a special message to the legislature on May 29, 1905.[80] His message called the original report not only "untrue, inaccurate and wholly unjustified by the fact but . . . in its tone and character scandalous and disreputable to a degree that one almost suspects it to have been inspired by other considerations than a fair and just, full and accurate investigation and consideration of all the facts. The report has afforded to a certain class of newspapers in this State a splendid opportunity for the exhibition of that character of journalism, which though so offensive to the gentility and refinement of the reading public, appeals strongly to the sensationalist and the scandalmonger."[81] In referring to the charges of immorality, Broward said: "This cruel, harsh attack upon the chastity of the female attendants and nurses at the hospital is unsupported by a single word of evidence. It seemed to have been begotten in the evil minds of those who would impute a lack of virtue to a lady who, in company with her escort, takes an evening stroll." The governor denied that a woman "sells her virtue when she consents to toil" and explained that the nurses had probably "sought employment as a means by which they might aid their parents in the maintenance of the home."[82]

The probing and the criticism brought results. Realizing that the people of Florida had been roused by these reports, the legislators voted appropriations for hospital buildings, supplies, and salaries. They also appointed a recess committee headed by Governor Broward to visit and inspect the hospital, and to make specific recommendations to the legislature in 1907.[83]

Governor and Mrs. Broward were not active members of Tallahassee society, as Mrs. Broward's large family gave her little time for entertaining. Friends were often invited for informal luncheons and dinners, but the Browards avoided as many formal parties and receptions as possible. It was customary, however, for the governor to entertain the legislature during the session. On Thursday morning, May 25, the following note from Governor Broward was received by Park M. Trammell in the Senate: "Mrs. Broward and I extend to you and all other members of the Legislature a cordial invitation to be present at the reception of the Legislature, Thursday, May 25, from 8 to 10:30 P.M., and I would be grateful should you extend this invitation to the House, upon convening this morning."[84] Although such affairs were usually stiff, formal, and boring, the Broward party was an exception. Miss Mary Whitfield and a group of Tallahassee musicians played during the evening. One newspaper reported that "the customary rule obtaining at public receptions of shaking hands with the host and hostess, partaking of light refreshments and then retiring, was suspended and everybody stayed for at least an hour."[85]

After the legislature adjourned, a state-wide controversy arose over the location of the college east of the Suwannee River. While it had been generally conceded that the Florida Female College[86] and the normal school for the colored should be left in Tallahassee, several other cities hoped to be chosen by the Board of Control as a site for the University of Florida. Many people thought that Lake City should be selected, since the university was already there, with several buildings, in-

cluding a gymnasium and swimming pool built by Henry M.
Flagler. A leading contender for the university was Gainesville.
Under the direction of William N. Wilson and W. R. Thomas,
an active campaign for the university was waged. Ocala, Bartow, Live Oak, Jacksonville, and Fernandina also entered the
contest. Charges and countercharges were hurled back and
forth among these communities. One Lake City resident sarcastically noted: "Of course, a great many places want the
University. That is perfectly natural. Did you ever see a poor
old horse with long hair that had run on the range with no
attention and nobody wanted him, but when taken up by some
good farmer and fed and groomed he became sleek and fat
and everybody wanted him?"[87]

Complaints against Gainesville asserted that her train service
was miserable and that "her trains are nothing but 'jerk-water'
trains and there is no Pullman service." Lake City citizens
reported that Gainesville's water "isn't an antidote for the
Gainesville fever . . . and there is an insufficiency of supply."
Gainesville citizens retaliated with similar criticisms of Lake
City.

The newspapers actively entered the campaign and one
editorial thus enumerated Fernandina's qualifications: "We've
got more ozone than both of those towns put together, and
if we once get them on the island, the boys can't run away
from school without getting caught at the drawbridge. We
can provide a magnificent site with an unobstructed view of
the Atlantic Ocean, with Europe and Africa in the background."[88] Dozens of people wrote Broward extolling the
virtues of their home cities. In answering these letters, the
governor said that the decision for locating the university
lay with the Board of Control. In reality, the Board of Education, of which the governor was a member, would also
vote on the site.

The new Board of Control and the Board of Education,
pursuant to the law, met in Tallahassee on July 6, to decide
on locations for the University of Florida and the Florida

Female College. Lobbyists thronged Tallahassee; both Gainesville and Lake City had chartered trains and sent delegations to the capital as they had when the Buckman Bill was being debated. After relatively little argument, the Female College was located in Tallahassee. That evening the two boards met in joint session to decide the heated question regarding the site for the university. Only a few Florida cities had backed up their desire to secure the school with concrete offers of money or land, and the real contest apparently was between Lake City and Gainesville. The boards considered offers by both communities. Lake City promised forty thousand dollars in cash and eight hundred seventy-one acres of land, valued at twenty thousand dollars, and backed her proposal with certified checks. Gainesville made two proposals. In one, she agreed to deed five hundred acres of land and give forty thousand dollars; in the other, she offered three hundred twenty acres of land in west Gainesville, fifteen acres in east Gainesville, and the use of all public school buildings and their grounds. In either case, Gainesville agreed to furnish free water to the university. Her citizens, moreover, offered to quarter all students who could not secure accommodations in dormitories, at a "price no higher than that charged by the state."[89] A few minutes later, the spokesman for the Gainesville delegation informed the boards that his city had decided to increase her proposal. The city was willing to deed five hundred and seventeen acres of land, give forty thousand dollars, allow the university to use the Gainesville High School, and, in addition, provide free water.[90]

It was nearly midnight before the public hearing was over and the members of the Board of Control and the Board of Education began the secret balloting. On the morning of July 7, 1905, the results were announced to the newspapers— Gainesville had been chosen by a vote of 6 to 4. The board stipulated that the university would remain in Lake City for one year, until buildings could be erected on the Gainesville campus. The transfer to Gainesville would take place in 1906.[9]

The members of the boards did not immediately reveal how they had voted, but many people concluded that the offer of free water made by Gainesville was the deciding factor in the final vote. The news caused considerable disturbance in Lake City. An angry crowd of people massed before the telegraph office and threatened the citizens of Gainesville, the Board of Control, the Board of Education, and Governor Broward. Any untoward action could have started a riot.

Several days later, Senator Adams, while addressing a protest meeting in Lake City, revealed that he had received promises from a majority of the members of the two boards that they would vote for Lake City. He stated bitterly that "evil influences" from Gainesville had caused two members to change their votes. Many people believed that Adams was referring to Governor Broward and Nathan P. Bryan. The citizens of Lake City later charged that the governor, in a campaign speech, had definitely promised to support Lake City's cause. Adams and the people of Lake City were not justified in suspecting Broward of breaking a promise. He later explained that, although he thought Gainesville a more suitable place for the university, he had kept his promise and had voted for Lake City.[92]

After announcing the site for the university, the Board of Control held another meeting on the same day and appointed Dr. Andrew Sledd president of the University of Florida, and Dr. Albert A. Murphree head of the Florida Female College.[93] There had been some opposition to Dr. Sledd ever since he had been chosen president of the university in Lake City in July, 1904, to succeed President Thomas H. Taliaferro. When members of the Board of Education learned that Sledd would continue as head of the university after it moved to Gainesville, they called a secret session on the evening of July 7 and resolved to annul Sledd's election and appoint Dr. Murphree instead. Denying the jurisdiction of the Board of Education in such matters, the Board of Control refused to accept this action. Nathan P. Bryan threatened to carry the controversy to the state supreme court, if necessary. When Governor Broward sided with the Board of Control, the Board of Education yielded. The salaries of Presidents Sledd and Murphree were set at twenty-five hundred dollars, and each president was permitted to choose his own faculty, subject to board approval.

A few days after the university issue was settled, Governor and Mrs. Broward and their family traveled to Chicago where Broward conferred with the engineers of the Featherstone Foundry and Machine Company about construction details of dredges and drainage equipment. The first dredge was being built according to plans drawn by the governor and the state engineers. Broward was informed by the Chicago company that one dredge would be ready for assembling in south Florida by the end of the year, and that the major part of the equipment would be completed and shipped to Florida by the fall of 1906.

After leaving Chicago, the governor and his family went to Hot Springs, Arkansas, for their vacation. Hot Springs had always been a favorite vacation spot for the family, and during the next few years, they visited there as often as possible.[94] Rested and relaxed, the family returned to Tallahassee in September so that the children could be enrolled in school. During the next few weeks the governor was occupied with details relating to the drainage program. Other activities also needed attention. On October 16, 1905, he appointed J. Emmett Wolfe of Pensacola as his private secretary to succeed M. A. Brown, who had returned to Jacksonville to accept a temporary appointment as sheriff of Duval County.[95] Later, Daniel A. Simmons was added to the governor's secretarial staff. During the latter part of the month, as was customary, the Florida State Troops went on their annual encampment. The 1905 camp was located in Lake City and had been named "Camp Broward." On October 20 the governor reviewed the troops, and in the evening he was guest of honor at a military reception and ball.[96]

He left that night for Jacksonville to welcome President Theodore Roosevelt and his party, who were visiting Florida. The presidential party arrived in Jacksonville on October 21. The city, largely rebuilt since the great fire, was decorated lavishly with pictures and giant "Welcome" signs. Clean new buildings and fresh-painted houses had been spangled with flags and red-white-and-blue bunting. The President rode with Broward in the official carriage, and in the bright noon sunlight they led a parade through Jacksonville's streets. After a large reception at the Seminole Club, President Roosevelt visited the Negro Florida Baptist College and addressed the student body in the afternoon. He left that evening for St. Augustine.[97]

Until this visit, Governor Broward had never been a warm admirer of President Roosevelt, and during the gubernatorial campaign of 1904 he had severely criticized Roosevelt's governmental policies and had berated his military exploits in the Spanish-American War.[98] Although the two men continued to oppose each other on many national issues, they became good friends after the meeting in Jacksonville. Governor Broward frequently called at the White House when he was in Washington, and several times he was invited to confer with the President about the problems of the Everglades drainage program.

◇ 15 ◇

"Save the People's Land!"

EVERGLADES DRAINAGE rapidly became a dramatic point of controversy for all Florida when the newly constituted Board of Drainage Commissioners imposed the special acreage tax. The Southern States Land and Timber Company, with large Everglades holdings, denied the constitutionality of the drainage law and refused to pay the tax. The company entered suit in the United States Circuit Court, asking that the law be declared null and void. Broward and the commissioners immediately filed a demurrer to this bill of complaint. The demurrer was overruled, however, and the court issued an injunction against collecting a drainage tax from the company.[1]

Meanwhile the governor worked unperturbed, and drainage plans proceeded. Anxious to mark the progress of the dredge being assembled at Fort Lauderdale, Broward and his family visited the New River area. In his special message of May 3, 1905, the governor had recommended that preliminary work begin in the St. Lucie River locale. On September 21, 1905, Captain J. O. Fries, civil engineer, suggested the practicability of this route in his survey report to the trustees.[2] Other areas were also surveyed, and on November 6, V. P. Keller prepared a map showing a profile of the drainage canals from Lake Okeechobee to Lake Worth.[3] John W. Newman, another civil engineer, made a hydrographical and topographical survey of New River from Fort Lauderdale to Lake Okeechobee.[4] On December 12 the trustees, adopting Newman's recommendations, designated the route for the first drainage canal, which was to start at the mouth of Sabate Creek and follow the open glades to the south end of Lake Okeechobee.[5] They ordered a second dredge and hired Newman as engineer in charge of operations.

Governor Broward and his staunchest supporters firmly believed that Everglades drainage and reclamation were of inestimable value to Florida. Their opponents, equally sure that the program would be a failure, asserted that huge sums of money were being spent on a worthless project. State newspapers quickly took sides in the bitter and heated conflict, and Florida citizens divided into drainage and anti-drainage factions. The *Jasper News,* one of the most vocal of the anti-drainage papers, declared emphatically: "Of all the foolish ideas that ever entered the brain of man the draining of the Everglades is the most nonsensical."[6] The *Levy Times-Democrat* insisted that "Broward's drainage scheme is the biggest elephant he ever tackled. It is believed the treasury will be drained before the Everglades."[7] Another journal, the *Volusia County Record,* repeated that "Broward's scheme to drain the Everglades is a great scheme to drain the State Treasury. . . . The attempt will simply result in a waste of the people's money."[8]

Early in March, 1906, Broward made arrangements for a meeting in Jacksonville at which he was scheduled for a debate with the anti-drainage editors of the *Florida Times-Union* and the *Jacksonville Metropolis.* Although the debate did not materialize, both newspapers agreed to print anything that Broward should write about his program. The governor, in his past speeches, had bluntly and consistently characterized the newspapers fighting drainage as "corporation papers," and he included in this category the *Florida Times-Union* and the *Metropolis.* He was determined that, regardless of opposition, he would fight for Everglades reclamation because he believed it to be for the state's welfare. In Jacksonville, Broward conferred with a group of his drainage supporters and told them that he planned to convince the Florida citizens of the merits of the project by canvassing the state and speaking in every community. The governor knew that his chief opponents

were the railroads and corporations of Florida, which had
land claims that would be jeopardized by successful drainage.[9]

Back in Tallahassee, the governor met with the commissioners, who ordered tax collectors in Dade, DeSoto, Lee, Osceola,
and St. Lucie counties to levy and collect the drainage tax,
except on lands belonging to the Southern States Land and
Timber Company.[10] The commissioners reasoned that this was
not an illegal action, as the court's injunction did not prevent
levying an assessment on other drainage lands. Nevertheless,
the drainage board was deluged with hundreds of letters from
citizens all over the state, protesting the tax. Five additional
lawsuits, four instigated by corporations, were filed, and the
court, following precedent, promptly granted additional in-
junctions. One corporation charged that the tax was a direct
violation of the Fourteenth Amendment.[11] In the face of this
storm of protest and court action, the board announced that
collection of drainage taxes was suspended, pending final
settlement of the injunction suits.

The drainage issue was rapidly brewing a great political
battle in Florida, and every weapon was being assembled for
the fight. Prominent in this conflict against Broward were
antagonistic newspapers whose accusations and smears were
loud, long, and bitter. The *Ocala Banner*, a strong conservative
journal, suggested that after the people had listened to
Broward they would cry out as did Cain, "My punishment is
greater than I can bear."[12] Numerous editorials insisted that
"it is a sinful waste of the dear people's money. . . . The lands
can't be drained. . . . Saw-grass muck is a peat bog that will
burn down to bedrock when drained. . . . We have countless
thousands of acres of land which ought to be tenanted before
attempting to open other territory. . . . These lands belong to
the railroads anyway." One journal branded reclamation enthusiasts as a "syndicate of land sharks";[13] another insisted
that the governor was "trying to court and retain favor and
pave the way for something better when his term as chief
executive of the State shall have expired."[14] Broward was

called a "hopeless chump,"[15] drainage a "wild cat scheme,"[16] and there was loud lamenting for "the hole made in the State Treasury."[17]

Other newspapers, many in south Florida, enthusiastically supported the program. The *Cocoa and Rockledge News*, connecting Henry M. Flagler with the campaign against Broward, argued that "if Mr. Flagler will come out and promise under bond to drain the Everglades at his own expense, then we say let the Governor come down. Until then, we bid him God Speed!"[18] Another editor wrote: "The attacks . . . led by the *Times-Union* and the *St. Augustine Record*, owned by the Flagler interests and joined in by that class of papers that past experience has proven are purchasable, remind us more of a sleeping lion surrounded by a pack of barking jackals than anything else in natural history. The governor will turn on them one of these days and when he does what a scurrying for holes there will be."[19] The governor's newly published open letter on drainage became a favorite target for attack. This pamphlet, which was mailed to voters throughout the state, set forth the drainage program at considerable length.[20]

On April 2, 1906, Broward, his family, and Captain R. E. Rose were in Fort Lauderdale for the christening of the first dredge, the *Everglades*, which was enthusiastically described as the "largest and finest dredge boat south of Philadelphia." She was forty-two by one hundred and eighty feet long, and powered with a five hundred horsepower engine. The christening provided an excuse for a lively celebration in Fort Lauderdale, and a large crowd gathered to watch the ceremonies. After Broward briefly outlined the scope of the drainage project and prophesied a bright future for south Florida, Miss Constance Bryan smashed a decorated bottle of champagne across the boat's bow.[21] The naming of a second dredge, the *Okeechobee*, was scheduled for the first week in May. The drainage problem consumed most of the governor's time, but during the spring and summer months of 1906 other duties also occupied his attention. On May 31 he and Mrs.

Broward attended commencement exercises at Stetson University. They spent several days in DeLand as guests of President and Mrs. Lincoln Hulley.[22] Broward spoke in Bronson on June 1, when the cornerstone for the new Levy County Court House was laid.[23] He made frequent trips to Fort Lauderdale during June to supervise construction of the dredges, and to Jacksonville for conferences with officials of the Merrill-Stevens Engineering Company, which supplied part of the dredging equipment used in drainage operations. The governor was in Fort Lauderdale the first week in July to watch the dredge *Everglades* move out in a direction northwest of New River. There was no definite technical survey to follow, and an engineering party, laying out stakes, preceded the dredge. Progress was slow, but the work of actual drainage had begun.

The governor returned to Tallahassee for a few days, and then on July 11 he traveled to Washington for conferences with the Secretary of Agriculture. Under consideration were plans for Federal aid for drainage and a Federal survey of swamp and overflowed lands.[24] As a result of these conferences, J. O. Wright, chief surveyor in the Department of Agriculture, was dispatched to Florida in November. For the next eighteen months groups of United States engineers, surveyors, and soil scientists were in and out of the drainage locale. While in Washington, Broward talked with various Democratic leaders about the problems and aims of the party in their relationship to the South. Broward's reputation as a prominent liberal was well known in the party.

After several days in New York, Broward returned to Florida to begin planning strategy for the approaching November elections. He hoped that a state legislature favorable to the drainage program would be elected. He was also anxious that the voters support the constitutional amendment providing for a permanent board of drainage commissioners. Determined to secure the people's endorsement of his project, Broward announced again that he was ready to stump the state and would campaign as vigorously as when he was running for public office.

In Pensacola, on the evening of August 20, a debate was scheduled between the governor and John S. Beard, a prominent and long-time opponent of the drainage program. In Seville Square, before an audience of fifteen hundred, Broward emphasized that he was fighting the people's battle against the railroads, which "had set out to steal the lands." The "designs of the railroads" could be defeated, he declared, if the drainage commissioners were made a constitutionally-delegated board. Berating railroad officials who were fighting him through state newspapers, the chief executive asserted: ". . . If I would just send a telegram to Mr. Flagler or a wire to Mr. Parrott containing the words 'the trustees are ready to deed you the land granted; meet us in Tallahassee tomorrow,' the *Times-Union* would come out in letters big and black and say 'Broward is the greatest governor that Florida has ever had,' and the little *Metropolis* would say 'me too.' "[25] The governor suggested that the railroads claiming Everglades lands were afraid to carry their suits to the United States Supreme Court because they feared defeat. Instead, they harassed the state with local litigation, and attempted to delay matters in the hope that "something would turn up in their favor."

John Beard was as tall as Napoleon Broward, over six feet, and according to the newspaper reports, his appearance was as pleasing and his arguments were as eloquent as Broward's.[26] He did not deny that the governor's program would be immensely valuable to Florida, but he did contend that the courts would eventually award lands to the railroads and that the huge drainage expenditure would be irrevocably lost to Florida. Disparaging the drainage tax scheme, Beard emphatically declared that "if the drainage of the Everglades will benefit the whole state it is unfair to place the burden of their drainage upon the people of the six counties directly interested."[27] In rebuttal Broward presented so many figures, court decisions, maps, and surveys, that a drainage supporter exclaimed: "The governor just naturally sweats dope about the Everglades and drainage. He is chock full of it and I believe he could talk all night on the subject without ever being at a loss for a word."²⁸

This Pensacola debate intensified the drainage issues. J. E. Ingraham, vice-president of the Florida East Coast railroad, called the governor's imputations "unjust, unfair, and most undeserved."²⁹ The *Florida Times-Union* sounded the cry of "machine politics," and called the project a "scheme for political power" and an initial step toward political dictatorship. "Given the power which the adoption of the drainage amendment would give them," continued that newspaper, "it would not be long before they inaugurated state liquor traffic and state insurance. With three such powerful engines of graft, they could do what they pleased with Florida affairs, and the people would be powerless to prevent it. Conservative people, temperance people, it is well for you to give this question prayerful thought."³⁰

On a hot night, late in August, Broward talked before a large group in Marion County. An Ocala newspaper editor endorsed the speaker's "frankness and cordiality, and sincerity and honesty of purpose, that flashes from his eye, pulsates in his soul and vibrates in his voice." After this "heart to heart talk with the common people . . . everybody was so in love with the governor and his splendid talk that they wanted to take the chief executive's hand, and he held a decided levee. . . . It was . . . one of those spontaneous outpourings that show the world the honest, untainted blood that courses in the veins of Florida's uncontaminated 'Crackers.'" The editor declared that "when a man can stand up in a plain, everyday talk, hold his audience spellbound from 11 to 2:30 o'clock, with an oncoming shower that promised to break up the gathering, and then when he said he would wait till the clouds rolled by, the shout rose from man, woman and child to go on and tell it all, it is proof positive that they did come to hear Napoleon B. Broward, governor of the state of Florida, and the true, tried and unbiased friend of the people . . . ."³¹

In a speech delivered in Madison, a few weeks later, the governor said he could find "no good reason why the Everglades should not be drained," because "only the railroad crowd is opposed to it."[32] In Jacksonville, he told his audience: "This rich, fertile land, so admirably situated, so rich in its soil, is your land. These corporations want it, and that is why they belittle it. They want to rock you to sleep and then take it away from you. But I warn you of the danger. There is an insidious enemy abroad in the land. Beware of him."[33]

Broward had been hard pressed for funds for many months. Although his salary had been increased and he was able to realize a small income from his dredging and wrecking business in Jacksonville, the expense of a large family, and the cost of publishing and dispatching the drainage literature, as well as his traveling expenses, were using up all the income he could raise. Moreover, his campaign for governor had depleted his finances. While he was governor his funds were low and he frequently renewed notes with various banks. Halfway through his administration, he told an acquaintance that "real cash has become almost obsolete with me."[34] As it was necessary somehow to secure additional money to carry on the drainage campaign, Broward issued, in August, 1906, a circular letter appealing for aid from "The People of Florida." He asked "every citizen to contribute at least a two-cent stamp, or other small contributions to defray the expense. . . . I think that it will cost about twenty-five hundred dollars, made up as follows, 100,000 one-cent stamps, $1,000; preparing and printing data, about $1,000; purchasing and addressing envelopes, $500. To everyone who contributes more than 50 cents, I promise to return to him his proportion of whatever sum in excess of that amount is contributed."[35] The response to this appeal was very satisfactory.

Broward's drainage plans progressed slowly but surely. Criticisms and obstacles continued, but they did not make the governor any less determined to see his project through. When someone suggested that careful investigation and detailed surveys should precede dredging, he answered: "I will be dead by that time. The state will be poor and the money thus expended will buy a couple of dredges. We can sell some land to build dredges and if my friends will hold the knockers in check, we can make a convincing ocular demonstration."[36]

An effective "ocular demonstration," a trip to the drainage district, was provided by the Trustees of the Internal Improvement Fund during the latter part of September for leading members of the legislature and several editors of state newspapers. State Chemist Rose and Chief Engineer Newman were in charge of inspecting the Everglades and its adjacent lakes. Boarding a vessel in Fort Myers, the party sailed up the Caloosahatchee River to Alva, where a barbecue was held in the shade of huge moss-festooned oaks, near the river's edge. After lunch, Governor Broward mounted a wooden platform and briefly outlined his drainage program to the assembled crowd. One of the party, Representative Syd L. Carter, of Alachua County, announced: "Already I was almost convinced that the drainage scheme is right, but I will not commit in favor of it until after our return to Fort Myers."[37]

From Alva the group continued their slow way up the Caloosahatchee to LaBelle, where Captain F. A. Hendry came aboard. It was nearly evening as the boat neared Fort Thompson, and Broward stood on deck to watch night darkening the land. His hands rested quietly on the railing of the boat, and his eye followed the winding ribbon of smooth brown water which reflected the last slanting rays of the sun. The river's edge was choked with rushes and thick-stemmed waterweeds. Frogs piped in the shallows, and wild birds swooped and screamed, their shrill calls vibrating through the Glades. On either side of the river stretched acres of marsh and forest. Swamp oaks and cypresses, heavy with swaying moss-scarves, were clumped along the bank. In the evening air there was a rich tropical fragrance of late summer jessamine and flowering wild azaleas.

Early the next morning the voyage was underway again. The river was narrow now, and the current hard to follow.

The steamer *Edison* joined the party and acted as guide through the canals and lakes. By midafternoon the boats had entered a canal leading from Bonnet Lake to Hichopchee, and that night they anchored near the dam on the edge of Hichopchee Lake.

Anxious to see the sun rise across the great saw-grass marshes, Governor Broward was on deck before dawn next morning. Rich swamplands stretched before him, with only an occasional palm or cypress tree to break the monotony of the vast expanses. Flocks of large birds swirled and circled the lowlands. The river's water was a brown ooze, laced with roots and lily pads. The air was moist and heavy with a rank smell of muck, decaying vegetation, and slow-running water. The sun shredded the early morning mist, lightened the shadows beneath the trees, and warmed the tall, broad-shouldered man standing near the ship's rail.

Throughout the trip, Broward detailed to his guests various phases of his drainage and reclamation program. Existing canals were investigated, map surveys explained, soundings taken, and experiments checked. As a result, the legislators and newspapermen acquired a fuller understanding of the huge scope and tremendous potentialities of this project. When the enthusiastic travelers returned to Fort Myers, they reported that the "entire party was in favor of immediate drainage to a man, the only difference of opinion being on the power given the commission under the amendment."[38] J. H. Humphries, of Bradenton, for instance, favored drainage and opposed the constitutional amendment.[39] John W. Henderson, of Tallahassee, and other owners of large Everglades holdings seemed impressed with what they saw, but it was questionable whether they were willing to go all the way with Broward's program.

In the election of 1906, the drainage issue threatened to disrupt the state. Broward's campaign for the constitutional amendment was as thorough as his campaign for the governorship. Although he was not running for any office, he was more vilified than the candidates. Newspaper attacks on him were equally absurd and satirical. The comment of the *Orlando*

Democrat was typical: "Some men believe the Everglades should be drained while others urge the annexation of the moon."⁴⁰ Carrying maps and suitcases filled with drainage literature, Broward went up and down the state, into every city, hamlet, and crossroad, campaigning as thoroughly as he had for the governorship. Not since the conflict over the Railroad Commission and Primary Law had there been so much excitement over proposed legislation. Broward and Beard argued their cause in a series of debates—in Pensacola, Jacksonville, Tallahassee, and other leading Florida cities. Both men were intimately acquainted with Everglades drainage and reclamation, and each was firmly convinced of the rightness of his cause. They answered questions without hesitancy and conducted their arguments in a dignified manner.

For Broward, the election results were disheartening. The margin between those voting for and those against the drainage amendment increased rapidly as returns came in. The governor acknowledged defeat when votes from the larger counties were tabulated. Twenty-seven counties voted against the constitutional amendment, which lost by five thousand votes.⁴¹ Even in the face of this crushing defeat, Broward refused to give up. After final tabulations were reported, he told newspapermen: "They have beat me, but I am not through fighting yet. In fact, I feel better prepared and more in the mood for fighting than at any time since I entered politics. I will have another constitutional amendment offered at the next session of the legislature, and I will have some bills put through which will cause weeping and gnashing of teeth in certain quarters."⁴²

Defeat on the drainage issue was not the only reversal suffered by the governor in this election. Two active anti-Browardites, Stephen M. Sparkman and Frank Clark, were elected to Congress with substantial majorities. Florida's third congressman, William B. Lamar, had leaned more toward Broward and his liberal faction in previous campaigns, but in the political fracas of 1906 he was more anti-Broward than otherwise.[43] Among the Broward opponents elected to the state legislature were H. H. Buckman, J. B. Johnson, W. Hunt Harris, F. W. Sams, John W. Watson, and A. S. Wells. His supporters in the legislature included Park M. Trammell, Fred M. Hudson, L. C. Massey, Fred P. Cone, L. W. Zim, Thomas F. West, James E. Broome, M. S. Knight, J. F. C. Griggs, James E. Calkins, R. Pope Reese, and Ion L. Farris.

The legislature of 1907 assembled on April 2 in Tallahassee with the usual fanfare of excitement, anticipation, and curiosity. Governor Broward's message, delivered during the first week of the session, was regarded by many of his supporters throughout Florida as a liberal and a realistic document which compared favorably with his famous first message delivered in 1905. Governor Broward recommended:

1. The construction of a state arsenal for handling and safeguarding Florida's military supplies.

2. Legislation authorizing the levying of a tax on franchises.

3. Designation of the Railroad Commission as a "constitutional branch of the State Government."

4. Increased pay for teachers, and the raising of their qualifications, particularly in the rural schools.

5. Codification of school laws, regulations, and rules into a uniform system.

6. Adoption of a uniform system of textbooks for state schools.

7. Enactment of compulsory school education and school attendance laws.

8. Enactment of conservation laws protecting fish, oysters, game, and Florida's forests.

9. Construction of a system of *good roads* throughout the state.

10. Advertisements designed to encourage tourists and settlers to come to Florida.

11. A statute requiring that all persons "desiring to present any matters to the Legislature or to the members thereof

should be registered with the Secretary or Clerk of either House, and should state their interests and the bills, claims, resolutions or reports in which they are interested, and what interests or persons they represent, and in what capacity."

12. A resolution memorializing the "Congress of the United States to purchase territory, either domestic or foreign, and provide means to purchase the property of the Negroes, at reasonable prices, and to transport them to the territory purchased by the United States. The United States to organize a government for them of the Negro race; to protect them from foreign invasion; to prevent white people from living among them on the territory; and to prevent Negroes from migrating back to the United States."

13. A statute making public mendacity "a misdemeanor and punishing any newspaper writer or editor or publisher who deliberately or intentionally writes or publishes an article that is untrue, and making the public printing of an untruth prima facie evidence of the misdemeanor."

14. Restrictions on child labor in industrial enterprises.[44]

Most of these recommendations were progressive, and were designed solely for the benefit of Florida and its citizens. There were no arguments against enacting conservation laws, regulating child labor, raising school standards and teachers' salaries, building good roads, and encouraging tourists and settlers to come into Florida. Admittedly, regulation of lobbying and lobbyists and a uniform textbook law were desirable for the state. However, many people felt that some of Broward's recommendations were based on his own prejudices rather than on sound judgment. His proposed mass removal of the Negro population was a heritage from Reconstruction days. The race question had been a frequently recurring issue in his past political campaigns. Broward's liberalism did not conflict with the theories of white supremacy. He contended that Negroes were "the wards of the white people, and that it is our duty to make whatever provision for them that would be best for their well-being."[45]

The governor's request for a libel law was severely criticized. The conservative newspapers chastised him for introducing factional political issues into his message. Nevertheless, many Broward supporters applauded his contention that "we have some newspapers that are not content with writing inaccuracies about candidates for office, who, if elected, would not serve the 'interests' . . . but continue to write falsehoods about the men after they become officials, with a view to impairing their influence for the good of the people. . . ."[46] The governor was infuriated with the papers that had persisted in making unnecessary attacks and allegations against him and his family during his political campaigns. These same journals, Broward held, were continuing their attacks on him and were, in addition, deriding the Trustees of the Internal Improvement Fund and the whole drainage and reclamation program. He bluntly told the legislators that "the Times-Union, Jasper News, St. Augustine Evening Record, Gainesville Sun, Lake City Index, Tampa Tribune, Tallahassee True Democrat, and two or three other small papers, have kept up the work of maligning your Trustees. . . ."[47]

In pressing for the restrictions against state newspapers, Governor Broward was concerned not only with the general antagonistic attitude of the conservative press toward him and his policies, but also with certain specific items published by these newspapers. He described three cartoons which had appeared in the *Florida Times-Union* on October 4, 1906, and February 23 and March 21, 1907. The drawings had intimated that funds which should have been used for the public schools had been diverted by the trustees for building dredges to be used on the drainage project. Broward branded the editorials which said that taxes were being used to pay attorneys' fees as "absolutely false." Using the sharpest language at his command, the governor reiterated that "not one dollar of taxpayers' money has been used in building dredges, drainage, or attorneys' fees. . . . Every dollar spent for these matters was derived from the sale of lands held by the Trustees for such purposes. . . ."[48]

The proposal for a libel law was not new to the Florida legislature. During the session in 1905, Senator Frank W. Sams had introduced a bill "entitled an act relating to the publication of libels in newspapers, magazines and other periodicals in the State; to provide a penalty for imparting false information to editors, owners, publishers and reporters of newspapers, magazines or other periodicals, and to provide where actions, civil and criminal, may be instituted and carried on."[49] This measure received an unfavorable committee report, and there had been no further attempt to resurrect the issue until 1907.

Still concerned with the attacks made against the Trustees of the Internal Improvement Fund, the governor sent the legislature a special message on April 2, 1907, the same day that he delivered his regular message.[50] He elaborated upon the points which he had made in his first message, and he continued his vigorous arraignment of the corporate interests who had "through newspapers and other publications, circulated many falsehoods against the present Trustees . . . , which may deceive the people as to the honor, integrity and ability of those State officials. By innuendo and otherwise, they have attempted to traduce not only your Trustees, but to create in the minds of the people, even beyond the confines of the State, the belief that the Trustees were guilty of mismanagement of the Internal Improvement Fund."[51] In order to answer these serious charges, the governor recommended that "a numerically strong committee, equipped with sufficient technical knowledge to make a searching investigation, be appointed at once, composed of members of each House, to investigate the charges and innuendoes . . . and make report of their findings at the earliest possible date."[52]

Such a committee was set up, and on May 31, 1907, the last day of the session, it announced that because the job was so large, and the time so short, it had not been able to make a thorough investigation and could not submit any findings.[53] The governor felt that a real report would have cleared up much of the suspicion held by many citizens in regard to the trustees. He was also disappointed when the legislators refused to enact a libel law.

Broward, however, was pleased with many of the other laws enacted by the legislature, as he considered them a fulfillment of his liberal program. Such a measure was the "Pure Drug and Food Law," which made it "unlawful for any person to manufacture, sell, keep or offer for sale . . . any article of food, drugs, medicine or liquors which is adulterated or misbranded, or which contains any poisonous or deleterious substance. . . ." The measure directed that examination of food and drug specimens be supervised by the state chemist.[54]

Broward was very happy when, on May 29, 1907, he signed into law the act which prohibited "the employment of minors under a certain age in factories, workshops, bowling alleys, barrooms, beer gardens, places of amusement where intoxicating liquors are sold, and in or about mine or quarry. . . ."[55] The recommendation to build a state arsenal was accepted by the legislators, and St. Francis Barracks in St. Augustine was chosen as a proper site.[56] The legislators also chose a permanent camp site for the Florida State Troops on the tract of land "at Black Point on the St. Johns River, known as Philbrofen."[57] A new law forbade selling or giving cigarettes to minors.[58] Influenced by several state patriotic groups, the legislature voted to place a statue of General Edmund Kirby Smith in Statuary Hall in Washington,[59] and to erect a monument on the Battlefield of Chickamauga in honor of the Florida soldiers who took part in that battle.[60] In the hope of establishing a popular tourist attraction, the legislators passed a law authorizing the transporting of Ponce de León's remains to Florida, if possible.[61] Senator H. H. McCreary tried unsuccessfully to push through the bill which would establish a state textbook commission and provide a uniform series of textbooks for the public schools.[62]

The senators and representatives were anxious to hear the report of the recess committee which had been established by the 1905 legislature to "inspect, examine into, report and recommend . . . whatever . . . is necessary or requisite and best suited to the welfare of the insane in this State. . . ."[63] On April 3, 1907, Governor Broward, on behalf of the committee, made the report which recommended that new buildings be erected in Chattahoochee, that a closer screening of applicants be effected so that only the insane be admitted, and that "every care and comfort . . . be given to a class of afflicted citizens whose very hopeless and childlike dependent condition appeals most strongly to every tender Christian sentiment in the human heart, and to philanthropic thought. . . ."[64] These recommendations were approved, and the legislators appointed still another committee to visit and inspect the hospital. This new committee found "recent improvements of a substantial and satisfactory character," but they criticized the fact that certain of the inmates in the hospital were not really insane. For instance, they announced that one "class, whose presence there is of doubtful propriety, consists of 'plain drunks,' who are sent to be sobered up and take the 'gold cure,' which is administered in the institution."[65]

During the legislative session of 1907, the members of the House of Representatives indignantly adopted a resolution in which they condemned an article on peonage in Florida, written by Richard Barry and published in the *Cosmopolitan Magazine*.[66] The resolution claimed that the statements "made by the said Barry were almost entirely false, and particularly that portion wherein it stated that the State of Florida was powerless to deal with alleged peonage conditions, and wherein it was stated that the people of Florida condoned alleged slavery conditions."[67] The governor had read the magazine article and its reproduction in the *New York Evening Journal*, and he endorsed the statements made in Congress by Frank Clark against Barry and Barry's publisher, William Randolph Hearst.[68]

Very late in the session, the legislators began debating the most important bill on their calendar, a new drainage measure.

Drafted by former Governor Jennings, and introduced by J. E. Crane of Hillsborough County, it sought to amend the weaknesses in the Act of 1905 and it explicitly stipulated boundaries of the drainage district.[69] In the House the bill was introduced by C. S. Wilson.[70] The measure was bitterly opposed by the anti-drainage factions in both houses. Leading the group in the Senate were John S. Beard, D. H. Baker, H. H. Buckman, E. S. Crill, J. H. Humphries, J. B. Johnson, F. W. Sams, and J. R. Willis. The anti-drainage group in the House included: B. C. Abernethey, John Bradshaw, A. E. Donegan, S. H. Melton, J. W. Watson, and A. S. Wells.

After a determined battle which lasted several days, the committee reported the bill favorably to the Senate on Friday, May 24. This bill had been of paramount interest to the assembly since the session opened, but final debate was begun in a surprise move by drainage supporters. The Humphries bill, designed to enforce stricter regulation of local option laws, was under discussion. While the Senate waited for a committee report on a proposed amendment to the Humphries bill, Senator Crane moved that the drainage measure be considered. When he assured the legislators that it would be disposed of in a few minutes, Senator Humphries yielded the floor. Immediately the anti-drainage forces collected every available weapon to fight the measure. The senators tried to stall debate, to talk the bill to death, and to amend it beyond recognition. Controversial arguments continued throughout the day, and it was evening before a final vote revealed that the drainage bill had passed by a majority of 20 to 12.[71] It also passed the House, on May 27, 1907, by a vote of 37 to 14,[72] and Governor Broward signed it into law on May 29, 1907.[73] The act established a board of drainage commissioners, determined a definite drainage district, and authorized a continuance of Everglades drainage and reclamation. It continued the annual tax of five cents per acre and authorized use of this revenue for financing the drainage program.[74] Governor Broward and his supporters hailed the passage of the drainage bill as a great victory.

Throughout the legislative session, many Florida newspapers continued their attacks on Governor Broward and denounced much of the liberal legislation for which he was responsible. Typical of these attacks were the following comments: "Let us be charitable if we cannot be good and let us hope that the sins of this legislature will never be itemized so that each member must carry his proportionate share—even a little bit would be bad. . . . Never in the history of Florida . . . has there been so much cheap demagoguery and reckless motives in legislation. . . . Had it not been for the sober-minded and level-headed members to act as balance wheels . . . confusion and unrest from one end of Florida to the other, would have been our shame."[75]

The conservative newspapers deplored the fact that the trend in the state seemed to be toward centralization and more governmental control. The *Florida Times-Union* reviewed with alarm the legislative proceedings, and particularly the action taken on drainage; they considered such measures dangerous. The editors of the paper were also disturbed by the indifference shown by a majority of the Florida citizens, who, the editors thought, could not or would not see the menace. They compared the apathy of the people with the stricken husband who had composed this epitaph:

> *My wife's dead and here she lies*
> *Nobody laughs and nobody cries;*
> *But where she's gone or how she fares,*
> *Nobody knows and nobody cares.*[76]

Particularly irritated with the *Florida Times-Union*, Broward filed a libel suit in the Circuit Court of Leon County early in April, 1907. He asked fifty thousand dollars damages for alleged malicious and false charges made against him as a public official and against the drainage commissioners. The governor's legal action, however, was not successful.

By midsummer of 1907 the drainage program was well under way. Two dredges, the *Everglades* and *Okeechobee*, were digging canals and drains.[77] At the beginning of Broward's administration in 1905, an audit had revealed that the Internal Improvement Fund totaled more than three hundred thousand dollars. Two years later this money was gone and the financial situation was serious. As a result of new litigation, drainage taxation failed to produce adequate revenue. The trustees still held over two and a half million acres of land, and Broward suggested general land sales to help make up the deficits. Consequently, lands were put on the market for as low as two dollars an acre.[78] The state school fund would receive 25 per cent of these proceeds, and the rest would be earmarked for drainage.

Drainage had assumed a Federal aspect, to some degree, during this period. Governor Broward conferred frequently with members of Congress who favored drainage projects, or who were members of Congressional committees supervising drainage and reclamation.[79] Many Floridians hoped eventually to secure Federal aid to help finance the Everglades project.

The governor became actively interested in the National Drainage Association and he hoped to use this organization to apply pressure for national drainage legislation. In a letter to Thomas L. Conner of St. Louis, the secretary of this association, Broward revealed the extent of Federal support for Florida drainage. "The United States, through the Bureau of Irrigation and Drainage Investigation," wrote Broward, "are aiding us by having engineers run lines of levels from the Gulf to the Atlantic Ocean, across the Everglades, and from Lake Okeechobee, in the Everglades, south. They will also lay out lines of canals. . . ."[80]

Broward's chief interest throughout his administration was to "save and reclaim the people's land."[81] Despite the great obstacles that confronted him, he never lost faith in his Everglades program. He frequently told those who opposed him: "It might be said of me, and perhaps of every other man who has a desire to accomplish something for the good of mankind, that he belongs to that class 'who rush in where angels fear to tread.' This land would have remained a wilderness and would have been inhabited by the Indians until the dawn of the millennium had those who preceded us been as weak as the majority of those who quibble now, and stand on the bank and shiver and shake, instead of plunging in and doing something."[82]

Broward's fight for drainage was also a battle against Florida's railroads and corporations. To him, they were predatory interests, ruthlessly encroaching upon the people's rights. His attitude toward Henry M. Flagler was typical of his attitude toward many railroad heads: "He desires to own all lands that are for sale or rent, by any means. . . ."[83] The governor's strong opposition to corporations appealed to public sentiment throughout the nation. His liberalism, progressive ideas, and demand for democratic government marked him as an outstanding personality of Florida, and as one of the most effective liberals in the South.

〜 16 〜

"Praised by
These--Blamed by Those"

ARLY IN SEPTEMBER, 1907, the stately new
Executive Mansion was completed in Tallahassee, and
in a few days the Broward family moved in.[1] The
large, white, frame house was colonial in style, with two-story
Ionic columns across its front. Surrounded by a spacious lawn,
attractively landscaped, the house occupied the middle of a
four-acre block, about half a mile from the capitol. A circular
carriage drive led from the street to the wide porch. The front
entrance opened into a large reception hall, with a graceful
stairway at the far end. On the first floor there were a drawing
room, front and back parlors, a dining room, the butler's pantry,
the kitchen, and the governor's study. In most of these, and in
several of the eight bedrooms on the second floor, were huge
marble mantels extending to the ceiling. There was also a
sewing room for Mrs. Broward, and a section of the attic was
arranged as a playroom for the children. The Cedar Rapids
Furniture Company submitted samples, and Mrs. Broward
spent many weeks selecting furniture for the house. The furniture, not including kitchen equipment, cost $4,444.75.[2]

The new era that was rapidly developing in Florida politics
was part of a general movement apparent in the Democratic
party. Progressives throughout the South overthrew conservative machines and elected reform governors. Many of the renowned political figures, prominent during the Civil War and
the Reconstruction era, had passed from the scene. New leaders were rapidly coming to the front—Napoleon Broward in
Florida, Hoke Smith in Georgia, James K. Vardaman and John

Sharpe Williams in Mississippi, Charles B. Aycock and William W. Kitchin in North Carolina, Thomas M. Campbell in Texas, and Braxton B. Comer in Alabama. For a time it seemed that the Populist dream of the 1890's might be finally realized during the first decade of the twentieth century; perhaps the progressives of the South and the West would join hands to redeem the farmer and the laborer. The "new" politician in the South stood on a truly progressive platform, and insisted, in the tradition of Thomas Jefferson, that the common man regain his rightful place in a free society. The reform period was characterized by a developing centralization of political powers, an increased emphasis on the importance of government for the majority, and a growing sense of responsibility of government to its citizens. In Florida, during the Broward Era, the continued shift in power from conservative to liberals, evident for many years, became almost a reality.

These changes were not concentrated wholly in the area of politics and government. There were social and economic changes, also, in Florida and throughout the nation. The frontier disappeared, and the diminishing importance of frontier life had a vital effect on the character of American civilization. America's population and wealth increased, her horizons broadened, and a new ideology permeated her people. The United States was in the midst of an economic revolution which had a transforming influence on the whole world. Railroad stretched across the land, connecting all parts of the country. Telegraph, telephone, and cable service daily grew more complete. There was wide circulation of newspapers, books, and periodicals. Inventions crowded forward in an impressive procession. Living was urbanized and people became more cosmopolitan. Easterners traveled west, and Westerners gained recognition in politics, in business, and in the professions. Thousands of Northern tourists and settlers moved south into states like Florida, and many from the South lived in Northern cities. The population was inextricably mixed, and many characteristics of one section of the country became similar to characteristics in other sections.

A new way of life developed in Florida. This was the period when "the old celluloid collar . . . passed out. Congress shoes were rapidly going. Silver finger rings were no longer worn by rural maidens. . . . Though the Florida Legislature still enrolled the bills it passed with pen and ink, no big business man by 1909 had his letters so written; he had already found out the advantages of the typewriter. . . . The old-fashioned hominy, ground at the country grist-mill, had practically disappeared from most family menus in Florida and grits had taken its place. . . . Gone were frock coats, Brandreth's pills, the old spinning wheel, the old home-sewed bonnet, the road cart, bullet molds, reloading tools, *McGuffey's Readers*, the 'blue-back' speller, and the 'vinegar and nails' treatment for puny children. . . . Women who wished to keep up with the fashions subscribed for the *Delineator*. . . . Religious denominations had about stopped excommunication of their members for dancing."[3] Moving pictures were rapidly becoming popular in the state, and during Broward's administration motion-picture theaters were built in several cities. The *Ocala Banner* proudly announced that the "Berlin Electrical Theater is attracting good crowds daily and nightly."[4] In Jacksonville, the managers of the Dixie Theater assured its patrons that "the Edison machine was utilized with fine results. The attachments to the 1907 model of the Wizard-make, enables the operator to obtain the best effect and without any perceptible jump or flicker. The pictures are sharp, clearly defined . . . the public gets all that can be drawn from moving pictures."[5] Many rural sections possessed regular telephone service, and there was hardly a Florida community with a population of five hundred which did not have electric lights. The state had advanced considerably since the day when someone described it as "the most fertile state . . . ever seen, the land producing forty bushels of frogs to an acre and alligators enough to fence them in."

As Governor Broward's administration progressed, his interest in a national drainage program quickened. He enthusiastically endorsed the program of the Inland Waterways Commission as outlined by Theodore Roosevelt on March 14,

1907, and he was pleased to note that the first commissioners included such men as Senator Francis G. Newlands of Nevada, Congressman John H. Bankhead of Alabama, and Gifford Pinchot, Chief Forester.[6] Broward believed that the Everglades drainage canals would not only reclaim thousands of acres of land for settlement but that a new inland waterway would be provided for Florida. He heartily supported President Roosevelt's argument that the "one complete remedy for the congestion of railroad traffic and the consequent crippling of the nation's business will be found in the development of a supplementary system of transportation by water."[7] Although Florida suffered no railroad congestion in 1907, Broward realized that better transportation facilities would be necessary, because when the drainage program was completed "millions of people might find homes and occupations" in the state.[8]

Broward had become recognized as a national authority on drainage, and during the late summer of 1907, he was invited to accompany President Roosevelt and his party in October on a trip down the Mississippi River to inspect various drainage projects.[9] Broward eagerly accepted the invitation and joined the group at Canton, Ohio, where Roosevelt dedicated the McKinley monument. While the steamboats moved slowly down the river en route to Memphis, and Roosevelt expounded his ideas, it became apparent to Broward that "the President's passionate interest in the national forests, in reclamation of arid Western lands by irrigation, in conservation of water power and other natural resources," was part "of his campaign against the malefactors of great wealth," and bore a strong resemblance to Broward's own fierce battle against the railroads and corporations of Florida. During the voyage, Broward and the President frequently talked about the Florida drainage program and national problems. One afternoon in Memphis the conversation turned to the Spanish-American War and the events leading up to the conflict. Roosevelt asked Broward,

"Governor, have you still got the Three Friends?"

"Yes," Broward replied.

"Well," said Mr. Roosevelt, "you ought to be mighty proud of her. If it had not been for the Three Friends you would not be governor now."

"You ought to be proud of her yourself," Governor Broward retorted, "because if it had not been for her you would not be president of the United States now."[10]

In connection with the drainage program, Broward, in late November of 1907, traveled to Baltimore for the National Drainage Congress, which assembled on the campus of The Johns Hopkins University. Gifford Pinchot spoke and revealed the progress that the Inland Waterways Commission was making. Broward had spent considerable time checking Everglades drainage, and when he delivered his talk on the third and last day of the meeting, he was able to give the latest information on the vast project.[11] The delegates endorsed a resolution to Congress, introduced by Senator Ashbury C. Latimer of South Carolina, which asked for Federal drainage legislation. At the conference Governor Broward met Major J. A. Dapray, temporary secretary of the National Drainage Congress, and the two men remained close friends until the governor's death. Before adjourning, the drainage conference elected Broward president for 1908. His officers and directors included Dr. James Bosely, W. S. Braddock, B. H. Griswold, James Cosgrove, F. J. Buck, and C. B. Brown.[12]

Governor Broward returned to Washington to confer with Pinchot, members of the Florida delegation, and other congressmen on certain aspects of the proposed national drainage program. While in Washington he accepted an invitation to dine with the President at the White House.[13]

There was much administrative detail connected with the Drainage Congress. Broward was active in securing funds to continue the work of the association, and devoted a considerable amount of his time to the enactment of Federal drainage legislation. He opposed the expenditure of the association's money for "publications calculated to influence legislation in Congress." He believed that "efforts should be made to avoid all seeming interference with Congress in the scheme of

legislative action, . . . simply urging upon Congress the wisdom
of Federal aid to drainage throughout the United States."¹
A Washington lobbyist, A. W. Bernard, worked against drainage legislation.¹⁵ Scornful of his influence, Broward wrote: "I
think Mr. Bernard is a humbug and grafter, pure and simple
and I cannot understand how any member of Congress car
be affected, either by his persuasion, or by any enlightenmen
that he can give them; he neither owns any swamp land, nor
has he anything to do with any. . . ."¹⁶

Bernard received a stinging letter from Broward, at which
he took great offense.¹⁷ Senator Moses E. Clapp of Minnesota
read it, and described it as a "damned insulting letter."¹⁸ In
Congress when Senator Clapp strongly opposed a drainage bil
introduced by Senator Latimer, the latter realized that some
Republican congressmen were planning to play partisan politic
with the national drainage program. Informing Broward of a
proposed meeting of drainage supporters with the Secretary
of the Interior, the Senator wrote: "They are determined to
have the bill that passes the Senate go to the country as a
Republican measure. . . ."¹⁹

Governor Broward paid little heed to the information he
read in Latimer's letter. Regardless of the political party re
ceiving credit he was primarily interested in seeing legislation
enacted. Victory seemed sure; Latimer had advised Broward
that he viewed the bill's passage as a certainty. Then Latimer
died suddenly in Washington, on February 20, 1908, and the
strongest drainage supporter in the Senate was gone. This was
a heavy blow to Broward and to the national drainage en
thusiasts. The governor immediately wired Major Dapray
and the latter went to Washington to confer with member
of Congress who had pledged their support. Meanwhile, the
governor wrote letters to John Sharpe Williams, Joseph Can
non, Champ Clark, and other leading Congressional figures.²
Latimer's death proved to be only a temporary setback
eventually Congress enacted the laws which helped assure the
realization of Governor Broward's far-reaching program.

Although much of the governor's time, during the closing months of 1907, was taken up by drainage problems and activities, he was also aware that political currents had begun to move, and especially that 1908 would be an election year. On the national level it seemed that some of the currents might run toward revolt. In Florida, Broward was determined that there would be no reversal of the trend toward liberalism.

Early in the fall of 1907, the state Democratic executive committee had met to plan a "coming out convention" to be held in Ocala on November 14. At that time, it was expected that most of the candidates for the state and Congressional offices would already be in the race and they would be given ample opportunity at the Ocala meeting to state their platforms. In October three candidates announced for the approaching gubernatorial nomination: General Albert W. Gilchrist, of Punta Gorda; Jefferson B. Browne, of Key West; and R. Hudson Burr, of Tallahassee, chairman of the Railroad Commission. Browne, formerly chairman of this commission, was a mild Broward supporter; Gilchrist, a rising political figure in the state, had been speaker of the Florida House of Representatives. John N. C. Stockton entered the race on Novmber 4.[21] Confessing that he had long "had the gubernatorial bee in his bonnet," he came out as a strong Broward man and sought an endorsement from the liberal factions in the state. Broward attended the Ocala meeting and while he did not announce himself in favor of any one candidate, it was obvious from his formal speeches and from his conversation that he would endorse the liberals in the race and would actively support them.[22]

John S. Beard of Pensacola announced that he was a candidate for the United States Senate against Stephen R. Mallory, who planned to run for re-election. Beard, a long-time foe of drainage, began an active speaking tour, and he had already visited the southern part of Florida before he arrived for the Ocala meeting. Governor Broward's former political ally and friend, Duncan U. Fletcher, also announced himself as a

268 Napoleon Bonaparte Broward

candidate for the Senate.²³ Fletcher was one of the early
Straightouts from Duval County, and had staunchly fought
for reform while mayor of Jacksonville. He had supported
Broward during the gubernatorial campaign of 1904, and for
several years had been chairman of the state executive committee. When Fletcher was appointed attorney for a railroad
company, early in 1905, he offered to resign from the executive
committee, but Broward dissuaded him. The governor wrote
Fletcher a note, and said, "I fear that you are too thin-
skinned."²⁴ During the early months of Broward's administration, Fletcher had been a frequent visitor in the Broward home
in Tallahassee. He and the governor often conferred about
personal and party problems. As the months passed, their
friendship cooled somewhat. Although there was no open
break, it became obvious that the old alliance had been rup-
tured. The rift widened as the governor continued to fight
against abuses sponsored by the interests with which Fletcher
was now aligned. Friction increased during the ensuing
months, and Broward and Fletcher became bitter political
enemies.

During the late summer and early fall of 1907, rumor
had circulated in the state that the governor would announce
himself for the Senate. Broward was only fifty years old and
he considered himself far too young to retire to slippered ease.
Politics was his true profession. He liked his job with it
powers and responsibilities and it was with regret that he saw
his term of office approaching its close. Nevertheless, he
seemed reluctant to throw his hat into the political ring; when
he was asked at Ocala whether he would run or not, he
jovially changed the subject. Supporters and friends had
strongly urged him to announce, and he had received dozens
of letters, of which the following was typical: "We have been
talking politics with Frank Adams and John M. Caldwell and
if you should run for the U. S. Senate they are both for you
Caldwell has promised to support you with his paper and
you know he has the farmer's Union paper. This would give you

both County papers and all the political following in Hamilton, and I think Columbia County. . . ."[25]

Broward decided not to become a candidate. After William James Bryan announced his own candidacy on November 15, 1908, the governor endorsed his old friend and campaign manager: "Bryan not only heartily supported me for nomination for Governor, in the sense that friends usually do, but he devoted much of his time and went to considerable expense in urging my nomination, and I feel that it is but just for me, at this time, to support him, taking into consideration that he is already a candidate. I believe that if he is nominated and elected, he will render the State splendid service."[26]

In November, while Broward was in Baltimore attending the National Drainage Congress, he was informed that Senator Mallory had suffered a stroke of paralysis, which at first was not thought serious. Mallory grew worse, and on December 19 he withdrew from the Senate race. Within a few hours after Mallory's announcement, the *Florida Times-Union* reported that "Governor Broward, John N. C. Stockton, William J. Bryan, Legal Advisor John Murdoch Barrs and Brother Nat" held an important political caucus in the Aragon Hotel in Jacksonville. "Brother Nat" (Nathan P. Bryan), according to the newspaper account, was "the power behind the throne and his advice . . . [was] heeded far more than that of professional Legal Advisor Barrs." The *Times-Union* also asserted that Broward intended entering the senatorial race if Stephen M. Sparkman became a candidate. "Napoleon I of Jacksonville will ask Wm. J. Bryan to withdraw. Bryan in turn will enter the Congressional race, the office upon which the Hon. Ion L. Farris had his eye."[27]

The political situation in the state became even more complicated when Senator Mallory died on the morning of December 23 in Pensacola. Two days later Governor Broward issued a statement to the press, announcing that he had named William James Bryan to complete Mallory's unexpired term. The governor said: "The particular qualities . . . that have actuated me in appointing him United States Senator, though he is but thirty-one years old, are: His intense patriotism. . . . His exceedingly clear grasp of the political problems of the day. . . . The great ability that he has shown. . . . His devotion to the cause of the people." Broward described his friend as "a man of great industry, of tireless energy. . . . He has every quality that fits a man for the great service to which he has been appointed."[28]

Bryan accepted the appointment and told the newspapermen who had come to his house for an interview: "I realize that in the Senate I shall be one of the representatives of all the people, and I shall try to so perform my duty in this responsible position that all of the people, whether rich or poor, whether they occupy prominent places or toil in obscurity for daily bread, will believe that I have done my duty."[29] When one of the reporters reminded Bryan that he would become the youngest member of the Senate, Bryan laughingly remarked: "I understand that I am the youngest member. Some day I will be the oldest. I am going to make the people of my state the best senator any state ever had, and it will take many years to do it."[30]

Conservative newspapers in the South severely criticized Bryan's appointment. The *Tampa Tribune*, for example, asserted that "if Mr. Bryan has given any symptoms of being worthy of this distinction we are utterly at a loss to know it— it must be a weighty secret hidden in the governor's brain. . . ."[31] Editor Frank Harris, of the *Ocala Banner*, dryly remarked: "The young man just seems to take it for granted that he is to homestead the office and become a permanent fixture in the upper branch of Congress."[32] A writer in the *Savannah News* advised, "Young fellow, when you go to Washington you had better wear a tag saying 'I'm old enough.' "[33] More favorable newspapers complimented Bryan's "native ability, his acquired fitness and the people's knowledge of him."[34] He accompanied Senator Taliaferro back to Washington on January 1, 1908. Presented to the Senate nine days later, he formally took his seat as junior United States Senator from Florida.

Meanwhile, as the national campaign began moving along at high tide, Governor Broward became increasingly interested in the candidates and the issues. He, like the rest of the Democratic party, had known for months that William Jennings Bryan wanted the presidential nomination for a third time. In the summer of 1907, Bryan had said that he would seriously consider "the question of candidacy" only if he knew that he could "advance the cause of Democracy by being a candidate."[35] As far as Bryan was concerned, this question had been settled by the time he landed in New York on August 29, 1907, after a tour of Europe. It was no surprise to Governor Broward, when, on August 30, Bryan made his bid for the Democratic nomination before a great crowd in Madison Square Garden. It was not an unwelcome action, as far as the governor of Florida was concerned. He had always considered himself a Bryan supporter, and he counted himself as one of Bryan's friends. Broward, however, did not endorse all of Bryan's speech. He certainly could not accept the idea "that the railroads . . . must ultimately become public property and be managed by public officials." Although the governor had waged an earnest fight for the Florida Railroad Commission and had opposed the Flaglers and the Plants in his state, he had not advocated an end of private ownership.

Governor Broward, like other Southern politicians in 1907 and 1908, was concerned over the clash of state and Federal rights.[36] He clearly saw the possibility of friction in the struggles for railroad and insurance regulation, the control of corporations, and the enactment of child-labor laws, employer liability laws, and laws regulating marriage and divorce. Although he supported centralization within the state, Broward could not fully condone the increasing concentration of powers in the Federal government. Bryan's New York speech showed Broward that the Commoner was a doubtful representative of the states' rights school, and the governor wondered whether the party should accept Bryan as its leader. Likewise, Governor Broward felt that William Jennings Bryan was too radical in his racial views. Although Broward was not so rabid on the Negro question as Tom Watson of Georgia or Ben Tillman of South Carolina, he was a loyal and consistent supporter of the white supremacy theory. Broward, however, did not feel called upon to speak for his constituents as did Watson, who announced that Bryan had proved himself "unworthy of Georgia's vote" by expressing sympathy for the Negro troops involved in the Brownsville riots of 1906.[37]

As the months passed and as Bryan started to back away from his views on government ownership of the railroads, Broward began to warm up to him. It was easier for the governor to support a Bryan who declared that perhaps the country was not ready for anything more drastic than strong railroad regulation and that he would not insist upon a government ownership plank in the Democratic platform in 1908. Broward felt that perhaps Bryan was advancing his racial ideas in an attempt to lure the Negro voters, already angry with Roosevelt and Taft over the Brownsville incident, from the Republican party and into the Democratic fold. When Broward visited Washington early in December, 1907, he noted that the Bryan campaign was already underway there. He conferred with Democratic leaders on plans for the approaching convention and in January, 1908, he accepted an invitation to meet with Bryan in Lincoln, Nebraska, to plan strategy for the campaign in the South.[38] Since there was little doubt that the Solid South would support the Democratic nominee, Bryan hoped that Broward would campaign for him in the North as well. When it appeared that Broward would not enter the senatorial race in Florida, it seemed likely that he would have time to take the stump for Bryan.

The governor returned to Tallahassee late in January, and almost immediately left for Miami. On February 3, 1908, he headed a motorcade of sixty south Florida businessmen to Fort Lauderdale. The governor, at luncheon, briefly explained the drainage project and announced that progress was being made. John N. C. Stockton, J. W. Watson, Mayor F. H. Wharton of Miami, and R. F. Daniel were present at the luncheon and accompanied Broward that afternoon on an inspection tour of the canals west of Fort Lauderdale.[39]

Broward had hoped to attend the meeting of the state Democratic executive committee in Jacksonville on February 11, but instead he returned to Tallahassee. The committee set the date for the primaries and announced the candidates. The newspaper story describing the meeting declared that "factionalism is not so rampant as it was in former years, and little is heard regarding the 'Antis' or 'Straightouts.' All the candidates are personally popular."[40] Nathan P. Bryan, Telfair Stockton, Mayor W. H. Sebring, of Jacksonville, John T. Alsop, P. A. Holt, former Governor Jennings, George C. Bedell, R. K. Knight, former Governor Fleming, and A. V. Wright were among the Florida politicians present.

Although the state campaign officially started with the meeting of the executive committee, in reality it had begun many months earlier, in November, 1907, at the Ocala "coming out convention." In January, the *Punta Gorda Herald* had raised the old cry of a "Broward-Barrs-Stockton ring," and had claimed that "they are out to elect Mr. Stockton."[41] Stockton began a speaking tour through west Florida in January, advocating state prohibition, control of the railroads, and continuance of the Everglades drainage program. He appeared in Ocala on January 24, 1908, to review a prohibition parade that had been organized by the ministers in the city. Three hundred school children, waving white flags and singing prohibition songs, marched through the streets. They stopped in front of each saloon in Ocala to sing and cheer, while the ministers went in to remonstrate and plead with the sinners at the bar. That evening Stockton, speaking before a huge crowd, endorsed the work of the prohibitionists, and bade them to "love God and fear no man and there will be a moral cleaning and regeneration."[42]

Gilchrist, Stockton's strongest opponent, was also busy during January and February, as he traveled through the state—talking, meeting voters, and shaking hands. The *Ocala Banner* was one of Gilchrist's strongest supporters, and Editor Frank Harris wrote: "No faction, machine or ring brought him out. He came out as a candidate, alone and single-handed. He will be glad to receive the support of the corporations, of the anti-corporations, the prohibitionists and the anti-prohibitionists, of the local optionists, the Christians and the Jews and of the Gentiles, the 'publicans and sinners.' He would even accept the support of the Pharisees."[43]

Meanwhile, Governor Broward received disturbing news from Washington. On February 19, forty days after he entered the United States Senate, William James Bryan was stricken with typhoid fever. This grave report shocked Florida. Most of the newspapers carried daily bulletins regarding his condition, and President Roosevelt sent a special messenger every day to the hospital to inquire about the Senator's health. Optimistic hospital bulletins revived hope that Bryan would recover, but on the morning of March 22 he died in Providence Hospital. Governor Broward was notified, and he left Tallahassee immediately for Jacksonville to attend the funeral. With Bryan's death, Broward lost a long-time friend, a close political ally, and a true and ardent supporter. The loss of the Senator was mourned by thousands throughout Florida, and by many persons throughout the nation. President Roosevelt telegraphed condolences; hundreds of people who had never seen Bryan wrote letters to his family, and many newspapers printed eulogies.

On March 27, Broward appointed William Hall Milton, of Marianna, to fill the vacancy until a Senator could be nominated in the coming primaries. The anti-Broward press in the state immediately denounced the governor's actions. The *Ocala Banner* had already predicted that if Milton were appointed, he would agree not to run again. The Ocala paper prophesied that if Broward subsequently announced himself as a candidate for Senator, Milton would lend him five thousand dollars for campaign expenses.[44]

By the first of April the governor had made up his mind, and he announced that he was officially entering the race. The *Florida Times-Union* greeted this decision with an "April Fool's Day" cartoon, which pictured the new candidate reaching down to pick up a pocketbook marked "United States Senate." Behind a fence, a man labeled "The People" was pulling a string which drew the pocketbook out of Broward's reach.[45] The *Tampa Tribune* wrote in similar vein: "Another B. enters the senatorial race and 'twill be up to every Florida voter to learn Hamlet's soliloquy which starts out 'To B. or not to B. that is the question,' when he casts his vote in the primary."[46]

In a letter, addressed "To The Great-Hearted People of Florida," which was printed in many of the state's newspapers, Broward explained that he had "concluded to be a candidate for the nomination of United States Senator," because "those nearest and dearest to . . . [Bryan] have expressed the wish that I should take up the fight where he was compelled by death to lay it down. . . . The time is very near before the primaries are to be held, and if I am to get the information to the people of Florida that I am a candidate, it is necessary to start at once."[47] In the ensuing campaign, the political opponents of the governor severely criticized him for announcing his candidacy so soon after Bryan's death. The *Ocala Banner* declared that Broward "shook off his sorrow like the lion in his strength shakes off the dew of the morning from his mane, and like another Minerva, springing in full armor from the forehead of Jupiter, he sprang into the senatorial arena clothed almost in ethereal glory as one specially anointed."[48] Broward considered this criticism unjust. Before naming Milton, he had offered the appointment to Nathan P. Bryan, who had refused it and had advised the governor to enter the Senate race himself.[49]

One of Broward's first moves in his campaign was to write

to various Florida papers, outlining his program and soliciting their support.[50] He opened campaign headquarters in Jacksonville and then, realizing that he would have to campaign strenuously to catch up with his opponents, he took the stump. He worked indefatigably throughout his campaign, arguing and debating from one end of Florida to the other. On April 15 he spoke in Lakeland. Five days later John S. Beard spoke there and severely criticized the Milton appointment. He charged that Milton, president of a national bank, belonged to corporation elements that Broward professed to oppose. On April 22 Broward returned to Lakeland to answer Beard's charges and to defend Senator Milton as "a clean, honest man, and one who is always to be found on the side of the people." Broward, as guilty of mudslinging as his opponents, hit directly at Beard in declaring that "when it becomes necessary for me to appoint a man to the position of United States Senator, I will not have to go to an inebriate asylum to find him."[51]

Beard returned to Lakeland for a second speech. Answering Broward's charge, he admitted that he "had been addicted to drink many years ago, but that is now in the past. All a person would have to do is look into my face to tell that I am not a drinking man. It has been years since I have touched anything stronger than coffee."[52] Beard again charged that "Mr. Broward appointed Milton not because he would represent the people, but because he would be of service to Mr. Broward. In appointing Milton he will not injure his race for the senate, as Milton will not oppose him but will support and assist him. . . . Broward possesses none of the elements of statesmanship and is nothing but a ward politician and one of the shrewdest and most successful political fakirs in the State of Florida."[53] Continuing this personal exchange, Broward called William B. Lamar "the nearest approach to a male fashion plate that I can find in human form," and he characterized Beard as a man "who looks like a wise owl and so far as I can discern, is just about as useful to the state as an owl."[54] Fletcher also received his share of abuse. When Broward's supporters claimed that Fletcher was irreligious and an infidel, the latter strongly repudiated the accusation. In a letter to the newspapers, Fletcher insisted that "he was and always had been a Christian."[55]

As the campaign continued, the mudslinging increased. Lamar, Beard, and Fletcher enthusiastically listed their charges against the governor, and the opposition press gleefully joined in the chorus. The *Gainesville Sun* said that Broward had come to an understanding with the Florida East Coast Railroad and that it was going to back him. In return, the story continued, Broward was supposed to make his home in a city other than Jacksonville, "so as not to be in Senator Taliaferro's way, two years hence." The Gainesville paper bluntly stated that Broward would "remove to hell if he thought he could be elected United States Senator by doing so."[56] The *Ocala Banner* reported a similar story, surmising that the Browards would move to Miami. Other newspapers suggested Tampa and Pensacola.

Meanwhile, the *Quincy Journal*, listing other specific charges against the governor, said that he had "spent money and the Everglades are not drained . . . worked and voted for the Flagler Divorce Bill . . . raised state taxes from 4 mills to 5½ mills . . . given railroads like the L & N thousands of acres of land and large sums of money."[57] The *Tampa Tribune* said he was "as mad as hops";[58] the *Jacksonville Floridian* denounced him as "a humbug and a hypocrite";[59] and the *Florida Times-Union* claimed that "he was a poor farmer and indifferent sheriff, a disobedient Democrat, a filibusterer scorning the law."[60]

Bitter attacks, insults, and newspaper opposition were anything but novel to Broward. With fierce determination he continued his campaign and reiterated his platform. At a Jacksonville political rally he stated: "I stand for the passage of a law that would give the Interstate Commerce Commission power to arbitrarily fix rates and classify freight, and in the passage of a law forbidding the issuing of bonds in excess of the money put into the physical property. . . . I stand for a law to give the commission proper control of the interstate rail-

roads and to give to each man what belongs to him. . . . I stand
for a careful revision and remodelling of the tariff, a revision
that would protect and benefit the people of this section . . . a
revision that would no longer force the people in this section
to buy in a protected market and sell in a free market. . . . I
stand for the passage of a national drainage law and a law
which will prevent the control of the prices of naval stores
produced in the State by trusts and combines. . . . I favor the
extension of the employer liability act and an 8 hour a day
law for manual labor."[61]

Duncan U. Fletcher also spoke in every hamlet and country
town he could reach. He toured west Florida as far as Escambia
County, circled back across the state to Jacksonville, and then
crossed to Tampa on the Gulf coast. He spoke throughout
south Florida, and went up the east coast. A few days before
the first primary, his travels ended with huge rallies in St.
Augustine and Jacksonville. Fletcher adopted a platform not
unlike Broward's. He favored Interstate Commerce Commission control of interstate carriers; increased government
appropriations for harbors, inland rivers, and waterways; a
duty on Egyptian cotton; currency reform; an income tax;
tariff revision; and increased benefits to Florida farmers and
fruit growers. He also opposed trusts and all monopolies.[62]

A heated issue which appeared in the senatorial campaign
in 1908 revived memories of the Buckman Bill and the fight
to locate the University of Florida in 1905. On April 9, 1908,
Governor Broward arrived in Gainesville and talked before
a large crowd gathered at the courthouse square. The *Gainesville Sun,* an anti-Broward journal, reported that "not a single
ripple of applause greeted the Governor's appearance, and his
speech . . . never elicited one iota of enthusiasm."[63] According
to the story in the Gainesville paper, Broward stated that although he had voted for Lake City, he had really wanted
the university in Gainesville and had consequently placed men
on the Board of Control who would vote for Gainesville.
Although the *Sun* approved the locating of the university in
Gainesville, it severely indicted Broward "for packing the

Board of Control." The editor, H. H. McCreary, caustically remarked that it was typical of the governor to admit that "Buck King would vote for Gainesville . . . and that Nat Adams would vote for Lake City."[64] The *Sun* termed the "packing" a reprehensible act. Broward was concerned because he realized that the antagonism of the *Sun* and a misunderstanding with the citizens of Gainesville might swing enough votes to defeat him in Alachua County. At the same time, if the people of Lake City were convinced that the governor had worked against their interests, he might lose the important vote of Columbia County. Realizing the danger, Broward issued a statement which strongly asserted that "three of the five who were appointed as members of the Board of Control, together with myself, voted for Lake City as the site of the University."[65] Denying the accusation made by the editor of the *Sun*, several prominent men from Gainesville, including W. R. Thomas, B. R. Colson, and Dr. J. F. McKinstry, Jr., submitted affidavits and showed that a wrong inference had been made from the governor's statement.[66]

The gubernatorial race rapidly reached its climax. Burr withdrew, leaving Stockton, Gilchrist, and Browne in the contest. The *Florida Times-Union*, supporting Gilchrist, opposed Stockton more strongly than it did Broward. Gilchrist, although often classified as a Broward man and a Progressive, did not sound like either in this campaign. The liberals charged that Gilchrist was trying to be "all things to all men" when he stated in a Tampa speech: "There are two kinds of men, the natural man and the artificial man. The artificial man is the corporation, the natural man is the laboring man. Both are essential to the public welfare. The corporation cannot do without the people, neither can the people do without the corporations. Neither should be allowed to oppress the other. Capital is organized. Labor should organize. . . . It has been said that the corporations are with me. Well, I am glad of it. I want everybody to be with me, and if they will, I will be governor and will surely protect the interests of all classes of its citizens. . . ."[67]

The question of prohibition, which was stirring the nation, became a major issue in this campaign. The Anti-Saloon League inspected the state in 1908 and reported that "Florida is bordering on prohibition. . . . There are only 330 saloons left in the entire State."[68] Several communities—Tallahassee, Live Oak, and Gainesville—had already "closed their gates against the saloon," and, as a result, had "immediately become prosperous."[69] The local option vote in Ocala, early in the year, stirred up considerable controversy in the state. The "wets" campaigned with parades, newspaper advertisements, speeches, mass rallies, and church meetings. The "Peace-Loving Women of Marion County" made a tearful plea to "The True and Noble Men of Marion County," asking them to "vote against the saloons that we may rejoice and be glad."[70] When the local option law failed to win, "drys" throughout the state assailed their opponents with bitter denunciations. For instance, they asserted that the "wets" had "lined up the Negro vote and had paid the poll tax of every Negro in the county that could vote."[71]

Although Broward was an avowed prohibitionist, his opponents resurrected the old charge that he favored whisky because he had supported the dispensary bill in the legislature of 1901. Broward refused to answer these obvious untruths. He pointed to his long record and his speeches favoring prohibition and vehemently assailed his opponents as "wets." In the gubernatorial race, Stockton advocated state-wide prohibition; Gilchrist declared for individual county regulation, or local option. Stockton supporters maintained that national liquor interests had contributed three hundred and sixty thousand dollars to Gilchrist's campaign. General Gilchrist stoutly denied these accusations, and offered to pay a thousand dollars to anyone who could prove the truth of his opponents' statements.[72]

A few months before the first primary, Carry Nation arrived in the state on a speaking tour. Heralded as "the great enemy of the saloon, the tobacco habit, and many other minor things" the peppery crusader attracted large crowds wherever she spoke. After inciting frenzy and enthusiasm in west Florida, she moved down into south Florida where, on March 21, she introduced Broward as "our dry governor" at a "big tent-meeting in Miami."[73] She arrived in Gainesville on April 4, 1908, and the *Gainesville Sun* reported: "The first lecture will be delivered Tuesday afternoon . . . and the woman who has made herself what beer did for Milwaukee, and who is known the world over, will appear again in the evening."[74] Scheduled to leave for Washington after her Gainesville lectures, Mrs. Nation, followed by a crowd of admirers who had come to see her off, arrived at the railroad station on the morning of April 8. The men and women waited on the platform of the clapboard station until they heard the whistle of the train in the distance. Just then Carry spied an old farmer relaxing on a chair in the waiting room and smoking a cigarette. With fire in her eyes, and her umbrella waving in the air, she advanced upon the culprit. Saved by a shout from the stationmaster, the man dashed into the washroom. The unabashed zealot probably would have followed if her friends had not persuaded her to board the train before it pulled away from the station.[75]

Primary day was May 19, but official returns were not announced until ten days later. In the senatorial race Broward led with 19,078 votes. Fletcher received 17,208 votes; Lamar, 12,527; and Beard, 4,592. Broward carried twenty-three counties—Baker, Brevard, Citrus, Clay, Dade, DeSoto, Franklin, Hamilton, Hernando, Holmes, Jackson, Lafayette, Lee, Liberty, Nassau, Polk, Putnam, St. Lucie, Sumter, Taylor, Volusia, Walton, and Washington. Broward lost Duval County by 709 votes. In Jacksonville, Fletcher carried every ward; in Ward Two, where Broward lived, the vote was 84 for the governor and 150 for Fletcher. In the gubernatorial contest, Gilchrist received 23,248 votes; Stockton, 20,068; and Browne, 8,936.[76]

Even before the official canvass was completed, the runoff candidates—Broward and Fletcher, Gilchrist and Stockton—assembled at a giant political rally near Micanopy on May 27.

The railroads from Tampa and Jacksonville had advertised special excursion rates, and many families packed picnic baskets and came to spend the day. Christopher Matheson, of Gainesville, was the chairman, and the political talks continued nearly all day. The *Gainesville Sun* reported that "everybody was there, from the grave and anxious politician and candidate to the lovely ladies of the land, and the little children, who, ignorant of the purpose of the meeting came to enjoy themselves. . . ."[77] Frank Harris drove over by auto from Ocala and boasted that he had made the twenty-seven-mile trip in "a little less than two hours, and through as pretty and picturesque country as one can see outside the mountain regions."[78]

When the executive committee announced the second primary candidates, the *Madison News Enterpriser* warned its readers: "Lookout for storms, squalls, earthquakes, and other casualties. There is going to be something doing in great big chunks during the next three weeks."[79] The newspaper prediction proved true; this runoff campaign was even more hectic than the first, and at times hysteria dominated the debate between the leading candidates. Fletcher insisted that Broward was head of a huge political machine, and he repeated an earlier charge that "the state bank examiners, convict lease inspectors, pure food inspectors, and other traveling state officials are all electioneering for the machine candidates."[80] Fletcher criticized the governor for "seeking an office while holding one and taking the pay for it to boost his candidacy for the Senate."[81] He frequently ridiculed the drainage program. Speaking in Pensacola, he branded "the great work" as nothing more than political capital, and predicted that if reclamation was carried on at "its present rate for the next hundred years, there would still be 1,000,000 of the 5,000,-000 acres . . . to be drained."[82]

There was to be no letup as far as the anti-Broward press was concerned. One newspaper complained that "the people should at least learn by painful experience and not be hoodwinked by Governor Broward's demagogic and ambiguous speeches, State reasons and booklets. He has been derelict to his duty and has broken his promises to the people by his compromises. He has also permitted unrestrained extravagance. He has been weighed and found wanting, and is not worthy of a greater trust."[83] Other newspapers asserted that the governor "had made a deal with Standard Oil . . . used public funds to defray his campaign costs . . . was personally dishonest . . . was unfriendly to soldiers pensions . . . and had held up executions so as not to antagonize the families of the condemned men."[84]

The governor continued his vigorous campaign, holding up to the voters his record in office. He took the offensive, trying to reawaken the citizens to the fact that corporate abuses still existed in Florida and that it was necessary to separate the liberals from the conservatives. He stoutly denied the accusations made on the speaking platforms and in the newspapers. He was indignant when journals like the *Ocala Banner* insinuated that he was in the pay of the *Florida Times-Union* and that he was at last a puppet of the very interests that he had denounced for so long. Broward hit back. He called Fletcher "a corporation tool and hireling that the people cannot trust"; and he threatened newspapers with libel suits.[85] He traveled everywhere, up and down the state, speaking long and loud at rallies and banquets, and to knots of farmers at the country crossroads.

Broward and his family arrived in Jacksonville the evening before the election and were met at the train by a crowd of supporters with a brass band. The governor was weary from the long campaign, the conferences and speeches, and the uncomfortable train ride from Tallahassee. Nevertheless, he doffed his slouch hat and waved it at the crowd. Responding to the insistence for a speech, Broward reminded his listeners that he had lost Duval County in the first primary, but assured them that he would win the county this time. He concluded with a simple plea for endorsement of his liberal program at the polls.

The governor voted early the next morning. In the evening,

shortly after dusk, he and Mrs. Broward drove to campaign headquarters to read the bulletins as they were telegraphed in and to watch the tabulations as they were chalked on a large wallboard. From the beginning the outcome looked dark. The first returns revealed that the Jacksonville precincts had gone solidly for Fletcher. Returns from the east coast began coming in by midnight and added to Fletcher's lead. Broward remained optimistic until he saw how the rural areas had voted. Counties in west and middle Florida that he had depended on had voted for Fletcher. The newspapers on the morning after the election headlined the news that Broward was losing and that Florida's conservative forces had scored a resounding victory. The *Ocala Banner* gleefully exclaimed: "Run over by his own 'machine'—Broward."[86] The final tabulations showed that Fletcher had won with 29,151 votes to 25,563 for Broward. Gilchrist defeated Stockton for governor by a vote of 32,465 to 23,291. In the Congressional race Stephen M. Sparkman, Frank Clark, and Dannitte H. Mays won the nominations.

The election over, telegrams and letters came in large numbers. Most of them reflected disappointment and sorrow; many predicted the end of the Broward Era. The governor admitted Fletcher's triumph with a bitter statement to the press. He recalled the unfair charges that had been leveled at him during the campaign, and scathingly denounced them as untruths. He called upon the people to uphold the liberal principles and the progressive legislation that he had fought for during his term of office. With the exception of this statement, Broward proved to be an excellent loser. He bore Fletcher no personal malice, and during the next few months relations between the two men became more cordial. On his trips to Washington, Broward frequently conferred with Fletcher about drainage problems, and they often lunched together in the Senate dining room.

People everywhere asked: "Why did Broward lose the election?" It was a difficult question for his supporters to answer. It was apparent that the campaign had not been fought on issues; the platforms of Broward and Fletcher were similarly progressive. There had been little argument between the candidates over the tariff, the income tax, the acceptance of railroad regulation, or the increased Federal benefits to the state. Although Fletcher had been connected with the railroads since 1905, before that time his identification with the liberal forces in Florida was an established fact. His record of Straightout activity in Duval County politics during the 1890's was as complete as Governor Broward's. After 1905 Fletcher was less outspoken in his demands for reform. Although the years had modified his liberalism, he did not become a conservative in the same sense as James P. Taliaferro or Robert W. Davis. The Broward backers further reasoned that if the election had been a contest of personalities the governor would have easily won. Despite his dignified and gracious appearance and his concise and forceful speeches, Fletcher lacked the colorful and dynamic personality of Broward. The governor's looks and mannerisms, his infectious grin, and his picturesque background appealed to the people. His progressivism and moral crusading had generated deep-seated loyalties; his courage and stamina in fighting the corporations had created a stable following in the state. Broward, perhaps more than any other chief executive in Florida history, had effectively established a factional group of supporters. The voters easily perceived that Governor Broward lacked neither a liberal platform nor personal magnetism. His victory in the first primary, however, had been precarious. Although he secured more votes than any other candidate in the race and held a majority of two thousand over Fletcher, Lamar and Beard also polled a substantial number of votes. In the second primary, many voters who had supported these two men switched to Fletcher. In addition, Broward lost votes for other reasons. The controversy over the location of the University of Florida encouraged some constituents in Alachua and Columbia counties to cast their ballots for Fletcher.

The conservative press, which was very strong in 1908, used every available weapon to fight Broward. These newspapers argued that Broward had a machine, that he was planning to build a political dynasty in Florida, and that he was trying to perpetuate his power by electing his coterie of lieutenants. Broward later claimed that the conservatives had employed a very shrewd political device to defeat him. He explained that, prior to the election, newspapers like the *Ocala Banner* had circulated a rumor that he had made a deal with the Florida East Coast Railroad. In return for the corporation's support in his election, Broward had allegedly agreed to further some of the company's state land claims. Broward labeled the story a "vicious lie" and dared anyone to prove its validity. Nevertheless, because in the first primary he had carried all the counties on the east coast, which was the route of the Florida East Coast Railroad, the newspapers insinuated that he had the support of the company. Then, just before the runoff election, the *Florida Times-Union* suddenly stopped criticizing Broward and his policies. Whether this was intentional on the part of the editor, Willis Ball, it is difficult to say, but it convinced many voters that the governor had decided to work with the vested interests in order to be elected.[87] Broward was an ambitious man and wanted very much to be a United States Senator; however, it is hardly likely that to achieve this goal he would have deserted the liberal cause which he had championed for so many years. Throughout the campaign, Broward had persisted in trying to prove that there was no basis for the charge. Nonetheless, he found that Fletcher was picking up strength constantly in the state.

A great many people thought that Broward had been too sure of himself in the campaign. He had traveled all over the state, had spoken frequently and campaigned hard, but he had tried to do too much. It was obvious that he had worked not only for himself, but for all the liberals in the race. Finally, although Broward had a strong factional group of supporters in Florida, party politics reveal that the "conditions of factional politics seem to be such that impermanence is the rule."[88] Perhaps the people wanted a change; perhaps they wanted to try something different.

Many newspapers predicted that Broward was through with politics; some said that never again could he be elected to public office. Broward made no predictions, and he refused to discuss publicly his plans for the future. He turned his attention to the national political scene, which was increasing in tempo as the presidential campaign got underway. Broward had known that with the support of Theodore Roosevelt and the lack of any concerted opposition, William Howard Taft would be the Republican party nominee. Thus, it was no surprise to Broward when he read that the delegates in Chicago had nominated Taft on the first ballot on June 18, 1908.[89]

The Democratic convention of 1908 was scheduled for Denver on July 7, and Broward planned to attend. During the senatorial race, he had been severely criticized for spending so much time away from Tallahassee. When it became known that he was traveling again, Claude L'Engle, the editor of the *Tallahassee Sun*, wrote sarcastically: "Please don't blame the governor for going. . . . He has been bitten by the migratory microbe and has wanderlust. This is not a new disease. It's name only is new. The Children of Israel had it in epidemic form for forty years. . . . I thought that when he came in from his last campaign among the 'greathearted' I thought that he would stay awhile. When three days passed, and the fourth found him within whooping distance of old Leon's red clay hills, I began to think that the crisis had passed. When the tolling of Tallahassee's church bells on two successive Sundays disturbed the executive slumber, I began to figure on convalescence. But no; it was not to be. The dread disease had too firm a grip; its strangle-hold could not be shaken off. . . . Once more they've nailed the old familiar sign on the executive door. It is dim and faded now . . . but a close inspection will even yet discover its legend to be—N. D., which translated means—nothing doing."[90]

En route to the convention in the West, many Democratic leaders stopped off in Lincoln, Nebraska, to pay homage to Bryan, "The Peerless One." On the Fourth of July over eight hundred delegates poured out of crowded trains and marched through the streets of Lincoln, waving banners, singing songs, and shouting the praises of their hero. The town was decorated with flags and pictures of Bryan, bearing the legend "Welcome To Bryan's Town." Many people brought baskets of food, and at noon scores of men and women ate in Mrs. Bryan's back yard. The Southern delegation, which included Governor and Mrs. Broward; Josephus Daniels, of North Carolina; Mr. and Mrs. John W. Tomlinson and their son Bryan, of Alabama; and Hoy Noel, of Mississippi, was invited to "Fairview" for luncheon with the Bryans.[91]

For weeks prior to the Democratic meeting, newspapers in Florida and throughout the South had mentioned Broward as a prominent candidate for the Vice-Presidency. Typical of these statements was the following in the *DeFuniak Herald*: "All honor to Gov. Broward. He would make an excellent man for the vice president on the ticket with Mr. Bryan. Let him go through the northern states and talk to the people and they would be assured that no harm would result to this nation if he were at its head. He is a great, broadminded, patriotic man, whose actions and words agree. If the south is to be recognized on the national ticket, Governor Broward is the man."[92] Broward's filibustering activities and his Everglades drainage program had made him not only a well-known Southern leader, but a publicized figure on the national level. Former Governor Jennings, a delegate from Florida, emphatically announced that Broward would be nominated. On the train en route to Lincoln, various Southern delegations held caucuses and pledged their support to Broward should his name be placed before the convention.[93] As he was governor of a "safe" Democratic state, however, there was little likelihood of his nomination.

Governor and Mrs. Broward arrived in Denver early on the morning of July 5, and made their headquarters with the Florida delegation in the Monroe Apartments. The hotel management had strung across the lobby of this hotel a mammoth silk banner reading: BRYAN, BROWARD AND BREAD.[94] The *Denver Republican* thus commented upon

Broward's chances for the nomination: "Napoleon Bonaparte
Broward of Florida, for vice-president, with a delegate from
Alabama to nominate him, and a Mississippi delegate to second
the nomination. This is the freshest product off the political
griddle and it's a hot one. N. B. Broward, governor of Florida,
president of the National Drainage Association, and filibusterer
of international repute, is one of the biggest men in the South
today, and when he arrived in Denver yesterday morning with
the Florida delegation another vice-presidential boom at once
swelled up in the public gaze. The South likes Governor
Broward, of Tallahassee, because he is the man who is draining
the Everglades of Florida and rendering 5,000,000 acres of
land available for cultivation in a region as fertile as the
valley of the Nile. . . . The successful carrying out of the
immense drainage scheme would add immeasurably to Governor Broward's popularity and if his name were placed in
nomination at the present convention as a candidate for vice-
president, he would undoubtedly receive hearty support from
the states of the Old South."[95]

On the eve of the convention, Southern delegates assembled
in the hotel room with Charles W. Bryan, the Great Commoner's brother. The delegates were anxious to get a direct
commitment from William Jennings Bryan as to whether he
would accept Broward as his running mate. Charles telegraphed
his brother in Lincoln, asking if he would support a man from
the South. Bryan wired back that he wanted a man from the
Midwest, since he was sure to get the Southern vote in any
event.[96] The Broward boom was punctured, but crowds still
paraded up and down the Monroe corridors chanting "Bryan,
Broward and Bread." In the streets, bands played and men
and women sang the "American Marseillaise":

You shall not press the crown of thorns upon the toiler's brow.
This we affirm in Freedom's name, with pledge and solemn
    vow.
You shall not crucify mankind upon a cross of gold.
The time has come when freedom true, shall not be bought
    or sold.

Our children cry aloud for bread, and while for them we
    strive,
The corporations shall combine and on our earnings thrive.
In vain we prayed! We beg no more! But on our cause we rely,
The trusts we now defy . . . . [97]

Thousands of Democrats crowded Denver. Every seat in
the convention hall was filled, bands played, banners waved,
and delegates hurried to and fro in last minute caucuses and
conferences. Mrs. Alice Roosevelt Longworth, dressed in "a
fetching gown and Lady Gap Spanker hat with flowing
plumes," sat in one box. Near her was Mrs. Ruth Bryan
Leavitt, waiting to see her father nominated for a third time.
On the speakers' platform, dressed in formal morning clothes,
were Count de Chambrun, of France; M. Kroupfsky, of Rus-
sia; H. F. Charteres, of England; and the ministers of
Argentina, Greece, Belgium, and Chile. Bryan's forces controlled the convention completely, and the Commoner was
able to write the platform and dictate his own nomination.

The presidential campaign in 1908 was comparatively dull.
The usual damning indictments were brought against all the
candidates. The editor of one religious newspaper insisted that
Taft, a Unitarian, was a "low, cunning imposter!" and an
infidel.[98] Carry Nation indignantly proclaimed that Taft was
not only an infidel but a foe of temperance, as well.[99] Bryan
was called a "wet," a "dry," a "slave of the Pope," the "anti-
Christ," a "reprobate," a "liar," a "spendthrift," and an
"enemy of the people." The Populist party was on the verge
of disintegration and while Tom Watson still raged against
the "millionaire plunderers and land-grabbing corporations,"
the election results were to strip him of many of his preten-
sions.[100] Bryan spent most of his oratorical energy in denouncing trusts, and remained, throughout the campaign,
confident of victory. Governor Broward noted this optimism
and enthusiasm when he visited the Bryan campaign headquarters in Washington three weeks before election. Bryan
and his supporters were whistling in the political darkness; it

was obvious almost from the earliest returns that their confidence had been misplaced. In his home at Oyster Bay, President Roosevelt tabulated the returns as they came in and kept repeating, "We have them beaten to a frazzle!"[101] The electoral vote was 321 for Taft and 162 for Bryan.

The campaign in Florida had been uneventful. After the runoff election, the Democratic nominees were assured of election, and the subsequent rounds of speechmaking were perfunctory. Official returns in Florida, which were not announced until almost a month after election, showed 33,036 for Albert W. Gilchrist and 6,453 for John M. Cheney, of Orlando, the Republican candidate. Duncan U. Fletcher had no Republican opposition, and his nomination was approved by legislative vote in 1909. Other Democratic nominees were elected by substantial majorities.[102]

Inauguration Day in 1909 was warm and springlike in Tallahassee. Governor Broward and Governor-elect Gilchrist rode in carriages to the capitol. Several black automobiles appeared in the inaugural parade. Crowds of people lined the route of the parade, and the cheers for Broward were as loud as those for the new governor. Since Gilchrist was unmarried, his mother became the new "First Lady," and that night she received at the Inaugural Ball with Mrs. Broward. Mrs. Gilchrist wore an elegant costume of "black, spangled with jet, elaborately trimmed with rose-point lace." Mrs. Broward's gown was of "heavy silver brocade, embroidered in clover leaves of gold, blue trimmings and white chiffon." Dorcas, Josephine, and Enid danced for the last time as daughters of the governor of Florida. Their ball dresses were new and imported from New York. Dorcas and Enid wore white silk and Josephine was dressed in a wide-skirted blue gown.[103] The next day the Browards moved back to their home in Jacksonville.

⌒ 17 ⌒

In the Hands
of the Common People

ALTHOUGH HIS POLITICAL OPPONENTS
thought otherwise, Broward retired from public
office without a fortune, and, indeed, poorer than he
was when he became governor. During the latter part of 1907
the state of his finances became so critical that he considered
planting ten acres of tomatoes as a quick cash crop. "Money
is very scarce," he wrote. "It would bring in about $1,000."[1]
Early in 1909 Broward worked for the Bolles Everglades
Land Company at a reported salary of four hundred dollars
a month.[2] This helped his financial condition tremendously.
He was still active in the Jacksonville Towing and Wrecking
Company, and much of his time was occupied with its business activities.

In October, 1909, Broward helped organize the Our Home
Life Insurance Company, with a capital of two hundred
thousand dollars and with twenty thousand shares of stock
available for sale. Florida's secretary of state issued a charter
on November 15, and Broward became company president.
Clifford R. Allen, R. J. Evans, J. J. Paul, Daniel A. Simmons,
Senator William Hall Milton, Henry E. Palmer, and George
L. Drew served as officers and directors.[3] Although Broward's
investment in the company was not large, the venture was not
a financial success for him.[4]

The former governor also found time for sports and amusement on Fort George Island, where the Browards owned a
large two-story beach home.[5] He fished on the "Snapper
Banks" and sailed the *Three Friends* when she was not busy

owing ships to and from St. Johns Bar. He also published
everal short articles on the Everglades and his drainage program in such national magazines as *Collier's* and *The Independent*.

During Gilchrist's administration, Broward followed with
lose interest legislation which provided for the publication
f campaign expenses, and which granted the Railroad Commission the power to regulate telephone and telegraph
ommunications. His frequently repeated demands for a
uniform school textbook law were finally answered by the
egislature with the passage of a bill in 1909. Broward was
n Tallahassee during much of the legislative session, and he
participated actively in the caucuses which debated the pro-
ibition question. By 1909 it was apparent to the former
overnor that the arid age was fast approaching both on the
tate and national level. He had always believed that the idea
f centralized control of liquor was sound, and he therefore
ndorsed the joint resolution adopted by the legislature to
ubmit a constitutional prohibition amendment to the vote
f the people in the general election in 1910.[6]

Broward was particularly concerned with the new governor's
ttitude toward drainage. Although Gilchrist had not openly
ondemned the project in his campaign speeches, he had
ssumed a lukewarm attitude toward continuing the program.
One of Broward's last acts before relinquishing his post as
hief executive was to take Gilchrist and the newly elected
abinet on a tour of the Everglades. The men rode on the
dredges, listened to the reports of Chief Engineer J. W.
Newman, checked the progress of the digging, and saw the
ich farmlands in the reclaimed areas.[7] Gilchrist was enthusi-
stic about what he saw, and he assured Broward that he
vould push the project.

Before the legislature assembled in Tallahassee in April,
909, Governor Gilchrist received an extract from a report
hat was to be released shortly by J. O. Wright, the chief
urveyor of the United States Department of Agriculture,

who had been working with the drainage project since November, 1906.[8] Although the report had not been officially
accepted by the Department of Agriculture, the Trustees of
the Internal Improvement Fund received the extract with much
enthusiasm. Broward was happy to see that nearly all Wright's
requests for canals coincided with his own recommendations;
in fact, work was already progressing along the New River
Canal, about twenty miles from Miami, and along the Caloosahatchee.[9] On May 27, 1909, a joint legislative committee
endorsed the Wright excerpt and declared that "the drainage
of the Glades is absolutely feasible and practical and its success
depends alone upon the number and size of the canals that
are cut through them to Lake Okeechobee." The members of
the committee thought that Federal aid could be secured if
the national government was made "acquainted with the facts
in this case, and the advantages to be derived from making a
canal from Jupiter or Hillsborough Inlets on the East Coast,
thence to Lake Okeechobee and down the Caloosahatchee River
to its mouth on the West Coast, . . . thus furnishing a public
highway from ocean to gulf."[10]

At the close of Broward's term, the dredges *Everglades*
and *Okeechobee* were operating, and contracts for two others,
the *Caloosahatchee* and the *Miami*, had been let in August,
1908.[11] The *Caloosahatchee* was launched in March, 1909.[12]
After the Broward administration, drainage was no longer the
personal bailiwick of the governor. A superintendent of drainage, P. F. Jenkins, was hired on January 27, 1909, and the
trustees took over active control of reclamation. By 1909,
much of the litigation relating to land titles had been settled
by the courts, and in January, 1910, the drainage commissioners made peace with representatives of the largest land
companies—The Southern States Land and Timber Company
directed by a syndicate of New Orleans capitalists and Herbert
H. Lehman of New York; the Consolidated Land Company
a subsidiary of the Consolidated Naval Stores Company; and
the Model Land Company, directed by Henry M. Flagler
and his associates. The companies agreed to liquidate their

unpaid drainage taxes provided the drainage work be handled by private construction companies.[13] Subsequently, a contract was let for the excavation of two hundred thirty-five miles of canal, and the four drainage dredges were sold to the Furst-Clark Construction Company of Baltimore, Maryland.

The question of financing so large a project remained critical. It was necessary to sell off large tracts of public land to secure additional funds for digging. Land was sold to J. H. Tatum and Company,[14] W. R. Comfort, of New York,[15] R. P. Davie, of Colorado,[16] and the Davie Realty Company.[17] The largest sale was to Richard J. Bolles, who has been described as "the most spectacular, most ingenious and most criticized promoter of and speculator in Everglades lands."[18] In December, 1908, Bolles signed a contract to purchase five hundred thousand acres of land for two dollars per acre. The agreement definitely stated that one of the two dollars was to be devoted by the state "solely and exclusively for drainage and reclamation purposes."[19] Broward's original drainage program did not envisage the land speculation and high-pressure business tactics which were instituted by the land companies. These land sales, however, gave impetus to drainage. The Bolles purchase provided a million-dollar fund which allowed the reclamation program to continue.

Many of the bills passed during the Gilchrist administration enacted into law ideas that Broward had long advocated and encouraged. Gilchrist had frequently been labeled a conservative by his political opponents, who argued that if he were elected governor the state would again be under the thumb of the railroad-corporation leaders. This proved a false assumption. In May, 1909, Daniel A. Simmons stated: "If the 'vested interests' expected any favors at his [Gilchrist's] hands, they have been disappointed."[20] Likewise, the anti-drainage forces in Florida were thwarted in their plan to halt the reclamation program. Simmons continued his analysis by reporting that the work was "going enthusiastically forward, and plans for the future [were] being made on a larger scale than ever before."[21] By thus encouraging the growth of liberal

government, the Gilchrist administration played an important
role in the Broward Era.

The year 1910 was pivotal for the nation and particularly
for the Democratic party. The issues which stirred the voter—
prohibition, internal improvements, labor, agitation for a direct
primary in national elections, and the race question—were to
bring Napoleon Broward back to public life. The liberal leaders in the South who had staged the revolt against the vested
interests came to power demanding reform in the name of the
people. These progressives had based their program in large
part upon the demands voiced by the Populists in the nineteenth century, and it appeared that Populist objectives would
be finally realized in the twentieth century. Gradually, however, there began an ominous undercurrent that was "fraught
with disastrous and even tragic consequences for the whole
future of social thought in the South."[22] As many of the
Southern rebels lost their control over the agrarian vote, they
resorted to dangerous and sensational devices—Negro baiting,
anti-Catholic crusades, and anti-Semitism—to retain power.[2]
Broward never became violently anti-Negro, and was never
identified with such demagogues as Tom Watson of Georgia,[2]
Ben Tillman of South Carolina,[25] or James K. Vardaman of
Mississippi.[26] His attitude toward the Negro followed generally the definition given by Supreme Court Justice Taney
in 1857 when he said that the "Negro had no rights or
privileges but such as those who held the power and the gov
ernment might choose to grant them."[27]

As the racial question brought about an important realign
ment in the Democratic party in the South, so new issues were
also changing the national political scene. Although Republican
leaders continued to insist that the Democratic party was
hopeless, it was apparent that such was not the true situation
The Pinchot-Ballinger controversy, the revolt in the House
of Representatives against the dictatorship of Joseph Cannon
the disturbances over the tariff bill, and the general ineptness
and lack of finesse and skill of President Taft had caused a
wide breach in the Republican party ranks. As a result, the

Democrats were hopeful of winning control of Congress in
1910 and paving the way for a return to presidential power
in 1912. In both the Congressional and presidential elections,
it was expected that the Solid South would swell the party's
vote.[28]

In Florida, after the date for the 1910 primaries had been
scheduled by the state Democratic executive committee, Senator James P. Taliaferro announced his candidacy for re-election. Most of the "big-city" newspapers warmly supported him
and asserted that anyone with Taliaferro's record of achieve-
ment in the Senate should be re-elected. Broward, after his
defeat in 1908, had been frequently mentioned as a possible
candidate against Taliaferro, and in the months following his
retirement from public office he seriously considered his
chances of success. He was ready to return to active politics
and listened with interest to the suggestions made by friends
throughout Florida that he should run. In January, 1910,
he traveled around the state, talking to political leaders, newspaper editors, and representative citizens. When he returned
to Jacksonville, he conferred with his friends and political
advisers, and early in February he officially became a candidate. The *Jacksonville Metropolis* greeted this announcement
with a cartoon which showed Taliaferro and Broward astride
horses running neck and neck. The drawing was labeled: "For
the Senatorial Stakes."

A third candidate was Claude L'Engle. During the campaign of 1904, L'Engle had been editor of the *Florida Sun
and Labor Journal*, in Jacksonville, and had opposed both
Broward and Barrs. Part of his opposition to J. M. Barrs
resulted from the latter's connection with the *Jacksonville
Metropolis*, a newspaper L'Engle hated. In more than one
issue of his paper L'Engle parodied the *Metropolis*, which he
called the *Mistake*. Instead of using their correct names—
William R. Carter and Rufus A. Russel—he called the editor
and the business manager of the *Metropolis* respectively
"Willie Ringworm Carter and Dufus A. Dussel." The Negro
column of the *Metropolis* was portrayed in black, and the lady

editor of "Talks with Girls," Mrs. Nellie Gray, was dubbed "Mrs. Yellow Bray."[29]

L'Engle's labor journal failed, and in 1905 he published a paper called the *Sun*.[30] Most of the advertising was withdrawn after he had printed a particularly offensive article, and the *Sun* also failed. L'Engle moved to Tallahassee, where he temporarily became Governor Broward's close friend and ally. Through some financial manipulation, and possibly through Governor Broward's influence, he bought stock in the Tallahassee *Capital*, a printing plant with a state printing contract. During the legislative session of 1907, L'Engle published the *Morning Star*, with an editorial policy directed against certain legislators and against the conservative newspapers that were criticizing Broward. He called the *Florida Times-Union* "the *Florida Crime-Onion*." L'Engle, who was in many ways not unlike Georgia's fiery demagogue, Tom Watson, was suggested for appointment to the United States Senate after the death of William James Bryan. A few months later he broke with Broward and refused to support him in the Senate race in 1908. During the legislative session of 1909, he opened a "People's Lobby" in Tallahassee near the capitol so that the legislators could have "a convenient place in which to assemble to informally discuss measures pending and to be introduced for the benefit of the people." He promised, "no attempt will be made by me to personally influence any member for or against any measure."[31] By 1910 L'Engle was again opposing Broward, and during the Senate campaign he sarcastically referred to his former friend as "Old Broward."[32]

Florida newspapers quickly chose sides for the approaching political battle. The conservative papers in the larger cities which supported Taliaferro severely criticized Broward, his administration, and the legislation identified with the Broward Era. The newspaper fight, however, lacked the color and sensationalism of earlier campaigns. The whole campaign before the primary was quiet and seemed almost spiritless.

Taliaferro remained in Washington until a few days before the May elections, and the major part of his campaigning was done by supporters and friendly newspapers. The *Miami Metropolis,* which supported Broward, and the *Florida Times-Union* were engaged in a journalistic fight more exciting than the campaigns of the rival candidates themselves. The Miami newspaper consistently indicted Taliaferro for allegedly favoring corporations and railroads. The *Times-Union* challenged the *Miami Metropolis* to present "some definite act of Senator Taliaferro's career to show that he was for the corporations. . . ."[33] This challenge was mildly accepted and the journals exchanged vague charges and countercharges which stirred little interest among the voters.

Many Florida newspapers, disgusted with the sham battle between the senatorial candidates, complained that the expected political fireworks were proving to be merely duds. For example, the *Gainesville Sun* wrote: "Of all the campaigns for United States senator we have witnessed this is certainly the deadest ever. Are the Broward and Taliaferro managers asleep?"[34] The *Fernandina Record* suggested that "Economy is certainly being practiced in politics this season."[35]

Particularly disappointed were Broward's supporters. One newspaper leveled this caustic criticism at the former governor: "The campaign of Captain Napoleon Broward . . . is a distinct disappointment to us. We had hoped to see him stride like a living colossus across the commonwealth, putting such ginger into the scrap that it would be memorable in our political annals; but either he has no hope of success, or he has devised a new plan of campaign in which he counts on masterly inactivity as a rabbit's foot to bring him luck. But that doesn't appeal to the Florida sovereign. It doesn't tickle his self-esteem. It depreciates his value, and he will resent such low appraisement of his importance and his vote."[36] Another newspaper suggested that Broward had delayed his speaking tour because he was busy playing with his nine children.[37]

Of the three senatorial aspirants, Claude L'Engle made the most active campaign. He traveled throughout Florida, speaking long and loud, early and late. He visited some communities three times. Upon Broward and Taliaferro he heaped unlimited abuse and criticism. His listeners were both amused and interested, but never seriously considered L'Engle as a candidate. The lady editor of the *Polk County Record* thus described his visit to her community: "Mr. L'Engle was loudly applauded by his friends, frowned at by his enemies and viewed with wonder by those who sat upon the fence."[38]

The conflict became more heated when Broward's political record was brought up for review, and when old issues, almost forgotten, were resurrected. Critics denounced Broward for his actions as Duval County's sheriff, belittled his drainage program, and derided much of the other liberal legislation enacted during his administration. Anti-Broward newspapers frequently questioned his business activities since his retirement from public affairs. When liberals, in turn, indicted Taliaferro for allegedly being a friend of Florida's corporate interests, and the *Perry Herald* called him "Standard Oil United States Senator James Piper Taliaferro,"[39] he became indignant and emphatically denied the charges. He also chastised the newspapers that said he had helped Negroes secure Federal appointments.[40]

The first primary was held May 10. Early returns showed Taliaferro leading by over 1,500 votes, but his margin rapidly declined. Three days after the primary, Taliaferro led by only 86 votes, and on May 17 by 27. Election news, however, was almost crowded off the front pages by fascinating reports of the progress of Halley's Comet—a phenomenon that entertained the whole nation. In Florida some counties ordered schools closed so that children could see the wondrous event Two weeks after the election, the Democratic executive committee announced official returns of the first primary. Broward received 21,146 votes, Taliaferro, 21,077, and L'Engle, 4,677 Broward carried twenty counties and, with Taliaferro, entered the second primary.[41]

The rivals campaigned with more energy in the runoff. Taliaferro opened his speaking tour with a giant political rally n Jacksonville on the evening of May 19. He claimed that 3roward was being supported by "the race track people." 'Broward's whole career," Taliaferro stated, "from his in- tuguration to the expiration of his term is marked, spot by spot, with broken promises. . . . I charge Broward . . . with being t stockholder in the Bolles Company, and I challenge him, or tny friend of his to deny it. . . ."⁴² Congressman Frank Clark, speaking for Taliaferro, charged that Broward possessed a private fortune, built up by using his "public office as an asset for trade and speculation." Clark claimed that Broward's "vociferous profession of eternal loyalty" was counterbalanced by his "record of treachery." He also suggested that "some people in the state seem to think that if Broward was sent to Washington, that as he walked up Pennsylvania Avenue, flags would be flying from the windows and streamers from the housetops. The truth of the matter is, if he was sent to the senate he would be placed at the tail end of the committee on waste paper."⁴³

Broward took to the road again. He spoke in Madison, Kissimmee, Tampa, Tallahassee, Pensacola, Orlando, Key West, Fort Myers, Miami, West Palm Beach, and the small communities along the east coast. He supported the platform of the National Democratic party and advocated an amend- ment to the Constitution providing for popular election of United States Senators; a bill fixing four-year terms for collectors of internal revenue; appropriations to aid agricul- tural high schools in each county, or a minimum of five in each state; a sub-health bureau in each state for studying the disease peculiar to that state and for gathering data concerning com- mon diseases; liberal expenditures for inland waterways; and Federal construction of coastal canals. Broward ably defended himself against all charges voiced by Senator Taliaferro and his supporters and by the conservative newspapers. He also denounced Taliaferro's corporation connections. He charged that although "the Atlantic Investment Company, of Savannah, pleaded guilty to violations of the anti-trust laws, . . . Senator Taliaferro was a stockholder in that company and received at least $7,500 in dividends from it."[44]

The campaign closed in Jacksonville on election eve, June 6, with a joint Taliaferro-Broward rally. Originally, individual meetings had been planned, but Broward accepted the Senator's invitation for a consolidated rally. A huge crowd assembled in the old St. James Hotel block and spilled across the narrow street into Hemming Park. It was a hot night. Men stood in their shirt sleeves, and women briskly fanned themselves with palmetto leaves.

R. P. Daniel presided and introduced Taliaferro, who devoted his speech to bitter attacks on Broward. When the Broward supporters began booing Taliaferro, the Senator became angry and increased his violent denunciations. Sporadic fights started on the fringes of the crowd as men shoved and pushed each other. The catcalls were so loud that the Senator could not make himself heard. Chairman Daniel rapped for order, and threatened to adjourn the meeting if Taliaferro were not allowed to continue. Former Governor Broward, who had been watching the proceedings with amusement, turned to Taliaferro and said, "Senator, if you like, I will be glad to try to get the crowd to shut up." Taliaferro's voice was cold and thin when he retorted angrily, "I will have no favors from you, sir." The agitation had infected the crowd, and the turmoil grew so loud that Senator Taliaferro, who could not continue, finally sat down.

Broward began his speech with a joke and then related several anecdotes to get the crowd laughing with him before he launched into the serious part of his talk. The former governor reiterated his political creed that government should be directed by the majority and that free people should exercise their fundamental liberties to express themselves. "For the benefit of the young men and young women of this country," he said, "for the protection of American institutions,

t is absolutely necessary that you control your own affairs.
Upon what theory will you turn over to the specially privileged
few the right to select your legislative officers? It is your duty,
t is my duty, to hold intact your institutions and to pass them
down to your children as pure as when they were turned over
o us."

Each sentence drew resounding applause from the crowd.
When Broward finished, the shouting, cheering, and shrill
whistling swelled into a crescendo of noise. Cowbells clanked.
Men clapped and yelled and pummelled each other. Chairman
Daniel banged his gavel for order and shouted impatiently,
"I can stand this as long as you can. I haven't a thing to do
until morning." Frank Clark and Robert W. Davis were
present to talk for Taliaferro, but it was Broward's night. In
front of the Windsor Hotel, Broward supporters started a
snake dance that wound around the park to the opera house.
Eager men with perspiring faces surged onto the speakers'
platform, reached Broward, and lifted him high on their
shoulders. Singing "There'll Be a Hot Time In the Old Town
Tonight," they marched through Jacksonville's streets to the
foot of Main Street, where Broward spoke again. Before the
Times-Union building a large bonfire blazed. Men swung signs
and banners reading: "Napoleon B. Broward Is Our Man,"
"Broward For Senator," and "The Friend of the Great-
Hearted People." Opposition newspapers claimed that this
widespread demonstration was started by Broward supporters
and that Duval County would support Taliaferro.[45]

Throughout election day a milling throng packed Jacksonville's business section. The crowd shoved and jostled along
streets and sidewalks for blocks. That night a group of shouting men discovered Broward talking to J. M. Barrs near Main
and Forsyth streets. They demanded a speech and Barrs willingly obliged. He had been speaking for about fifteen minutes
when the dry-goods box upon which he had been standing
collapsed abruptly and precipitated him into the street. Barrs
got up, brushed himself off, and completed his talk. By mid-

night enough returns had come in from all sections of Florida
to assure Broward's nomination. Someone sent for the First
Regiment Band, and when it arrived the cheering crowd formed
a parade. Broward climbed into an open automobile, and
marchers followed him through the business and residential
sections, yelling and singing. Dawn broke before Broward
finally reached home.[46]

The official canvass, announced on June 22, gave Broward
25,780 votes and Taliaferro, 23,193. Broward carried twenty-
six counties—Brevard, Calhoun, Clay, Citrus, Dade, DeSoto,
Franklin, Gadsden, Hamilton, Holmes, Jackson, Lee, Levy,
Madison, Marion, Nassau, Osceola, Palm Beach, Putnam,
Santa Rosa, St. Lucie, Sumter, Taylor, Volusia, Walton, and
Washington.

Tired from the long campaign and plagued by recurring
gallstone attacks, Broward spent the remaining days of June
with his family at Fort George. Although his doctor thought
it unwise, Broward spoke at a large Fourth of July celebration in Perry, Florida, and in August he and his sister Hortense
traveled to New York. Following a whim, he revisited New
Gloucester, the scene of his early fishing and shipping days.
He searched along the water front and found the boardinghouse in which he had lived that winter many years before.
The owners were gone, but the house was there, more shoddy
and decrepit than Broward remembered it.[47]

Returning to Florida early in September, Broward rejoined
his family in their Fort George Island home. The days passed,
each one bright and serene. Broward, rested and refreshed,
played in the ocean with his children, sailed and fished and
swam, and lay on the soft grass for long hours reading or
writing. The last Sunday in September was a languorous day.
Sunlight fell through the trees and warmed the gray stones
protruding from grass and weeds. Gulls swooped from the
sky, touched the water lightly with their wings, and soared
skyward again. In the morning Broward walked along the
wet beach, pushing through clumps of sea grass and nettles,

and after lunch he rearranged and played with his ship models. In midafternoon his daughters persuaded him to race along the beach with them. Later, hot and tired, he swam in the surf.

Back in the house Broward complained of being tired, and reported sharp pains in his stomach and chest. The next morning his fever was high, but he remained cheerful and took nourishment so there seemed no great cause for alarm. On Tuesday he was in great pain, and Mrs. Broward decided to take him to Jacksonville. His brother Montcalm wrapped him in warm blankets and carried him aboard a riverboat. Dr. S. A. Morris, Broward's physician, diagnosed the case as a gallstone attack caused by jaundice, and revealed that the Senator-elect was critically ill. For many months Broward had shown symptoms of gallstone trouble. He was repeatedly warned of his danger by Dr. Morris, but he was always too busy to undergo an operation. Tired from his hectic years in Tallahassee, and further exhausted by his campaign for the Senate, he was an easy prey to disease.

News of his condition spread rapidly through Jacksonville. Newspaper reporters arrived morning and night to read the doctor's bulletins. On Thursday morning Doctors J. R. Boyd and C. Drew, of Jacksonville, and Dr. J. Y. Porter, of Key West, were called in for consultation. Broward's condition had taken a turn for the worse, but it was still too soon to decide whether he could undergo a needed operation. By 11 o'clock Thursday night, the patient's temperature was 104, and he rested uneasily.[48]

On Friday morning two more specialists were called in on the case. The bulletin that evening reported a fever of 104, with low pulse and weak respiration.[49] Saturday morning Broward was removed from his home to DeSoto Sanitorium, in the Springfield section of the city. Mrs. Broward, his sister Hortense, and his brother Montcalm kept a constant vigil. Crowds of people gathered anxiously in front of the hospital to read the bulletins now posted every hour.

The patient's pulse continued weak and his breathing be-

came harsh and rasping. Still the doctors refused to admit that
the fight was lost or that Broward was dying. They hoped that
an operation might be successful. Broward lay motionless,
the dawn grayly sculpturing his face. His eyes were closed.
Once he roused himself and smiled weakly, recognizing his
wife who sat by his bedside. He spoke, but the words were
confused. Sounds from the busy street echoed softly. It was
near noon when attendants wheeled Broward into the operating
room. As he was laid on the operating table he coughed, his
face contorted painfully. There was no other sound or movement.[50]

They shrouded him. His dark features were full and sharp,
and he looked like a marble statue in his coffin. On Tuesday,
October 4, 1910, he was buried. Stores throughout the city,
and many through the state, shut their doors. Public offices
closed, and flags on all buildings hung at half-mast. All morning thousands of people filed solemnly past the body, which
lay in state in the City Hall rotunda. Huge crowds had waited
quietly and patiently since early dawn. They were from all
walks and stations of life and of many creeds and faiths—
ladies in starched and rustling gowns, plain farmers and their
wives, and poor "cracker" families from the piney woods.
Governor Gilchrist and his cabinet, Florida's congressmen and
senators, the justices of the supreme court, and public officials
from every county came to pay Broward their last respectful
homage.

Services were held in the First Presbyterian Church and
were read by the Reverend J. Walton Graybill and by
Broward's old friend, the Reverend W. H. Dodge. Active
pallbearers were J. M. Barrs, P. A. Dignan, Frank Brown,
D. T. Gray, James E. Dodge, W. M. Bostwick, Jr., J. C.
Connally, and Edward Williams. The church was draped in
mourning and giant baskets of flowers banked the walls. Hundreds of people, unable to get into the church, stood quietly
in the streets for blocks around.

When the last hymn was sung, the casket, covered with a

huge cross of white carnations and Maréchal Niel roses, was placed in a black carriage and the long trek to Evergreen Cemetery began. It was a bright, warm afternoon, filled with sunshine. Grass, weeds, and flowers along the roads were thick and fresh. A gentle breeze blew in across the land from the St. Johns. The procession stretched interminably. Thousands of mourners lined the way to watch the funeral pass. By five o'clock the slow-moving train reached its destination. Napoleon Broward was buried under towering moss-festooned trees. Standing beside the raw, naked sod, militiamen from the Dixie Guards fired volleys across the peaceful land. Taps were sounded, and through the still air soft echoes stirred. Night moved in to cover the green breast of the earth.

The news of Broward's death shocked and stunned the state. Hundreds of civic, religious, and social organizations met and prepared resolutions of sorrow and respect. Governor Gilchrist issued a special proclamation. Memorial services were held in many churches. In practically every newspaper in Florida, and in many throughout the country, editorials commenting on Broward's untimely passing appeared.[51]

On the day of the funeral, the black-bordered pages of the *Jacksonville Metropolis* solemnly observed:

Today all that is mortal of Napoleon B. Broward will be returned to the earth from which it sprang, but the real Broward is not dead, and will never die. His spirit will be a moving mighty force for good throughout the ages, as it was when he was with us in life.
To sing the praise of the lamented Floridian in these columns seems useless, and the song would be pitifully inadequate— the man's life, public and private, his deeds and his achievements, constitute the only adequate chorus of praise that could be sung in his honor. He was a great man in every sense of the word, and the most marked characteristic of his greatness was his goodness and gentleness.[52]

The editor of the *Florida Times-Union* wrote:

Today there are thousands who, like the *Times-Union*, always opposed the big man so recently crowned with laurel and now clothed in a shroud, who see so clearly the qualities that all admired that past differences refuse to intrude and the opponent craves a place among the mourners.

And there are many thousands who were always ready to follow where he led. These grieve for him today as for one of their own. We do not believe that more sorrow has ever oppressed the state at the loss of an honored one than the people of Florida feel today. While Gov. Broward lived Floridians were his friends or his foes. There was nothing in his nature that tolerated neutrality or permitted lukewarmness. Those who knew him gave him less credit than he deserved. . . . Among Gov. Broward's supporters were a number of able men, but his was the biggest brain, the most masterful power. It was his brain, his force, his power that won for him the position of leadership.[53]

Napoleon Broward had the good fortune to fit the needs of his generation with a completeness that has been rare among the political leaders of the South. He came upon the political stage at a moment when Florida desperately needed some strong personality to rally and lead the forces of liberalism. His was an astonishing career; that of a man seemingly doomed to mediocrity and obscurity, yet whose worth and unremitting efforts for the betterment of his fellow men gave him a place among those who have done most for Florida. Apparently a man of plain and simple talents, he had latent powers which were slowly revealed. His magnetism and strength of character made these powers count with singular force in public affairs. He impressed himself upon his time as no mediocre man could have.

Like many other great leaders, Broward allowed the needs of the people to determine his political action; the common man became his highest level of measure. Moved by the wrongs of economic privilege, by human suffering and exploitation, he performed great services. He left to subsequent generations an example of courage and truth—the rarest elements in the political life of modern democracies. Broward's name may perhaps fade with the years, but his deeds will remain as lasting evidence of his services. Honored, revered, and respected, he lived a grand life, and in death he has not suffered at the hands of the common folk. In truth, he lives today in his achievements. Primarily a man of the people, he was their spokesman in a troubled age, when they were divided by resentful sectionalism and bitter memories. With sincere effort he encouraged Florida's citizens toward a broader and more wholesome political life and a wider understanding of government.

Broward's efforts to unify the institutions of higher learning in Florida made him a statesman. His drainage program made him a benefactor of the people. His invincible determination to crush railroad and corporate abuses made him a crusader. Of his many distinguished achievements, perhaps the greatest —and the one which will make his name live longest in history—was that he put into motion dormant and dispersed forces of liberalism, and gave government back to its citizens. To Broward, democracy was a gigantic weapon to be wielded not for the privileged few, but for the masses, as its founders and preservers always intended that it should be.

As the termination of a potentiality for even greater influence, and for broader public service, the death of Napoleon B. Broward was a tragedy. He had been nominated to a seat in the United States Senate, and his service in Washington would have been closely identified with a truly liberal Democratic administration. In President Woodrow Wilson he would have found a man whose fight for the "New Freedom" was similar in many respects to his own battles in Florida. In the Senate chambers he would have found himself in congenial company, working with men who also had fought in the long, hard struggle for liberal democracy. But for Broward it was not to be. Other hands would have to take up his unfinished task.

Broward's example will never cease to be a challenge and an inspiration to courageous fighting in the people's cause. So long as Floridians speak of "Browardism" or recall the Broward Era, Napoleon Bonaparte Broward, Florida's fighting Democrat, will not be forgotten.

Notes

I

The Birthright of a Fighting Democrat

1. William Watson Davis, *The Civil War and Reconstruction in Florida* (New York, 1913), 153.
2. Frank Moore (comp.), *The Rebellion Record: A Diary of American Events, with Documents, Narratives, Illustrative Incidents, Poetry, etc.* (New York, 1861-1863; 1864-1868), IV, 229.
3. Lieutenant Commander Franklin E. Smith, *U.S.S. Bienville*, to his wife, March 10, 1862, in Franklin E. Smith Papers, Duke University Manuscript Collection. David Levy Yulee was appointed United States Senator by the Florida legislature in 1845, and he held this position, with only a brief interruption, until the Civil War.
4. Mills M. Lord, Jr., "David Levy Yulee, Statesman and Railroad Builder" (unpublished master's thesis, University of Florida, 1940), 153.
5. Napoleon B. Broward, Sr., to Oscar Hart, July 30, 1864, in Broward Papers, Jacksonville.
6. Pleasant D. Gold, *History of Duval County, Florida: Also Biographies of Men and Women Who Have Done Their Part in Making Duval County's Past and Present* (St. Augustine, 1928), 131.
7. T. Frederick Davis, *History of Early Jacksonville, Florida* (Jacksonville, 1911), 160.
8. *Ibid.*
9. *The War of the Rebellion: A Compilation of the Official Records of the Union and Confederate Armies* (Washington, 1880-1901), Ser. 1, Vol. VI, 414.
10. Davis, *History of Early Jacksonville, Florida*, 157.
11. *Ibid.*

12. *New York Times*, March 30, 1862, quoting the *Savannah Republican*, March 14, 1862.

13. *Ibid.*, March 20, 1862.

14. *Ibid.* See also T. Frederick Davis, *History of Jacksonville, Florida and Vicinity, 1513 to 1924* (St. Augustine, 1925), 119-120.

15. The Broward name has had several different spellings. Originally it was *Breur*, but in the public land documents in the *American State Papers* . . . the name is spelled as both *Breward* and *Brevard*.

16. Arthur H. Hirsch, *The Huguenots of Colonial South Carolina* (Durham, N. C., 1928), 7.

17. Jared Sparks (ed.), *The Library of American Biography* (Boston, 1855), IV, 36.

18. Florida and Margaret Broward, "Biographical Sketch of Broward Family" (typed copy of original in Broward Papers).

19. The three older children were Charles Broward, Francis Broward, Jr., and Sarah Elizabeth Broward.

20. This Spanish order, communicated to the American government on October 29, 1790, by "the captain general of the Island of Cuba and the two Floridas," provided, among other things, "that to foreigners who, of their free will, present themselves to swear allegiance to our Sovereign, there will be granted to them lands gratis in proportion to the workers each family may have." Ashbury Dickens and John W. Forney (eds.), *American State Papers, Documents of the Congress of the United States in Relation to the Public Lands* (Washington, 1860), V, 430.

21. Davis, *History of Jacksonville, Florida,* 26.

22. Dickens and Forney, *American State Papers*, IV, 566.

23. *Ibid.*, 619-620.

24. John Broward's Obituary (typed copy in Broward Papers).

25. These grants were usually five miles square and consisted of sixteen thousand acres of land. Dickens and Forney, *American State Papers*, V, 428.

26. Walter Lowrie and Walter S. Franklin, *American State Papers, Documents, Legislative and Executive of the Congress of the United States* (Washington, 1832), III, 805.

27. *Ibid.*
28. Broward, "Biographical Sketch of Broward Family."
29. *Ibid.*
30. *Marriage Records, Book O,* 3, Office of the County Judge, Duval County, Florida. According to Gold (*History of Duval County, Florida,* 119), the marriage was performed by the groom's brother, Charles Broward, who was a well-known Methodist minister in the community. Margaret Tucker, the daughter of Andrew Tucker, was born in Florida in 1801. In 1804 her father received a grant of land and established a plantation at Black Hammock, near the mouth of the Nassau River. The family remained in Florida until the East Florida Revolution in 1812, when all its members moved to Georgia. After Margaret's marriage to John Broward, the Tuckers returned to Florida, and in 1825 the title of their land was confirmed by the United States Land Commissioners.
31. Some of the foundations of the house and parts of the dam were seen by the author, January, 1942.
32. John Broward's Obituary.
33. *Journal of the Proceedings of the First General Assembly of the State of Florida* (Tallahassee, 1845). During this same session, John Broward introduced a measure in the Senate for adoption of the state flag with the motto "Let Us Alone" (Florida *Senate Journal,* 170); Charles Broward was appointed as a commissioner of fisheries by the assembly (Florida *Senate Journal,* 168).
34. Charles F. McRory was born in 1843 from this union. He was later adopted by John Broward and was mentioned in John Broward's will.
35. Gold, *History of Duval County, Florida,* 121.
36. Broward, "Biographical Sketch of Broward Family."
37. Mrs. Josephine Broward Beckley to author, November, 1941.
38. *Records of Wills, Book C-1,* 3, Office of the County Judge, Duval County, Florida.
39. Laura Buxton Hobbes, "Parsons Family Genealogy Record" (typed copy of original in Broward Papers).
40. Frederick Adams Virkus (ed.), *The Compendium of American Genealogy* (Chicago, 1933), V, 777.

41. Robert Francis Seybolt, *The Town Officials of Colonial Boston, 1634-1775* (Cambridge, Mass., 1939), 71.
42. *Ibid.*, 119. See also Hobbes, "Parsons Family Genealogy Record."
43. Governor William Badger was the son of Elizabeth Parsons Badger and was a direct descendant of Joseph Parsons, the first of the family in America.
44. The Parsons mill was purchased from Joseph Finnegan, who later achieved fame in the Confederate army. See Gold, *History of Duval County, Florida,* 119.
45. Miss Hortense Broward to author, February, 1950.
46. Halstead Parsons died in childhood. His father's mill partner, Halstead Hoeg, was mayor of Jacksonville at the time of the Federal invasion in 1862. See Davis, *History of Jacksonville, Florida.*
47. Mary Dorcas Parsons to Joseph Burke, December 12, 1849, in Broward Papers.
48. Mary Dorcas Parsons to William Parsons, October, 1851, in Broward Papers.
49. Broward, "Biographical Sketch of Broward Family."
50. Davis, *History of Jacksonville, Florida,* 112.
51. *Ibid.* See also Frank Mortimer Hawes, "New Englanders in the Florida Census of 1850," *New England Historical and Genealogical Register* (January, 1922), 47. Hawes gives the name incorrectly as *Tarsons.*
52. Traces of this highway were observed by the author, January, 1942.
53. Davis, *Civil War and Reconstruction in Florida,* 42.
54. "Ladies of Broward's Neck, Through Editors of the Papers, to the Politicians of Florida, as to Their Present and Future Protection against Abolition Emissaries of the North," November 6, 1860 (typed copy in Broward Papers).
55. Gold, *History of Duval County, Florida,* 127.
56. Fred L. Robertson (comp.), *Soldiers of Florida in the Seminole Indian, Civil and Spanish-American Wars* (Live Oak, Fla., 1903), 301.
57. Mary Elizabeth Dickison, *Dickison and His Men. Reminiscences of the War in Florida* (Louisville, 1890), 11.

58. Miss Hortense Broward to author, November, 1949; and Gold, *History of Duval County, Florida*, 274.
59. *Ibid.*
60. Dickison, *Dickison and His Men*, 12.
61. Gold, *History of Duval County, Florida*, 277.
62. George Seitner to Napoleon B. Broward, Sr., June 24, 1861, in Broward Papers.
63. Napoleon B. Broward, Sr., to Colonel Oscar Hart, July 30, 1864, in Broward Papers.

2

Winds of Adversity

1. Napoleon Bonap. te Broward, *Napoleon B. Broward, Candidate for Governor of Florida, Autobiography, Platform, Letter and Short Story of the Steamer "Three Friends," and a Filibustering Trip to Cuba* (1904), 1. Henceforth referred to in manuscript and footnotes as *Autobiographical Sketch*.
2. *Ibid.*
3. *Ibid.*
4. Mrs. Josephine Broward Beckley to author, January, 1942.
5. *Autobiographical Sketch*, 2.
6. *Ibid.*
7. *Ibid.*
8. *Ibid.*
9. Joseph Parsons operated a lumber camp in the woods at Mill Cove, a small settlement on the south side of the St. Johns River.
10. Broward, "Biographical Sketch of Broward Family." Margaret Tucker Broward is buried in the Old City Cemetery, Jacksonville, Florida.
11. Records of John Broward's estate are in the Office of the County Judge, Duval County, Florida. This bill was listed for the last time on February 17, 1871, and the debt was paid soon afterward.
12. The offices were on the second floor of a building located near the corner of Bay and Newnan streets. As Charles Broward's business prospered, he repurchased large amounts of the family

property that had been lost in the tax sales after the Civil War. After Charles Broward's death in 1873, this property was divided among his heirs. (A. W. Cockrell, the Broward family attorney, to author, February, 1942.)

13. Osceola Broward died in childhood and California Broward died in infancy. Gold, *History of Duval County, Florida*, 274. One of the aunts, Margaret Broward, was teaching school in the Bahama Islands in 1871 (Mrs. Napoleon B. Broward to author, April, 1942). Caroline Broward had married J. O. C. Jones and was living in Live Oak, Florida.

14. Wanton S. Webb (comp.), *Webb's Jacksonville Directory* (New York, 1873). This address was listed every year until 1882.

15. Miss Hortense Broward to author, November, 1941.

16. *Autobiographical Sketch*, 2.

17. *Ibid.*, 3.

18. *Ibid.*, 2.

19. *Ibid.* Scenic descriptions of the Florida woods during this period are found in Ledyard Bill, *A Winter in Florida* (New York, 1870); Daniel G. Brinton, *A Guide Book to Florida and the South, for Tourists, Invalids and Immigrants* (Philadelphia, 1869); and Sidney Lanier, *Florida—Its Scenery, Climate and History* (Philadelphia, 1876).

20. *Autobiographical Sketch*, 3.

21. *Ibid.* Aunt Lizzie was Elizabeth Turner Broward.

22. Amander Parsons is buried in the Parsons family cemetery at Newcastle.

23. *Autobiographical Sketch*, 3.

24. *Ibid.*, 4.

25. Mrs. Napoleon B. Broward to author, February, 1942.

26. These military breastworks have never been filled in and may still be seen (1950).

27. The *Kate Spencer* was named for Mrs. Kate Spencer, the postmistress of Fort George Island, Florida, and the wife of Captain Charles Spencer.

28. Mrs. Maggie Kemps Jenkins (Georgiana Carolina's sister) to author, February, 1942.

29. Mr. and Mrs. Dill lived in Jacksonville at the Broward boardinghouse for several winters. It was there that they met and grew

to love Hortense. They wanted to take her back with them to their Northern home for a visit, but the aunts objected strenuously. Hortense was able to accompany them only after she had been legally adopted by her grandmother, Elizabeth Burke Parsons. (Miss Hortense Broward to author, March, 1942.)

30. *Autobiographical Sketch,* 4.
31. *Ibid.,* 4-5.
32. *Ibid.,* 5.
33. Sheriff Uriah Bowden was appointed administrator of the estate on March 15, 1879. The estate records of Napoleon B. Broward, Sr., are filed in *Book O,* 147, Office of the County Judge, Duval County, Florida.
34. "Reminiscences of Captain R. G. Ross," quoted in Davis, *History of Jacksonville, Florida,* 387-389.
35. Description from a picture in the home of Napoleon Broward Kemps, son of Captain David Kemps.
36. *Florida Times-Union,* January 4, 1883. John McDonald was a boyhood friend of Napoleon Broward.
37. Mrs. Maggie Kemps Jenkins to author, 1942.
38. Papers dated May 25, 1883, authenticating this bond, are in the "Broward Family Scrapbook." The scrapbook, which was compiled by Mrs. Dorcas Beckley Foster, Broward's granddaughter, is part of the Broward Papers.
39. "Broward Family Scrapbook." License granted by P. McQuaid, chairman, Board of Pilot Commissioners.
40. *Acts of the Legislative Council of the Territory of Florida, Fifth Session, 1826-1827* (Tallahassee, 1827), 159-160.
41. *Acts of the Legislative Council of the Territory of Florida, Seventeenth Session, 1839* (Tallahassee, 1839), 26-27.
42. *Acts and Resolutions of the Legislative Council of the Territory of Florida, Nineteenth Session* (Tallahassee, 1841), 23; *Acts and Resolutions Adopted by the Legislature of Florida, Passed at its Ninth session, 1877, under the Constitution of 1868* (Tallahassee, 1877), 105.
43. The receipt for this furniture, dated September 29, 1883, is in the Broward Papers.
44. Mrs. Maggie Kemps Jenkins to author, February, 1942.
45. Obituary in *Florida Times-Union,* October 31, 1883.

46. The vessel was lent by Dr. J. C. L'Engle, a close family friend.
47. *Florida Times-Union,* November 1, 1883.
48. Mrs. Maggie Kemps Jenkins to author, February, 1942.

3

River Runs and a Romance

1. Chairman of the Pilot Commissioners to Broward, May 8, 1884, in Broward Papers.
2. Annie Isabell Douglass' grandfather, Henry Mitchell Douglass, emigrated from Scotland and settled near New Bern, N. C., early in the nineteenth century. He was a sailor by profession, and followed the sea until he was drowned in a hurricane off the Florida Keys. Her father, Alexander Douglass, was born on April 15, 1834. During his early years he worked for a cousin, Captain Joseph Hartick, and then moved to New York City to marry Margaret Hutchinson. (The Hutchinson family were Scotch and had emigrated to the United States from the Orkney Islands.) Annie Isabell Douglass was born in New York on March 13, 1867. After attending the public schools in that city, she moved with her family to Florida in 1883. Her father had sailed to Florida earlier on his schooner, the *J. E. Woodhouse.* (Details of the Douglass family history furnished the author by Mrs. Napoleon B. Broward.)
3. The Douglass home was located on Mount Pleasant Creek, near St. Johns Bluff. Captain Douglass had purchased an orange grove and built a large frame house which he named "Idle Wild."
4. An undated letter by Broward describing the transaction, in the Broward Papers.
5. *Florida Times-Union,* June and July, 1885.
6. Davis, *History of Jacksonville, Florida,* 160.
7. *Ibid.,* 491. See also John P. Varnum (ed.), *Jacksonville, Florida: A Descriptive and Statistical Report* (Jacksonville, 1885), 46-48. For a general picture of Jacksonville at the time, see Wanton S. Webb (ed.), *Webb's Historical, Industrial and Biographical Florida* (New York, 1885), Part I, 44-46.
8. *Florida Times-Union,* July 14, 1885; and Davis, *History of Jacksonville, Florida,* 361.

9. *Ibid.*, July 29, 1885.
10. *Ibid.*, June 26, 1885.
11. *Ibid.*, July 5, 1885.
12. Description taken from a picture of Broward photographed while he was captain of the *Kate Spencer*.
13. John E. Hartridge to Emory Speer, July 3, 1886, in Broward Papers.
14. Mrs. Napoleon B. Broward to author, February, 1942.
15. Mrs. Napoleon B. Broward to author, March, 1942. Captain Rice was mayor of Jacksonville in 1885.
16. Mrs. Napoleon B. Broward to author, March, 1942.
17. *Jacksonville Metropolis*, May 5, 1887.
18. Mrs. Napoleon B. Broward to author, March, 1942.
19. This section of East Jacksonville was the former site of the plantation of the Reverend and Mrs. Johnson. Mrs. Johnson was the daughter of Charles Broward and a niece of John Broward. The property was sold several times and was finally inherited by Mrs. Broward before her marriage. (Mrs. Josephine Broward Beckley to author, November, 1949.)
20. Wanton S. Webb (comp.), *Webb's Jacksonville and Consolidated Directory, 1887* (Jacksonville, 1887). Property listed as being at 111 Maggie Street. The house faced Church Street, so the address given was probably where the family received its mail. Maggie Street was named for Margaret Broward, John Broward's daughter.
21. Mrs. Napoleon B. Broward to author, February, 1942.
22. *Florida Times-Union*, October 20, 1886.
23. *Ibid.*, May 29, 1887.
24. *Ibid.*, August 23, 1887.
25. According to *Webb's Jacksonville and Consolidated Directory, 1887*, the woodyard was located at 92 East Bay Street, near the corner of Liberty Street.
26. *Florida Times-Union*, January 28, 1888.
27. *Ibid.*, February 3, 1888.
28. *Ibid.*, February 16, 1888.
29. *Ibid.*
30. *Ibid.*, February 19, 1888.
31. *Florida Weekly Times*, February 23, 1888.

32. John L. Crawford to Broward, February 20, 1888. This date is incorrectly shown as 1887 in the *Autobiographical Sketch*, 4.
33. *Florida Times-Union*, February 28, 1888.
34. *Ibid.*, March 3, 1888.
35. *Ibid.*
36. *Ibid.*, March 4, 1888.
37. M. A. Brown to author, March, 1942.
38. *Florida Times-Union*, March 10, 1888.

4

Politics and the Plague

1. *Florida Times-Union*, April 25, 1888.
2. *Ibid.*, April 29, 1888.
3. *Ibid.*, April 30, 1888.
4. *Ibid.*, July 18, 1888.
5. Charles S. Adams (ed.), *Report of the Jacksonville Auxiliary Sanitary Association of Jacksonville, Florida, Covering the Work of the Association during the Yellow Fever Epidemic, 1888* (Jacksonville, 1889), 11.
6. *Ibid.*, 12. See also Margaret C. Fairlie, "The Yellow Fever Epidemic of 1888 in Jacksonville," *The Florida Historical Quarterly*, XIX (October, 1940), 97.
7. Adams, *Report of the Jacksonville Auxiliary Sanitary Association*, 26.
8. Davis, *History of Jacksonville, Florida*, 180.
9. Adams, *Report of the Jacksonville Auxiliary Sanitary Association*, 13.
10. *Ibid.*, 24.
11. *Florida Times-Union*, October 4, 1888.
12. *Congressional Record*, 50 Cong., 1 Sess., XIX, 8719.
13. Adams, *Report of the Jacksonville Auxiliary Sanitary Association*, 19.
14. *Ibid.*, 18.
15. Fairlie, "The Yellow Fever Epidemic of 1888 in Jacksonville."
16. Adams, *Report of the Jacksonville Auxiliary Sanitary Association*, 65. An account of the epidemic is given in Webster Mer-

ritt's *A Century of Medicine in Jacksonville and Duval County* (Gainesville, 1949), 146-161.

17. Mrs. Napoleon B. Broward to author, February, 1942. Miss Hortense Broward returned to Florida on the *Ozama* early in November and lived in Mayport until the order was given that refugees could return to the city.

18. According to Fairlie ("The Yellow Fever Epidemic of 1888 in Jacksonville," 106), the Board of Health had announced that refugees could not return home until December 15, 1888.

19. *Florida Times-Union*, October 17, 1888.

20. *Ibid.*, November 7, 1888.

21. *Ibid.*, November 17, 1888.

22. *Ibid.*, November 22, 1888.

23. *Ibid.*, December 18, 1888.

24. *Ray P. Moody* v. *W. D. Barnes* in *Florida Reports*, XXV (1889), 298-310.

25. *Florida Times-Union*, March 27, 1889. This newspaper consistently supported Broward and endorsed his policies until 1897. The paper began with the *Florida Union*, a four-page weekly, started by John K. Stickney in 1864. During the Reconstruction era, the *Union* was bitterly partisan to the Republican party, but after the election of 1876 it became a Democratic paper. In 1877 the Reverend H. B. McCallum and W. W. Douglass purchased the *Union*, and turned it first into an afternoon daily and finally a morning daily in November, 1879. In 1883 the *Daily Florida Union* was merged with the *Florida Daily Times* to form the *Florida Times-Union*, the first issue of which appeared on February 4, 1883. In 1888 T. T. Stockton, Telfair Stockton, and John N. C. Stockton organized the Florida Publishing Company, which purchased and began publishing the *Florida Times-Union*. For a brief account of the history of the *Florida Times-Union*, see Davis, *History of Jacksonville, Florida*, 452-454, and J. Pendleton Gaines, Jr., "A Century in Florida Journalism" (unpublished master's thesis, University of Florida, 1949), 64-65.

26. *Florida Times-Union*, July 2, 1889.

27. *A Journal of the Proceedings of the House of Representatives of the Regular Session of the Legislature of the State of Florida,*

1889 (Tallahassee, 1889), 51. Henceforth referred to as *Florida House Journal.*

28. *Laws of the State of Florida, Adopted by the Legislature at Its Second Session, 1889* (Tallahassee, 1889), 190-194. Henceforth referred to as *Laws of Florida.*

29. *Florida Times-Union,* January 5, 1890.

30. *Ibid.,* January 6, 1890.

31. Herbert D. Mendenhall, "What the Phosphate Industry Means to Florida Engineers" (Tallahassee, 1938), 1.

32. *Autobiographical Sketch,* 5.

33. *Florida Times-Union,* July 19, 1890.

34. *Ibid.,* July 24, 1890.

35. *Ibid.,* July 25, 1890.

36. *Ibid.*

37. *Ibid.,* August 5, 1890.

38. *Ibid.,* October 17, 1890.

39. *Ibid.,* October 25, 1890.

40. *Ibid.,* October 30, 1890.

41. *Ibid.,* November 8, 1890.

42. John L. Crawford to Broward, November 11, 1890, in Broward Papers.

43. *Florida Times-Union,* January 16, 1892.

44. *Ibid.,* January 22, 1892.

5

Breaking with Bourbonism

1. For a brief account of Drew and his administration, see Rowland R. Rerick, *Memoirs of Florida* (Atlanta, 1902), I, 339-347; and the *Tallahassee Sentinel,* June 16, 1876.

2. The platforms of the national political parties in this period, 1876-1892, are in Kirk H. Porter, *National Party Platforms* (New York, 1924), 86-158.

3. For an analysis of Whig party strength in Florida prior to the Civil War, see Henry J. Doherty, Jr., "The Florida Whigs" (unpublished master's thesis, University of Florida, 1949). The political scene in Florida during the 1850's is described in Arthur

W. Thompson, "Political Nativism in Florida, 1848-1860: A Phase of Anti-Secessionism," *The Journal of Southern History,* XV (February, 1949), 39-65.

4. There is no published biography of Bloxham. The best source for his life is Ruby Leach Carson, "William Dunnington Bloxham, Florida's Two-Term Governor" (unpublished master's thesis, University of Florida, 1945). See also Ruby Leach Carson, "William Dunnington Bloxham: The Years to the Governorship," *The Florida Historical Quarterly,* XXVII (January, 1949), 207-236.

5. *Minutes of the Trustees of the Internal Improvement Fund, 1881* (Tallahassee, 1881), II, 433. Henceforth referred to as *Trustees I.I.F. Minutes.* See also T. Frederick Davis, "The Disston Land Purchase," *The Florida Historical Quarterly,* XVII (January, 1939), 206-209. For accounts of Disston's life, see Alfred J. Hanna and Kathryn A. Hanna, *Lake Okeechobee, Wellspring of the Everglades* (Indianapolis, 1948), 93-95. See also obituary in *New York Times,* May 1, 1896.

6. Junius E. Dovell, "A History of the Everglades of Florida" (unpublished doctoral dissertation, University of North Carolina, 1947), 124.

7. Hanna and Hanna, *Lake Okeechobee,* 96.

8. William D. Bloxham, "The Disston Sale and the State Finances" (1884), 6-7.

9. For an account of the controversy over the calling of the constitutional convention, see Eldridge R. Collins, "The Florida Constitution of 1885" (unpublished master's thesis, University of Florida, 1939), 14-29; and J. B. Whitfield (comp.), *Florida State Government: An Official Directory of the State Government* (Tallahassee, 1885), 7.

0. *Florida Times-Union,* May 6, 1884.

1. Carson, "William Dunnington Bloxham, Florida's Two-Term Governor," 237-243.

2. William T. Cash, *History of the Democratic Party in Florida* (Live Oak, 1936), 76.

3. Sigsbee C. Prince, Jr., "Edward Alysworth Perry, Florida's Thirteenth Governor" (unpublished master's thesis, 1949), 87-90.

14. Cash, *History of the Democratic Party in Florida*, 77 (date of convention incorrectly listed as May 17, 1884). See also *Florida Times-Union*, June 19, 1884; and *Land of Flowers*, June 21, 1884.

15. Edward C. Williamson, "Independentism: A Challenge to the Florida Democracy of 1884," *The Florida Historical Quarterly*, XXVII (October, 1948), 137.

16. *Ibid.*, 154-155.

17. James O. Knauss, "The Farmers' Alliance in Florida," *South Atlantic Quarterly*, XXV (July, 1926), 301; Kathryn T. Abbey, "Florida Versus the Principles of Populism, 1896-1911," *The Journal of Southern History*, IV (November, 1938), 462.

18. The Alliance published a series of newspapers in Florida, which included: *The Florida Alliance* (Lakeland); *The Alliance Farmer* (Selman); the *Banner of Liberty* (Live Oak); the *Farmers' Advocate* (Tampa); *The Alliance* (Tallahassee); the *Alliance Farmers* (Chipley); and the *Ocala Demands* (Ocala). *The Florida Dispatch, Farmer and Fruit-Grower* was the official state paper.

19. Samuel Proctor, "The National Farmers' Alliance Convention of 1890 and Its 'Ocala Demands,'" *The Florida Historical Quarterly*, XXVIII (January, 1950), 161-181. See also *The Florida Dispatch, Farmer and Fruit-Grower*, December 11, 1890.

20. John D. Hicks, *The Populist Revolt* (Minneapolis, 1931), 177-178; C. Vann Woodward, *Tom Watson, Agrarian Rebel* (New York, 1937), 160-161.

21. Edward C. Williamson, "Wilkinson Call: A Pioneer in Progressive Democracy" (unpublished master's thesis, University of Florida, 1946), 160-169. For partisan discussions of the Call controversy in 1891, see W. D. Chipley, *A Review of the Record of Hon. Wilkinson Call* (1890); and Francis P. Fleming, *Did the Florida Legislature of 1891 Elect a Senator?* (Tallahassee, 1891). See also *R. H. M. Davidson v. Wilkinson Call, Brief of Eppa Hunton, Counsel for Davidson, Before the Committee on Privileges and Elections of the United States Senate, 52 Congress Contested Election from the State of Florida* (1891), 1-21; and *Proceedings in the United States Senate Admitting Hon. Wilkin-*

    son Call as a Senator from Florida, December 7 and 8, 1891 (Washington, 1891), 3-7.

22. Abbey, "Florida Versus the Principles of Populism, 1896-1911," 463-464.

6

A Fight and a Riot

1. *Florida Times-Union*, April 15, 1892.
2. *Ibid.*, April 16, 1892.
3. *Ibid*. By 1892, the *Florida Times-Union* had begun taking a strong stand, in its editorials and news columns, against the railroads and corporations in Florida.
4. *Ibid.*, April 17, 1892.
5. *Ibid.*
6. M. A. Brown to author, March, 1942.
7. *Florida Times-Union*, April 17, 1892.
8. *Ibid.*, April 22, 1892.
9. Appeared daily in the *Florida Times-Union*, April 20-April 30, 1892.
10. *Ibid.*, May 19, 1892.
11. *Ibid.*, May 20, 1892.
12. *Ibid.*, June 4, 1892.
13. *Ibid.*
14. *Ibid.*, July 5, 1892.
15. Lang to Broward, July 6, 1892, in Broward Papers. Broward had wired the governor for the troops, but the governor was away from Tallahassee, and the adjutant general answered the telegram.
16. *Florida Times-Union*, July 6, 1892.
17. Davis, *History of Jacksonville, Florida*, 197.
18. *Ibid.*
19. *Florida Times-Union*, July 8, 1892.
20. *Report of the Adjutant-General, January 1, 1893* in *Annual Reports, 1893*, 18-20.
21. *Florida Times-Union*, July 20, 1892.
22. *Ibid.*, August 2, 1892.

23. Duncan U. Fletcher was mayor of Jacksonville and later United States Senator from Florida. There is no published biography of Fletcher. For a brief account of his life, see *Makers of America, Florida Edition* (Atlanta, 1909), I, 211-215; and William James Wells, "Duncan Upshaw Fletcher, Florida's Grand Old Man" (unpublished master's thesis, John B. Stetson University, July, 1936).

24. *Florida Times-Union*, August 4, 5, and 6, 1892.

25. *Ibid.*, August 7, 1892.

26. *Ibid.*, October 5, 1892. The Antis, through a group of Jacksonville attorneys, petitioned Attorney General Lamar to bring *quo warranto* proceedings against the elected officials and oust them from office, but Lamar refused to take such action. See *Report of the Attorney-General, March 20, 1893* in *Annual Report 1893*, 8-9.

27. *Ibid.*, November 15, 1893.

28. *Ibid.*, November 12, 1893.

29. *Ibid.*

30. Broward to Mitchell, November 17, 1893, in Broward Papers; Mitchell to Broward November 22, 1893, in Broward Paper

31. *Florida Times-Union*, November 20, 1893. Newspapers throughout the country reported the activities in Jacksonville (*Florida Times-Union*, November 23 and 24, 1893, quoting the *New York World, Washington Post, Knoxville Tribune, Memphis Appeal-Avalanche*, and *Cincinnati Tribune*).

32. Near the present site (1950) of the Gator Bowl Stadium in Jacksonville.

33. A copy of this advertisement, which was mailed by Broward to Mitchell, December 2, 1893, is in the Broward Papers. The Florida law at the time (as cited in the *Revised Statutes of Florida*, 1892, Title II, Chapter III, Act. III, 781) was designed to prevent duels, but the state officials considered the law broad enough to outlaw prize fights.

34. Mitchell to Broward, January 2, 1894, in Broward Papers.

35. Houstoun to Broward, January 13, 1894, in Broward Papers.

36. *Florida Times-Union*, January 20, 1894.

37. *Ibid.*, January 24, 1894.

8. *Report of the Attorney-General, March 20, 1895,* in *Annual Reports, 1895,* 13-14; *Report of the Adjutant-General, January 1, 1895,* in *Annual Reports, 1895,* 12-13. In addition to Cockrell, the Athletic Club also hired as counsel Marshall McDonald, a well-known attorney from St. Louis, who was in Jacksonville for the fight. Arguing the case for the state were State's Attorney A. G. Hartridge and Attorney General William B. Lamar.
9. "Broward Family Scrapbook."
0. *Florida Times-Union,* January 26, 1894.
1. *Ibid.* See also James J. Corbett, *The Roar of the Crowd* (New York, 1930), 217.
2. Eight letters to firms in New York ordering boilers and similar equipment Undated except for 1894, in Broward Papers.

7

"Iniquity of the Corporation People"

1. *Florida Times-Union,* July 8, 1894.
2. *Ibid.*
3. *Ibid.* (editorial), July 9, 1894.
4. *Ibid.,* July 11, 1894.
5. *Ibid.*
6. The Florida Central and Peninsular Railroad, and the Jacksonville, Tampa and Key West Railroad.
7. The Savannah, Florida and Western Railroad, and the East Tennessee, Virginia and Georgia Railroad.
8. *Autobiographical Sketch,* 20.
9. *Ibid.,* 20-21.
0. *Florida Times-Union,* January 5, 1892. For an account of Plant's life, see G. Hutchinson Smyth, *The Life of Henry Bradley Plant* (New York, 1898).
1. *Ibid.,* July 12, 1894.
2. *Ibid.,* July 13, 1894.
3. *Ibid.*
4. *Ibid.,* July 15, 1894.
5. *Ibid.,* July 19, 1894.
6. Dr. C. Joyner and C. E. Ringland.

17. *Florida Times-Union,* July 20, 1894.
18. *Ibid.*
19. *Ibid.,* July 25, 1894.
20. *Ibid.,* August 1, 1894. It was alleged that Chipley was using his influence to defeat Congressman Stephen R. Mallory.
21. *Daily Florida Citizen,* September 22, 1894.
22. *Autobiographical Sketch,* 23.
23. *Daily Florida Citizen,* October 2, 1894.
24. Mitchell to Broward, September 30, 1894, in Broward Papers.
25. *Ibid.,* October 1, 1894, in Broward Papers.
26. *Ibid.*
27. *Ibid.*
28. *Daily Florida Citizen,* October 2, 1894.
29. *Ibid.* Actually the adjutant general had arrived about four in the morning and established his headquarters at the Carlton Hotel, but he did not announce himself until several hours later (Houstoun to Mitchell, October 3, 1894, in *Adjutant-General's Report, 1895,* 13).
30. *Florida Times-Union,* October 3, 1894.
31. *Ibid.*
32. *Ibid.*
33. *Ibid.* Immediately after this interview, Taliaferro asked Houstoun to call out the troops, but the latter refused (*Adjutant-General's Report, 1895,* 13).
34. *Ibid.,* October 2, 1894.
35. *Ibid.,* October 3, 1894; *Adjutant-General's Report, 1895,* 15.
36. *Ibid.* Houstoun did not mention the parade in his report; he merely stated that the troops "were relieved from further duty." See *Adjutant-General's Report, 1895,* 16.
37. *Ibid.,* October 7, 1894.
38. *Ibid.,* October 4, 1894.
39. *Ibid.*
40. *Ibid.,* October 3, 1894.
41. *Ibid.*
42. *Ibid.,* October 5, 1894.
43. Among those who signed this petition were: Charles Marvin, E. W. Fleming, E. W. Gillen, W. A. Bours, E. J. Triay, E. J. E. McLaurin, A. G. Hartridge, J. B. Christie, forme

Governor Francis P. Fleming, John E. Hartridge, H. H. Buck-
man, Porcher L'Engle, J. C. L'Engle, Julius Saloman, James
P. Taliaferro, E. C. Pickett, J. B. Coachman, and Bion H.
Barnett. See *The Free Lance*, February 16, 1895.

4. *The Free Lance*, February 16, 1895.
5. *Ibid.*
6. *Florida Times-Union*, October 3, 1894; *Adjutant-General's Report, 1895*, 16.
7. *Adjutant-General's Report, 1895*, 16.
8. Mitchell's secretary (no name on letter) to Broward, October 12, 1894, in Broward Papers.
9. *Florida Times-Union* (editorial), October 13, 1894.
0. *Ibid.*, October 17, 1894.
1. Original copy, October 18, 1894, in Broward Papers.
2. Broward to Mitchell, October 20, 1894, in Broward Papers.
3. *The Free Lance*, February 16, 1895.
4. *Ibid.*
5. *Annual Report of the Secretary of State of Florida* in *Messages and Documents of Florida, 1895* (Tallahassee, 1895), 19.
6. Call to Broward, December 24, 1894, in Broward Papers.
7. *Florida Times-Union*, April 25, 1895.

8

Bearding the Spanish Lion

1. *Florida Times-Union*, June 19, 1895.
2. Mrs. Napoleon B. Broward to author, March, 1942.
3. The house is still standing (1950) at 935 East Church Street.
4. Ralph D. Paine, "From Deck Hand to Governor: The Pictur-esque Career of Napoleon Broward," *Everybody's Magazine*, XX (February, 1909), 191.
5. *Autobiographical Sketch*, 27.
6. *Florida Times-Union*, February 3, 1895.
7. Walter Millis, *The Martial Spirit* (Boston, 1931), 1. See also the *Tampa Morning Tribune*, February 27, 1895, for a descrip-tion of the joyous Cuban population in Tampa and Ybor City when the news of the insurrection arrived.

8. For an account of American newspaper interest in the revolt in Cuba, see Oliver Carlson and Ernest S. Bates, *Hearst, Lord of San Simeon* (New York, 1937), 92-109; and James W. Barrett, *Joseph Pulitzer and his World* (New York, 1941), 174-178. The interest shown by the rural newspapers in the South is described by Thomas D. Clark in *The Southern Country Editor* (Indianapolis, 1948). Clark states: "After 1895 events leading to the Spanish-American War took the country papers, for the first time, well beyond the pale of their communities. Highly colored accounts of this international conflict appeared in the ready-print pages and boiler-plate matter."

9. *Papers Relating to the Foreign Relations of the United States,* House of Repr., 54 Cong., 1 Sess., Doc. 1, Pt. 2, 1187-1209; French E. Chadwick, *The Relations of the United States and Spain* (New York, 1909), 418; and Orestes Ferrara, *The Last Spanish War* (New York, 1937), 36 (quoting the Spanish memorandum of July, 1896). For a description of American interest in Cuba during the nineteenth century, see John Bassett Moore, *A Digest of International Law* (Washington, 1906, VI, 121; John H. Latané, *America as a World Power* (New York, 1907), 7; Allan Nevins, *Hamilton Fish: The Inner History of the Grant Administration* (New York, 1936), 871-886; Parker T. Moon, *Imperialism and World Politics* (New York, 1927), 385; and John H. Latané, "The Diplomacy of the United States in Regard to Cuba," American Historical Association, *Annual Report* (1897).

10. Broward suggested that they were called Conchs "probably because they can be seen engaged in their work on the reefs by day, and at night they disappear as completely as do the conch fish in their shells." See Napoleon B. Broward, "Filibustering in Florida," *The Florida Life* (November, 1897), reprinted in *Autobiographical Sketch,* 24.

11. James D. Richardson (comp.), *A Compilation of the Messages and Papers of the Presidents, 1789-1905,* IX (Washington, 1907), 591; and Allan Nevins, *Grover Cleveland: A Study in Courage* (New York, 1932), 714.

12. *Autobiographical Sketch,* 26. For a description of the organization and functions of the Cuban *junta* in the United States, see

Richard V. Rickenbach, "A History of Filibustering From Florida to Cuba, 1895-1898" (unpublished master's thesis, University of Florida, 1948), 16-26; H. S. Rubens, "The Insurgent Government in Cuba," *North American Review*, LCXVI (May, 1898), 560-569; and H. S. Rubens, *Liberty: The Story of Cuba* (New York, 1932), 140-212.

13. *Autobiographical Sketch*, 28; Elbert J. Benton, *International Law and Diplomacy of the Spanish-American War* (Baltimore, 1908), 49.
14. *Daily Florida Citizen*, January 15, 1896.
15. *Autobiographical Sketch*, 28; Paine, "From Deck Hand to Governor," 191.
16. *Autobiographical Sketch*, 28.
17. *Ibid.*, 29.
18. *Ibid.*, 29-30.
19. *Daily Florida Citizen*, March 18, 1896. As Alphonso Fritot, Huau's nephew, was the agent in charge of all railroads entering and leaving Jacksonville, it was a relatively easy matter to have the merchandise unloaded from the railroad car.
20. *Ibid.*
21. Burton Barrs, brother of John M. Barrs, to author, October, 1941.
22. *Daily Florida Citizen*, March 18, 1896.
23. *Ibid.*
24. *Ibid.*
25. *Autobiographical Sketch*, 31.
26. *Ibid.*
27. *Ibid.* Broward (*Autobiographical Sketch*, 31) states that when Kilgore arrived back in Jacksonville, the newsboys were calling, "Morning paper, tell all about the Three Friends going to Cuba with Gen. Colasso and the whole Cuban army aboard!"
28. *Ibid.*
29. *Ibid.*, 32.
30. *Ibid.*
31. *Ibid.*
32. *Ibid.*, 33.
33. *Ibid.*, 34.
34. *Ibid.*, 36.

35. *Ibid.*, 37.

36. *Ibid.*

37. *Ibid.*, 38.

38. *Ibid.*

39. *Ibid.* See also Chadwick, *The Relations of the United States and Spain*, 316; and John H. Latané, "Intervention of the United States in Cuba," *North American Review*, LCXVI (March 1898), 355. Rickenbach ("A History of Filibustering From Florida to Cuba," 12) states that the *Virginius* belonged to General Quesada, a prominent member of the Cuban *junta*, and that it had been illegally flying the American flag at the time of capture.

40. *Autobiographical Sketch*, 39.

41. *Ibid.*

42. *Florida Times-Union*, March 23, 1896.

43. *Ibid.*

44. *Daily Florida Citizen*, March 26, 1896.

45. *Ibid.*, March 31, 1896.

46. *Ibid.*, March 21, 1896.

47. *Ibid.*

48. *Ibid.*, May 22, 1896.

49. *Florida Times-Union*, May 23, 1896.

50. *Papers Relating to the Foreign Relations of the United States*, House of Repr., 55 Cong., 1 Sess., Doc. 326, 15.

51. *Daily Florida Citizen*, May 23, 1896.

52. *Evening Times-Union*, May 23, 1896.

53. *Florida Times-Union*, May 23, 1896.

54. *Ibid.*

55. *Daily Florida Citizen*, May 23, 1896.

56. *Papers Relating to the Foreign Relations of the United States*, Doc. 326, 15. Hamelin's message to Bisbee was quoted in the *Daily Florida Citizen*, May 23, 1896.

57. Calderon Carlisle, *Report to the Spanish Legation* (Washington, 1896), I, 32.

58. *Daily Florida Citizen*, June 4, 1896.

59. *Ibid.*

60. *Florida Times-Union*, June 10, 1896. Scrapia Arteago was staff officer under the command of General Gomez. Arteago

had come to the United States from Cuba to expedite a shipment of guns and men to the rebel armies.

1. *Florida Times-Union,* June 18, 1896.
2. United States Commissioner Locke should not be confused with Judge James W. Locke.
3. *Florida Times-Union,* June 18, 1896.
4. *Evening Times-Union,* June 18, 1896.
5. *Florida Times-Union,* June 28, 1896.
6. *Ibid.*
7. *Ibid.*
8. "Broward Family Scrapbook," unidentified newspaper clipping dated July 19, 1896; Carlisle, *Report to the Spanish Legation,* II, app. I, 21. Another source states that the landing took place between July 1 and July 13, 1897 (*Appleton's Annual Cyclopaedia and Register of Important Events of the Year, 1897,* II).
9. *Florida Times-Union,* July 7, 1896.
10. *Ibid.,* July 14, 1896.
11. *Daily Florida Citizen,* July 14, 1896.
12. *Florida Times-Union,* July 20, 1896, quoting the *Atlanta Journal,* July 18, 1896.

9

"A Price on His Head"

1. *Florida Times-Union,* July 22, 1896. According to Benton (*International Law and Diplomacy,* 44), before the *Three Friends* was placed in dry dock, she made a fourth filibustering voyage on July 17, and landed guns and supplies for the Cubans.
2. *Florida Times-Union,* July 31, 1896.
3. *Ibid.,* August 11, 1896.
4. *Ibid.,* August 15, 1896.
5. *Ibid.,* August 21, 1896. Benton (*International Law and Diplomacy,* 44) states that earlier in the month the *Three Friends* had attempted an unsuccessful filibustering expedition.
6. *New York Herald,* September 20, 1896.
7. *Florida Times-Union,* September 16, 1896.
8. *Ibid.,* September 23, 1896.

9. *New York Herald*, September 19, 1896.

10. *Florida Times-Union*, September 29, 1896.

11. *Ibid.*, October 20, 1896.

12. The unsuccessful filibustering expedition attempted on November 8, 1896, is reported by Benton in *International Law and Diplomacy*, 44. The Spanish authorities had been alerted to the preparations, and when they notified the American government about the plans of the *Three Friends*, the attorney general ordered the United States District Attorney in Jacksonville to seize the vessel. (Carlisle, *Report to the Spanish Legation*, II, app. I, 23, 24.)

13. *United States* v. *The Steamer Three Friends*, 166, U.S., 1-83; Carlisle, *Report to the Spanish Legation*, II, app. II, pt. 1, 2.

14. *Florida Times-Union*, November 15, 1896.

15. *Ibid.*, November 20, 1896. George DeCottes was no longer connected with the *Three Friends*. Earlier in the year, soon after the steamer had returned from her first filibustering trip, DeCottes sold his interest in the *Three Friends* to A. W. and J. M. Barrs for twelve thousand dollars (*Florida Times-Union*, May 24, 1896). Napoleon Broward owned fifty-eight shares of stock, Montcalm two shares, and the two Barrs brothers owned the remaining forty shares (*Florida Times-Union*, November 15, 1896).

16. *Ibid.*, November 28, 1896.

17. Clark cited the decision of 1883 by the United States Court for the Southern District of New York, in the libel against the steamer *Mary N. Hogan*, in which the court had ruled that bond could not be given. He stated that the circumstances in the libel of the *Three Friends* were similar to those in the earlier case.

18. *Florida Times-Union*, December 3, 1896.

19. John Bassett Moore, *A Digest of International Law*, VII, 966.

20. *Ibid.*, 965.

21. *Revised Statutes of the United States* (Washington, 1877), XX, 1029.

22. Broward signed a new contract with Huau on December 9, 1896, in which he agreed to haul to Cuba a cargo of munitions, not to exceed thirty-five tons, and a group of patriots. Huau stated that he would pay for all provisions and coal and give Broward

ten thousand dollars as soon as the *Three Friends* was at sea. Huau further agreed that if the steamer failed to return, Broward would receive an additional ten thousand dollars and twenty thousand dollars in Cuban bonds. The *Jacksonville Journal* of August 23, 1939, carried a reproduction of the photostat made of the original contract.

3. Horace Smith, *A Captain Unafraid: The Strange Adventures of Dynamite Johnny O'Brien* (New York, 1912), 141-143; Ralph D. Paine, *Roads of Adventure* (Boston, 1925), 63. Rickenbach ("A History of Filibustering From Florida to Cuba, 1895-1898," 73) tells the following story: "Fernandina had been chosen for the port of embarkation of this expedition. The collector of that port, George L. Baltzell, had made a boast that thus far no filibustering expedition had been made from his town since he had become collector. He was quite fond of poker and on the night of this venture, Broward 'sat in' with Baltzell in a session of his favorite card game. Knowing what was transpiring, Broward undoubtedly had to keep a good 'poker face' the entire evening."

4. According to a later report, the pilothouse on the Spanish boat had been torn away (Rickenbach, "A History of Filibustering From Florida to Cuba, 1895-1898," 77, footnote). The Hotchkiss on the *Three Friends* was torn away from its lashings as a result of the strong recoil, and the gun almost pushed through the bulwarks (Smith, *A Captain Unafraid*, 150). Mike Walsh, a member of the group, boasted later that he had fired the shot. See Ralph D. Paine, "The Log of a Filibuster-Correspondent," *The Outing*, XLIII (November, 1903), 216; and Ruby Leach Carson, "Florida, Promoter of Cuban Liberty," *The Florida Historical Quarterly*, XIX (January, 1941), 286.

5. *Florida Times-Union*, January 1, 1897.

6. *New York Herald*, December 25, 1896.

7. See Ralph D. Paine, "On No-Name Key," *The Outing*, XLII, (September, 1903); and Paine, *Roads of Adventure*, 150. Paine was a war correspondent for the *New York American*. Before leaving the United States, Paine was instructed by William Randolph Hearst to deliver a two thousand dollar, gem-encrusted sword to General Gomez. Paine still had the valuable gift when

he landed on No-Name Key. The sword eventually reache General Gomez through the office of the Jacksonville *junta*. See Paine, *Roads of Adventure*, 63; and Carson, "Florida, Pro moter of Cuban Liberty," 287.

28. *Florida Times-Union*, December 29, 1896.
29. *Ibid.*
30. *United States* v. *The Steamer Three Friends*, 166, U.S., 71.
31. *Florida Times-Union*, January 6, 1897.
32. *Ibid.*, February 7, 1897.
33. *United States* v. *The Steamer Three Friends*, 166, U.S., 11.
34. *Ibid.*, 63-66.
35. *Ibid.*
36. *Ibid.*, 70.
37. Benton, *International Law and Diplomacy*, 56.

10

Fireworks in Florida

1. For a description of the national political scene in 1896 and th events leading up to it, see James Ford Rhodes, *The McKinle and Roosevelt Administrations* (New York, 1927), 1-29; Alla Nevins, *Grover Cleveland: A Study in Courage*, 677-712; C Vann Woodward, *Tom Watson, Agrarian Rebel*, 302-331 Woodrow Wilson, "Mr. Cleveland as President," *Atlanti Monthly*, LXXIX (March, 1897); and Ray Ginger, *The Bend ing Cross* (New Brunswick, 1949), 187-201.
2. M. R. Werner, *Bryan* (New York, 1929), 96.
3. *Evening Times-Union*, June 16, 1896.
4. *Florida Times-Union*, June 16, 1896.
5. *Ibid.*, June 17, 1896.
6. *Ibid.* See also O. L. Parker, "William N. Sheats, Florida Edu cator" (unpublished master's thesis, University of Florida, 1949) 105.
7. *Ibid.*, July 24, 1896.
8. *Ibid.*, July 29, 1896.
9. *Evening Times-Union*, July 28, 1896.
10. *Florida Times-Union*, July 29, 1896.

11. *Ibid.*, August 2, 1896.

12. *Ibid.*, August 13, 1896.

13. For a description of the convention and the Broward demonstration, see the *Florida Times-Union*, August 16, 1896.

14. *Florida Times-Union*, August 5, 1896; Carson, "William Dunnington Bloxham, Florida's Two-Term Governor," 290-292.

15. *Ibid.*

16. *Ibid.*, August 24, 1896.

17. *Ibid.*, September 7, 1896.

18. *Ibid.*, October 3, 1896.

19. *Ibid.*

20. *Ibid.*, October 4, 1896.

21. *Ibid.*

22. *Ibid.*, October 6, 1896.

23. *Ibid.*, October 7, 1896.

24. *Ibid.*, October 10, 1896. An unofficial tabulation of votes by precincts is in the Broward Papers.

25. Certification of bond, signed by sureties, is in the Broward Papers.

26. Mitchell to Broward, November 29, 1896, in Broward Papers.

27. *Florida Times-Union*, January 6, 1897.

28. Carson, "William Dunnington Bloxham, Florida's Two-Term Governor," 296-299; *Florida Times-Union*, October 21, 1896. For national election results, see Werner, *Bryan*, 111; Rhodes, *The McKinley and Roosevelt Administrations*, 29; and the *New York Times*, November 4, 1896.

29. Mrs. Napoleon B. Broward to author, February, 1942.

30. *Acts and Resolutions of the General Assembly of the State of Florida, Seventh Session, 1855*, 16.

31. *Acts and Resolutions Adopted by the Legislature of Florida at its Eleventh Session, 1881*, 217-218.

32. *Weekly Floridian*, July 7, 1887; Prince, "Edward Alysworth Perry," 111-112. The first commissioners were George G. McWhorter, Enoch J. Vann, and William Himes.

33. *Autobiographical Sketch*, 9.

34. "Napoleon B. Broward on Important Issues," *Autobiographical Sketch*, 24.

35. *Autobiographical Sketch*, 10.

36. Florida *House Journal, 1897*, 63.

37. *Ibid.*
38. Florida *Senate Journal, 1897,* 563-564; *Laws of Florida, 1897,* 82-94.
39. *First Annual Report of the Railroad Commission of the State of Florida, March, 1898* (Jacksonville, 1898), 17.
40. *Ibid.,* 18.
41. *Ibid.,* 20-21.
42. *Autobiographical Sketch,* 10.
43. Cash, *History of the Democratic Party in Florida,* 106.
44. *Laws of Florida, 1897,* 62-64.
45. *Florida Times-Union,* April 29, 1897.
46. The future policy of the paper was announced in an editorial by Editor George W. Wilson on September 9, 1897. See also Gaines, "A Century in Florida Journalism," 80.
47. Williamson, "Wilkinson Call: A Pioneer in Progressive Democracy," 180; Carson, "William Dunnington Bloxham, Florida's Two-Term Governor," 304-305; and the *Ocala Banner,* March 19, 1897.
48. *Biographical Directory of the American Congress, 1774-1927* (Washington, 1928), 447.
49. Albert H. Roberts, "The Senatorial Deadlock of 1897," *Apalachee* (1944), 3-4; Carson, "William Dunnington Bloxham, Florida's Two-Term Governor," 305-306.
50. For a sketch of Chipley's life, see Edward C. Williamson, "William D. Chipley, West Florida's Mr. Railroad," *The Florida Historical Quarterly,* XXV (April, 1947), 333-355.
51. Cash, *History of the Democratic Party in Florida.* Carson ("William Dunnington Bloxham, Florida's Two-Term Governor") suggests that Perrenot and Mays were Call supporters.
52. Florida *House Journal, 1897,* 252-253.
53. In Call's behalf, Frank Pope read a speech which had been written by Frank E. Harris, editor of the *Ocala Banner* and a warm supporter of Wilkinson Call. Entitled "What Has Call Done?" the speech is dated 1892, but it was first printed in the *Ocala Banner* on October 25, 1896. It is reprinted in Francis Eppes Harris' *Frank Harris, More Than Fifty Years Editor Ocala Banner* [n.d.], 87-90.

54. *Daily Florida Citizen,* May 8, 1897; Florida *Senate Journal, 1897,* 470.
55. Florida *House Journal, 1897,* 715.
56. *Ibid.,* 728.
57. Mallory was chosen by an anti-Call caucus. This event is described by Williamson in "William D. Chipley, West Florida's Mr. Railroad," 350 (quoting the *Pensacola Daily News* of May 14 and June 7, 1897). See also Roberts, "The Senatorial Deadlock of 1897," 7. Call explained his withdrawal from the race in the "Letter of Wilkinson Call to the People of Florida" [n.d.], 1-20.
58. Florida *Senate Journal, 1897,* 676. The Call-Chipley fight is described by Williamson in "Wilkinson Call: A Pioneer in Progressive Democracy," 182-194.

II

Liberalism Comes to Power

1. Description and data relating to vessel in Broward Papers.
2. Camp Cuba Libre was established near Jacksonville on May 26, 1898. Under the command of General Fitzhugh Lee, it was considered the best-managed major army camp in the United States. See Rerick, *Memoirs of Florida,* I, 400.
3. John D. Miley, *In Cuba With Shafter* (New York, 1899), 1-14; Richard Harding Davis, *The Cuban and Porto Rican Campaigns* (New York, 1898), 45-85; and R. A. Alger, *The Spanish-American War* (New York, 1901), 62-82.
4. Sketches of Jennings' life are found in *The National Cyclopaedia of American Biography,* XI, 383, and in *Makers of America,* IV, 252-261.
5. *Florida Times-Union and Citizen,* May 20, 1900.
6. *Ibid.,* June 19, 1900. For a description of Jacksonville at this time, see the letter from Robert Chaffin to his mother, July 30, 1900, in the Washington Sanford Chaffin Papers, Duke University Manuscript Collection.
7. *Ibid.,* June 21, 1900.
8. *Ibid.,* June 22, 1900.
9. *Ibid.*

10. *Ibid.*, June 23, 1900.
11. *Ibid.* Davis states that only forty-three ballots were cast (*History of Jacksonville, Florida,* 218).
12. Mrs. Napoleon B. Broward to author, April, 1950.
13. *Florida Times-Union and Citizen,* June 23, 1900.
14. *Ibid.*, September 14, 1900.
15. *Ibid.*, September 20, 1900.
16. *Ibid.*, October 26, 1900.
17. *Ibid.*, September 28, 1900.
18. *Ibid.*, October 25, 1900.
19. Official certification of the vote count was forwarded to Broward by Secretary of State John L. Crawford on December 14, 1900. See Broward Papers.
20. William T. Cash, *The Story of Florida* (New York, 1938), II, 514.
21. During this period Broward was also organizing the anti-corporation legislators into a secret caucus which he called the "Before Day Club." The "Before Day Club" operated throughout the legislative session of 1901 and was responsible for most of the liberal legislation enacted. (James M. Carson, "The Background of Broward and the Everglades," 6; and Carson to author, November 20, 1947, and January 14, 1948.)
22. Florida *House Journal, 1901,* 55-57.
23. *Ibid.*, 61. See also Florida *House Journal, 1901,* 35; and *Message and Documents, 1901,* 31.
24. Escambia, Santa Rosa, Walton, Holmes, Washington, Jackson, Calhoun, Franklin, Gadsden, Liberty, Leon, Wakulla, Jefferson, Madison, and Taylor counties.
25. Hamilton, Columbia, Alachua, Baker, Duval, Putnam, Suwannee, Lafayette, Bradford, Nassau, Clay, and St. Johns counties.
26. Levy, Marion, Citrus, Hernando, Sumter, Lake, Orange, Pasco, Hillsborough, Polk, Osceola, Brevard, Manatee, DeSoto, Lee, Dade, Monroe, and Volusia counties.
27. Florida *Senate Journal, 1901,* 97-98.
28. Florida *House Journal, 1901,* 580, 582.
29. *Laws of Florida, 1901,* 47-48.
30. Florida *House Journal, 1901,* 167.
31. Florida *Senate Journal, 1901,* 234-235; Florida *House Journal, 1901,* 314.

32. *Laws of Florida, 1901,* 118-121.
33. Sidney Walter Martin, *Florida's Flagler* (Athens, Georgia, 1949), 169-186; Johnson and Malone (eds.), *Dictionary of American Biography,* VI, 452.
34. Martin, *Florida's Flagler,* 185-186.
35. *Ibid.,* 187, quoting the *Pensacola Journal,* May 28, 1901.
36. M. A. Brown to author, January, 1942. See also Pat Murphy, *Legislative Blue Book, 1917: "Through Green Glasses"* (Tallahassee, 1917), 7.
37. *Ocala Banner,* May 31, 1901.
38. Martin, *Florida's Flagler,* 187, quoting the *Palmetto News,* May 27, 1901.
39. *Ibid.,* 194. For a sketch of the Kenan family, see William R. Kenan, Jr., *Incidents By the Way, Lifetime Recollections and Reflections* (1946), 9-10; and William R. Kenan, Jr., *Incidents By the Way, More Recollections* (1949), 12-13.
40. *New York Herald,* March 30, 1902. For a description of Whitehall, see Martin, *Florida's Flagler,* 195-201; and Kenan, *Incidents By the Way, Lifetime Recollections and Reflections,* 55-59.
41. Florida *House Journal, 1901,* 487.
42. MS. copy of bill in Broward Papers.
43. Florida *House Journal, 1901,* 968.
44. Florida *Senate Journal, 1901,* 1119.
45. *The Daily Capital,* May 28, 1901.
46. According to *The Daily Capital,* May 28, 1901, M. A. Brown of Jacksonville was working in Tallahassee as secretary to the House Committee on Finance and Taxation.
47. *Florida Times-Union and Citizen,* May 4, 1901.
48. Mrs. Napoleon B. Broward to author, February, 1942. See also *Weekly Tallahassean,* May 28, 1901.
49. Mrs. Josephine Broward Beckley to author, September, 1949.
50. M. A. Brown to author, January, 1942.
51. For a detailed description of the Jacksonville fire, see *Florida Times-Union and Citizen,* May 4, 1901; Rerick, *Memoirs of Florida,* I, 411-412; Benjamin Harrison, *Acres of Ashes* (Jacksonville, 1901); Walter S. Wagstaff (ed), *Jacksonville in Flames: An Artistic Description of a Gloomy Affair* (Jacksonville, 1901); and Charles H. Smith (comp.), *Report of the Jacksonville Relief Association,* (Jacksonville, 1901).

52. Mrs. Josephine Broward Beckley to author, January, 1942.
53. Mrs. Napoleon B. Broward to author, January, 1942.
54. Florida *House Journal, 1901,* 631.
55. *Ibid.,* 992-993.
56. *Jacksonville Metropolis,* May 22, 1901.
57. *Laws of Florida, 1901,* 368-369.
58. Cash, *History of the Democratic Party in Florida,* 105; and James O. Knauss, "The Growth of Florida's Election Laws," *The Florida Historical Quarterly,* V (July, 1926), 3-17.
59. *Autobiographical Sketch,* 7.
60. Florida *House Journal, 1901,* 301.
61. *Ibid.,* 382.
62. *Ibid.,* 550.
63. *Ibid.,* 910.
64. *Laws of Florida, 1901,* chap. 5014, 160-165.
65. *Autobiographical Sketch,* 7-8.
66. *Laws of Florida, 1901,* 160-165.
67. *Ibid., 1903,* 242-243.
68. Jennings' official commission to Broward in Broward Papers.
69. Harry Fozzard, Jr., to author, November, 1941.
70. Mrs. Napoleon B. Broward to author, April, 1950.
71. Mrs. Josephine Broward Beckley to author, March, 1942.
72. *Ibid.*
73. Mrs. Napoleon B. Broward to author, April, 1950.

12

The Battle of the Giants

1. Mrs. Napoleon B. Broward to author, April, 1942. See also Paine, "From Deck Hand To Governor," 192; and Alston W. Cockrell, "Reminiscences of Tallahassee," *Tallahassee Historical Society Annual,* II (1935), 39.
2. *Autobiographical Sketch,* 12; Carson, "The Background of Broward and the Everglades," 6; and Carson to author, January 14, 1948.
3. *Jacksonville Metropolis* clipping in "Broward Family Scrapbook." The clipping is undated, but from all evidence it appeared early in December, 1903.
4. *Ibid.,* quoting the *Tampa Herald.*

5. *Ocala Banner*, December 22, 1903, clipping in "Broward Family Scrapbook."
6. *Florida Times-Union*, January 5, 1904; *Jacksonville Metropolis*, January 4, 1904.
7. This description of Broward is based upon various pictures taken during this period of his life and upon interviews with members of Broward's family by the author. See also Rivers H. Buford, "Napoleon B. Broward," *Apalachee* (1946), 4.
8. *Semi-Weekly Times-Union*, October 23, 1903.
9. *Ibid.*
10. *Florida Times-Union*, November 17, 1903.
11. *Ibid.*, November 18, 1903.
12. For brief biographical sketches of Davis, see *Biographical Directory of the American Congress, 1774-1927*, 888; and Rerick, *Makers of America*, I, 131-135.
13. "Open Letter As Candidate For Governor," *Autobiographical Sketch*, 13-14.
14. *Ibid.*
15. *Ibid.* See the brief biographical sketches of Mays in the *Biographical Directory of the American Congress, 1774-1927*, 1302; and in Rerick, *Memoirs of Florida*, I, 624-625.
16. Cash, *History of the Democratic Party in Florida*, 101.
17. *Florida Times-Union*, March 6, 1904.
18. *Ibid.*, May 9, 1904.
19. William T. Cash to author, February, 1947.
20. *Florida Times-Union*, December 15, 1903.
21. In addition to Barrs and Clark, the Second District Congressional candidates included J. E. Alexander of DeLand, former secretary to Senator Wilkinson Call; Charles Dougherty, congressman from Florida from 1885-1889; and W. P. Watson, of Orlando.
22. Cash, *History of the Democratic Party in Florida*, 98.
23. *Ibid.*, 99.
24. Gaines, "A Century in Florida Journalism," 101.
25. Cash, *History of the Democratic Party in Florida*, 99-100.
26. *Ibid.*, 99.
27. For brief biographical sketches of Taliaferro, see *The National Cyclopaedia of American Biography*, X, 175; and the *Biographical Directory of the American Congress, 1774-1927*, 1594.
28. *Florida Times-Union*, February 16, 1904.

29. *Ibid.*, January 23, 1904.
30. *Ibid.*, February 27, 1904.
31. Hanna and Hanna, *Lake Okeechobee*, 123.
32. *Florida Times-Union*, March 20, 1904.
33. *Ibid.*, February 27, 1904.
34. *Jacksonville Metropolis*, May 7, 1904.
35. W. P. Douglass, son of W. W. Douglass, to author, March, 1942. W. P. Douglass worked as a reporter on the *Metropolis* during the campaign of 1904.
36. M. A. Brown to author, April, 1942.
37. The sojourn in Jacksonville was well timed, as Mrs. Broward gave birth to the fifth Broward daughter, Florida Douglass, April 13, 1904.
38. *Jacksonville Metropolis*, May 5, 1904.
39. *Ibid.*, May 7, 1904.
40. *Autobiographical Sketch*, 7.
41. *Ibid.*, 18-19.
42. *Autobiographical Sketch*, 19.
43. *Jacksonville Metropolis*, April 23, 1904, quoting the *Madison News Enterprise*.
44. *Florida Times-Union*, April 20, 1904, quoting the *Brooksville Star*.
45. *Jacksonville Metropolis*, April 30, 1904, quoting the *Brooksville Star*.
46. *Florida Times-Union*, May 10, 1904.
47. *Jacksonville Metropolis*, May 12, 1904.
48. Copy of ballot tabulations by counties in Broward Papers. The final vote was published in the *Florida Times-Union*, May 22, 1904.
49. *Ibid.*
50. *Jacksonville Metropolis*, May 24, 1904.
51. *Ibid.*, May 20, 1904.

13

A Crusader Becomes Governor

1. *Florida Times-Union*, May 24, 1904, quoting the *Punta Gorda Herald.*
2. *Ibid.*

3. *Daily Tallahassean,* May 28, 1904.
4. *Jacksonville Metropolis,* May 19, 1904.
5. *Florida Times-Union,* June 5, 1904.
6. *Autobiographical Sketch,* 14.
7. *Ibid.*
8. *Ibid.*
9. MS. speech in Broward Papers.
10. *Ibid.*
11. *Florida Times-Union,* May 27, 1904, quoting the *Miami Metropolis.*
12. *Ibid.,* May 25, 1904.
13. *Jacksonville Metropolis,* May 28, 1904.
14. Carson, "The Background of Broward and the Everglades," 7.
15. M. A. Brown to author, January, 1942.
16. *Jacksonville Metropolis,* May 28, 1904.
17. *Ibid.,* July 2, 1904.
18. *Florida Times-Union,* June 18, 1904; and *Ocala Banner,* June 18, 1904.
19. *Ibid.* Unofficial ballot tabulation sheet in Broward Papers.
20. *Ibid.*
21. *Ibid.*
22. *Ibid.*
23. *Ibid.*
24. *Weekly Tallahassean,* June 24, 1904.
25. *Jacksonville Metropolis,* May 26, 1904.
26. *Ibid.,* June 18, 1904.
27. B. J. Lennard to Broward, June 24, 1904, in Broward Papers.
28. Unsigned letter to Broward, April 30, 1904, in Broward Papers.
29. *Florida Times-Union,* September 6, 1904.
30. *Jacksonville Metropolis,* October 14, 1904.
31. *Florida Times-Union,* November 8, 1904.
32. MS. speech in Broward Papers. Speech delivered at Ocala, October 4, 1904.
33. *Florida Times-Union,* October 4, 1904.
34. *Ibid.,* October 29, 1904.
35. Official notification of election results by Secretary of State H. Clay Crawford to Broward, December 1, 1904, in Broward Papers.

36. Mrs. Napoleon B. Broward to author, April, 1942. The house, constructed in 1847, stood at 404 N. Monroe Street. There is a brief sketch of the history of the house in Evelyn Whitfield Henry's "Old Houses in Tallahassee," *Tallahassee Historical Society Annual*, I (February, 1934), 50.
37. Inauguration program in Broward Papers.
38. *Florida Times-Union*, January 4, 1905.
39. MS. speech in Broward Papers.
40. *Ibid.*
41. *The Tallahassee Capital*, January 11, 1905.
42. Miss Hortense Broward to author, February, 1942.
43. A. W. Cockrell to author, February, 1942.
44. Florida *Senate Journal, 1905*, 378.
45. *Semi-Weekly Times-Union*, February 14, 1905; and Florida *Senate Journal, 1905*, 378-380.
46. In addition to Miss Elsie Douglass, who served throughout the Broward administration, the governor's secretaries included: C. H. Dickerson, January, 1905-July 31, 1905; M. A. Brown, August 1, 1905-October 16, 1905; J. Emmett Wolfe, October 16, 1905-February 15, 1907; Daniel A. Simmons, March 20, 1907-January, 1909.
47. M. A. Brown to author, March, 1942.
48. *Jacksonville Metropolis*, March 3, 1905.
49. *Florida Times-Union*, January 4, 1905.
50. Florida *House Journal, 1905*, 3-47; and *Message of N. B. Broward, Governor of Florida, to the Legislature, Regular Session, 1905* (Tallahassee, 1905), 1-36.
51. Cash, *History of the Democratic Party in Florida*, 115.

14

The Broward Era Begins

1. Florida *Senate Journal, 1905*, 378-413; *Message and Documents, 1905*, I, 1-36; *Message of N. B. Broward, Governor of Florida, to the Legislature, Regular Session of 1905*, 1-36.
2. The preamble and resolution, relative to Everglades drainage, passed the Florida Senate on December 2, 1845, and the Florida

House of Representatives on December 4, 1845. It was signed by Governor William D. Moseley on December 10, 1845.

3. Thomas A. Jesup to James D. Westcott, Jr., February 12, 1848, quoted in *Everglades of Florida*, Senate Doc. 89, 62 Cong., 1 Sess. (Washington, 1911), 56.

4. *Report of Buckingham Smith, Esq., on His Reconnoissance of the Everglades*, 1848 (submitted to R. J. Walker, Secretary of the Treasury, June 1, 1848), and *Appendix to Report of Buckingham Smith*, in Senate Doc. 89, *Everglades of Florida*, 46-66.

5. *Ibid.*, 53; Florida *Senate Journal*, 1905, 382.

6. *Trustees I.I.F. Minutes*, II, 473, 490, 503; Dovell, "The History of the Everglades of Florida," 122-123; and J. E. Dovell, "The Everglades of Florida—Florida's Frontier," *Economic Leaflets*, VI (April, 1947), Pt. I, 3.

7. Florida *Senate Journal*, 1905, 390; *Trustees I.I.F. Minutes*, VII, 532. See also *The Eighth Biennial Report of the Commissioner of Agriculture, State of Florida* (Tallahassee, 1905), 415-417. According to this report, the number of acres patented to the state prior to January 1, 1905, was 20,133,900.67.

8. *Trustees I.I.F. Minutes*, I, xv-xxi; *Laws of Florida, 1855*, Chap. 610, 9-19. See also Hanna and Hanna, *Lake Okeechobee*, 56-57.

9. Senate Doc. 89, *Everglades of Florida*, 8-9; Hanna and Hanna, *Lake Okeechobee*, 120.

10. *Message and Documents, 1903*, 67.

11. *Patent to the Everglades*, 1903, in Senate Doc. 89, *Everglades of Florida*, 91-93.

12. *Annual Report, General Counsel of the Trustees of the Internal Improvement Fund*, December 21, 1908, in *Trustees I.I.F. Minutes*, VII, 532.

13. Senate Doc. 89, *Everglades of Florida*, 13.

14. *Message and Documents, 1903*, 71-72. Jennings referred to the observations and findings of W. H. Caldwell, assistant United States engineer, December, 1901, and the earlier surveys and reports by Charles Hopkins, V. P. Keller, J. W. Newman, and others.

15. *Ibid.*, 78.

16. *Trustees I.I.F. Minutes*, V, 267.

17. Senate Doc. 89, *Everglades of Florida,* 24-25.
18. *Trustees I.I.F. Minutes,* VI, 10.
19. Jennings to Broward, January 21, 1905, in Senate Doc. 89, *Everglades of Florida,* 25-26.
20. Florida *Senate Journal, 1905,* 383.
21. *Ibid.,* 390.
22. The Louisville and Nashville Railroad Company had two bills of complaint, April 19, 1902, in the United States Circuit Court, the first claiming 1,447,391 acres of land, and the second 1,772,679 acres. The attorneys for the railroad filed another suit, March 23, 1905, claiming an additional 1,447,321 acres.
23. The Florida East Coast Railway Company filed a bill of complaint, November 12, 1903, claiming 2,040,000 acres of land under the provisions of Chapter 4260, *Laws of Florida.*
24. The Florida Coast Line Canal and Transportation Company brought suit, June 6, 1904, in the Circuit Court of the Second Judicial Circuit of Florida, claiming that it was entitled to 3,840 acres of land per mile for the distance from St. Augustine to Biscayne Bay, under the provisions of Chapters 3641 and 3995, *Laws of Florida.*
25. Two bills of complaint had been filed by Matilde C. Kittel as executrix of the will of Joseph J. Kittel. The first bill, filed November 23, 1904, claimed 40,000 acres of land; the second, filed December 14, 1904, claimed an additional 72,349.18 acres.
26. Florida *Senate Journal, 1905,* 398-399.
27. *Ibid.,* 399-404. The report is incorrectly dated 1896 in the *Senate Journal* and in Senate Doc. 89, *Everglades of Florida,* 104.
28. Spreckels to Disston, March 22, 1890, in Senate Doc. 89, *Everglades of Florida,* 106.
29. Florida *Senate Journal, 1905,* 412.
30. *Ibid.,* 413.
31. *Florida Times-Union,* May 5, 1905.
32. *Ibid.,* May 10, 1905, quoting the *Miami Record.*
33. Florida *Senate Journal, 1905,* 700.
34. Florida *House Journal, 1905,* 915.
35. *Ibid.*
36. Senate Doc. 89, *Everglades of Florida,* 15.

37. *Laws of Florida, 1905,* Chap. 5377, 22-23; Senate Doc. 89, *Everglades of Florida,* 15.
38. Florida *Senate Journal, 1905,* 1062-1063.
39. *Ibid.,* 1423.
40. *Laws of Florida,* 1905, Chap. 5377, 22-23. See also Fritzie P. Manuel, "Land Development in the Everglades," *Hearings Before the Select Committee Investigating National Defense Migration,* House of Repr., 77 Cong., 2 Sess., 12870.
41. Hanna and Hanna, *Lake Okeechobee,* 127.
42. Florida *House Journal, 1905,* 19.
43. Florida *Senate Journal, 1905,* 13-14.
44. *Ibid., 1903,* 973-974.
45. *Ibid., 1905,* 704-705; Florida *House Journal, 1905,* 418.
46. Florida *House Journal, 1905,* 1668.
47. *Message of N. B. Broward, 1905,* 17. For a history of the institutions referred to by Broward, see Francis A. Rhodes, "The Legal Development of State Supported Higher Education in Florida" (unpublished doctoral dissertation, University of Florida, 1948), 1-142; L. M. Bristol, *The Buckman Act: Before and After: A Study in Historical Sociology* (unpublished MS. in P. K. Yonge Library of Florida History, 1946); C. L. Crow, "The University of Florida" (unpublished MS., University of Florida Archives, 1932); Orland K. Armstrong, *The Life and Work of Dr. A. A. Murphree* (St. Augustine, 1928), 39-43; William G. Dodd, "Early Education in Tallahassee and the West Florida Seminary now Florida State University," *The Florida Historical Quarterly,* XXVII (July, 1948), Pt. I, 1-27, and *ibid.,* XXVIII (October, 1948), Pt. II, 157-180; George G. Bush, *History of Education in Florida* (Washington, 1889); and Venila L. Shores, "Some Historical Notes Concerning Florida State College for Women," *Tallahassee Historical Society Annual,* III (1937), 103-120.
48. *Message of N. B. Broward, 1905,* 17.
49. Florida *House Journal, 1905,* 795-799. For the early action in the Florida Senate, relative to the education measure, see Senate Bill No. 74, introduced by Telfair Stockton (Florida *Senate Journal, 1905,* 74), and the ensuing debate on the proposed board of regents (Florida *Senate Journal, 1905,* 373, 376).

50. Florida *House Journal, 1905,* 1031.
51. *Florida Times-Union,* May 19, 1905.
52. *Ibid.*
53. *Ibid.*
54. Florida *House Journal, 1905,* 1358-1359.
55. *Ibid.,* 1359.
56. Florida *Senate Journal, 1905,* 1337.
57. *Ibid.,* 1336.
58. *Laws of Florida, 1905,* Chap. 5384, 37-60.
59. *Florida Times-Union,* June 22, 1905; and *Pensacola Journal,* June 22, 1905. According to the *Pensacola Journal,* as quoted by Rhodes ("The Legal Development of State Supported Higher Education in Florida," 180): "The Board of Control appointed by Governor Broward under the provisions of the Buckman educational law, is being generally commended as one from which the people have every reason to expect honest and intelligent effort. Its personnel is not made up of old political 'has been's' or those dead to trespasses and sin in factional politics, but of men generally unknown in their immediate home neighborhoods. There are times when the introduction of new blood into the working force of public affairs is to be especially commended. The present seems to be one of those times."
60. Florida *Senate Journal, 1905,* 1252-1256; Florida *House Journal, 1905,* 502-503. Up until this time, the private homes of the governors had served as their executive mansions. Governor Bloxham's home at 410 North Calhoun Street was used as the Executive Mansion during his two administrations (Henry, "Old Houses of Tallahassee," 47).
61. *The Executive Mansion, Tallahassee, Florida* [n. d.], 1.
62. Florida *House Journal, 1905,* 1737-1738.
63. Florida *Senate Journal, 1905,* 116.
64. *Ibid.,* 575.
65. *Florida Times-Union,* April 26, 1905, quoting the *Suwannee Democrat.*
66. Taft to Broward, March 25, 1905, quoted in Florida *House Journal, 1905,* 99-100.
67. Foster to Broward, April 10, 1905, quoted in Florida *House Journal, 1905,* 98-99.

68. Florida *Senate Journal, 1905,* 121-122.
69. *Ibid.,* 992.
70. *Ibid.,* 1487.
71. Florida *House Journal, 1901,* 1148.
72. *Ibid., 1903,* 1732.
73. *Ibid., 1905,* 27-29.
74. *The Testimony Taken Before the Special Committee to Investigate the Report on the Asylum* (1905); and Florida *House Journal, 1905,* 2273.
75. Florida *House Journal, 1905,* 3. The committee, appointed under House Concurrent Resolution No. 5, included W. K. Jackson, J. W. Knight, J. T. Fillingham, and James A. Sledge.
76. The report was submitted to Park M. Trammell, president of the Senate, May 17, 1905.
77. *Report of the Special Committee Appointed by the Legislature of Florida on the Hospital for the Insane, Session of 1905* (Tallahassee, 1905), 3-5. See also Florida *Senate Journal, 1905,* 920-967.
78. Florida *House Journal, 1905.*
79. *The Testimony Taken Before the Special Committee to Investigate the Report on the Asylum,* 1-276.
80. Florida *Senate Journal, 1905,* 1720-1744.
81. *Ibid.,* 1720.
82. *Ibid.,* 1742-1743.
83. *Laws of Florida, 1905,* Chap. 5454, 145-146.
84. Florida *Senate Journal, 1905,* 1249-1250. A similar invitation, received by Albert W. Gilchrist, speaker of the House, was read to the House of Representatives on May 25, 1905.
85. *Florida Times-Union,* May 27, 1905.
86. The Florida Female College, so named in the Buckman Act, became Florida State College for Women in 1909 and Florida State University in 1947. See *Report of the Board of Control for the Period Beginning January 1, 1907 and Ending January 1, 1909* (Tallahassee, 1909), 11; and *Laws of Florida,* 1947, Chap. 23669, 112-113.
87. *Florida Times-Union,* June 20, 1905.
88. *Ibid.,* June 22, 1905, quoting the *Fernandina Star.*
89. *Jacksonville Metropolis,* July 6, 1895. The Gainesville spokesman was Dr. J. F. McKinstry, Jr., and A. B. Small made the

offer for Lake City. See Rhodes, "The Legal Development of State Supported Higher Education in Florida," 184-185, quoting *Minutes of the State Board of Education*, Minute Book Number Three, October 8, 1895-April 9, 1909; and *Minutes of the Board of Control*, July 6, 1905.

90. *Florida Times-Union*, July 7, 1905. In the *Board of Control Minutes* there is no mention of a lapse of time between the two Gainesville offers.

91. *Gainesville Sun*, July 10, 1905; *Florida Times-Union*, July 7, 1905. See also Rhodes, "The Legal Development of State Supported Higher Education in Florida," 188-189.

92. *Gainesville Sun*, April 10 and April 21, 1908.

93. *Florida Times-Union*, July 9, 1905. See also *Report of the Board of Control for the Period Beginning June 5, 1905 and Ending January 1, 1907* (Tallahassee, 1907).

94. Mrs. Napoleon B. Broward to author, March, 1942.

95. *Florida Times-Union*, October 5 and October 17, 1905.

96. *Jacksonville Metropolis*, October 20, 1905.

97. *Florida Times-Union*, October 22, 1905.

98. *Ibid.*, September 24, 1904.

15

"Save the People's Land!"

1. Senate Doc. 89, *Everglades of Florida*, 15; *Report of the Joint Commission Created by the Legislature of 1907, Chapter 5632, Session Laws of 1907, to Investigate the Acts and Doings of the Trustees of the Internal Improvement Fund* (Tallahassee, 1909), 10.

2. *Trustees I. I. F. Minutes*, VI, 79; and Senate Doc. 89, *Everglades of Florida*, 14 and 26.

3. *Trustees I. I. F. Minutes*, VI, 89.

4. *Ibid.*, VI, 91.

5. *Ibid.*, VI, 96.

6. *Jasper News*, March 3, 1906.

7. *Florida Times-Union*, March 4, 1906, quoting the *Levy Times-Democrat*.

8. *Ibid.*, March 5, 1906, quoting the *Volusia County Record*.

9. *Ibid.*, March 4, 1906.

10. *Ibid.*, March 23, 1906.

11. *Ibid.*, April 5, 1906.

12. *Ocala Banner*, March 11, 1906.

13. *Bradenton Herald*, June 14, 1906.

14. *Miami Metropolis*, March 3, 1906.

15. *Florida Times-Union*, March 13, 1906, quoting the *Tampa Tribune*.

16. *Ibid.*, March 19, 1906, quoting the *Lakeland Sun*.

17. *Volusia County Record*, March 12, 1906.

18. *Cocoa and Rockledge News*, March 23, 1906.

19. *DeFuniak Breeze*, March 15, 1906.

20. *Open Letter of Governor Broward to the People of Florida* (1906). See also *St. Augustine Evening Record*, April 4, 1906.

21. *St. Augustine Evening Record*, April 6, 1906. The *Everglades* was launched July 4, 1906, and the *Okeechobee* in October, 1906. See Senate Doc. 89, *Everglades of Florida*, 16.

22. *Florida Times-Union*, June 1, 1906.

23. *Ibid.*, June 22, 1906.

24. Senate Doc. 89, *Everglades of Florida*, 15-16. See also *Florida Times-Union*, July 18, 1906.

25. *Florida Times-Union*, August 20, 1906. An editorial satirizing the opposition of the *Times-Union* and the *Jacksonville Metropolis* to the drainage program appeared in the Jacksonville *Sun* on March 10, 1906, and was reproduced in the pamphlet issued by Broward, *Open Letter of Governor N. B. Broward to the People of Florida*, 5.

26. For a biographical sketch of Beard, see *Makers of America*, I, 264-267.

27. *Florida Times-Union*, August 20, 1906.

28. *Ibid.*

29. *Ibid.*, August 30, 1906.

30. *Ibid.*, September 10, 1906.

31. *Ocala Evening Star*, August 31, 1906.

32. *Madison Recorder*, October 9, 1906.

33. *Florida Times-Union*, October 19, 1906.

34. Broward to A. J. Knight, Tampa, November 7, 1907, in Broward Papers.

35. *Cocoa and Rockledge News*, August 23, 1906.

36. John Gifford, *The Everglades and Other Essays Relating to Southern Florida* (Kansas City, Mo., 1911), 99.
37. *Miami Evening Record,* September 24, 1906.
38. *Ibid.*
39. *Ibid.*
40. *Florida Times-Union,* September 13, 1906, quoting the *Orlando Democrat.*
41. *Ibid.,* November 11, 1906; Hanna and Hanna, *Lake Okeechobee,* 128.
42. *St. Augustine Evening Record,* November 12, 1906.
43. Cash, *History of the Democratic Party in Florida,* 115.
44. Florida *House Journal, 1907,* 1-70. Many of these recommendations appeared in a pamphlet issued by Broward, *Gov. Napoleon B. Broward on Certain Live Public Questions of interest to the People of Florida. Being a discussion of STATE LIFE INSURANCE, the DRAINAGE OF THE EVERGLADES and other problems that will require solution by the Legislature of Florida in 1907 Session* (Tallahassee, 1907), 1-16.
45. Florida *House Journal, 1907,* 63-64.
46. *Ibid.,* 65
47. *Ibid.,* 68.
48. *Ibid.,* 67-69.
49. Florida *Senate Journal, 1905,* 902, 1916.
50. *Ibid.,* 1907, 2-4.
51. *Ibid.,* 2.
52. *Ibid.,* 3.
53. *Ibid.,* 1884-1889.
54. *Laws of Florida, 1907,* Chap. 5662, 151-160.
55. *Ibid.,* Chap. 5686, 194-197.
56. *Ibid.,* Chap. 5670, 167-169.
57. *Ibid.,* Chap. 5672, 175-176.
58. *Ibid.,* Chap. 5716, 229-230.
59. *Ibid.,* Chap. 5714, 226-228.
60. *Ibid.,* Chap. 5711, 223-224. Pulaski Broward, Governor Broward's uncle, was a member of the Chickamauga Monument Commission appointed by the legislature of 1907 to erect the monument on the Chickamauga Battlefield. See Gold, *History of Duval County, Florida,* 274.
61. *Ibid.,* Chap. 5715, 228-229.

62. Florida *Senate Journal, 1907,* 26 and 636.
63. The recess committee included Governor Broward, Comptroller A. C. Croom, State Health Officer Joseph Y. Porter, S. B. Cameron, and W. E. Boggs.
64. Florida *Senate Journal, 1907,* 2-9.
65. *Ibid.,* 1542-1546.
66 Richard Barry, "Slavery in the South Today," *Cosmopolitan Magazine,* XLII (March, 1907), 481-491. This article carried a picture of Broward which was captioned "Napoleon Bonaparte Broward, Governor of Florida, who is willing but powerless to put an end to peonage in his state." See also the *New York Evening Journal,* February 24, 1907. The Frederick C. Cubberly Papers in the P. K. Yonge Library of Florida History describe the alleged peonage conditions in Florida as suggested by Barry's article.
67. Florida *House Journal, 1907,* 5-6.
68. *Congressional Record,* XLI, Pt. V, 59 Cong., 2 Sess., 4659-4663.
69. Florida *Senate Journal, 1907,* 1292: Senate Doc. 89, *Everglades of Florida,* 15; Hanna and Hanna, *Lake Okeechobee,* 130; and Dovell, "A History of the Everglades of Florida," 224.
70. Florida *House Journal, 1907,* 1170.
71. Florida *Senate Journal, 1907,* 1526.
72. Florida *House Journal, 1907,* 1571.
73. Florida *Senate Journal, 1907,* 1964.
74. *Laws of Florida, 1907,* Chap. 5709, 220-222; and Senate Doc. 89, *Everglades of Florida,* 27-28.
75. *Florida Times-Union,* June 3, 1907.
76. *Ibid.*
77. Broward to F. G. Havens, California, March 27, 1907, in Broward Papers.
78. *Ibid.* See also Dovell, "A History of the Everglades of Florida," 229-232; and *Trustees I. I. F. Minutes,* VII, 89.
79. F. G. Newlands to Broward, January 10, 1908, in Broward Papers.
80. Broward to Conner, April 10, 1907, in Broward Papers.
81. Daniel A. Simmons, "The Florida Everglades. How They Happened; What They Are; What They Will Be," *The World Today* XVI (May, 1909), 530-538.
82. Broward to C. Horace McCall, Atlanta, July 5, 1907.

83. Broward to Freeman Tilden, New York, April 6, 1907, in Broward Papers.

16

"Praised by These—Blamed by Those"

1. Unaddressed letter from Broward, September 21, 1907, in Broward Papers.
2. Paid memorandum for furniture in Broward Papers. For a brief description of the house, see *The Executive Mansion, Tallahassee, Florida,* 1-4.
3. Cash, *The Story of Florida,* II, 550-551.
4. *Ocala Banner,* February 4, 1908.
5. *Florida Times-Union,* June 3, 1907.
6. Theodore Roosevelt, *Theodore Roosevelt: An Autobiography* (New York, 1916), 422-423.
7. "Back To Water Transportation," *The Literary Digest,* XXXIV (March 30, 1907), 491.
8. Napoleon B. Broward, "Draining the Everglades," *The Independent,* LXIV (June 25, 1908), 1448-1449.
9. "The President's Tour," *The Literary Digest,*" XXXV (October 12, 1907), 509-512; "Wasting the Nation's Resources," *The Literary Digest,* XXXV (October 19, 1907), 553-555.
10. Carson, "Florida, Promoter of Cuban Liberty," 291. See also Henry F. Pringle, *Theodore Roosevelt: A Biography* (New York, 1931), 430-431.
11. *Florida Times-Union,* November 26, 1907.
12. *Ibid.,* November 27, 1907.
13. Roosevelt to Broward, November 16, 1907, in Broward Letter Book.
14. Broward to Dapray, January 9, 1908, in Broward Letter Book.
15. Latimer to Broward, January 20, 1908, in Broward Letter Book.
16. Broward to Latimer, January 24, 1908, in Broward Letter Book.
17. Bernard to Broward, January 20, 1908, in Broward Letter Book.
18. Latimer to Broward, February 1, 1908, in Broward Letter Book.
19. *Ibid.*
20. Copies of letters in Broward Letter Book. Senator Latimer had suggested in January that Broward contact the leading members

of Congress. (Latimer to Broward, January 20, 1908, in Broward Letter Book.)

21. *Florida Times-Union,* November 12, 1907.
22. *Ocala Banner,* November 16, 1907.
23. *Florida Times-Union,* November 18, 1907.
24. Broward to Fletcher, May 9, 1905, in Broward Papers.
25. I. J. Call, Callahan, Florida, to Broward, November 17, 1907, in Broward Papers.
26. Broward to J. C. Wills, Tampa, Florida (undated), in Broward Papers.
27. *Florida Times-Union,* December 19, 1907.
28. *Ocala Banner,* January 3, 1908.
29. *Ibid.*
30. *Florida Times-Union,* January 1, 1908, quoting the *New York Evening Sun.*
31. *Ibid.,* quoting the *Tampa Tribune.*
32. *Ocala Banner,* January 3, 1908.
33. *Ibid.,* January 24, 1908, quoting the *Savannah News.*
34. *Florida Times-Union,* January 1, 1908, quoting the *St. Augustine Record.*
35. *Ibid.,* June 3, 1907. See also Werner, *Bryan,* 157.
36. "The Clash of State and Federal Rights," *The Literary Digest,* XXXIV (March 30, 1907), 485-486.
37. Woodward, *Tom Watson, Agrarian Rebel,* 399.
38. *Ocala Banner,* January 24, 1908. See also Richard Hofstadter, *The American Political Tradition and the Men Who Made It* (New York, 1948), 195; and Arthur F. Mullen, *Western Democrat* (New York, 1940), 129.
39. *Ocala Banner,* February 7, 1908, quoting the *Miami News.*
40. *Jacksonville Metropolis,* February 12, 1908.
41. *Ocala Banner,* January 24, 1908, quoting the *Punta Gorda Herald.*
42. *Ibid.*
43. *Ibid.,* March 20, 1908.
44. *Ibid.*
45. *Ibid.,* April 3, 1908.
46. *Florida Times-Union,* April 14, 1908, quoting the *Tampa Tribune.*
47. *Ocala Banner,* April 3, 1908. Copy of letter in Broward Papers.

48. *Ibid.*
49. Mrs. Napoleon B. Broward to author, April, 1942.
50. *Florida Times-Union*, April 16, 1908, quoting the *Palatka News.* Copy of letter to newspapers in Broward Papers.
51. *Ibid.*, April 25, 1908.
52. *Ibid.*
53. *Ibid.*
54. *Ibid.*, May 4, 1908.
55. *Gainesville Sun*, June 9, 1908.
56. *Ibid.*, May 11, 1908.
57. *Ibid.*, June 7, 1908, quoting the *Quincy Journal.*
58. *Ibid.*, May 11, 1908, quoting the *Tampa Tribune.*
59. *Ibid.*, May 7, 1908, quoting the *Jacksonville Floridian.*
60. *Florida Times-Union*, May 9, 1908.
61. Napoleon B. Broward, *For United States Senator—Napoleon B. Broward* (1908), 15. See also *Florida Times-Union*, May 6, 1908.
62. *Gainesville Sun*, April 30, 1908.
63. *Ibid.*, April 10, 1908.
64. *Ibid.*
65. *Ibid.*, April 21, 1908.
66. *Ibid.*, May 3, 1908.
67. *Florida Times-Union*, April 11, 1908.
68. Ernest H. Cherrington (ed.), *The Anti-Saloon League Year Book, 1909* (Columbus, Ohio, 1909), 27.
69. *Ocala Banner*, January 17, 1908.
70. *Ibid.*
71. *Ibid.*
72. *Florida Times-Union*, May 16, 1908.
73. *Ocala Banner*, March 27, 1908, quoting the *Miami News-Record.*
74. *Gainesville Sun*, April 4, 1908.
75. *Ibid.*, April 10, 1908.
76. *Florida Times-Union*, May 29, 1908; and *Gainesville Sun*, June 6, 1908. Unofficial vote tabulation by counties in Broward Papers.
77. *Gainesville Sun*, May 28, 1908.
78. *Ocala Banner*, May 28, 1908.
79. *Ibid.*, June 5, 1908, quoting the *Madison News Enterpriser.*

80. *Ibid.*, March 27, 1908, quoting the *Key West Citizen.* These charges, made during the first primary, were reiterated by Fletcher during the runoff.
81. *Ibid.*, May 9, 1908, quoting the *Orlando Reporter-Star.*
82. *Florida Times-Union*, June 14, 1908.
83. *Gainesville Sun*, June 11, 1908.
84. *Ocala Banner*, June 26, 1908.
85. Broward, *For United States Senator*, 17-18.
86. *Ocala Banner*, June 26, 1908. Broward carried eighteen counties: Baker, Brevard, Clay, Dade, Hamilton, Holmes, Jackson, Lafayette, Lee, Liberty, Nassau, Santa Rosa, St. Johns, St. Lucie, Sumter, Taylor, Volusia, and Washington counties.
87. George W. Wilson, editor of the *Florida Times-Union*, died on June 2, 1908, and was succeeded by Willis M. Ball. There was no change in the policy of the paper. For a brief sketch of Wilson, see *Makers of America*, III, 44-50. There are brief sketches on Ball in Cash, *The Story of Florida*, IV, 422; and W. T. Cash, "The Dean of Florida Newsmen," *Florida Newspaper News*, XXVII (April, 1945), 6-8.
88. V. O. Key, Jr., *Southern Politics in State and Nation* (New York, 1949), 105.
89. Henry F. Pringle, *The Life and Times of William Howard Taft* (New York, 1939), I, 349-353.
90. *Ocala Banner*, July 10, 1908, quoting the *Tallahassee Sun.*
91. Mrs. Napoleon B. Broward to author, May, 1942; and *Florida Times-Union*, July 5, 1908.
92. *Ocala Banner*, March 27, 1908, quoting the *DeFuniak Herald.*
93. Mrs. Napoleon B. Broward to author, May, 1942.
94. *Ibid.*
95. *The Denver Republican*, July 6, 1908, clipping in "Broward Family Scrapbook."
96. Mrs. Napoleon B. Broward to author, May, 1942.
97. Werner, *Bryan*, 83-84.
98. Pringle, *The Life and Times of William Howard Taft*, I, 374, quoting the *Pentecostal Herald*, July 15, 1908.
99. *Ibid.*, 375.
100. Woodward, *Tom Watson, Agrarian Rebel*, 400-401.
101. Pringle, *The Life and Times of William Howard Taft*, I, 377.

102. *Florida Times-Union,* December 7, 1908.
103. Inauguration program in Broward Papers. The inauguration proceedings were described in the *Florida Times-Union,* January 6, 1909.

17

In the Hands of the Common People

1. Broward to T. H. Milton, Marianna, Florida, December 16, 1907, in Broward Papers.
2. *Florida Times-Union,* March 29, 1910, quoting the *DeLand Record.*
3. *Ibid.,* October 8, 1909. See also *Report of the Secretary of State of the State of Florida for the Period Beginning January 1, 1909, and Ending December 31, 1910* (Tallahassee, 1911), 519.
4. Mrs. Napoleon Broward to author, March, 1942.
5. Mrs. Napoleon B. Broward still owns this home on Fort George Island (1950).
6. There were thirty-five "dry" counties in Florida in 1909, and four-fifths of the total population lived in "dry" territory *(The Anti-Saloon League Year Book, 1910,* 63). The constitutional amendment in which Broward was interested was defeated by a majority of more than 4,900 votes in the general election of November, 1910. One authority stated that "the defeat of prohibition was due to the negro vote, which was handled by the liquor interests" (*The Anti-Saloon League Year Book, 1911,* 44).
7. *Ocala Banner,* December 29, 1908.
8. James Wilson, Secretary of Agriculture, to Gilchrist, March 27, 1909, in Senate Doc. 89, *Everglades of Florida,* 130.
9. Broward, "Draining the Everglades," 1448. The extract from the drainage report by J. O. Wright, February 25, 1909, is in Senate Doc. 89, *Everglades of Florida,* 130-137.
10. *Report of the Special Joint Committee of the Florida Legislature for the Year 1909, on the Drainage of the Everglades,* in Senate Doc. 89, *Everglades of Florida,* 121-138. See also Florida *Senate Journal, 1909,* 1590-1624.
11. Broward, "Draining the Everglades," 1448. See also *Trustees I.I.F. Minutes,* VII, 277, 287-293, 302, 492.

2. Dovell ("A History of the Everglades of Florida," 233) says that the machinery for the *Caloosahatchee* and the *Miami* had been shipped to Tampa, where the dredges were assembled early in 1909. In April the *Caloosahatchee* began working in the upper channel of the Caloosahatchee River.

3. *Trustees I.I.F. Minutes*, VIII, 351-361; Dovell, "A History of the Everglades of Florida," 241-242; Hanna and Hanna, *Lake Okeechobee*, 132.

4. *Trustees I.I.F. Minutes*, VII, 457-458. J. H. Tatum and Company of Miami purchased 12,000 acres of land at two and three dollars an acre on November 14, 1908.

5. *Ibid.*, 438-440. W. R. Comfort purchased 6,422 acres for two dollars an acre on October 12, 1908.

6. *Ibid.*, 261. R. P. Davie, of Colorado Springs, Colorado, purchased 27,500 acres at two dollars an acre on June 3, 1908. Dovell ("A History of the Everglades of Florida," 230) states that this was the first large sale of Everglades land in this period. Everglades lands had increased in market value at the time of the sale in 1908. In 1905 a tract of 1,500,000 acres had been offered for sale at twelve and a half cents an acre; in 1907 an option was taken on 25,000 acres at one dollar an acre. See also Rufus E. Rose, *The Swamp and Overflowed Lands of Florida: The Disston Drainage Company and the Disston Purchase* (Tallahassee, 1916), 8-9; *Trustees I.I.F. Minutes*, VII, 89; and Marjory Stoneman Douglas, *The Everglades: River of Grass* (New York, 1947), 316.

7. *Trustees I.I.F. Minutes*, VII, 471-475. The Davie Realty Company purchased 80,000 acres in Dade County early in December, 1908, for one dollar and a quarter an acre. According to Dovell ("A History of the Everglades of Florida," 231), W. S. Jennings handled the negotiations for this sale and received a fee of thirty-seven hundred and fifty dollars for his services.

8. Bolles was a fabulous figure, who allegedly had made and lost several fortunes, and who had purchased a seat on the New York Stock Exchange when he was only twenty-three years of age. One of his close personal friends was F. E. Bryant, an Englishman who later became prominent as a promoter of the city of Lake Worth, Florida, and as the organizer of the Florida Sugar and Food Products Company. Bryant had studied American irri-

gation problems and was interested in Bolles' plan to reclaim
Western farm lands. When Bolles and Bryant were investigating
lands in New Mexico, they once chanced to spend the night at a
sheep ranch where they met Harvey Duval, a Jacksonville man
who had gone out West for his health. Upon hearing of Bolles'
interest, Duval suggested that he look into the Everglades area
as a possible source of investment. Bolles' flamboyant activities
in promoting the sale of farm lands in Oregon had been reported in the newspapers and had come to the attention of
Governor Broward in Florida. When Broward heard, through
Duval, that Bolles was interested in Florida land, he was determined to meet him. Consequently, after the Democratic National Convention adjourned in July, 1908, Broward and former
Governor Jennings visited Bolles at his Colorado home. Soon
afterwards Bolles arrived in Florida. See Hanna and Hanna, *Lake
Okeechobee*, 137-138. The account of the meeting between
Broward and Bolles, as related in *Lake Okeechobee*, was secured
by Dr. and Mrs. A. J. Hanna from the Howard Sharp Collection
of manuscripts dealing with the Everglades and drainage. See also
Florida Times-Union, March 26, 1917; *New York Times*
March 27, 1917; Carson, "The Background of Broward and
the Everglades," 8-9; and Douglas, *The Everglades*, 316-317.

19. *Trustees I.I.F. Minutes*, VII, 502-519; *Everglades of Florida
Hearings before the Committee on Expenditures in the Depart-
ment of Agriculture, February 3-August 9, 1912* (Washington
1912), VII, 261, and IV, 143-144; and J. E. Dovell, "A Brief
History of the Florida Everglades," *The Soil Science Society of
Florida, Proceedings*, Vol. IV-A (1942), 133.

20. Simmons, "The Florida Everglades. How They Happened; What
They Are; What They Will Be," *The World Today*, 530-538

21. *Ibid.* See also extract from Broward letter in *Concerning Everglades Land*, 10-11.

22. C. Vann Woodward, *The South in Search of a Philosophy*, Phi
Beta Kappa Series, No. 1 (Gainesville, Florida, 1938), 13.

23. For a description of anti-Catholic sentiment in Florida, see John
R. Deal, Jr., "Sidney Johnston Catts, Stormy Petrel of Florida
Politics" (unpublished master's thesis, University of Florida,
1949), 28-32. See also C. P. Sweeney, "Bigotry in the South;

Anti-Catholic Prejudice," *Nation,* CXI (November 24, 1920);
Michael Williams, *The Shadow of the Pope* (New York, 1932);
Gustavus Myers, *History of Bigotry in the United States* (New
York, 1943); T. A. Hill, *The Negro and Economic Recon-
struction* (Washington, 1937); Charles S. Mangum, Jr., *The
Legal Status of the Negro* (Chapel Hill, 1940); Christopher P.
Connolly, *The Truth About the Frank Case* (New York, 1915);
Paul Lewinson, *Race, Class, and Party: A History of Negro
Suffrage and White Politics in the South* (New York, 1932);
Gilbert T. Stephenson, *Race Discrimination in American Law*
(New York, 1910); and Arthur S. Link, "The Progressive
Movement in the South," *The North Carolina Historical Re-
view,* XXIII (April, 1946).

4. The best biography on Tom Watson is C. Vann Woodward's
Tom Watson, Agrarian Rebel. See also C. Vann Woodward,
"Tom Watson and the Negro in Agrarian Politics," *The Journal
of Southern History, IV* (February, 1938), 14-33.

5. Francis Butler Simkins, *The South, Old and New* (New York,
1948), 404-405; Francis Butler Simkins, *The Tillman Movement in South Carolina* (Durham, 1926); Francis Butler Simkins, "Ben Tillman's View of the Negro," *The Journal of
Southern History,* III (May, 1937), 161-174; and Francis Butler Simkins, *Pitchfork Ben Tillman, South Carolinian* (Baton
Rouge, 1944).

6. See Harris Dickson, "The Vardaman Idea," *Saturday Evening
Post* (April 27, 1907); Frederick Palmer, "Williams versus
Vardaman at Meridian," *Collier's* XXXIV (July 27, 1907)
11-12; and Archibald S. Coody, *Biographical Sketch of James
Kimble Vardaman* (Jackson, 1922). See also the references to
Vardaman in George C. Osborn, *John Sharp Williams, Planter-
Statesman of the Deep South* (Baton Rouge, 1943); and George
C. Osborn, "John Sharp Williams Becomes a United States
Senator," *The Southern Historical Quarterly* VI (May, 1940),
222-236.

7. Woodward ("Tom Watson and the Negro in Agrarian Politics,"
29-30) states that in 1908 Tom Watson had arrived somewhere
near this position in his attitude toward the Negro. According
to Woodward, "This was as reactionary a policy as any serious
leader of the South dared advance in Watson's period. Yet he

was destined to carry his position even further toward reaction
ism."

28. Pringle, *The Life and Times of William Howard Taft*, I
557-579; and Pringle, *Theodore Roosevelt: A Biography*,
540-547.

29. Cash, *History of the Democratic Party in Florida*, 120. Gaine
lists the *Florida Sun* in his "A Century in Florida Journal
ism," 101.

30. *Ibid.* .

31. Florida *House Journal, 1909*, 5-6.

32. Cash, *History of the Democratic Party in Florida*, 121.

33. *Florida Times-Union*, April 1, 1910; *Florida Times-Union*
April 5, 1910, quoting the *Miami Metropolis*.

34. *Gainesville Sun*, April 5, 1910.

35. *Florida Times-Union*, April 6, 1910, quoting the *Fernandin*
Record.

36. *Ibid.*, April 18, 1910, quoting the *Suwannee Democrat*.

37. *Ibid.*, April 11, 1910, quoting the *Plant City Courier*. The name
and birth dates of the nine children to whom the newspaper re
ferred were: Annie Dorcas, September 30, 1889; Josephine
October 20, 1892; Enid Lyle, December 8, 1894; Elsie Hor
tense, December 1, 1896; Ella, May 21, 1899; Agnes Carolyn
October 25, 1901; Florida Douglass, April 13, 1904; Elizabet
Hutchinson, August 31, 1906; and Napoleon Bonaparte Broward
Jr., March 18, 1910. The birth dates of the Broward childre
were furnished the author by Mrs. Napoleon B. Broward. Th
births are also recorded in the Broward Family Bible.

38. *Florida Times-Union*, May 2, 1910, quoting the *Polk Count*
Record.

39. *Ibid.*, April 20, 1910, quoting the *Perry Herald*.

40. *Ibid.*

41. *Ibid.*, May 25, 1910. Broward carried Baker, Brevard, Calhoun
Clay, Dade, Franklin, Gadsden, Hamilton, Holmes, Jackson
Lafayette, Lee, Leon, Liberty, Marion, Suwannee, Taylor
Volusia, Washington, and West Palm Beach counties. L'Eng
carried two counties, and Taliaferro the remainder.

42. *Florida Times-Union*, May 20, 1910.

43. *Ibid.*

44. *Ibid.*, June 7, 1910.

5. *Ibid.* An eyewitness account of the meeting was furnished by Alston Cockrell, January 9, 1950.
6. *Ibid.*, June 8, 1910.
7. Miss Hortense Broward to author, May, 1942. Before returning to Florida, Broward attended the meeting of the National Inland Waterways Association in Providence, Rhode Island.
8. *Florida Times-Union*, September 30, 1910.
9. *Ibid.*, October 1, 1910.
10. The details of Broward's last illness were furnished the author by Dr. S. A. Morris, April, 1942.
11. The *Florida Times-Union* of October 9, 1910, reprinted tributes and eulogies from the following newspapers: *Gainesville Sun, Key West Citizen, Miami Metropolis, Miami News-Record, Ocala Banner, Ocala Star, Orlando Citizen, Pensacola Evening News, Pensacola Journal, St. Augustine Record, St. Petersburg Independent, Tampa Times, Tampa Tribune,* and *West Palm Beach Tropical Sun.*
12. *Jacksonville Metropolis*, October 4, 1910.
13. *Florida Times-Union*, October 4, 1910.

Bibliography

Manuscripts and Private Papers

THE BROWARD PAPERS, owned by Mrs. Napoleon B. Broward, constitute a large and valuable source of biographical materials relating to the life and career of Governor Broward. The collection includes family letters, pictures, and genealogy records; thirty-five file boxes of miscellaneous letters to and from Broward; six bound ledgers of typed copies of official letters written in the period from 1905-1908; two telegram books (one containing telegrams congratulating Broward on his gubernatorial victory in 1904, and the other telegrams expressing sorrow over Broward's death in 1910); and miscellaneous pamphlets, books, drainage literature, handbills, newspaper clippings, and campaign literature. The file boxes contain personal and business letters, check stubs, bank statements, manuscripts of speeches, original drafts of legislative bills, vote counts of county and state elections, campaign itinerary plans, and a few newspaper clippings. Broward did not keep copies of his own letters, except the few he preserved while he was governor, and there are large gaps in the letters addressed to him, particularly in the period up to 1893. The Papers contain large and valuable files of campaign literature which was issued by Broward and his political opponents during the campaigns of 1904, 1908, and 1910. The Papers also include a number of Florida newspapers, covering the years 1900-1910, with particular emphasis on the drainage issue in 1905 and 1906.

Miss Hortense Broward possesses a few Broward family letters, including letters written to her father, Napoleon Broward, Sr. Mr. Carlton Beckley, a grandson of Governor Broward, has in his possession several letter files containing correspondence to and from Broward during the years 1900-1910. This correspondence is valuable because most of the letters are from well-known Florida political leaders and relate to important legislation enacted in 1901, 1905,

[367]

and 1907. A scrapbook, compiled by Mrs. Josephine Broward Beckle and her daughter, Mrs. Dorcas Beckley Foster, is a valuable bio graphical source. The scrapbook contains materials relating to fili bustering and includes an undated handwritten list of passengers fo one of the filibustering voyages, as well as a number of newspape clippings. It also includes two letters from Mary Dorcas Parsons the St. Johns River Bar Pilot license, official commissions from Governors Fleming, Mitchell, Bloxham, and Jennings, and a numbe of family items.

The Frederick C. Cubberly letters in the P. K. Yonge Librar of Florida History at the University of Florida relate to the allege peonage conditions in Florida in 1907 and to the Richard Barr article which created so much controversy in the state. The Thoma E. Will collection in the P. K. Yonge Library of Florida Histor includes letters and papers dealing with the Everglades drainag program and Everglades land sales. Although the major part of th Will correspondence begins about 1913, it discusses many of th issues in which Broward was involved. The letters are, therefore valuable as a related source.

The Franklin E. Smith Papers in the Duke University Manuscrip Collection contain letters describing the Federal invasion of Florid in March, 1862, the conditions in Fernandina and Jacksonville, an the evacuation of the planters to the interior of the state. A fev letters in the Edmund Kirby Smith Papers in the Library of th University of North Carolina, written by General Kirby Smith' mother, describe conditions in Florida when the Federal army move in. Several letters detail the economic situation after the capture o Fernandina, Jacksonville, and St. Augustine. The Edward M. L'Engl Papers in the Library of the University of North Carolina wer consulted for a description of railroad activities in Florida durin the 1880's and 1890's. L'Engle was president of the Florida Centra Railroad Company, and there is a vast amount of material con cerning the business activities of this organization. An interesting lette in the L'Engle Papers describes the election of 1876 and discusse its effect upon Florida and the other Southern states. A single lette in the Washington Sanford Chaffin Papers in the Duke Universit Manuscript Collection describes Jacksonville at the time of th Democratic State Convention in 1900.

Official Records and Documents

NATIONAL RECORDS

Carlisle, Calderon: *Report to the Spanish Legation*, Washington, 1896.

Congressional Record, XIX, 50 Congress, 1 Session; XLI, Part V, 59 Congress, 2 Session.

Dickens, Ashbury, and Forney, John W. (eds.): *American State Papers, Documents of the Congress of the United States in Relation to the Public Lands*, Vols. IV and V, Washington, 1860.

Everglades of Florida, Hearings before the Committee on Expenditures in the Department of Agriculture, February 3-August 9, 1912, Ralph W. Moss, Chairman, 3 vols., Washington, 1912.

Everglades of Florida: Acts, Reports, and Other Papers, State and National, Relating to the Everglades of the State of Florida and Their Reclamation, Senate Document No. 89, 62 Congress, 1 Session, Washington, 1911.

Hearings Before the Select Committee Investigating National Defense Migration, House of Representatives, Seventy-Seventh Congress, Second Session, Pursuant to House Resolution 113, Washington, 1942.

Lowrie, Walter, and Franklin, Walter (eds.): *American State Papers, Documents, Legislative and Executive of the Congress of the United States* (18 Congress, 2 Session—19 Congress, 2 Session), Vol. III, Washington, 1932.

Papers Relating to the Foreign Relations of the United States, House of Representatives, 54 Congress, 1 Session, Document 1, Part 2.

Papers Relating to the Foreign Relations of the United States, House of Representatives, 55 Congress, 1 Session, Document 326.

Revised Statutes of the United States, 1877, Washington, 1877.

The War of the Rebellion: A Compilation of the Official Records of the Union and Confederate Armies, Series I, Vol. VI, Washington, 1880-1901.

United States Reports, Cases Adjudged in the Supreme Court at October Term, 1896, Vol. 166, New York, 1897.

United States Senate Reports, 55 Congress, 1 Session, Washington, 1897.

STATE RECORDS

Acts of the Legislative Council of the Territory of Florida, 1826-
1827, 1839, and 1841, Tallahassee.

Acts and Resolutions of the General Assembly of the State of Florida
1845 and 1855, Tallahassee.

*Acts and Resolutions Adopted by the Legislature of Florida . .
under the Constitution of 1868*, 1877, and 1881, Tallahassee

*Acts and Resolutions Adopted by the Legislature of Florida . .
under the Constitution of A.D. 1885*, for the Sessions of 1887
1889, 1891, 1893, 1895, 1897, 1899, 1901, 1903, 1905, 1907
1909, and 1947, Tallahassee.

Adjutant-General of the State of Florida, Biennial Reports for 1893
and 1895, in *Annual Reports*, 1893 and 1895.

Attorney-General of the State of Florida, Biennial Reports for 1893
and 1895, in *Annual Reports*, 1893 and 1895.

Board of Control, Report for the Period Beginning June 5, 1906
and Ending June 1, 1907, Tallahassee, 1907.

Board of Control, Report for the Period Beginning January 1, 1907
and Ending January 1, 1909, Tallahassee, 1909.

Commissioner of Agriculture of the State of Florida, Eighth Biennial
Report, Tallahassee, 1905.

Florida Reports. Cases Argued and Adjudged in the Supreme Court
of Florida, During the Year 1889, Vol. XXV, Tallahassee, 1890

General Counsel of the Trustees of the Internal Improvement Fund
Annual Report, December 21, 1908, in *Minutes of the Trustees*
of the Internal Improvement Fund, Vol. VIII, Tallahassee

Journal of the Proceedings of the First General Assembly of the
State of Florida, Tallahassee, 1845.

Journal of the Proceedings of the House of Representatives of the
Regular Session of the Legislature of the State of Florida, Held
under the Constitution Adopted by the Convention of 1885 for
the sessions of 1889, 1891, 1893, 1895, 1897, 1901, 1903
1905, 1907, and 1909, Tallahassee.

Journal of the Proceedings of the Senate of the Regular Session of
the Legislature of the State of Florida, Held under the Con-
stitution Adopted by the Convention of 1885 for the sessions of
1889, 1891, 1893, 1895, 1897, 1899, 1901, 1903, 1905
1907, and 1909, Tallahassee.

1essage and Documents, 1893, 1895, 1897, 1899, 1901, 1903, and 1905, Tallahassee.

1essage of N. B. Broward, Governor of Florida, to the Legislature, Regular Session of 1905, Tallahassee, 1905.

1inutes of the Trustees of the Internal Improvement Fund, 1855-1910, 8 vols., Tallahassee.

ailroad Commission of the State of Florida, First Annual Report, March, 1898, Jacksonville, 1898.

eport of the Joint Commission Created by the Legislature of 1907, Chapter 5632, Session Laws of 1907, to Investigate the Acts and Doings of the Trustees of the Internal Improvement Fund, Tallahassee, 1909.

eport of the Special Committee Appointed by the Legislature of Florida on the Hospital for the Insane, Session of 1905, Tallahassee, 1905.

eport of the Special Joint Committee of the Florida Legislature for the Year 1909, on the Drainage of the Everglades, Tallahassee, 1909.

evised Statutes of the State of Florida, 1892, Jacksonville, 1892.

ecretary of State of Florida, Annual Report, 1895, in Message and Documents, 1895, Tallahassee, 1895.

ecretary of State of Florida, Report for the Period Beginning January 1, 1909, and Ending December 31, 1910, Tallahassee, 1911.

he Testimony Taken Before the Special Committee to Investigate the Report on the Asylum, Tallahassee, 1905.

UNPUBLISHED RECORDS

Book of Records, Duval County, Florida," Deeds of Land: Books 12, 13, and 19, in the main vaults of the Duval County Courthouse.

Order Book, Duval County, Florida," Book B, Office of the County Judge, Duval County, Florida.

Plat Book, Duval County, Florida," Number 1, in the main vaults of the Duval County Courthouse.

Record of Deaths, Duval County, Florida," Bureau of Vital Statistics, Jacksonville, Florida.

"Record of Estates, Duval County, Florida," recorded in Books 1 and C, Office of the County Judge, Duval County, Florida
"Record of Marriages, Duval County, Florida," Books 0 and 7 Office of the County Judge, Duval County, Florida.
"Records of Wills, Duval County, Florida," Book C-1, Office o the County Judge, Duval County, Florida.

Collected Source Materials

Adams, Charles S. (ed.): *Report of the Jacksonville Auxiliary Sani tary Association of Jacksonville, Florida, Covering the Wor. of the Association during the Yellow Fever Epidemic, 1888* Jacksonville, 1889.
Appleton's Annual Cyclopaedia and Register of Important Event . . . Embracing Political, Military and Ecclesiastical Affairs Public Documents; Biography, Statistics, Commerce, Finance Literature, Science, Agriculture, and Mechanical Industry, 3r Series, 7 vols., New York, 1897-1903.
Cherrington, Ernest H. (ed.): *The Anti-Saloon League Year Boo. . . . An Encyclopedia of Facts and Figures Dealing with th Liquor Traffic and the Temperance Reform, 1909, 1910, 1911* Columbus, 1909-1911.
Moore, Frank (comp.): *The Rebellion Record: A Diary of America Events, with Documents, Narratives, Illustrative Incidents Poetry, etc.,* 11 vols., New York, 1861-1863; 1864-1868.
Richardson, James D. (comp.): *A Compilation of the Messages an Papers of the Presidents, 1789-1905,* 11 vols., Washington, 1907
Smith, Charles H. (comp.): *Report of the Jacksonville Relief Asso ciation, Jacksonville,* 1901.
Virkus, Frederick Adams (ed.): *The Compendium of America Genealogy,* Chicago, 1933.
Webb, Wanton S. (ed.): *Webb's Jacksonville Directory, 1873, 1874 1875, 1876, 1877, 1878, 1879, 1880, 1881, 1882, 188(1887, 1888, 1889, 1890, 1891, 1892, 1893, 1894, 189: 1896, 1897, 1898, 1899, 1900, 1901, 1902, 1903,* Jacksonvill and New York, 1873-1903.
——, *Webb's Jacksonville and Consolidated Directory, 1887* Jacksonville, 1887.

Whitfield, J. B. (comp.): *Florida State Government: An Official Directory of the State Government,* Tallahassee, 1885.

Newspapers and Periodicals

Bradenton Herald, June, 1906.
Cocoa and Rockledge News, May-August, 1906.
Collier's The National Weekly, 1906-1910.
Daily Capital (Tallahassee), May, 1901.
Daily Florida Citizen (Jacksonville), 1894-1897.
Daily Tallahassean, May, 1904.
DeFuniak Breeze, March, 1906.
Denver Republican, July, 1908.
Evening Times-Union (Jacksonville), June-July, 1896.
Florida Dispatch, Farmer and Fruit Grower, 1890.
Florida Times-Union (Jacksonville), 1883-1910.
Florida Times-Union and Citizen (Jacksonville), 1900.
Florida Weekly Times (Jacksonville), 1888.
Free Lance (Jacksonville), 1895.
Gainesville Sun, 1905-1906; 1908-1910.
Jacksonville Journal, August, 1939.
Jacksonville Metropolis, 1887-1901; 1903-1910.
Land of Flowers (Tallahassee), June, 1884.
Literary Digest, 1905-1910.
Madison Recorder, October, 1906.
Miami Evening Record, September, 1906.
Miami Metropolis, March, 1906.
New York Evening Journal, February, 1907.
New York Herald, 1896-1897; 1902; 1908-1910.
New York Times, 1862-1864; 1896; 1907-1910; 1917.
Ocala Banner, 1897-1910.
Ocala Evening Star, 1906.
Pensacola Daily News, May-June, 1897.
Pensacola Journal, June, 1905.
St. Augustine Evening Record, April-November, 1906.
Semi-Weekly Times-Union (Jacksonville), 1903-1905.
Tallahassee Capital, January, 1905.
Tallahassee Sentinel, June, 1876.
Tampa Morning Tribune, 1895-1896.
Volusia County Record, March, 1906.

Weekly Floridian (Tallahassee), 1887.
Weekly Tallahassean, April-May, 1901; January-June, 1904.

Articles

Abbey, Kathryn T.: "Florida Versus the Principles of Populism
    1896-1911," *The Journal of Southern History,* IV (November
    1938).
"Back to Water Transportation": *The Literary Digest,* XXXIV
    (March 30, 1907).
Barry, Richard: "Slavery in the South Today," *Cosmopolitan Maga*
    zine, XIII (March, 1907).
Broward, Napoleon B.: "Draining the Everglades," *The Independ*
    ent, LXIV (June 25, 1908).
————: "Filibustering in Florida," *The Florida Life* (November
    1897).
————: "Homes for Millions: Draining the Everglades," *Collier's*
    XLIV (January 22, 1910).
Buford, Rivers H.: "Napoleon B. Broward," *Apalachee* (1946).
Carson, Ruby Leach: "Florida, Promoter of Cuban Liberty," *The*
    Florida Historical Quarterly, XIX (January, 1941).
————: "William Dunnington Bloxham: The Years to the Gov
    ernorship," *The Florida Historical Quarterly,* XXVII (January
    1949).
Cash, William T.: "The Dean of Florida Newsmen," *Florida News*
    paper News, XXVII (April, 1945).
"Clash of State and Federal Rights": *The Literary Digest,* XXXIV
    (March 30, 1907).
Cockrell, Alston W.: "Reminiscences of Tallahassee," *Tallahasse*
    Historical Society Annual, II (1935).
Davis, T. Frederick: "The Disston Land Purchase," *The Florida*
    Historical Quarterly, XVII (January, 1939).
Dickson, Harris: "The Vardaman Idea," *Saturday Evening Post*
    (April 27, 1907).
Dodd, William G.: "Early Education in Tallahassee and the West
    Florida Seminary Now Florida State University," *The Florida*
    Historical Quarterly, XXVII (Part I, July, 1948; Part II
    October, 1948).
Dovell, Junius E.: "The History of the Everglades of Florida,"
    Economic Leaflets, VI (Part I, April, 1947).

Bibliography 375

Dovell, Junius E.: "A Brief History of the Florida Everglades," Soil Science Society of America *Proceedings*, IV-A (1942).

Fairlie, Margaret C.: "The Yellow Fever Epidemic of 1888 in Jacksonville," *The Florida Historical Quarterly*, XIX (October, 1940).

Hawes, Frank M.: "New Englanders in the Florida Census of 1850," *New England Historical and Genealogical Register* (January, 1922).

Knauss, James O.: "The Farmers' Alliance in Florida," *South Atlantic Quarterly*, XXV (July, 1926).

————: "The Growth of Florida's Election Laws," *The Florida Historical Quarterly*, V (July, 1946).

Henry, Evelyn Whitfield: "Old Houses in Tallahassee," *Tallahassee Historical Society Annual*, I (February, 1934).

Latané, John H.: "Intervention of the United States in Cuba," *North American Review*, XCXVI (March, 1898).

————: "The Diplomacy of the United States in Regard to Cuba," American Historical Association, *Annual Report* (1897).

Link, Arthur S.: "The Progressive Movement in the South, 1870-1914," *The North Carolina Historical Review*, XXIII (April, 1946).

Osborn, George C.: "John Sharp Williams Becomes a United States Senator," *The Southern Historical Journal*, VI (May, 1940).

Paine, Ralph D.: "From Deck Hand to Governor: The Picturesque Career of Napoleon Broward," *Everybody's Magazine*, XX (February, 1909).

————: "On No-Name Key," *The Outing*, XLII (September, 1903).

————: "The Log of a Filibuster-Correspondent," *The Outing*, XLIII (November, 1903).

Palmer, Frederick: "Williams versus Vardaman at Meridian," *Collier's*, XXXIX (July 27, 1907).

"The President's Tour," *The Literary Digest*, XXXV (October 12, 1907).

Proctor, Samuel: "The National Farmers' Alliance Convention of 1890 and Its 'Ocala Demands,'" *The Florida Historical Quarterly*, XXVIII (January, 1950).

Roberts, Albert H.: "The Senatorial Deadlock of 1897," *Apalachee* (1944).

Rubens, H. S.: "The Insurgent Government in Cuba," *North American Review*, LCXVI (May, 1898).

Shores, Venila L.: "Some Historical Notes Concerning Florida State College for Women," *Tallahassee Historical Society Annual*, III (1937).

Simkins, Francis B.: "Ben Tillman's View of the Negro," *The Journal of Southern History*, III (May, 1937).

Simmons, Daniel A.: "The Florida Everglades. How They Happened; What They Are; What They Will Be," *The World Today*, XVI (May, 1909).

Sweeney, C. P.: "Bigotry in the South; Anti-Catholic Prejudice," *Nation*, XCI (November 24, 1920).

Thompson, Arthur W.: "Political Nativism in Florida, 1848-1860: A Phase of Anti-Secessionism," *The Journal of Southern History*, XV (February, 1949).

"Wasting the Nation's Resources," *The Literary Digest*, XXXV (October 19, 1907).

Wilson, Woodrow: "Mr. Cleveland as President," *Atlantic Monthly*, LXXIX (March, 1897).

Williamson, Edward C.: "Independentism: A Challenge to the Florida Democracy of 1884," *The Florida Historical Quarterly*, XXVII (October, 1948).

————: "William D. Chipley, West Florida's Mr. Railroad," *The Florida Historical Quarterly*, XXV (April, 1947).

Woodward, C. Vann: "Tom Watson and the Negro in Agrarian Politics," *The Journal of Southern History*, IV (February, 1938).

Pamphlets

Broward, Napoleon B.: *For United States Senator—Napoleon B. Broward*, 1908.

————: *Gov. Napoleon B. Broward on Certain Live Public Questions of interest to the People of Florida, Being a discussion of STATE LIFE INSURANCE, the DRAINAGE OF THE EVERGLADES and other problems that will require solution by the Legislature of Florida in 1907 Session*, Tallahassee, 1907.

————: *Open Letter of Governor N. B. Broward to the People of Florida*, 1906.

Bloxham, William D.: *The Disston Sale and the State Finances*, Jacksonville, 1884 (speech delivered by Bloxham in the Park Opera House, Jacksonville, August 26, 1884).

Bush, George D.: *History of Education in Florida*, Bureau of Education, Circulars of Information No. 7, Washington, 1889.

Chipley, W. D.: *A Review of the Record of Hon. Wilkinson Call*, 1890.

Concerning Everglades Land, ca. 1910 (promotional pamphlet in the Thomas E. Will Collection, P. K. Yonge Library of Florida History).

The Executive Mansion, Tallahassee, Florida, Tallahassee.

Fleming, Francis P.: *Did the Florida Legislature of 1891 Elect a Senator?* Tallahassee, 1891.

Mendenhall, Herbert D.: *What the Phosphate Industry Means to Florida Engineers* (speech delivered at the meeting of the American Society of Civil Engineers, Jacksonville, April, 1938), Tallahassee, 1938.

Proceedings in the United States Senate Admitting Hon. Wilkinson Call as a Senator from Florida, December 7, and 8, 1891, Washington, 1891.

R. H. M. Davidson v. *Wilkinson Call, Brief of Eppa Hunton, Counsel for Davidson, Before the Committee on Privileges and Elections of the United States Senate, 52 Congress, Contested Election from the State of Florida*, 1891.

Woodward, C. Vann: *The South in Search of a Philosophy*, Phi Beta Kappa Series, No. 1, University of Florida, 1938.

Autobiographies, Biographies, Memoirs, and Reminiscences

Armstrong, Orland K.: *The Life and Work of Dr. A. A. Murphree*, St. Augustine, 1928.

Barrett, James W.: *Joseph Pulitzer and his World*, New York, 1941.

Biographical Directory of the American Congress, 1774-1927: The Continental Congress, September 5, 1774 to October 21, 1788 and the Congress of the United States From the First to the Sixty-Ninth Congress, March 4, 1789 to March 3, 1927 Inclusive, Washington, 1928.

Broward, Napoleon B.: *Napoleon B. Broward, Candidate for Governor of Florida: Autobiography, Platform, Letter and Short Story of the Steamer "Three Friends," and a Filibustering Trip to Cuba,* 1904. Reprinted privately in Miami, 1938.

Carlson, Oliver, and Bates, Ernest S.: *Hearst, Lord of San Simeon,* New York, 1937.

Coody, Archibald: *Biographical Sketch of James Kimble Vardaman,* Jackson, 1922.

Corbett, James J.: *The Roar of the Crowd,* New York, 1930.

Dickison, Mary Elizabeth: *Dickison and His Men. Reminiscences of the War in Florida,* Louisville, 1890.

Ginger, Ray: *The Bending Cross,* New Brunswick, 1949.

Johnson, Allen, and Malone, Dumas (eds.): *Dictionary of American Biography,* 20 vols., New York, 1928-1936.

Kenan, William R., Jr.: *Incidents By the Way, Lifetime Recollections and Reflections,* 1946.

————: *Incidents By the Way, More Recollections,* 1949.

Martin, Sidney W.: *Florida's Flagler,* Athens, 1949.

Mullen, Arthur: *Western Democrat,* New York, 1940.

Nevins, Allan: *Grover Cleveland: A Study in Courage,* New York, 1932.

————: *Hamilton Fish: The Inner History of the Grant Administration,* New York, 1936.

Osborn, George C.: *John Sharp Williams, Planter-Statesman of the Deep South,* Baton Rouge, 1943.

Pringle, Henry F.: *The Life and Times of William Howard Taft,* 2 vols., New York, 1939.

————: *Theodore Roosevelt: A Biography,* New York, 1931.

Roosevelt, Theodore: *Theodore Roosevelt: An Autobiography,* New York, 1916.

Simkins, Francis B.: *Pitchfork Ben Tillman, South Carolinian,* Baton Rouge, 1944.

Smith, Horace: *A Captain Unafraid: The Strange Adventures of Dynamite Johnny O'Brien,* New York, 1912.

Smyth, Hutchinson G.: *The Life of Henry Bradley Plant,* New York, 1898.

Sparks, Jared (ed.): *The Library of American Biography,* Second Series, Vol. IV, Boston, 1855.

The National Cyclopaedia of American Biography, Being the History of the United States as Illustrated in the Lives of the Founders, Builders, and Defenders of the Republic, and of the Men and Women Who Are Doing the Work Moulding the Thought of the Present Time, 34 vols., New York, 1893-1948.

Werner, M. R.: *Bryan,* New York, 1929.

Woodward, C. Vann: *Tom Watson, Agrarian Rebel,* New York, 1937.

Special Studies and General Works

Alger, R. A.: *The Spanish-American War,* New York, 1901.

Benton, Elbert J.: *International Law and Diplomacy of the Spanish-American War,* Baltimore, 1908.

Bill, Ledyard: *A Winter in Florida,* New York, 1870.

Brinton, Daniel G.: *A Guide Book to Florida and the South, for Tourists, Invalids, and Immigrants,* Philadelphia, 1869.

Cash, William T.: *History of the Democratic Party in Florida,* Live Oak, 1936.

————: *The Story of Florida,* 4 vols., New York, 1938.

Chadwick, French E.: *The Relations of the United States and Spain,* New York, 1909.

Clark, Thomas D.: *The Southern Country Editor,* Indianapolis, 1948.

Connolly, Christopher P.: *The Truth About the Frank Case,* New York, 1915.

Davis, T. Frederick: *History of Early Jacksonville, Florida,* Jacksonville, 1911.

————: *History of Jacksonville, Florida and Vicinity, 1513 to 1924,* St. Augustine, 1925.

Davis, Richard Harding: *The Cuban and Porto Rican Campaigns,* New York, 1898.

Davis, William Watson: *The Civil War and Reconstruction in Florida,* Vol. LIII, *Studies in History, Economics, and Public Law,* New York, 1913.

Douglas, Marjory Stoneman: *The Everglades: River of Grass,* New York, 1947.

Ferrara, Orestes: *The Last Spanish War,* New York, 1937.

Gifford, John: *The Everglades and Other Essays Relating to Southern Florida,* Kansas City, 1911.

Gold, Pleasant D.: *History of Duval County, Florida: Also Biographies of Men and Women Who Have Done Their Part in Making Duval County's Past and Present,* St. Augustine, 1928.

Hanna, Alfred J., and Kathryn A.: *Lake Okeechobee, Wellspring of the Everglades,* Indianapolis, 1948.

Harris, Francis Eppes: *Frank Harris, More Than Fifty Years Editor Ocala Banner, ca.* 1920.

Harrison, Benjamin: *Acres of Ashes,* Jacksonville, 1901.

Hicks, John D.: *The Populist Revolt,* Minneapolis, 1931.

Hill, T. A.: *The Negro and Economic Reconstruction,* Washington, 1937.

Hirsch, Arthur H.: *The Huguenots of Colonial South Carolina,* Durham, 1928.

Hofstadter, Richard: *The American Political Tradition and the Men Who Made It,* New York, 1948.

Key, V. O., Jr.: *Southern Politics in State and Nation,* New York, 1949.

Latané, John H.: *America As a World Power, 1897-1907. The American Nation: A History,* Vol. XXV, New York, 1907.

Lanier, Sidney: *Florida—Its Scenery, Climate, and History,* Philadelphia, 1876.

Lewinson, Paul: *Race, Class, and Party: A History of Negro Suffrage and White Politics in the South,* New York, 1932.

Makers of America, Florida Edition, 4 vols., Atlanta, 1909.

Mangum, Charles S., Jr.: *The Legal Status of the Negro,* Chapel Hill, 1940.

Merritt, Webster: *A Century of Medicine in Jacksonville and Duval County,* Gainesville, 1949.

Miley, John D.: *In Cuba With Shafter,* New York, 1899.

Millis, Walter: *The Martial Spirit,* Boston, 1931.

Moon, Parker T.: *Imperialism and World Politics,* New York, 1927.

Moore, John Bassett: *A Digest of International Law,* Washington, 1906.

Murphy, Pat: *Legislative Blue Book, 1917: "Through Green Glasses,"* Tallahassee, 1917.

Myers, Gustavus: *History of Bigotry in the United States,* New York, 1943.

Paine, Ralph D.: *Roads of Adventure,* Boston, 1925.

Porter, Kirk H.: *National Party Platforms*, New York, 1924.

Rerick, Rowland R.: *Memoirs of Florida*, 2 vols., Atlanta, 1902.

Rhodes, James Ford: *The McKinley and Roosevelt Administrations*, New York, 1927.

Robertson, Fred L. (comp.): *Soldiers of Florida in the Seminole Indian, Civil and Spanish-American Wars*, Live Oak, 1903.

Rose, Rufus E.: *The Swamp and Overflowed Lands of Florida: The Disston Drainage Company and the Disston Purchase*, Tallahassee, 1916.

Rubens, Horatio S.: *Liberty: The Story of Cuba*, New York, 1932.

Seybolt, Robert F.: *The Town Officials of Colonial Boston, 1634-1775*, Cambridge, 1939.

Simpkins, Francis B.: *The South, Old and New*, New York, 1948.

—————: *The Tillman Movement in South Carolina*, Durham, 1926.

Stephenson, Gilbert T.: *Race Discrimination in American Law*, New York, 1910.

Varnum, John P., (ed.): *Jacksonville, Florida: A Descriptive and Statistical Report*, Jacksonville, 1885.

Wagstaff, Walter S., (ed.): *Jacksonville in Flames: An Artistic Description of a Gloomy Affair*, Jacksonville, 1901.

Webb, Wanton S., (ed.): *Webb's Historical, Industrial and Biographical Florida*, New York, 1885.

Williams, Michael: *The Shadow of the Pope*, New York, 1943.

Unpublished Monographs

Bristol, L. M.: "The Buckman Act: Before and After: A Study in Historical Sociology," bound MS. in P. K. Yonge Library of Florida History, University of Florida, 1946.

Broward, Florida and Margaret: "Biographical Sketch of Broward Family," typed MS. in Broward Papers.

Carson, James C.: "The Background of Broward and the Everglades," typed copy in author's library.

Carson, Ruby Leach: "William Dunnington Bloxham, Florida's Two-Term Governor," master's thesis, University of Florida, 1945.

Collins, Eldridge R.: "The Florida Constitution of 1885," master's thesis, University of Florida, 1939.

382 Bibliography

Crow, C. L.: "The University of Florida," MS. in University of Florida Archives.

Deal, John R., Jr.: "Sidney Johnston Catts, Stormy Petrel of Florida Politics," master's thesis, University of Florida, 1949.

Doherty, Henry J., Jr.: "The Florida Whigs," master's thesis, University of Florida, 1949.

Dovell, Junius E.: "A History of the Everglades of Florida," doctoral dissertation, University of North Carolina, 1947.

Gaines, J. Pendleton, Jr.: "A Century in Florida Journalism," master's thesis, University of Florida, 1949.

Lord, Mills M., Jr.: "David Levy Yulee—Statesman and Railroad Builder," master's thesis, University of Florida, 1940.

Parker, O. L.: "William N. Sheats, Florida Educator," master's thesis, University of Florida, 1949.

Prince, Sigsbee C., Jr.: "Edward Alysworth Perry, Florida's Thirteenth Governor," master's thesis, University of Florida, 1949.

Rickenbach, Richard V.: "A History of Filibustering From Florida to Cuba, 1895-1898," master's thesis, University of Florida, 1948.

Rhodes, Francis A.: "The Legal Development of State Supported Higher Education in Florida," doctoral dissertation, University of Florida, 1948.

Wells, William J.: "Duncan Upshaw Fletcher, Florida's Grand Old Man," master's thesis, John B. Stetson University, 1936.

Williamson, Edward C.: "Wilkinson Call: A Pioneer in Progressive Democracy," master's thesis, University of Florida, 1946.

Histories and General References
(*Not cited in footnotes*)

Bemis, Samuel Flagg: *The American Secretaries of State and Their Diplomacy*, Vol. IX, New York, 1929.

Brevard, Caroline Mays: *A History of Florida From the Treaty of 1763 to Our Own Times*, Vol. II, DeLand, 1924.

Brown, S. Paul: *The Book of Jacksonville*, Poughkeepsie, 1895.

Chapin, George M.: *Florida, 1513-1913, Past, Present and Future, Four Hundred Years of Wars and Peace and Industrial Development*, 2 vols., Chicago, 1914.

Commager, Henry S. (ed.): *Documents of American History Since 1865*, New York, 1943.
————: *The American Mind*, Chapters 1 and 2, New Haven, 1950.
Connor, R. D. W., and Poe, Clarence: *The Life and Speeches of Charles Brantley Aycock*, Garden City, 1912.
Cotterill, R. S.: *The Old South*, Glendale, 1936.
Cutler, H. G. (ed.): *History of Florida Past and Present*, 3 vols., Chicago, 1923.
Dabney, Virginius: *Liberalism in the South*, Chapel Hill, 1932.
Dau, Fred W.: *Florida Old and New*, New York, 1934.
Hamilton, J. G. de Roulhac: *History of North Carolina: North Carolina Since 1860*, Chicago, 1919.
Hanna, Kathryn A.: *Florida: Land of Change*, Chapel Hill, 1941.
Moore, Albert B.: *History of Alabama and Her People*, Vol. I, New York, 1927.
Morison, Samuel Eliot, and Commager, Henry S.: *The Growth of the American Republic*, Vol. II, New York, 1942.
Nevins, Allan: *Letters of Grover Cleveland, 1850-1908*, Chapters 14 and 15, Boston, 1933.
Parkes, Henry B.: *The American Experience*, Chapter 13, New York, 1947.
Parrington, Vernon Louis: *Main Currents in American Thought*, Vol. III, New York, 1927.
Patrick, Rembert W.: *Florida Under Five Flags*, Gainesville, 1945.
Phillips, Ulrich B.: *Life and Labor in the Old South*, Chapters 17 and 18, Boston, 1929.
Raines, C. W.: *Speeches and State Papers of James Stephen Hogg*, 1905.
Richardson, Rupert N.: *Texas, the Lone Star State*, New York, 1943.
Schlesinger, Arthur M., and Fox, Dixon R. (eds.): *A History of American Life: The Quest For Social Justice, 1898-1914*, Vol. XI, New York, 1931.

Index